negotiating
in
organizations

negotiating in organizations

edited by

MAX H. BAZERMAN
AND
ROY J. LEWICKI

SAGE PUBLICATIONS
Beverly Hills / London / New Delhi

For information address:

SAGE Publications, Inc.
275 South Beverly Drive
Beverly Hills, California 90212

SAGE Publications India Pvt.
Ltd.
C-236 Defence Colony
New Delhi 110 024, India

SAGE Publications Ltd
28 Banner Street
London EC1Y 8QE, England

Printed in the United States of America

Library of Congress Cataloging in Publication Data

Main entry under title:

Negotiating in organizations.

  Bibliography: p.
  1. Negotiation in business—Congresses.
2. Organizational behavior—Congresses.
I. Bazerman, Max H. II. Lewicki, Roy J.
HD58.6.N43   1983   658.4   83-10156
ISBN 0-8039-2035-0
ISBN 0-8039-2036-9 (pbk.)

FIRST PRINTING

Contents

Preface

When two or more parties within one or in different organizations jointly make decisions and do not have the same preferences, they are negotiating. They may not be sitting at the bargaining table; they may not act like they are competing; they may not be making offers and counteroffers; they may not threaten a strike or lockout. Negotiating is a pervasive activity that is central to organizational life. Most previous work on the topic of negotiation has concerned the labor/management context or had a specific disciplinary focus. This book responds to this state of affairs by bringing together chapters that develop new theories and applications of negotiation inside organizations.

The seed of this book dates back to the Academy of Management Annual Meeting in San Diego in the summer of 1981. Max had organized a symposium on third-party intervention. A group of us met after the session, and everyone said something vague about moving negotiation research into the mainstream of organizational behavior. In addition, everyone agreed that a conference might be a good vehicle for initiating this activity, but nobody volunteered to do anything about it. Without negotiating a clearer distribution of work, very little occurred immediately. Max, believing the concreteness of the conversation, proposed to Roy that we would jointly coordinate a conference; Roy agreed.

In December 1981, we identified a number of creative individuals working in the general field of negotiation and conflict and sent a letter to them requesting their participation in a conference on negotiating in organizations. Seventeen responded that they had something to contribute, thought the conference was needed, and would be glad to be included. We successfully negotiated with the one respondent who required travel funding in order to participate: We told that person that we had no money, and the individual gave in to our position—funding the trip from personal resources. The potential success of the conference was also confirmed by a number of offers from publishers to publish the book that you are now reading.

The actual conference was held the weekend of October 15-17, 1982. Presentations of previously distributed papers were limited to summaries in order to allow the majority of the time to be spent on discussion. The four major parts of this book reflect the four different sessions of the conference (Part I provides a general introduction). Authors were asked to use the feedback from the conference to revise the final drafts of their chapters. Each of the resulting parts contains these chapters, as well as the ideas of our discussants.

Part II deals with the decision-making processes of negotiators. As Bacharach and Lawler noted in *Bargaining: Power, Tactics, and Outcomes,* "For too long bargaining theory has neglected or assumed away the calculative thought patterns of actors in bargaining" (p. ix). The chapters in Part II suggest that the area of human cognition offers fertile ground for exploring a variety of ways that negotiations occur in organizations.

Part III focuses on the use of third parties in conflict resolution. The institutions of arbitration and mediation have been used extensively in the labor/management arena. These techniques, as well as other third-party approaches, have recently been applied to a wide variety of other conflict settings. This group of chapters examines various dimensions of third-party effectiveness and the benefits that can accrue from specific organizational uses of third-party intervention.

The emphasis in Part IV is on negotiating between organizations and their environments. How does an organization negotiate with its environment to reduce the uncertainty caused by various external factors and forces? It is common for the "macro" organizational literature to ignore the role of explicit and implicit negotiating as a means of uncertainty reduction. The chapters in Part IV provide a unique perspective on an important aspect of organizational management.

Part V addresses ways that negotiation theory and principles can be applied to specific organizational settings. This group of chapters looks specifically at influence—the strategy and tactics managers use, a case example of a successful and influential manager, and the understanding of a complex organizational process—performance appraisal—from a negotiating perspective.

The chapters included in each part were not meant to form a firmly cohesive, closely integrated set; rather, they were meant to represent various aspects of the four subtopics. We, the editors, will try to highlight some of the missing pieces in our conclusion; we will leave other parts of the mosaic to be completed by the reader and to provide the initiative for future research.

The contributors to and editors of this volume are indebted to those who provided logistical, financial, and moral support for this conference and this book. These parties include the Fuqua School of Business, Duke University; the Graduate School of Management of Boston University; and a National Science Foundation grant (BSN-8107331) to Max Bazerman. We thank all of our authors for willingly providing the contribution of their essays and their presence at the conference. We also thank them for actively cooperating with our editorial suggestions for revisions and with our manuscript deadlines. Finally, we thank the people at Sage Publications for their helpful advice and suggestions at every stage of manuscript preparation.

You may be wondering how editors of a book on negotiation negotiate the order of authorship. At some point we needed to put it on paper and had not discussed the issue previously. Max was in Boston, Roy in Durham. In a phone conversation, Max suggested flipping a coin. Roy (having recently read about the need for verifiability in any nuclear freeze) asked how we would handle verifiability. Max suggested that Roy could be in charge of flipping and verifiability. Roy agreed. Roy lost the flip. Roy went back and reread his paper for this volume on lying.

—*MHB* and *RJL*

—I—

INTRODUCTION

1

NEGOTIATIONS IN ORGANIZATIONS

Blending Industrial Relations and Organizational Behavior Approaches

Thomas A. Kochan
Anil Verma

Massachusetts Institute of Technology

The purpose of this chapter is to set the stage for the analysis of the role played by negotiations in organizations, by examining how negotiation as a theoretical construct had evolved in our broader theories of organizations and industrial relations. Our thesis is that a stage of evolution has been reached, in both organization and industrial relations theory, that allows us to move beyond broad and abstract conceptualizing about negotiating phenomena to more concrete analysis and practical application. Indeed, unless a negotiations perspective can be successfully translated from the level of broad

Authors' Note: Support for this research was provided by the Alfred P. Sloan Foundation. However, the views expressed are solely the responsibility of the authors. We wish to thank Robert McKersie and Michael Tushman for their helpful comments on an earlier draft.

theory into useful guides for organizational participants, these theories will continue to remain aloof from organizational application. Industrial relations, on the other hand, does have a long tradition of moving from broad theoretical premises about conflict and negotiations in organizations to application through formal negotiations and conflict resolution structures. Thus it provides a rich body of concepts, experience, and data from which we can draw. Indeed, by paying attention to industrial relations theory, research, and experience, we can avoid a tendency that has become the legacy of organization theory—to "rediscover" periodically, using new terminology, ideas from the past only to abandon them again at about the same level of development achieved in their earlier life.

We will proceed by providing a brief historical overview of the treatment of negotiations as a theoretical construct in various organizational theories. We will then compare that treatment to what we consider to be some fundamental assumptions about organizations arising out of industrial relations theory. This should facilitate an understanding of the role played by negotiations and closely allied concepts such as "conflict," "goals," "power," and the like. Finally, we draw on some of the emerging literature in industrial relations, as well as on the work presented at this conference, to illustrate the contributions that an understanding of the role of negotiations can make to organizational analysis and practice.

FADS AND CYCLES IN ORGANIZATION THEORY

Before a coherent view of the role that negotiations play in organization theory can be developed, we first need to establish why negotiations arise in organizations. Negotiations represent a special form of social interaction or decision making that (1) involves more than one party, (2) who hold some potentially conflicting interests as well as sufficient common interests or interdependence to motivate each to remain within the relationship or complete the exchange, and (3) involves reciprocity. Because conceptualizing exchanges or interactions among organizational participants as forms of negotiations makes sense only if the parties have or perceive different interests, we must first examine how the concept of conflict has been treated in organization theory.

The treatment of the role of conflict in organization theory tends to run in cycles. Early (pre-1960) managerial theories of organizations tended to ignore conflict in organizations (Fayol, 1949; Barnard, 1938) in the rush to find optimal strategies for designing and structuring organizations in ways that maximized efficiency. Then the rejection of the "management principles" approach to organization theory (March & Simon, 1958; Cyert & March, 1963), along with the social turmoil of the 1960s, helped organizational theorists to begin to bring conflict out of the closet and to recognize that conflict may not only be a naturally occurring organizational phenomenon but that it would have positive as well as negative consequences for different organizational actors (Coser, 1956; Pondy, 1967). Little progress was made in going beyond this elementary point, however, and the treatment of conflict tended to get lost in what we are now coming to describe as the "rationalist" and, to a lesser extent, contingency-based theories that were most popular in the later 1960s and early 1970s (Blau & Scott, 1962; Blau & Schoenherr, 1972; Perrow, 1967; Thompson, 1967; Lawrence & Lorsch, 1967; Pugh et al., 1968). It is not that these organizational theorists necessarily ignored conflict. Instead as Bacharach and Lawler (1981) note, they tended to be *apolitical*. Rational organizational decisions could be made in response to different environmental and technological contexts. Correct decisions would allow organizations to adapt, grow, and be effective. Interest group resistance, divergent preferences, and sub-group or subunit autonomy (the loose coupling of later years) did not get prominent attention in these models.

More recently, however, there has been considerable backlash against the rationalistic paradigms by those preferring to take a more interpretive approach to organizational theory. This has once again moved to the forefront of organization theory the ideas of researchers who view parties in organizations as having different preferences or goals, acting out their roles on the basis of their individual or organizational subunit preferences, drawing on diverse sources of power and influence, and engaging in open conflict. Indeed, several recent works have attempted to do so (Strauss, 1978; Goldman & Van Houten, 1974; Bacharach & Lawler, 1980, 1981; Pfeffer, 1981).

Yet much of this conceptual discussion has been heard before. The framework for studying organizations as political systems, and the discussion of conflict, power, and negotiations, is insightful and refreshing, but all of these works still focus on the level of paradigm development and articulation. None of them take us far enough down the conceptual ladder to suggest strategies for organizational design and principles for guiding organizational activities that can be used by individuals interested in influencing or changing organizations or the behavior of individuals within them. Works such as Pfeffer (1981), Kanter (1976), and Pettigrew (1973), for example, imply a variety of implications for organization design and change, but all stop short of fully articulating them. In short, both the Pondy (1972) and the Arygris (1972)—strange bedfellows indeed—critiques of conflict theory and organization theory, respectively, are still valid. Both have argued that little progress has been made in moving from theoretical statements to strategies for promoting and managing change in organizations that serve the interests of organizational participants or society at large. In short, *useful* theories of negotiations within and between (among) organizations have yet to be developed. Brown's (1983) recent book on conflict management, however, both represents an exception to this general argument and illustrates the value of pursuing conflict and negotiations theory to the applied level.

There is both a cost and a threat to this lack of progress. While the study of conflict and organizational negotiations has remained at its abstract level, those who view organizations from a competing paradigm—as largely cooperative and unitary systems—have filled the void in middle-range theory and guides to administrative (largely managerial) practice. In the 1930s the cooperative paradigm produced the human relations movement (Mayo, 1933). In the 1950s through the 1960s and early 1970s it produced, among others, studies of leadership (Fleishman et al., 1955); participative management (Likert, 1961, 1967) and organizational development and change strategies that stressed the building of interpersonal trust, openness, and communications; and other strategies that assume a natural congruence between the goals of individuals and organizations (Argyris, 1964; Schein, 1969; Beckhard, 1969). The most recent version of this school centers around the concept of organizational culture (Ouchi, 1981) and its implied efforts to change behavior in a manner that is consistent with the values and philosophies of the top executives in the organization. As normative or action-oriented theories, all of these approaches rest on the assumption that organizations are homogeneous units and that strategies for changing or controlling behavior in a way that is consistent with a single value system are functional for individuals, organizations, and society as a whole.

The challenge, for those who see organizations as political systems composed of multiple sets of interests, is both to build a coherent organizational theory and to apply it in ways that can also ultimately be useful to organizational actors. This does not necessarily require rejection of the theoretical and empirical insights of the work on organizational culture or any of its predecessors within the "cooperation" school. Indeed, as we review the assumptions about organizations coming out of industrial relations, the need to draw on *both* conflict-based and cooperation-based theories and strategies in order to develop useful guides for organizational action will be demonstrated.

CONFLICT AND NEGOTIATIONS IN INDUSTRIAL RELATIONS THEORY

In contrast to the varying assumptions about conflict and negotiations found in organization theory, the pluralist tradition of American industrial relations theory, derived from the work of John R. Commons and his associates and followers, has maintained a coherent and consistent set of assumptions about the nature and role of conflict within organizations around issues pertaining to the determination and administration of the employment relationship (Commons, 1934; Perlman, 1928; Kerr & Fisher, 1957; Kerr, Dunlop, Harbison, & Myers, 1960; Barbash, 1964). Furthermore, these broad theoretical views have been translated into public policy and private practice through the various protective labor laws of the 1930s and the 1960s, through the National Labor Relations Act and its amendments, and through the evolving practice of collective bargaining.

The employment relationship and—by extension—organizations are viewed as mixed-motive relationships (Walton & McKersie, 1965); i.e., the actors are separated by some conflicting interests and tied together by some common interests. Therefore, conflict is accepted as a naturally occurring phenomenon among organizational participants but one that can have either positive or negative consequences for the different parties. The mixed-motive nature of organizations implies that the parties also share a range of common interests that can be effectively pursued by improving problem solving or integrative bargaining potential that exists within organizations. The normative objective of industrial relations theory, therefore, is to foster effective negotiations and conflict resolution or management processes that can allow for the orderly accommodation of conflicting interests and the pursuit of integrative (Walton & McKersie, 1965) or joint-gain solutions as well. Thus the central theoretical proposition that emerges out of these broad assumptions is that effective management and resolution of conflict will contribute to organizational effectiveness and individual welfare.

Since industrial relations is focused on the employment relations issues and interactions, its theories have traditionally stressed the dichotomy between labor and management. It has always been recognized, however, that this is an overly simplistic distinction and that multiple interests exist within as well as across these two broad groups (Walton & McKersie, 1965; Raskin & Dunlop, 1967; Kochan, Cummings, & Huber, 1976). Indeed, outside the context of employment decisions, the configurations of interest groups or coalitions may become considerably more fluid and temporary in nature. It is still essential, however, that the configuration of shared and divergent interests be analyzed in order for a negotiations perspective to achieve any analytical power. Thus in the sections to follow we will attempt to generalize these basic theoretical premises to a wider range of organizational phenomena and merge them with some of the recent work within the "political" school of organization theory.

BASIC ASSUMPTIONS FOR A NEGOTIATIONS PERSPECTIVE

Combining the basic assumptions of industrial relations with those of the emerging political models of organizations provides a useful foundation for moving to a lower level of theoretical abstraction. While the following summary list of basic premises may not be exhaustive, it distills what we believe are the main points of consensus found in these two literatures and provides a parsimonious foundation upon which more applied work can then build.

(1) Organizations are inherently mixed-motive in nature.
Participants share some common interest and have some conflicting
ones as well. It is the mixed-motive nature of these interests that
provides the motivation for negotiations and more cooperative forms
of decision making. The parties share enough interdependence or
common interests to continue rather than terminate their relationships.
At the same time, parties are assumed to act sufficiently on the basis
of self or suborganizational interests (Shull, Delbecq, & Cummings,
1970) to engage in negotiating processes. Thus the first requirement
for a social interaction to be described as a form of negotiations exists
in organizations, namely that there are diverse parties bound together
by a mix of common and divergent interests (Ikle, 1968).

*(2) The "goals" or "interests" that separate parties within
organizations can vary considerably* from "hard" or objective differences that are embedded in the different economic interests or
structural roles the parties occupy and represent in organizations (as
the traditional industrial relations literature tends to stress) to highly
subjective, interpersonal, or socially constructed perceptions of
differences (as some of the more recent interpretive and information-
processing organization theories [e.g., Strauss, 1978] emphasize). In
addition, some interest group configurations are relatively fixed and
enduring in organizations (e.g., workers versus employers in employment contract bargaining), while other interests are situational, fluid,
and can better be studied within a coalition framework (Bacharach &
Lawler, 1981). One need not rigidly adhere to or reject either an
objective reality or rationalist perspective, or a socially constructed
view of reality to accept the role of negotiations within organizations.
Indeed, most mixed-motive processes involve both objective and
subjective differences in goals and perceptions. Consequently, most
theories of bargaining (or resolution strategies that stress problem
solving and consensus building) need to consider both the real or
enduring and the perceived or constructed differences in interests or
goals (Walton & McKersie, 1965). Furthermore, different resolution
or conflict management strategies vary in their ability to cope with
conflicts arising out of different degrees of "objective" or "socially
constructed" interest configurations.

(3) To understand the dynamics of interactions among organiza-tional participants, one must draw on some concept of power. While the conceptual and operational definitions of power vary widely, any organizational analysis that considers negotiations to be an impor-tant phenomenon will need to consider power as an important source of influence and part of the dynamics of decision making. The indus-trial relations literature, for example, treats power as not only a natural but also an essential aspect of negotiations that helps to produce an employment contract between employees and employers (Chamberlain & Kuhn, 1965).

(4) Overt forms of conflict are a natural byproduct of negotiations. While the occurrence of conflict per se cannot be viewed as inherently functional or dysfunctional because its outcomes may have differen-tial effects for different organizational participants or constituents, the lack of effective conflict management or resolution processes or procedures is likely to lead to lower levels of goal attainment for all parties. This is perhaps the least well articulated premise underlying most negotiations theories, yet one that is implicit in most industrial relations and organizational politics research.

(5) Those who take a negotiations' perspective to organizational activity need to take a multiple constituency perspective toward the assessment of organizational outcomes or organizational effective-ness (Freidlander & Pickle, 1968; Goodman & Pennings, 1977). That is, assessments of outcomes of conflict, negotiations, or other organizational processes need to be made in terms of the extent to which they contribute to the goals of each of the different parties. Thus only in cases where parties share common goals can organiza-tional effectiveness be judged against a single criterion.

MOVING TOWARD A USEFUL THEORETICAL FRAMEWORK

The above general premises provide only the starting point for making our theories and research on negotiations useful to organizational theory and practice. The next step is to develop an understanding of the dynamics of conflict and negotiations within organizations. Pondy (1967, 1969) earlier developed the concept of conflict episodes and stressed the need to examine the sequence of conflict events from latency, feeling, perception, and manifestation, through to its aftermath. Schmidt and Kochan (1972) used a similar argument by suggesting the need to move from the analysis of the *motivational states* or underlying *sources* of conflict, to the assessment of the *configuration of goals or interests,* through the *sources of interdependence* or power, and to the *interaction process* in which conflict occurred and/or was resolved. We believe that the analysis of conflict episodes provides a viable way of making conflict and negotiations theory useful to organizational practitioners and provides the link needed for moving from abstract conceptualization to organizational application. It can be made more useful by drawing on both the Pondy and the Schmidt and Kochan frameworks and extending them to examine the outcomes of negotiations or conflict and their effects on the goal attainment of the parties. We will attempt to illustrate how this might be done by drawing on some of the material included in this volume and on some selected industrial relations research.

Motivational States, Goals, and Latent Conflict

No issue is more intensely debated among organizational, conflict, and industrial relations researchers than the question of what are the most basic underlying sources of differences in goals, perceptions, or environmental conditions that produce the potential for conflict, and therefore give rise to negotiations within organizations. Yet most of the literature on this topic is nonempirical and simply asserts the beliefs of the theorist/researchers. Thus Marxist theorists turn to the inherent conflict of class interests embedded within organizations by capitalist social relations (Hyman, 1975; Goldman & Van Houten, 1977). Pluralist industrial relations theorists (Commons, 1934; Barbash, 1964; Kochan, 1980) assume that the different economic interests and structural roles (Dahrendorf, 1959) provide the underlying differences in goals that give rise to the potential for conflict. Others who see organizations as cooperative systems look to interpersonal and intergroup tensions and individual perceptions or cognitions as the key sources of conflict (Argyris, 1964; Likert, 1967; Schein, 1969). While these ideological differences make for stimulating debate within the field, too strong adherence to the premises of any one of these schools at the expense of the other limits our ability to develop effective conflict management processes. This is especially true if effective conflict management requires the matching of resolution strategies to the source or type of conflict (Kochan & Jick, 1978). Thus we need to begin to explore the various potential sources of conflict within organizations and trace their effects on the choice of influence strategies, power relations that develop among individuals or groups, the effectiveness of conflict management efforts, and their ultimate effects on the parties' goals. Some examples from this volume and from other organizational and industrial relations research will help illustrate this point.

The Browns' analysis of the contexts of negotiations that are shaped by the carryover of social and cultural tensions of the larger society provides a starting point for analyzing one source of organizational conflict. The more the boundaries of organizaitons are open to the influence of cultural, racial, or political tensions in the larger society, the greater the potential for organizational conflicts. The Browns go a step further and suggest that conflicts arising out of cultural differences are likely to take on ideological overtones. This leads to a more general hypothesis that is being pursued by those interested in organizational demographics (Pfeffer, 1981), namely that the more heterogeneous the cultural, social, economic, and demographic characteristics of the participants in an organization, the greater the potential for conflict. In contrast, the more homogeneous the participants, the more they can be subject to the same values and norms, the more they can be influenced by the same influence strategies, and the lower the level of conflict.

Murray, Jick, and Bradshaw's chapter on the effects of economic scarcity on organizations moves us beyond the standard industrial relations assumption that differences in economic interests within organizations will lead to incentives to bargain among interest groups. By exploring how changes in the degree of economic scarcity or slack will influence the nature and intensity of conflict and bargaining and the strategies available for managing conflicts, their work provides a look at the effects of changes in those economic pressures on the patterns of negotiations and the intensity of conflict.

The Bazerman/Neale and Greenhalgh/Neslin papers explore underlying variables relating to cognitive styles, value systems, and preferences, all of which respresent important individual-level variables for understanding the origins of conflict in organizational interactions. Work on the effects of variations in individuals' initial interpretation of their organizational setting is necessary if we want to pursue the view of organizational structures, strategies, and outcomes as forms of negotiated order (Strauss, 1978).

These chapters provide good starting points for exploring the origins of a conflict episode and relating them to later stages. Together they illustrate the multiple external and internal sources of organizational conflicts and the need to move away from the search for the single, dominant cause of conflict. Other work in the organizational literature has focused more on structural sources of differences in goals across departmental subunits (Kochan et al., 1976), on interpersonal perceptions and tensions (Walton, 1969), and on group membership or identity (Shull et al., 1970). More empiricial work along these lines is necessary to understand the effectiveness of different strategies for managing conflict and structuring decision making among parties whose potential conflicts arise from different sources.

From Latent Conflict to Organizational Processes

The second stage of a conflict episode involves the movement from the motivational origins and configuration of interests to the actions parties take to make decisions. Understanding this stage requires analysis of the distribution of power and resources among the participants and their choice of influence strategies and tactics. Two key theoretical propositions, both of which are amenable to empirical research, are central to developing an understanding and to managing this stage of the conflict episode and its relationship to negotiations. First, in order for latent conflicts or differences in actual or perceived interests to be translated into a negotiations process, each interest group must have some power over the others. In the absence of shared power or mutual interdependence, one party can unilaterally decide the outcome without negotiating with the others. An extension of this proposition would be that the more unequal the distribution of power, the higher the probability of a unilateral rather than a negotiated outcome, and the higher the likelihood that the differences in interest will be suppressed, smoothed over, or ignored by the stronger party or not pursued by the weaker party. The second key proposition relates to the effectiveness of the structures and processes used to manage or resolve conflicts and follows from the earlier discussion of the need to match the conflict management strategy to the source of the conflict. The general proposition is that effective conflict management requires that the conflict management or resolution process be able to deal with the underlying sources of the conflict. This is a vague and almost tautological proposition and requires more specific application to be useful. Several examples may, however, help illustrate its importance to developing an understanding of the management of conflict and negotiations.

Kochan and Jick (1978) found that the labor mediation process used in most public sector jurisdictions is more effective in resolving impasses that arise because of lack of experience or expertise of the negotiating teams or some breakdown in the process of negotiations (e.g., one or both of these parties getting overly committed to a negotiating position and needing help to save face). The mediation process was less able to achieve settlements in disputes in which the conflicts were extremely intense (multiple sources of conflict were present), the economic objectives of the parties were highly divergent, or the parties had well thought out strategic or political reasons for continuing the impasse. Thus the mediation process was more effective in resolving some types of conflicts than others.

The Goldberg and Brett experiments with mediation of the grievances that otherwise would have gone to arbitration represents another application and testing of this general proposition. Their preliminary results suggest that a significant percentage of grievances are amenable to a more informal mediation process and need not be referred to the more formal and costly arbitration process.

Another visible example of this proposition is currently being played out in labor/management relations in many of our basic industries. Within the past several years, many unions and firms have embarked on employee participation programs designed to foster greater communications, commitment, motivation, and involvement of individual workers and to overcome some of the costs of adversarial relationships at the workplace. These strategies have drawn very heavily on organizational development techniques of training people in problem solving, team building, and consensus decision making. The choice of these approaches represented a recognition that the standard formal negotiation and grievance-handling mechanisms of collective bargaining were not well suited for introducing the types of organizational changes on nonfinancial issues that required modifying deeply ingrained perceptions of the roles of individual workers, supervisors, and managers and the sharing of information and knowledge.

In putting these efforts in place, however, most union and management officials have learned (from previous failures) to maintain a separation between the formal contract negotiations and grievance procedures, and the more flexible worker participation processes. The current strategy is to use formal negotiations processes and grievance procedures to handle the highly distributive issues that lie within the traditional scope of collective bargaining (e.g., wages and fringes) while allowing problem solving to proceed more informally at the workplace. Maintaining viable distributive and problem-solving processes over time is proving to be a significant challenge in many of these efforts. Indeed, the compatibility of these two approaches is being put to a severe test in situations in which employers have gone to their employees and negotiated through the traditional structures and bargaining processes (although in some cases transformed in significant ways) to achieve economic concessions (wage freezes, deferrals, work rule changes, and so on).

Since whether parties to an interdependent relationship will initiate a negotiations process depends on the extent to which power is shared or distributed among the participants, the analysis of the distribution of power is essential to the study and practice of negotiations. Yet it is perhaps one of the most difficult concepts to define and measure. The industrial relations literature has relied on Chamberlain's (1955) analysis of the costs of agreement and disagreement as its most popular approach to the definition of bargaining power. Emerson's (1962) power/dependence approach (A has power over B to the extent that A controls resources B values and B has few alternative means of obtaining these resources) continues to be popular in the behavioral literature. Both of these are helpful conceptual tools. However, in order to examine the forces affecting the ability of either party to achieve its goals in a specific negotiation, one is normally forced to adopt some version of the French and Raven (1960) approach by identifying those aspects of the situation that serve as sources of power for one party over another.

Several of the chapters in this volume illustrate the diverse sources of power that can influence a party's ability to negotiate and the importance of power to the dynamics of negotiations processes. Hall's essay on the power of human resource management departments seeking to obtain the status, resources, and organizational influence needed to carry out their programs extends Strauss's (1962) earlier analysis of the dynamics of lateral relations among organizational units. Human resource or industrial relations departments illustrate the generic nature of the power of boundary units in organizations. These units derive their power from both the severity of the threat that their part of the environment poses to an organization, and paradoxically, from their ability to control or limit the impact of that external threat. Yet as Hall emphasizes, boundary units must use their power to achieve results that are instrumental to the mission or objectives of the organization.

Identifying the sources of power of boundary units requires starting well outside of the organization and looking at the environment with which the unit interacts. For example, the traditional environmental sources of power that have affected the internal power of human resource departments are the pressures of tight labor markets, unions, and government regulations (Kochan & Cappelli, 1983). In the case of marketing departments it is likely to be the degree of market competition and potential for market penetration that can put marketing professionals in powerful negotiating positions with manufacturing, finance, and other lateral groups. Thus understanding the rise and fall of the ability of boundary units to command resources and organizational influence can only be understood by first assessing the sources of external power they derive from the environment they face.

Murray's discussion of the growing importance of strategic planning and decision making describes the role that formal structures and units designed to aid and formalilze decision making can play in influencing the distribution of power by controlling the information and the criteria or premises used to make decisions.

Grigsby presents an illustration of an interaction involving hierarchical relations that is seldom analyzed as a negotiations framework, namely, the performance appraisal process. Looking at performance appraisal as a negotiating activity, however, helps go beyond the search for technical reasons why most performance appraisal systems suffer from systematic sources of error (Cooper, 1981). It looks more intensively at the interpersonal and organizational dynamics of the appraisal process, the benefits and costs to the appraiser and appraisee of positive or negative performance evaluations, and the larger political context of the supervisor/subordinate relationship.

The Kipnis and Schmidt chapter builds on a long line of empirical research that has documented the variety of influence tactics individuals draw on and the process by which parties alter their tactics as conflicts escalate or continue through time. This type of work is necessary if we take seriously one of the key conceptual arguments in the industrial relations literature on bargaining power—that power is not a static quantity that can be measured at any single point in the negotiations process or in a relationship but is altered over time by changing events and over the course of a negotiations process by the behavior and tactics of the parties. It is this dynamic component to the distribution of power, and the different tactics Kipnis and Schmidt have identified, which now must be added to the typologies of earlier students of influence processes such as French and Raven, that makes power so difficult to measure and study. Yet to either study negotiations from the outside or intervene as a third party or an active participant, one must be able to assess the distribution of power and the tactics and other forces that alter that distribution over time.

In a related vein, Lewicki's chapter on lying as an influence tactic demonstrates how norms or accepted "rules of the game" influence the range of tactics parties will view as acceptable in a given context. Lying may be acceptable in some contexts but not others. So may physical violence, as in disputes between warring tribes, nations, or crime families.

Negotiation Processes and the Management/Resolution of Conflict

An enormous amount of empirical research has focused directly on the dynamics of negotiations and conflict management or resolution processes. This concentration is reflected in the mix of chapters included here. Most research on negotiations attempts to describe the dynamics of negotiations, explain variations in negotiation outcomes, or predict the conditions under which an agreement or an impasse will occur. Another branch of research addresses the same sets of questions with respect to conflict resolution or third-party intervention processes (describing the dynamics, predicting how outcomes are affected, and predicting whether the process will produce an agreement or not). The industrial relations literature experienced a growth spurt in this area in recent years from the expansion of public sector collective bargaining. Its heavy reliance on formal third-party procedures of mediation, fact finding, and various forms of arbitration stimulated the development of new theories (Stevens, 1966) and extensive laboratory and field research. Pruitt's chapter represents a second generation of theorizing as he extends and modifies earlier theories of integrative bargaining and problem solving in light of his and others' more recent empirical studies on this topic.

Notz and Starke build on much of this work in their chapter and go on to extend some of its empirical insights to options for structuring and resolving conflicts in organizational budgeting processes. It is in decision-making contexts that share some of the highly structured and recurring forms of disputes that these collective bargaining procedures have the most insight to offer. This point is also illustrated in Wall's examination of the role of mediation in civil court cases. As we move to less highly structured activities (i.e., where coalitions are more fluid and the goals and power of the parties are more uncertain), these formal impasse procedures can less easily stand alone and must be integrated with more of the problem-solving strategies described in Pruitt's essay. Ebert and Wall's chapter builds on this premise by developing a more generic framework for treating decision making as a negotiations process.

Sheppard also brings the study of third-party roles and processes directly into an organizational and managerial process. His analysis of managers as conflict resolvers represents an important step toward the goals of making a negotiations perspective on organizations relevant to organizational participants.

The central questions for those studying this stage of a conflict episode are: (1) How well do the various negotiations processes and third-party dispute resolution mechanisms allow the various interests at stake to participate and have their concerns voiced? (2) How effective are the processes in achieving a resolution to the dispute? Data that address these questions can help complete Sheppard's taxonomy of third-party intervention procedures and expand the tools available to those attempting to improve conflict management processes in organizations.

The Effects of Negotiations and Alternative Conflict Management Strategies

Ultimately, a negotiations paradigm needs to relate the processes used to manage or resolve conflicts to the goals of the parties. Unfortunately, it is at this stage of the conflict cycle or episode where the least empirical research exists. Most work stops short of relating different patterns of conflict management to the key organizational outcomes valued by the parties. Yet this is the type of work most needed to test explicitly the general proposition driving this entire line of organizational and industrial relations research, namely that effective conflict management can make an important contribution to organizational effectiveness. Some current industrial relations research is moving in this direction. In two studies (Katz, Kochan, & Gobielle, in press; Katz, Kochan, & Weber, 1983), a strong direct relationship was found between the effectiveness of the management of industrial relations conflicts at the workplace and organizational effectiveness.

APPLICATION OF RESEARCH ON NEGOTIATIONS

What can be done with the type of research results that might flow from the work suggested above and is represented in this volume? Clearly one direct beneficiary of this type of work should be the teaching of organizational behavior, industrial relations, and negotiations/conflict resolution. The teaching of organizational behavior can benefit from moving beyond an elementary statement of forces that give rise to negotiations in organizations to a broadened set of insights into the effects of alternative structural arrangements on the oportunities for negotiations and the strategies for resolving conflicts among organizational interest groups. It can also lead to a critical assessment of the extent to which alternative organizational strategies lead to the smoothing over or suppression of diverse organizational interest groups and to the longer-term consequences of effective and ineffective conflict management.

For the teaching of industrial relations and human resource management, research on organizational negotiations and conflict management can provide greater insight into both the contributions and limitations of formal procedures most closely identified with collective bargaining. Perhaps more important, it can break down a traditional misperception that unfortunately still dominates much of the teaching of human resource management: namely the treatment of negotiations as synonomous with, and limited to, unionized environments. A negotiations perspective can give further impetus to the teaching of human resource management from a governance (Beer, 1982) or diversity of interests perspective. Finally, for the growing number of courses on organizational negotiations that are being taught in universities, a more complete perspective on analysis of the different stages of conflict and negotiations in organizations can provide a useful organizing theme and framework.

Ultimately, this work should produce better participants and interveners in organizational negotiations processes. Each of the chapters that follow help move organization theory and research in this direction. Taken together, they demonstrate the power a negotiations perspective holds for students of and practitioners in organizations.

REFERENCES

Argyris, C. *Integrating the individual and the organization.* New York: John Wiley, 1964.

Argyris, C. *The applicability of organizational sociology.* New York: Cambridge University Press, 1972.

Bacharach, S. B., & Lawler, E. J. *Power and politics in organizations.* San Francisco: Jossey-Bass, 1980.

Bacharach, S. B., & Lawler, E. J. *Bargaining.* San Francisco: Jossey-Bass, 1981.

Barbash, J. The elements of industrial relations. *British Journal of Industrial Relations,* 1964, *2,* 66-78.

Barnard, C. *The functions of the executive.* Cambridge, MA: Harvard University Press, 1938.

Beckhard, R. *Organization developmment.* Reading, MA: Addison-Wesley, 1969.

Beer, M. *Report on the first year human resource management course* (Working Paper 82-50). Boston: Harvard University, Graduate School of Business Administration, 1982.

Blau, P. M., & Schoenherr, R. A. *The structure of organizations.* New York: Basic Books, 1971.

Blau, P. M., & Scott, W. *Formal organizations.* San Francisco: Chandler, 1962.

Brown, L. D. *Managing conflict at organizational interfaces.* Reading, MA: Addison-Wesley, 1983.

Chamberlain, N. W. *A general theory of economic process.* New York: Harper, 1955.

Chamberlain, N. W., & Kuhn, J. *Collective bargaining* (2nd ed.). New York: McGraw-Hill, 1965.

Commons, J. R. *Institutional economics: Its place in the political economy.* New York: Macmillan, 1934.

Cooper, W. H. Ubiquitious halo. *Psychological Bulletin,* 1981, *90,* 218-244.

Coser, L. *The functions of social conflict.* Glencoe, IL: Free Press, 1956.

Cyert, R. M., & March, J. G. *A behavioral theory of the firm.* Englewood Cliffs, NJ: Prentice-Hall, 1963.

Dahrendorf, R. *Class and class conflict in industrial society.* London: Routledge, 1959.

Emerson, R. M. Power-dependence relations. *American Sociological Review,* 1962, *27,* 31-40.

Fayol, H. *General and industrial management.* London: Pitman & Sons, 1949.

Fleishman, E. A., Harris, E. G., & Burtt, H. E. *Leadership and supervision in industry.* Columbus: Bureau of Educational Research, Ohio State University, 1955.

French, J.R.P., Jr., & Raven, B. H. The bases of social power. In D. Cartwright & A. Zander (Eds.), *Group dynamics: Research and theory.* Evanston, IL: Row Peterson, 1960.

Friedlander, F., & Pickle, H. Components of effectiveness in small organizations. *Administrative Science Quarterly,* 1968, *13,* 289-304.

Goldman, P., & Van Houten, D. R. Managerial strategies and the worker: A Marxist analysis of bureaucracy. *Sociological Quarterly,* 1977, *18,* 108-125.

Goodman, P. S., & Pennings, J. M. (Eds.). *New perspectives on organizational effectiveness.* San Francisco: Jossey-Bass, 1977.

Hyman, R. *Industrial relations: A Marxist introduction.* London: Macmillan, 1975.

Ikle, F. C. "Negotiation." In *International encyclopedia of the social sciences.* New York: Macmillan, 1968.

Kanter, R. M. *Men and women of the corporation.* New York: Basic Books, 1976.

Katz, H., Kochan, T. A., & Weber, M. *Assessing the effects of industrial relations and quality of working life efforts on organizational effectiveness.* Working Paper, Sloan School of Management, M.I.T., 1983.

Katz, H., Kochan, T. A., & Gobielle, K. Industrial relations performance, economic performance and the effects of the quality of working life efforts: An interplant comparison. *Industrial and Labor Relations Review,* in press.

Kerr, C., Dunlop, J. T., Harbison, F. H., & Myers, C. A. *Industrialism and industrial man.* New York: Oxford University Press, 1964.

Kerr, C., & Fisher, L. H. Plant sociology: The elite and the aborigines. In M. Komarovsky (Ed.), *Common frontiers of social sciences.* New York: Free Press, 1957.

Kochan, T. A. *Collective bargaining and industrial relations.* Homewood, IL: Irwin, 1980.

Kochan, T. A. and Cappelli, P. The transformation of the industrial relations and personnel function. In Paul Osterman (Ed.), *Employment policies of larger firms.* Cambridge, MA: MIT, 1983.

Kochan, T. A., Cummings, L. L., & Huber, G. P. Operationalizing the concept of goals and goal incompatibilities in organizational research. *Human Relations,* 1970, *29,* 527-554.

Kochan, T. A., & Jick, T. The public sector mediation process: A theory and empirical examination. *Journal of Conflict Resolution,* 1978, *22,* 209-240.

Lawrence, P., & Lorsch, J. *Organization and its environment.* Cambridge, MA: Harvard University Press, 1967.

Likert, R. *New Patterns of Management.* New York: McGraw-Hill, 1961.

Likert, R. *The human organization.* New York: McGraw-Hill, 1967.

March, J. G., & Simon, H. A. *Organizations.* New York: John Wiley, 1958.

Mayo, E. *The human problems of an industrial civilization.* New York: Macmillan, 1933.

Ouchi, W. *Theory Z.* Reading, MA: Addison-Wesley, 1981.

Perlman, S. *A theory of the labor movement.* New York: Macmillan, 1928.

Perrow, C. A framework for the comparative analysis of organizations. *American Sociological Review,* 1967, *32,* 194-208.

Pettigrew, A. M. *The politics of organizational decision making.* London: Travistock, 1973.

Pfeffer, J. *Power in organizations.* Marshfield, MA: Pitman, 1981.

Pondy, L. R. Organizational conflict: Concepts of models. *Administrative Science Quarterly,* 1967, *17,* 296-320.

Pondy, L. R. Varieties of organizational conflict. *Administrative Science Quarterly.* 1969, *14,* 499-520.

Pondy, L. R. A reviewer's comment. *Administrative Science Quarterly,* 1972, *17,* 408-409.

Pugh, D. S., et al. Dimensions of organizational structure. *Administrative Science Quarterly,* 1968, *13,* 65-103.

Raskin, A. H., & Dunlop, J. T. Two views of collective bargaining. In Lloyd Ulman (Ed.), *Challenges to collective bargaining.* Englewood Cliffs, NJ: Prentice-Hall, 1967.

Schein, E. H. *Process consultation.* Reading, MA: Addison-Wesley, 1969.

Schmidt, S. M., & Kochan, T. A. Conflict: Towards conceptual clarity. *Administrative Science Quarterly,* 1972, *17,* 359-370.

Shull, F. M., Delbecq, A. L., & Cummings, L. L. *Organizational decision making.* New York: McGraw-Hill, 1970.

Stevens, C. M. Is compulsory arbitration compatible with collective bargaining? *Industrial Relations,* 1966, *5,* 38-52.

Strauss, A. L. *Negotiations.* San Francisco: Jossey-Bass, 1978.

Strauss, G. Tactics of lateral relationships: The purchasing agent. *Administrative Science Quarterly,* 1962, *7,* 161-186.

Thompson, J. *Organizations in action.* New York: McGraw-Hill, 1967.

Walton, R. E. *Interpersonal peacemaking: Confrontations and third party consultation.* Reading, MA: Addison-Wesley, 1969.

Walton, R. E., & McKersie, R. B. *A behavioral theory of labor negotiations.* New York: McGraw-Hill, 1965.

—II—

NEGOTIATED DECISION MAKING IN ORGANIZATIONS

2

ACHIEVING INTEGRATIVE AGREEMENTS

Dean G. Pruitt

State University of New York at Buffalo

Integrative agreements in bargaining are those that reconcile (i.e., integrate) the parties' interests and hence yield high joint benefit. They can be constrasted with compromises, which are reached when the parties concede along an obvious dimension to some middle ground and which usually produce lower joint benefit (Follett, 1940). Consider, for example, the story of two sisters who quarreled over an orange (Fisher & Ury, 1981). A compromise agreement was reached to split the fruit in half, whereupon one sister squeezed her portion for juice while the other used the peel from her portion in a cake. For whatever reasons, they overlooked the integrative agreement of giving the first sister all the juice and the second all the peel.

Integrative agreements sometimes make use of known alternatives, whose joint value becomes apparent during the controversy. But more often they involve the development of novel alternatives. Hence it is proper to say that they usually emerge from creative problem solving. Integrative alternatives (those that form the basis for integra-

Author's Note: *This research was supported by National Science Foundation grant BNS80-14902.*

tive agreements) can be devised by either party acting separately, by the two of them in joint session, or by a third party such as a mediator.

In the story of the sisters, the situation had unusually high *integrative potential* in the sense of allowing the development of an agreement that totally satisfied both parties' aspirations. Not all situations are so hopeful. For example, in negotiating the price of a car, both dealer and customer usually must reduce their aspirations in order to reach agreement.

However, most situations have more integrative potential than is commonly assumed. For example, car dealers can often sweeten the deal by throwing in a radio or other accessory that costs them little but benefits their customer a lot. Hence problem solving is often richly rewarded.

There are four main reasons for bargainers (or the mediators assisting them) to seek integrative agreements rather than compromises (Pruitt, 1981);

(1) If aspirations are high and both sides are resistant to conceding, it may not be possible to resolve the conflict unless a way can be found to reconcile the two parties' interests.

(2) Integrative agreements are likely to be more stable. Compromises are often unsatisfactory to one or both parties, causing the issue to come up again at a later time.

(3) Because they are mutually rewarding, integrative agreements tend to strengthen the relationship between the parties. This has a number of benefits, including facilitating problem solving in later conflicts.

(4) Integrative agreements ordinarily contribute to the welfare of the broader community of which the two parties are members. For example, a firm will usually benefit as a whole if its departments are able to reconcile their differences creatively.

METHODS FOR ACHIEVING INTEGRATIVE AGREEMENTS

Five methods for achieving integrative agreements will now be described. These are means by which the parties' initially opposing demands can be transformed into alternatives that reconcile their interests. They can be used by one party, both parties working together, or a third party such as a mediator. Each method involves a different way of refocusing the issues under dispute. Hence potentially useful refocusing questions will be provided under each heading. Information that is useful for implementing each method will also be mentioned, and the methods will be listed in order of increasing difficulty of getting this information.

The methods will be illustrated by a running example concerning a husband and wife who are trying to decide where to go on a two-week vacation. The husband wants to go to the mountains, his wife to the seashore. They have considered the compromise of spending one week in each location but are hoping for something better. What approach should they take?

Expanding the Pie

Some conflicts hinge on a resource shortage. For example, time, money, space, and automobiles are in short supply but long demand. In such circumstances, integrative agreements can be devised by increasing the available resources. This is called expanding the pie. For example, our married couple might solve their problems by persuading their employers to give them four weeks of vacation so that they can take two in the mountains and two at the seashore. Another example (cited by Follett, 1940) is that of two milk companies vying to be first to unload cans on a platform. The controversy was resolved when somebody thought of widening the platform.

Expanding the pie is a useful formula when the parties reject one another's demands because of opportunity costs; for example, if the husband rejects the seashore because it keeps him away from the mountains and the wife rejects the mountains because they deny her the pleasure of the seashore. But it is by no means a universal remedy. Expanding the pie may yield strikingly poor benefits if there are inherent costs in the other's proposal, e.g., the husband cannot stand the seashore or the wife the mountains. Other methods are better in such cases.

Expanding the pie requires no analysis of the interests underlying the parties' demands. Hence its information requirements are slim. However, this does not mean that a solution by this method is always easy to find. There may be no resource shortage, or the shortage may not be easy to see or to remedy.

Refocusing questions that can be useful in seeking a solution by pie expansion include: How can both parties get what they want? Does the conflict hinge on a resource shortage? How can the critical resource be expanded?

Nonspecific Compensation

In nonspecific compensation, one party gets what he or she wants and the other is repaid in some unrelated coin. Compensation is nonspecific if it does not deal with the precise costs incurred by the other party. For example, the wife in our example might agree to go to the mountains, even though she finds them boring, if her husband promises her a fur coat. Another example would be giving an employee a bonus for going without dinner.

Compensation usually comes from the party whose demands are granted. But it can also originate with a third party or even with the party who is compensated. An example of the latter would be an employee who pampers him- or herself by finding a nice office to work in while going without dinner.

Two kinds of information are useful for devising a solution by nonspecific compensation: (a) information about what is valuable to the other party; for example, knowledge that he or she values love, attention, or money; (b) information about how badly the other party is hurting by making concessions. This is useful for devising adequate compensation for these concessions. If such information is not available, it may be possible to conduct an "auction" for the other party's acquiescence, changing the sort of benefit offered or raising one's offer, in trial-and-error fashion, until an acceptable formula is found.

Refocusing questions that can help locate a means of compensation include: How much is the other party hurting in conceding to me? What does the other party value that I can supply? How valuable is this to the other party?

Logrolling

Logrolling is possible in complex agendas where several issues are under consideration and the parties have differing priorities among these issues. Each party concedes on low priority issues in exchange for concessions on issues of higher priority to itself. Each gets that part of its demands that it finds most important. For example, suppose that in addition to disagreeing about where to go on vacation, the wife in our example wants to go to a first-class hotel while her husband prefers a tourist home. If accommodations are a high priority issue for the wife and location for the husband, they can reach a fairly integrative solution by agreeing to go to a first-class hotel in the mountains. Logrolling can be viewed as a variant of nonspecific compensation in which both parties instead of one are compensated for making concessions desired by the other.

To develop solutions by logrolling, it is useful to have information about the two parties' priorities so that exchangeable concessions can be identified. But it is not necessary to have information about the interests (e.g., the aspirations, values) underlying these priorities. Solutions by logrolling can also be developed by a process of trial and error in which one party moves systematically through a series of possible packages, keeping his or her own outcomes as high as possible, until an alternative is found that is acceptable to the other party (Kelley & Schenitzki, 1972; Pruitt & Carnevale, 1982).

Refocusing questions that can be useful for developing solutions by logrolling include: Which issues are of higher and lower priority to myself? Which issues are of higher and lower priority to the other party? Are some of my high-priority issues of low priority to the other party and vice versa?

Cost Cutting

In solutions by cost cutting, one party gets what he or she wants and the other's costs are reduced or eliminated. The result is high joint benefit, not because the first party has changed his or her demands but because the second party suffers less. For instance, suppose that the husband in our example dislikes the beach because of the hustle and bustle. He may be quite willing to go there on vacation if his costs are cut by renting a house with a quiet inner courtyard where he can read while his wife goes out among the crowds.

Cost cutting often takes the form of specific compensation in which the party who concedes receives something in return that satisfies the precise values frustrated. For example, the employee who must work through dinner time can be specifically compensated by provision of a meal in a box. Specific compensation differs from nonspecific compensation in dealing with the precise costs incurred rather than providing repayment in an unrelated coin. The costs are actually canceled out rather than overbalanced by benefits experienced in some other realm.

Information about the nature of one of the parties' costs is, of course, helpful for developing solutions by cost cutting. This is a deeper kind of information than knowledge of that party's priorities. It involves knowing something about the interests—the values, aspirations, and standards—underlying that party's overt position.

Refocusing questions for developing solutions by cost cutting include: What costs are posed for the other party by our proposal? How can these costs be mitigated or eliminated?

Bridging

In bridging, neither party achieves its initial demands but a new option is devised that satisfies the most important interests underlying these demands. For example, suppose that the husband in our vacation example is mainly interested in fishing and hunting and the wife in swimming and sunbathing. Their interests might be bridged by finding an inland resort with a lake and a beach that is close to woods and streams. Follett (1940) gives another homely example of two women reading in a library room. One wanted to open the window for ventilation, the other to keep it closed so as not to catch cold. The ultimate solution involved opening a window in the next room, which satisfied both the need for fresh air and the need to avoid a draft.

Bridging typically involves a reformulation of the issue(s) based on an analysis of the underlying interests on both sides. For example, a critical turning point in our vacation example is likely to come when the initial formulation, "Shall we go to the mountains or the seashore?" is replaced by "Where can we find fishing, hunting, swimming, and sunbathing?" This new formulation becomes the basis for a search model (Simon, 1957), which is employed in an effort to locate a novel alternative. The process of reformulation can be done by either or both parties or by a third party who is trying to help.

People who seek to develop solutions by bridging need information about the nature of the two parties' interests and their priorities among these interests. Priority information is useful because it is rare to find a solution, like opening the window in the next room of the library, that bridges all of the two parties' interests. More often, higher-priority interests are served while lower-priority interests are discarded. For example, the wife who agrees to go to an inland lake may have foregone the lesser value of smelling the sea air and the husband may have foregone his preference for spectacular mountain vistas.

In the initial phase of search for a solution by bridging, the search model can include all of the interests on both sides. But if this does not generate a mutually acceptable alternative, some of the lower-priority interests must be discarded from the model and the search begun anew. The result will not be an ideal solution but, it is hoped, one that is mutually acceptable. Dropping low-priority interests in the development of a solution by bridging is similar to dropping low-priority demands in the search for a solution by logrolling. However, the latter is in the realm of concrete proposals, while the former is in the realm of the interests underlying these proposals.

Refocusing questions that can be raised in search of a solution by bridging include: What are the two parties' basic interests? What are their priorities among these interests? How can the two sets of high-priority interests be reconciled?

THE ANALYSIS OF INTERESTS

To devise integrative solutions involving cost cutting or bridging, it is usually necessary to know something about the interests underlying

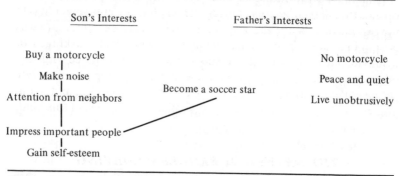

Figure 2.1   Son's Interest Tree in a Controversy With Father

one or both parties' proposals. The only other possible approach is one of trial and error, which is usually inferior.

Interests are commonly organized into hierarchical trees, with more basic interests underpinning more superficial ones. Hence it is often useful to go deeper than the interests immediately underlying a party's proposals to the interests underlying these interests, or even to the interests underlying the interests underlying the interests. If one goes far enough down the tree, an interest may be located that can be easily reconciled with the opposing party's interests.

An example of an interest tree can be seen on the left in Figure 2.1. It belongs to a hypothetical boy who is trying to persuade his father to allow him to buy a motorcycle. At the top right are listed those of the father's interests that conflict with the son's. At the top of the tree is the boy's initial proposal (buy a motorcycle), which is hopelessly opposed to this father's proposal (no motorcycle). Analysis of the boy's proposal yields a first-level underlying interest, to make noise in the neighborhood. But this is opposed to his dad's interest of maintaining peace and quiet. Further analysis of the boy's position reveals a second-level interest underlying the first level, to gain attention from the neighbors. But again this conflicts with one of his father's basic interests, to live unobtrusively. The controversy is only resolved when someone (the father, the boy, the boy's mother) discovers an even more basic interest underlying the desire for a motorcycle—the boy's desire to impress important people. This discovery is helpful because there are ways of making such an impression that do not contradict the father's interests, for example, going out for the high school soccer team. At the bottom of the boy's tree is a fourth-level interest, self-esteem. But it is unnecessary to go down this far, because the controversy can be resolved at the third level.

Analysis of the interests underlying divergent positions often reveals that the initial area of disagreement had different meanings to the two parties. While there appeared to be disagreement, there was no fundamental opposition in what they were really asking. For example, one party may be more concerned with substance while the other cares more for appearances, one may be seeking an immediate settlement while the other is seeking a long-term solution, and so on. Fisher and Ury (1981, p. 77) list nine other dimensions of this kind.

THE NATURE OF PROBLEM SOLVING

Bargainers are sometimes able to "luck into" a highly integrative agreement as, for example, when prior creative activity has produced a good standard solution. But more often they, or some third party working with them, must engage in problem solving, that is, must seek a new option that better satisfies both parties' interests than those currently available. The more vigorous is this problem solving, the more integrative is the final agreement likely to be, up to the limits imposed by the integrative potential.

Problem solving takes a variety of forms. For example, one can raise refocusing questions of the kind described earlier or seek and provide information about priorities and interests. (When both parties provide such information, it is called *information exchange*). An important aspect of problem solving is openness to new alternatives, that is, a willingness to seek them oneself and give them serious consideration when suggested by the opponent or some third party.

In seeking new alternatives, it is necessary to adopt a policy of *firm flexibility*.[1] One must be *firm* with respect to one's *ends* (i.e., one's interests), giving them up only if they are clearly unobtainable. Otherwise the solution will be one-sided in favor of the other party rather than represent a true integration of the two parties' needs. Yet one must also be *flexible* with respect to the *means* to these ends, continually seeking new alternatives until a mutually acceptable one can be found.

An example of firm flexibility can be seen in actions taken by President John F. Kennedy in 1961 during the second Berlin crisis. The Russians, led by Premier Nikita Khrushchev, had been trying to end American occupation of West Berlin by threatening to sign a separate peace treaty with East Germany and buzzing planes in the Berlin Corridor. Recognizing that some concessions had to be made,

Kennedy "decided to be firm on essentials but negotiate on non-essentials" (Snyder & Diesing, 1977, p. 566). In a speech on July 25, he announced three fundamental principles that ensured the integrity and continued American occupation of West Berlin. The firmness of these principles was underscored by a pledge to defend them by force and a concomitant military buildup (Pruitt & Holland, 1972). Yet Kennedy also indicated flexibility and a concern about Russian priorities by calling for negotiations to remove "actual irritants" to the Soviet Union and its allies. Two results were achieved: the building of the Berlin Wall, which can be viewed as a bridging solution that solved the problem of population loss from East Germany without disturbing American rights in West Berlin, and eventual negotiations that put these rights clearly in writing.

CONDITIONS ENCOURAGING THE DEVELOPMENT OF INTEGRATIVE SOLUTIONS

In three recent studies, the antecedents of integrative agreements by means of a simulated negotiation task with logrolling potential were explored. The subjects, playing the roles of buyer and seller in a wholesale appliance market, were expected to reach agreement on prices for television sets, vacuum cleaners, and typewriters. Profit schedules were arranged so that the buyer's highest profits were achieved on television sets and the seller's on typewriters. Hence the best agreement for both parties involved a low price for television sets and a high price for typewriters. (This method is described in more detail in Kimmel, Pruitt, Magenau, Konar-Goldband, & Carnevale [1980] and Pruitt and Lewis [1975].)

Theoretical guidance was derived from a *dual concern model* based on the writings of Blake and Mouton (1979), Filley (1975), and Thomas (1976). This postulates that problem solving and hence (when there is integrative potential) high joint benefit will arise to the extent that bargainers are concerned about both their own and the other party's outcomes. If they are mainly concerned about their own outcomes, they will engage instead in contentious behavior designed to elicit concessions from the other party. As a result, they will be inflexible with respect to means and thus achieve low joint benefit. If they are concerned primarily about the other party's outcomes, they will be overly flexible with respect to ends, also leading to low joint benefit.

All three studies employed 2 × 2 factorial designs, involving various interpretations of concern about own and other's outcomes. All variables were manipulated bilaterally in the sense that both bargainers received identical instructions and experiences.

In the first two studies, concern about own outcomes was interpreted as resistance to reducing one's aspirations (i.e., forsaking one's interests). High resistance was produced by sending the bargainers' private communications from their companies instructing them to reach an agreement involving a total profit of $4600 or more. (This figure was chosen because past experience had shown that it was a moderately difficult goal.) Low resistance was produced by saying nothing about a lower limit on profit. In Study 1 (Ben Yoav & Pruitt, 1982), concern about the other party's outcomes was encouraged by inducing a concern about the relationship with the other party. We told the bargainers that they would have to work together toward a common goal on a task following the negotiation. In the contrasting condition, they were told that they would be working alone on a subsequent task. In Study 2 (Nachajsky, Carnevale, Van Slyck, & Pruitt, 1982), high concern about the other party's outcomes was encouraged by putting the bargainers in a good mood. Shortly before the beginning of negotiation, each bargainer received a gift from a confederate of the experimenter. Earlier research (Isen & Levin, 1972) suggests that gifts induce a good mood that encourages a desire to help others. There was no gift in the low-concern condition.

The results of both studies supported the predictions from the dual-concern model. High resistance to reducing aspirations in conjunction with either a concern about the relationship or a good mood encouraged the development of agreements involving high joint benefit. A content analysis of verbalizations showed that the bargainers in these conditions tended to exchange information about their profit schedules, a form of problem solving. However, the separate elements of this combination led to low joint benefit. Resistance to reducing aspirations alone encouraged contentious behavior, often leading to failure to reach agreement. Concern about the relationship and a good mood produced the worst joint outcomes of all, presumably by encouraging efforts to seek a simple compromise.

These results lead to interesting conclusions about conditions that foster a desire to be cooperative or helpful. When people are also motivated to hold fast to their basic aspirations, such conditions encourage creative problem solving and hence high joint benefit. But when aspirations are free to vary, such conditions encourage too rapid concession making and hence result in low joint benefit. It follows that conditions that foster cooperativeness must be balanced by conditions that support aspirations if they are to produce creative problem solving in interpersonal and intergroup relations.

In Study 3 (Ben Yoav & Pruitt, 1983) concern about own outcomes was produced by making the bargainers highly accountable to constituents. Two confederates served as constituents. Under high accountability, the constituents were able to divide the money earned in the negotiation and to write an evaluation of the outcome achieved by their negotiators. Under low accountability, the bargainers divided the money earned and no evaluations were written. Concern about the other's outcomes was produced as in Study 1 by the expectation of cooperative future interaction.

Again, the winning combination involved a combination of both concerns. Highly accountable representatives who were concerned about their relationship with the other party achieved unusually high joint benefit. But accountability alone or concern about the relationship alone had no such effect. Both conditions produced low joint benefit, the former in conjunction with heavy contentious behavior.

These last findings have interesting implications for bargaining between group representatives. Accountability is shown to be a two-edged sword. Under normal conditions, it encourages contentious behavior and low joint benefit. But in association with good relations between the opposing representatives, it fosters problem solving and high joint benefit. Good relations between opposing representatives are also shown to be a two-edged sword. When coupled with high accountability, they foster creative problem solving, leading to a productive resolution of intergroup controversy. But when accountability is low, they encourage "cozy" arrangements in which the representatives lose track of their constituent's interests and end up with simple, unimaginative compromise agreements.

These findings also relate to the impact of role conflict. The combination of high accountability and concern about the relationship places bargainers in a conflict between constituent expectations and a desire to please the other bargainer. Our research suggests that such role conflict can, under some circumstances, encourage a creative synthesis of the two sets of demands rather than the sort of debilitating psychological reaction found by Kahn, Wolfe, Quinn, Snoek, and Rosenthal (1964).

THE ROLE OF CONTENTIOUS BEHAVIOR

Contentious behavior[2] consists of all those actions that are designed to elicit concessions from the other party. Examples include persuasive arguments, threats, and positional commitments.

Contentious behavior has traditionally been assumed to militate against the development of integrative agreements (Blake & Mouton, 1979; Deutsch, 1973; Walton & McKersie, 1965), and there is solid research evidence supporting this assumption (Pruitt & Carnevale, 1982), including some reported just above. There are four reasons why this should be true:

(1) Contentious behavior ordinarily involves standing firm on a particular proposal that one seeks to foist on the other party. This is incompatible with the flexibility about means that is an important element of successful problem solving.

(2) Contentious behavior encourages hostility toward the other party by a principle of psychological consistency. This diminishes one's willingness to contribute to the other's welfare and hence one's willingness to devise or accept jointly beneficial alternatives.

(3) Contentious behavior encourages the other party to feel hostile and engage in contentious behavior in return. A conflict spiral may ensue in which both parties becomes increasingly rigid and progressively more reluctant to take any actions that benefit the other.

(4) Contentious behavior signals to the other party that one has a win/lose orientation, calling into question the possibility of achieving a jointly beneficial agreement. In other words, it tends to reduce the integrative potential perceived by the other party.

However, the indictment against contentious behavior has been clearly overdrawn. Under some circumstances, this behavior can actually make problem solving more likely or contribute to the effectiveness of problem solving. This can occur in two ways:

(1) It encourages the other party to face the controversy when he or she benefits from the status quo. If present circumstances favor the other party, it is often necessary to employ threats to force his or her attention to one's concerns. Such threats run the risk of eliciting

contentious behavior in return and a conflict spiral. But they can encourage problem-solving behavior by the other party (Pruitt & Gleason, 1978).

An example can be seen at the beginning of the second Berlin crisis, when Russian Premier Nikita Khrushchev threatened to sign a separate peace treaty with East Germany if the status of West Berlin were not settled to his liking. At the same time, he proposed negotiation. Had he not made this threat, which was tantamount to a proposal to give East Germany control of the access routes to West Berlin, it is doubtful that the West would have accepted his offer of negotiation.

(2) It underlines one's areas of firmness. Threats and other contentious actions are means of communication. They can be used to emphasize the rigidity of one's high priority interests, making it doubly clear that certain elements of one's position are nonnegotiable. An example would be the Kennedy speech mentioned earlier in which he threatened to use force to defend the integrity of and American access to West Berlin. Concomitant troop movements added emphasis to his message. Such a message can contribute to the development integrative solution in two ways:

(a) It makes the other party less likely to try to dislodge one from one's areas of firmness. Instead the other is motivated to try to devise a way to live within these constraints, i.e., to engage in problem solving.

(b) It makes one more likely to take problem-solving actions, since there is less need to fear that the other side will misinterpret them as signs of weakness. Thus shielded by his own threats from being misinterpreted, Kennedy was able to call for negotiations to remove "actual irritants" to the Soviet Union.

In short, contentious behavior has the capacity of both contributing to and militating against the development of integrative agreements.

How can the advantages of this kind of behavior be achieved while avoiding the pitfalls? Four tentative answers to this question are proposed:

(1) Send signals of flexibility and a concern about the other party's interests in conjunction with contentious displays. Khrushchev did this by coupling his threat with hints of a willingness to make concesssions; Kennedy, by offering to negotiate about "actual irritants." Such maneuvers are designed to make the integrative

potential seem large enough to the other party that problem solving seems warranted.

(2) Insulate contentious behavior from problem-solving behavior so that neither undermines the other. The most common form of insulation is the "black-hat/white-hat" routine, in which contentious behavior is assigned to one team member (the black hat) and problem-solving behavior to another (the white hat). In the context of the black hat's threats, the white hat's offer of cooperation is more likely to be reciprocated by the target. In the context of the white hat's blandishments, the black hat's escalation is less likely to be reciprocated by the target.

(3) Use contentious tactics to defend basic interests rather than a particular solution to the controversy. It is possible for the other party to cope with such rigidities.

(4) Employ deterrent rather than compellent threats. Deterrent threats indicate that a particular action or solution favored by the other is intolerable but do not judge the adequacy of other solutions. They involve saying "no" to the other party without demanding that the other say "yes."

NOTES

1. Called "flexible rigidity" in a prior publication (Pruitt, 1981).

2. The term "contentious" is used in preference to "competitive" because the latter carries the excess meaning of trying to do better than the other party and in preference to "distributive" so as to avoid confusion with distributive justice.

REFERENCES

Ben Yoav, O., & Pruitt, D. G. *Level of aspiration and expectation of future interaction in negotiation.* Paper presented at the annual convention of the American Psychological Association, Washington, August 1982.

Ben Yoav, O., & Pruitt, D. G. *Accountability, a two edged sword: Friend and foe of integrative agreements.* Paper presented at the annual convention of the Eastern Academy of Management, Pittsburgh, May 1983.

Blake, R. R., & Mouton, J. S. Intergroup problem solving organization: From theory to practice. In W. G. Austin & S. Worchel (Eds.), *The social psychology of intergroup relations.* Monterey, CA: Brooks/Cole, 1979.

Deutsch, M. *The resolution of conflict.* New Haven, CT: Yale University Press, 1973.

Filley, A. C. *Interpersonal conflict resolution.* Glenview, IL: Scott, Foresman, 1975.

Fisher, R., & Ury, W. *Getting to YES.* Boston: Houghton Mifflin, 1981.

Follett, M. P. Constructive conflict. In H. C. Metcalf & L. Urwick (Eds.) *Dynamic administration: The collected papers of Mary Parker Follett.* New York: Harper, 1940.

Isen, A. M., & Levin, P. F. Effect of feeling good on helping: Cookies and kindness. *Journal of Personality and Social Psychology.* 1972, *21,* 384-388.

Kahn, R. L., Wolfe, D. M., Quinn, R. P., Snoek, J. D., & Rosenthal, R. A. *Organizational stress: Studies in rule conflict and ambiguity.* New York: John Wiley, 1964.

Kelley, H. H., & Schenitzki, D. P. Bargaining. In C. G. McClintock (Ed.), *Experimental social psychology.* New York: Holt, Rinehart & Winston, 1972.

Kimmel, M. J., Pruitt, D. G., Magenau, J. M., Konar-Goldband, E., & Carnevale, P.J.D. Effects of trust, aspiration and gender on negotiation tactics. *Journal of Personality and Social Psychology,* 1980, *38,* 9-23.

Nochajski, T. H., Carnevale, P.J.D., Van Slyck, M. R., & Pruitt, D. G. *Positive mood, aspirations, and negotiation behavior.* Paper presented at the annual convention of the Eastern Psychological Association, Baltimore, March 1982.

Pruitt, D. G. *Negotiation behavior.* New York: Academic, 1981.

Pruitt, D. G., & Carnevale, P.J.D. The development of integrative agreements. In V. J. Derlega & J. Grzelak (Eds.), *Cooperation and helping behavior.* New York: Academic, 1982.

Pruitt, D. G., & Gleason, J. M. Threat capacity and the choice between independence and interdependence. *Personality and Social Psychology Bulletin,* 1978, *4,* 252-255.

Pruitt, D. G., & Holland, J. *Settlement in the Berlin crisis, 1958-1962.* Special Study No. 18 of the Council on International Studies, State University of New York at Buffalo, 1972.

Pruitt, D. G., & Lewis, S. A. Development of integrative solutions in bilateral negotiation. *Journal of Personality and Social Psychology,* 1975, *31,* 621-633.

Simon, H. A. *Models of man.* New York: John Wiley, 1957.

Snyder, G. H., & Diesing, P. *Conflict among nations.* Princeton, NJ: Princeton University Press, 1977.

Thomas, K. Conflict and conflict management. In M. D. Dunnette (Ed.), *Handbook of industrial and organizational psychology.* Chicago: Rand McNally, 1976.

Walton, R. E., & McKersie, R. B. *A behavioral theory of labor negotiations.* New York: McGraw-Hill, 1965.

3

HEURISTICS IN NEGOTIATION
Limitations to Effective Dispute Resolution

Max H. Bazerman

Massachusetts Institute of Technology

Margaret A. Neale

University of Arizona

Negoitation is a decision-making process in which multiple parties jointly make decisions to resolve conflicting interests. The research literature typically classifies the study of negotiations in organizations as part of labor/management relations. However, negotiations extend over a much broader range of organizational processes, occurring in

Authors' Note: This research was funded by National Science Foundation grant BNS9107331. This chapter benefited from the helpful comments of Roy Lewicki. It was written while the first author was at Boston University.

the acquisition of supplies, salary negotiation, personnel transfers within organizations, performance appraisal, budget determination, the acquisition of financing, selling output, and so on. In addition to limiting its application to labor/management relations, the literature has concentrated on two major categories of research: the industrial relations approach and the social psychological approach (Kochan, 1980). The industrial relations approach encompasses three major components of negotiating: (1) legal issues, (2) the historical/institutional aspects, and (3) the neoclassical economic. The social psychological perspective focuses on the individual differences of the negotiators (e.g., interpersonal orientation) and structural interventions (e.g., forms of third-party interventions). Further, both these lines of investigation have emphasized the *outcomes* of negotiation (resolution or impasse, value of the contract, and so forth) to the virtual exclusion of the *process* involved in negotiation. The purpose of this chapter is to suggest an alternative direction for negotiation research—that of defining the negotiator as a decision maker, focusing on the effects of the negotiator's decision-making process on the negotiator's success and the likelihood of reaching a negotiated settlement. Specifically, five decisional biases will be suggested that systematically and predictably alter negotiator performance and dispute resolution behavior.

To more clearly understand how these inferential biases work, it is useful to make the argument that negotiator behavior often deviates from rationality. To allow us to discuss the existence of systematic deviations from rationality by negotiators, consider Walton and McKersie's (1965) "bargaining zone" concept. Their framework can be illustrated through the use of the following simplified diagram:

$$\text{M}_t \qquad \text{U}_r \qquad \text{M}_r \qquad \text{U}_t$$

M_t = management's target
U_r = union's resistance point
M_r = management's resistance point
U_r = union's target

Walton and McKersie suggested that each negotiator has a resistance point, below which he or she would choose to sustain a strike (or whatever alternative exists when an impasse is reached) rather than settle. Further, they suggested that the resistance points typically represent greater compromise than is suggested by the two parties' target points and initial offers/demands. If a gap exists between resistance points—that is, the employer's (in a labor/management context) resistance point is less than the union's resistance point—a "*negative* contract zone" exists. Where the resistance points overlap (e.g., the above diagram), a "*positive* contract zone" exists. If the negotiators are rational, a settlement would never occur when a negative contract zone exists, while a settlement would always occur when a positive contract zone exists. In contrast, common observation is that the two parties often fail to agree despite overlapping resistance points. Walton and McKersie asserted that "intangibles," or psychological factors and conflict dynamics, result in the disappearance of the bargaining zone during negotiations. *If it is rational for a settlement to occur whenever a positive contract zone exists, what specific processes account for negotiators failing to reach an agreement despite overlapping resistance points?* The alternative direction to understanding the negotiation process that we propose here offers some answers to this question.

The lack of rationality in the negotiation process can further be seen by considering the recent normative work of Farber and Katz (1979). They argued that negotiators who do not reach agreement under conditions of binding arbitration may still be acting in a rational manner, considering their particular risk attitudes. They suggested that if both parties are risk averse, a negotiated settlement should occur rather than the parties accepting the uncertainty of giving an outside third party the power to determine a settlement (a riskier option without increasing the aggregated expected value). A resolution is also predicted if risk aversion is so strong in one party that he or she is willing to pay the premium required by the more risk seeking party in order to forego the uncertainty of arbitration. Conversely, if both parties are risk seeking, or if risk seeking dominates, arbitration will be invoked. Thus based on this work, it is suggested that individuals choosing to invoke binding arbitration are probably risk seeking. It is, however, widely accepted in the decision theory literature that individuals and organizations tend to be risk averse (Holloway, 1979). Given that organizations and individuals are risk averse, the increasing number of negotiations reaching impasse illustrates a critical paradox of negotiator behavior: *If failing to reach an agreement is a risk-seeking alternative, why do typically risk-averse negotiators (individuals and/or organizations) exhibit increasing utilization of arbitrators?* Resolution of this paradox may be facilitated by an understanding of the systematic biases that negotiators incorporate into their decision-making processes. Further, while Farber and Katz developed their logic in the context of parties' going to binding arbitration, the paradox analyzed here is applicable to a broad range of conflict situations.

Following March and Simon's (1958) concept of bounded rationality, the literature on behavioral decision theory has identified a number of ways in which systematic biases bound a decision maker's rationality. This chapter proposes five specific biases that affect negotiators and demonstrates how these biases may explain the paradox defined above. For each bias, logic and empirical evidence will be presented to demonstrate the effect and examine the impact of that bias in the negotiation domain.

THE FRAMING OF NEGOTIATION

Bazerman's (1982) adaptation of Kahneman and Tversky's (1979) prospect theory presents the following question:

> A large car manufacturer has recently been hit with a number of economic difficulties and it appears as if three plants need to be closed and 6000 employees laid off. The vice-president of production has been exploring alternative ways to avoid this crisis. She has developed two plans:
>
> Plan A: This plan will save 1 of the 3 plants and 2000 jobs.
>
> Plan B: This plan has a ⅓ probability of saving all 3 plants and all 6000 jobs, but has a ⅔ probability of saving no plants and no jobs.
>
> Which plan would you select?

Organizational behavior research has identified a number of content issues that are relevant to consider in evaluating the plans. However, a more fundamental question underlies this subjective situation and the resulting decision. Reconsider the above problem, replacing the choice options provided above with the following alternative choices:

Plan C: This plan will result in the loss of 2 of the 3 plants and 4000 jobs.

Plan D: This plan has a ⅔ probability of resulting in the loss of all 3 plants and all 6000 jobs, but has a ⅓ probability of losing no plants and no jobs.

Which plan would you select?

Close examination of the two sets of alternative plans finds them to be *objectively* the same. For example, saving 1 of 3 plants and 2000 of 6000 jobs (Plan A) is the same objective outcome as losing 2 of 3 plants and 4000 of 6000 jobs (Plan C). Empirically, however, *most* (80+ percent) individuals choose Plan A (objectively the same as Plan C) in the first set, while *most* (80+ percent) individuals choose Plan D (objectively the same as Plan B) in the second set. While the two sets of choices are objectively identical, changing the description of the outcome states from job and plants saved (gains) to jobs and plants lost (losses) was sufficient to shift prototypic choice from risk averse (taking the sure thing) to risk seeking.

These findings are consistent with a growinng body of literature (Tversky & Kahneman, 1981; Thaler, 1980; Kahneman & Tversky, 1979) that indicates that individuals treat the prospect of gain (e.g., saving jobs and plants) differently from the prospects of losses (e.g., losing jobs and plants). Kahneman and Tversky's (1979) prospect theory states that potential gains and losses are evaluated relative to their effect on current wealth. Choice is explained by an S-shaped value function—a value function that is convex (indicating a risk-averse orientation) for gains and concave (indicating a risk-seeking orientation) for losses.

Figure 3.1 shows that the value individuals typically place on *saving* one plant and 2,000 jobs is more than one-third of the value placed on *saving* three plants and 6,000 jobs. In contrast, the "value" of a loss suffered by *losing* three plants and 6,000 jobs is not three times as great as the "value" of losing one plant and 2,000 jobs.

Now consider a prototypic labor/management situation: The union claims it needs a raise to $12 per hour and that any lesser raise would represent a *loss* to members given the current inflationary environment. Management, in contrast, claims that it cannot pay more than $10 per hour and that any greater payment would impose an unacceptable *loss* to the company. Given this simplified, one-issue case,

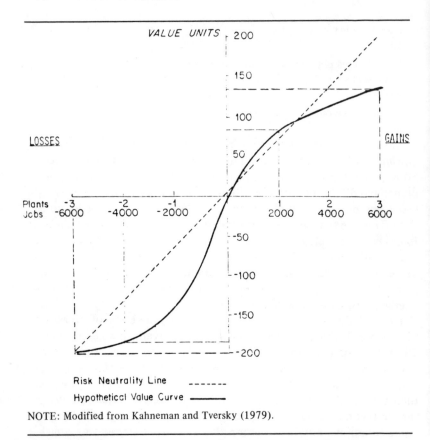

NOTE: Modified from Kahneman and Tversky (1979).

Figure 3.1 Hypothetical Value Function Accounting for Framing

imagine what would happen if each side had the option of settling for $11 per hour or going to arbitration? Since each party is viewing the negotiation in terms of what it has to lose, following Kahneman and Tversky's basic propositions, each will respond in a risk-seeking manner and arbitration is likely to be chosen. Presenting the same objective specified above but changing the *subjective* gain/loss situation results in a very different predicted outcome. If the union views anything about $10/hour as a gain and management views anything under $12/hour as a gain, a positive frame will exist, risk aversion will tend to dominate, and a negotiated settlement will generally occur (Neale and Bazerman, 1983). Empirically, Neale and Bazerman found that a positive frame led to significantly greater concessionary behavior and more successful performance than a negative frame did.

The implications of the above framework are of critical importance. Both sides in negotiations often talk in terms of why they *need* a certain wage, thus setting the referent point (the benchmark by which gains or losses are determined) along the same lines as their public target goals. If this is indeed the case, the negotiators would adopt negative frames, exhibit risk-seeking attitudes, and be less likely to reach a settlement. Because of the tendency to view the potential outcome from this perspective, a critical aspect of the potential success of the negotiation hinges upon how various participants in the interaction are able to influence the position of the referent point and thus the frame of the negotiation. A critical role of interested third parties may therefore be their skill at influencing the parties to alter their negative frame (and concomitant risk-seeking orientation) toward a neutral or positive frame that is more conducive to a negotiated settlement. Thus as Rubin (1980) suggests, the primary role of the third party may not be simply to add uncertainty associated with third-party intervention strategies but to increase the options of the participants by altering the situational frame of the parties in conflict. Second, in collective bargaining it is generally recognized that the actual participants negotiate not only with identified opponents but also with their constituencies to influence the position of the referent points (and thus the frame) through intraorganizational bargaining (Walton & McKersie, 1965). Negotiator skill in interaction with the constituency to manipulate their aspirations levels—as the equivalent third-party skill at influencing negotiator frame—is likely to result in a higher settlement rate because the referent point is altered thus allowing a greater range of settlement options to be viewed as gains (i.e., from a positive frame). Finally, while this framework was developed in the labor/management negotiating domain, the importance of the frame of a dispute is relevant to *any* negotiation context in which two parties have the option of accepting a settlement or in some way risking the escalation of the dispute (e.g., divorce, transfer pricing, salary negotiation).

OVERCONFIDENCE IN JUDGMENT

A substantial amount of research on clinical judgment, decision making, and probability estimation has demonstrated many systematic deviations from rationality. Yet evidence also shows that individuals have unwarranted confidence in their fallible judgments (Einhorn & Hogarth, 1978; Einhorn, 1980). Laboratory subjects are known to be overconfident in their assessment of the probability (confidence judgment) that their response to uncertain decisions will be accurate. Because it is hard to observe overconfidence based on a single confidence judgment, research has examined the quality of a set of confidence judgments, each representing the subjective probability that a response to a two-choice question (e.g., yes/no) is correct (Lichtenstein, Fischhoff, & Phillips, 1977). An appropriately confident individual within this methodology should, for example, be accurate on 80 percent of the judgments to which they give confidence judgments of 80 percent. Typical laboratory studies, in contrast, find overconfidence to be the commonly observed finding (Fischhoff, 1981). For example, with a large group of two-choice questions for which subjects were 75 percent confident that their judgment was correct, typically only 60 percent of the questions would have been answered correctly. For confidence judgments of 100 percent, it is common for subjects to be correct only 85 percent of the time (Fischhoff, 1981). Finally, when people put confidence intervals around numerical judgments (e.g., "I am 95 percent certain that there are between 500 and 700 pennies in that jar"), it is common for the actual number (of pennies) to fall outside the 95 percent boundaries for 50 percent of all subjects.

In the negotiation context, Farber (1981) discusses this problem in terms of the existence of divergent expectations by negotiators. That is, each negotiator has an optimistic view of the point at which a neutral third party will choose to adjudicate the dispute. For example, assume the union is demanding $8.75 per hour, while management is offering $8.25 per hour. In addition, assume that the "appropriate" wage is $8.50 per hour. Farber (1981) suggests that the union will typically expect the neutral third party to adjudicate at a wage somewhat over $8.50/hour, while management will expect a wage somewhat under $8.50/hour. Given these divergent expectations, neither side is willing to compromise on $8.50/hour (or on any other mutually agreed upon wage). Both sides will thus incur the costs of impasse and aggregately do no better than they would through the use of a third party.

In general, existing research demonstrates that negotiators tend to be overconfident that their positions will prevail if they do not "give in" during negotiations. Specifically, Neale and Bazerman (1983, in press) show that negotiators consistently overestimate by 15 percent the probability that, under final-offer-by-package arbitration, their final offer will be accepted by the arbitrator. That is, while only 50 percent of all final offers submitted to the arbitrator can be accepted, the average subject estimated that there was a much higher probability that his or her own offer would be accepted. In terms of Walton and McKersie's bargaining zone, overconfidence may inhibit a variety of settlements, despite the existence of a reasonable bargaining zone. Neale and Bazerman (1983) found "appropriately" confident negotiators to exhibit more concessionary behavior and to be more successful than overly confident negotiators. Once again, while these arguments have been developed relative to an industrial relations perspective, they can be generalized to suggest that any joint venture may fail to occur as each side is overconfident that the other side will eventually give in to one's own "superior" position/argument.

THE LACK OF PERSPECTIVE TAKING

The biases of framing and overconfidence just presented suggest that individuals are generally affected by systematic deviations from rationality. Yet experience and empirical evidence suggest that there are some individuals who are more accurate in their interpersonal judgments (Bernstein & Davis, in press; Davis, 1981) or less influenced by the frame of the situation. These individual differences may be related to the ability of a negotiator (individual) to take the perspective of his or her opponent. It is important to note that taking the perspective of an opponent is not done for purely philanthropic reasons; rather, in achieving any set of objectives, there is valuable information to be gleaned from taking the perspective of the other negotiating party. Davis (1981) recently developed a construct and measure of the ability to take others' perspective and see things from their point of view. He found that individuals with high perspective-taking ability (PTA) are more accurate than are those with low PTA in judging others. Further, the accuracy with which those with high PTA judge others increased with experience, while those with low PTA did not exhibit similar improvement in accuracy (Bernstein & Davis, in press). Interestingly, this systematic limitation to effective interpersonal judgment is not related to standard measures of intelligence.

In a bargaining context, it is expected that individuals with high PTA would be better able to adopt the perspective of their bargaining opponents. They would also be more aware of the perspective of the opponent's constituency (e.g., labor or management) than would individuals with low PTA. This added information from perspective taking should increase one's ability to predict accurately the opponent's goals and expectations. This is extremely important in developing bargaining strategy (Siegel & Fouraker, 1960; Rubin & Brown, 1975) and facilitating compromise. Neale and Bazerman (in press) found that perspective-taking ability postively affects the concessionary tendencies of negotiators and the likelihood that a settlment will be reached. In addition, perspective-taking ability was found to affect positively the outcome obtained by a negotiator. Further, Bazerman and Neale (1982) have suggested that training mechanisms should be developed to increase the perspective-taking ability of negotiators. This is consistent with the literature on negotiator role reversal—that having each bargainer verbalize the viewpoint of the other increases the likelihood of a negotiated resolution (see Pruitt, 1981). Perhaps increasing the tendency of negotiators to take their opponents' perspective is the central focus of mediators. Research (Kochan & Jick, 1978; Neale & Bazerman, in press) suggests that increased information that is derived in this way often results in behavior that is more conducive to a negotiated settlement.

ESCALATION

There are many organizational contexts in which an employee can become trapped into a costly course of action. The escalation of commitment to a failing course of action has recently become a topic of interest among decision researchers (Bazerman, Geekun, & Schoorman, 1982; Brockner, Shaw, & Rubin, 1979; Conlon & Wolf, 1980, Staw, 1976, 1981; Teger, 1979). Individuals and groups who are personally responsible for negative consequences consistently commit the greatest amount of resources to a previously chosen course of action. America's involvement in Vietnam is often cited as a classic example of escalation (Teger, 1979). Policymakers of that time gradually increased the nation's commitment in such a manner that no major political force could retrospectively argue that the actions taken were rational.

Staw (1976) provided initial experimental evidence of the escalation effect. In this study, one group of subjects (high responsibility) was asked to allocate research and development funds to one or two operating divisions of an organization. Subjects were then told that after three years, the investment had either proved successful or unsuccessful and that they were faced with a second allocation decision concerning the division to which they had previously given funds. A second group (low responsibility) was told that another financial officer of the firm made a decision that had been either successful or unsuccessful (the same content information was provided to both groups of subjects) and that they were to make a second allocation of funds concerning that division. When the outcome of the previous decision was negative (an unsuccessful investment), high-responsibility subjects allocated significantly more funds to the original division in the second allocation than did low-responsibility subjects. For successful initial decisions, the amount of money allocated in the second decision was not related to responsibility.

Following the logic of the escalation literature, negotiators can be expected to escalate nonrationally their commitment to a previous course of action. Unfortunately, the most common form for distributive negotiation leads both sides to make extreme demands initially. If negotiators become committed to their initial public statements, we can expect them nonrationally to adopt a nonconcessionary stance. Further, if both sides incur losses as a result of a lack of agreement (e.g., a strike), their commitment to their respective positions will increase and the willingness to change to a different course of action (i.e., compromise) may decrease. For example, it could be argued that in the Malvinas/Falklands conflict, once Argentina had suffered the initial loss of life, it had the information necessary rationally to pursue a negotiated settlement. The escalation literature, in contrast, accurately predicts that the loss of life (a significant commitment to a course of action) would lead Argentina to a further escalation of its commitment not to compromise on the return of the Malvinas to Britain.

One important result from the escalation literature is that public announcement of one's commitment increases one's tendency to escalate nonrationally (Staw, 1981). Once this general public (or constituency) is aware of the commitment, the decision maker is far less likely to retreat from his or her previously announced position. This suggests that escalation can be reduced if negotiators and third parties avoid the formation of firmly set public positions, for this provides the ignition for the nonrational escalation of conflict. Implementation of this recommendation is, however, contradictory to everything known about how negotiators (e.g., labor leaders, representatives of management) behave when they represent constituencies. A firmly set public position is typically perceived as necessary to build constituency support and allegience. Thus it may be that what is best for the constituency is not the same as what the constituency will reward.

THE MYTHICAL FIXED PIE

Walton and McKersie (1965) suggested four models of negotiation. Two of them present drastically different perspectives of the bargaining process. The distributive bargaining model views the bargaining process as a procedure for the division of a fixed pie of resources. That is, what one side gains, the other side loses. In contrast, the integrative bargaining model focuses on the means of making tradeoffs or solving problems to the mutual benefit of both sides. Walton and McKersie suggest that most negotiators view the bargaining process as a distributive task.

We argue that Walton and McKersie's observation of the perceptions of labor/management negotiators represents a fundamental bias in human judgment. It is common to take a win/lose perspective. Some people would argue that acting as if all conflicts are of a fixed pie nature is likely to be perceived as hard-headed, tough-minded, and realistic. It may be that the competitive nature of our education, athletic activities, and the like fosters fixed pie conflict behavior. Regardless of the basis for this mythical fixed pie perception of bargaining, we agree with Pruitt (this volume) that most conflicts are not purely distributive problems. Why?

Most conflicts have more than one issue at stake, with the parties placing different values on the differing issues. Once this condition exists, the conflict is objectively no longer a fixed pie. Consider a Friday evening on which you and your spouse are going to dinner and a movie. Unfortunately, you prefer different restaurants and different movies. It is easy to adopt a distributive attitude toward each event to be negotiated. In contrast, if you do not assume a fixed pie, you may find out that you care more about the restaurant selection and your spouse cares more about the movie choice. Similarly, purchasing goods is often treated as a distributive problem. Often, however, a retailer is suddenly willing to reduce the purchase price if payment is made in cash (no receipt, and so on). While you care only about price, he or she also cares about the form of payment. In a tight, inflationary housing market, many deals are possible when it becomes clear that the seller cares more about the sales price while the buyer is largely concerned about the existence of secondary sources of financing. Again, tradeoffs to both sides may be possible.

Reaching a negotiated settlement in the above situations is likely to depend on determining the favorable tradeoffs that are viable. Such solutions, however, are possible only when the negotiators eliminate fixed pie perceptions. The literature on creativity (Winkelgren, 1974) points out that we are often limited in finding creative problem solutions by the false assumptions that we make. We apply this position to negotiation by arguing that the fixed pie perception is a fundamentally false assumption that hinders the resolution of conflict, despite the potential existence of mutually agreeable resolutions. A fundamental role of mediators should be to break such false assumptions and to look for mutually favorable tradeoffs.

CONCLUSION

While negotiation is often defined as a decision-making process, the research literature has failed to consider the critical role of the social-cognitive decision processes of negotiators and its impact on their behavior. This chapter has attempted to highlight conceptually the negative impact of limitations in human judgment on the performance of negotiators and the likelihood that these negotiators will reach a mutually agreed-upon solution to their conflict. Specifically, five unique systematic biases that affect the judgments of negotiators have been identified. Future research is needed to provide empirical support for the existence of these biases in actual and varied negotiation contexts. Further, it is likely that these biases are merely a sampling of the population of systematic deficiencies in human judgment. Thus continued research is necessary to identify these biases and to provide possible solutions to the problems they present.

The description of systematic biases that affect negotiators is a critical step in the development of the conflict literature. However, research on this topic needs to advance to provide prescriptive recommendations for improving resolution behaviors. While systematic research is needed to explore alternatives for improving the personal and societal effectiveness of the process of negotiation, some guidelines for such improvement can be provided. In the literature on behavioral decision theory, Nisbett and Ross (1980) have begun to focus on remedies for these decision-making limitations. With respect to the negotiation context, there are at least two approaches to overcoming the biases of negotiators in probability assessment: (1) improve the selection criteria used for negotiators and (2) train negotiators to eliminate decision-making biases. In developing selection criteria, it is important to select for the defined task—negotiating. Thus it becomes particularly important to have, at hand, remedies for the biases to which negotiators are particularly vulnerable. Choosing negotiators on characteristics other than job title or elected position may provide considerable relief for the observed deviations from rationality identified here. Second, a number of systematic decision biases exist due to the effects of statistics and their interpretation on the human inference process. If individuals can be trained to deal with the common task of negotiating in a "rational" manner, the probability of reaching a negotiated settlement will be enhanced. This chapter identifies a number of specific items that should affect the training of negotiators. The remaining question concerns how to train negotiators to eliminate the biases identified. The first step would be awareness—most negotiators are not aware of these biases. Most scholars in the area of creating change would quickly point out, however, that it is far easier to identify behavioral dispositions than to change them. To respond to this criticism, we advocate using an unfreezing-change-refreezing approach to improving the judgment of negotiators. That is, before negotiators change their judgmental strategies, their current strategies need to be unfrozen. How? One change strategy adopted by the authors in the classroom is to develop negotiation exercises that lead to failure because of the manner in which the participants deviate from rationality. Once a negotiator attends to the fact that his or her biases led to failure, the likelihood increases that change will occur and persist. Finally, an aware mediator can facilitate the negotiation process by using the information in this chapter to point out to the parties the judgmental deficiencies in each side's arguments

In conclusion, this chapter has identified a new direction for increasing the likelihood that negotiators will achieve a resolution by improving the quality of their decision-making processes. This area of inquiry complements the existing literature that has identified structural interventions and relevant personality characteristics of negotiators (Rubin & Brown, 1975; Pruitt, 1981) as predictors of their success.

REFERENCES

Bazerman, M. H. *The framing of organizational behavior.* Paper presented at the annual meeting of the Academy of Management, 1982.

Bazerman, M. H., Beekun, R. K., & Schoorman, F. D. Performance evaluation in a dynamic context: A laboratory study of the impact of a prior commitment to the ratee. *Journal of Applied Psychology,* 1982, *67*, 873-876.

Bazerman, M. H., & Neale, M. A. Improving negotiation effectiveness under final offer arbitration: The role of selection and training. *Journal of Applied Psychology,* 1982, *67*, 543-548.

Bernstein, W., & Davis, M. Perspective taking, self-consciousness, and accuracy in person perception. *Basic and Applied Social Psychology,* in press.

Brockner, J., Shaw, M. C., & Rubin, J. Z. Factors affecting withdrawal from an escalating conflict: Quitting before it's too late. *Journal of Experimental Social Psychology,* 1979, *15*, 492-503.

Conlon, E. J., & Wolf, G. The moderating effects of strategy, visibility, and involvement on allocation behavior: An extension of Staw's escalation paradigm. *Organizational Behavior and Human Performance,* 1980, *26,* 172-192.

Davis, M. A multidimensional approach to individual differences in empathy. *JSAS Catalogue of Selected Documents in Psychology,* 1981, *10,* 85.

Einhorn, H. J. Overconfidence in judgment. In R. A. Shweder and D. W. Fiske (Eds.), *New directions for methodology of behavior research: Fallible judgment in behavioral research.* San Francisco: Jossey-Bass, 1980.

Einhorn, H. J., & Hogarth, R. M. Confidence in judgment: Persistence of the illusion of validity. *Psychological Review,* 1978, *85,* 395-416.

Farber, H. & Katz, H. Interest arbitration, outcomes, and the incentives to bargain. *Industrial and Labor Relations Review,* 1979, *33,* 55-63.

Farber, H. S. An analysis of "splitting-the-difference" in interest arbitration. *Industrial and Labor Relations Review,* 1981, *34,* 66-74.

Fischhoff, B. Debiasing. In D. Kahneman, P. Slovic, & A. Tversky (Eds.), *Judgment under uncertainty: Heuristics and biases.* New York: Cambridge University Press, 1981.

Holloway, C. *Decision making under uncertainty: Models and choices.* Englewood Cliffs, NJ: Prentice-Hall, 1979.

Kahneman, D., & Tversky, A. Prospect theory: An analysis of decision under risk. *Econometrica,* 1979, *47,* 263-291.

Kochan, T. Collective bargaining and organizational behavior research. In B. Staw & L. Cummings (Eds.), *Research in organizational behavior* (Vol. 2). Greenwich, CT: JAI, 1980.

Kochan, T., & Jick, T. A theory of public sector mediation process. *Journal of Conflict Resolution,* 1978, *22,* 209-240.

Lichtenstein, S., Fischhoff, B., & Phillips, L. D. Calibration of probabilities: The state of the art. In H. Jungermann & G. de Zeeuw (Eds.), *Decison making and change in human affairs.* Amsterdam: D. Reidel, 1977.

March, J., & Simon, H. *Organizations.* New York: John Wiley, 1958.

Neale, M. A., & Bazerman, M. H. *Systematic deviations from rationality in negotiator behavior: The framing of conflict and negotiator overconfidence.* Working paper, 1983.

Neale, M. A., & Bazerman, M. H. The impact of perspective taking ability on the negotiation process under alternative forms of arbitration. *Industrial and Labor Relations Review,* in press.

Nisbett, R., & Ross, L. *Human inference: Strategies and shortcomings of social judgment.* Englewood Cliffs, NJ: Prentice-Hall, 1980.

Pruitt, D. G. *Negotiation behavior.* New York: Academic, 1981.

Rubin, J. Z., & Brown, B. R. *The social psychology of bargaining and negotiation.* New York: Academic, 1975.

Rubin, J. Experimental research on third party intervention in conflict: Toward some generalizations. *Psychological Bulletin,* 1980, *87,* 379-391.

Siegal, S., & Fouraker, L. E. *Bargaining and group decision making: Experiments in bilateral monopoly.* New York: McGraw-Hill, 1960.

Staw, B. M. Knee-deep in the big muddy: A study of escalating commitment to a chosen course of action. *Organizational Behavior and Human Performance,* 1976, *16,* 27-44.

Staw, B. M. The escalation of commitment to a course of action. *Academy of Management Review,* 1981, *6,* 577-587.

Teger, A. I. *Too much invested to quit: The psychology of the escalation of conflict.* New York: Pergamon, 1979.

Thaler, R. Toward a positive theory of consumer choice. *Journal of Economic Behavior and Organization,* 1980, *1,* 39-80.

Tversky, A., & Kahneman, D. The framing of decisions and the psychology of choice. *Science,* 1981, *211,* 453-458.

Walton, R. E., & McKersie, R. B. *A behavioral theory of labor negotiations: An analysis of a social interaction system.* New York: McGraw-Hill, 1965.

Winklegren, W. A. *How to solve problems.* San Francisco: Freeman, 1974.

4

LYING AND DECEPTION
A Behavioral Model

Roy J. Lewicki

Duke University

As defined by Rubin and Brown (1975, p. 2), bargaining is "the process whereby two or more parties attempt to settle what each shall give and take, or perform and receive, in a transaction between them." Bargaining is typically characterized by a conflict of interest—the parties have conflicting preferences or priorities for attaining their objectives—and interdependence, such that they are dependent on the other's behavior for attaining their own goals. Activity in bargaining is concerned with the division or exchange of resources and the resolution of "intangibles," or with the satisfaction of the psychological objectives and motivations of the negotiating parties.

Since negotiators are interdependent and their preferred outcomes conflict, they are faced with choices regarding the strategy and tactics required to achieve those outcomes. Each party would like to reach an agreement that maximizes his or her own goals—or at least achieve some outcome above a minimum level of satisfaction. As a result, the activity of negotiating traditionally involves the presentation of demands or proposals by one party—those that will maximize that party's outcomes—followed by counterdemands and counterpro-

Author's Note: The author is indebted to Blair Sheppard and Max Bazerman for their comments on earlier drafts of this chapter.

posals by the opponent. Each party then expects that it will have to make concessions and conciliations away from most-preferred objectives toward some middle ground of compromise and agreement.

As noted by Kelley and Thibaut (1969), the process of achieving compromise is based on "information dependence." At the outset of negotiation, each party knows only his or her own preferences. Advantage in negotiation is obtained by two independent but related processes: successful determination of the other's true preferences and priorities, and successful disguise of one's own preferences and priorities. As Rubin and Brown (1975, p. 14) note,

> To the extent that the other party knows both what the first wants as well as the least that he will accept, [the other] will be able to develop a more effective, more precise bargaining position than would be possible in absence of this information about the other's preferences, while at the same time disclosing minimal (or misleading) information about his own postion.

Kelley (1966) has noted that this information dependence creates two major dilemmas in bargaining. First, negotiators must resolve the "dilemma of trust"—that is, they must infer the other's true intentions or preferences while knowing that the other is attempting to inflate, magnify, and justify those preferences. As Kelley writes, "To believe everything the other says is to place one's fate in his hands, and to jeopardize the full satisfaction of one's own interests. . . . On the other hand, to believe nothing the other says is to eliminate the possibility of accepting any arrangement with him" (p. 60). Correlatively, negotiators must also resolve their own "dilemma of honesty and openness"—that is, how frank and candid they should be about their own true preferences and priorities. If the negotiator is completely honest and candid, he or she may be vulnerable to exploitation by his or her opponent, become committed to a position that allows no further concessions, or sacrifice gains that might have been successfully derived through less candid approaches. "To sustain the bargaining relationship, each party must select a middle course between the extremes of complete openness toward, and deception of, the other. Each must be able to convince the other of his integrity while not at the same time endangering his bargaining position" (Rubin & Brown, 1975, p. 15).

Kelley's dilemmas are at the root of successful negotiation. On the one hand, concerns for honesty and integrity are essential to a successful negotiating relationship; on the other hand, deception and disguise of one's true position are essential to maximizing objectives. Deception and disguise may take a number of forms.

Misrepresentation of position to opponent. The negotiator lies about his or her preferred settlement point or resistance point. A management representative who is prepared to pay the union $9.00 base pay but says that he or she can only afford $8.50 would be misrepresenting his or her true maximum settlement. This is the most common form of deception in negotiation, and it is frequently described as bluffing. Chertkoff and Baird (1971) demonstrated that negotiators who made extreme demands were more likely to have opponents accede to those demands and to achieve highly favorable settlements.

Bluffing. The negotiator falsely states his or her intentions to commit an action. False threats and false promises would be examples of bluffs. A false threat would be the stated intention of a negotiator to walk out if the opponent does not make a desirable concession when the negotiator does not actually intend to walk out. A false promise would be the stated intention to make additional concessions to the opponent if quick agreement is reached on a contract when the negotiator has no intention of actually making them.

Falsification. Erroneous and factually incorrect information is introduced as though it were true. As an example, a union negotiator may introduce the results of an "industry survey" that shows ten other unions successfully obtaining cost-of-living clauses in their latest contract settlements, while in fact only four unions actually had the clause included in the final package. In this context, falsification is most commonly called "lying."

Deception. A collection of arguments are made that lead the opponent to draw an incorrect conclusion or deduction. A negotiator may put forward ten different arguments as to why a particular course of action is undesirable, without ever specifically stating that he or she would not agree to the course of action. Statements that create implications or lead the opponent to draw conclusions that are never explicitly tested by the opponent create successful deception by the negotiator.

Selective disclosure or misrepresentation to constituencies. Partial truths—or complete truths—are told in representing other parties in the negotiating relationship. Negotiators may selectively disclose or misrepresent their constituencies' desires and wishes to an opposing negotiator or misrepresent events in the negotiating relationship when describing these activities to constituencies.

This is not meant to be an exhaustive list of the ways that lying and deception can enter into negotiation, nor is it designed to create confusion over semantic distinctions between various forms of truth distortion. It does serve to point out, however, that (1) lying and deception are an active part of the negotiating process, (2) some forms of deception may be traditionally acceptable within the definition of negotiation while others may not, and (3) these same deceptive tactics—bluffing, falsifying, misrepresenting, and lying—may be viewed as immoral or inappropriate, either within a negotiating context or in other social contexts. When used, they may be successful in helping the negotiator to achieve objectives (tangibles) but may be destructive to the relationship between negotiators and their constituencies (intangibles). The manner in which deceptive tactics are perceived and employed has received little attention in bargaining research (or in broader situations of social influence) and will be the focus of this chapter.

LYING AND DECEPTION: A BROADER VIEW

There is a widespread concern in today's society with a deterioration in the ethical and moral concern for the truth. Each week, newspapers and magazines report the examples. Politicians are accused of lying to their constituencies or covering up the exploitative use of their office. Trusted and distinguished scientists are exposed for falsifying their research studies. It is revealed that bright and capable students have cheated on examinations and plagiarized papers or stolen from other students in order to maximize grades and career opportunities. Businesspeople have secured confidential data from their competitors in order to gain competitive market advantage.

Several authors (see Lewicki, 1982) have identified truth telling as one of three major dimensions of ethical conduct. Standards for truth telling are concerned with the societal and moral standards for observing adherence to telling "the truth, the whole truth, and nothing but the truth." For centuries, philosophers, theologians, and scholars have debated the degree to which any deviation from the truth—for whatever reason—could be considered morally justifiable (Augustine, 1847; Oates, 1948). These arguments can be readily extended to contemporary problems of moral and ethical conduct: whether it is ethical for physicians to give placebos to their patients, whether political leaders may justifiably lie to the public for any reason (e.g., national security), or whether businessmen and-women are unethical if they bluff and distort information to increase their chances of winning.

In the past, efforts to understand the reasoning, motivation, and behavior of individuals who perform unethical acts have generally been restricted to the domains of religious and philosophical ethics. While there are exceptions that will be noted below, behavioral science is amenable to scientific explanation and investigation. Such examination would require efforts to separate the moral and normative "oughts" of human conduct from the predictions and descriptions of actual behavior.

It is the purpose of this chapter to perform this analysis of lying and truth-telling behavior. It will be proposed that lying is a purposeful human activity, often used as a tactic in a negotiation process, and that the "decision" to lie can be better examined and understood within a behavioral decision-making model. Lying is often perceived to have certain social functions and benefits, but it also has deleterious consequences that may be underestimated and undervalued at the time of the decision. Perceptions of these advantages and disadvantages, or benefits and costs, are likely to be strongly affected by one's *perspective.* Perspective will be explored in two major ways: in terms of the personality, background, and situational variables that (positively or negatively) influence the actor's decision to lie, and in terms of the evaluation of the behavior by the actor, by his or her target, or by audiences who can observe and evaluate the actor's behavior. Finally, lies and other deviations from the truth are often strategic elements in a bargaining scenario. While attention will often focus on the broader process of lying in social environments, specific attention will be given to the use of deception in negotiation.

While this chapter will endeavor to separate the behavioral science perspective on lying from the moral perspective, numerous authors—

the present one included—have found this process easier to promise than to deliver. In part, this may be due to the forced reliance on moral and ethical writings in order to deduce behavioral principles. In this chapter, reliance on philosophical writings will be most clear cut in the proposed definition of lying and in defining many of the dimensional concepts that are used to evaluate and judge lies. In particular, the work of Bok (1978) will be frequently cited as an insightful integration of earlier philosophical and theological treatises and as an application of the moral rules of truth telling to a wide variety of contemporary social problems and situations.

LYING DEFINED

A lie is defined as "any intentionally deceptive message which is stated" (Bok, 1978, p. 13). There are several key elements to this definition that must be clarified. First, truth is discernible—it is possible to establish that information which is factually accurate and verifiable, and that information which is deceptive, not accurate, and not verifiable. As the ability to distinguish and factually discern the truth becomes problematic, so will the definition of lying and truth telling. Second, lying *intends* to deceive. Deception that is made in error—by mistake—is not lying. Error may be used as an *excuse* by the liar, but this is merely an effort to use error as a cover-up for the original intent. Finally, it is proposed that lies are *stated* deceptions. This implies that lies are a subcategory of a wider group of intentional deceptions and that unstated deceptions may not be treated as lies. This is the most complex and problematic element of a definition. Consider a huckster who is selling the public his or her wares—be they vacation condominiums, kitchen gadgets, or miracle cures for diseases. The huckster may play on the biases of his or her audience, stimulate their fantasies and imaginations, and lead them to entirely false conclusions about his or her product without ever explicitly making a false statement. Moreover, we know that human communication is fragile and frequently prone to error and distortion (e.g., the many studies on the psychology of rumor) and that the individual receiver is often prone to denial and distortion of information. Has the huckster lied in his or her transaction? Is the failure to tell the whole truth the same as intentionally misstating the truth? While this question receives continued debate among moral philosophers and ethicists, it is proposed that this behavior is *not* within the bounds of lying as defined here. Consideration of lying behavior will be restricted to those cases in which the communicator has intentionally misstated the truth—"lies where the intention to mislead is obvious, where the liar knows what he is communicating is not what he believes, and where he has not deluded himself into believing his own deceits" (Bok, 1978, p. 16).

In proceeding with the proposed definition, two further distinctions should be drawn between the philosophical/ethical approach to lying and the behavioral perspective. First, all lies represent some deviation from the "truth"; hence "truth" will be used as the benchmark and anchor by which lies are measured. Whereas philosophers and ethicists express a profound commitment to the truth for moral and ethical reasons, this analysis will affirm a commitment to the truth as a definitional anchor and as essential to the social fabric of human relations. The need for the truth, and the ability to distinguish truth from deception, is at the foundation of our social order. The accurate exchange of information, and the ability to determine the veracity of that information, is absolutely essential to human social functioning. Individuals must be able to rely on the information given to them by others; they cannot test every statement for themselves to determine its accuracy. Lies therefore distort the quality of information that people receive and their ability to make accurate and informed choices about how to behave. Second, many ethical and moral treatises on lying have paid attention to various types and magnitudes of lies as deviations from "the truth." Ethicists are primarily concerned with articulating whether *any* deviation from the truth is morally viable, and if so, under what conditions lying ought to be justifiable and appropriate. In contrast, the approach considered here will be to evaluate those factors that lead individuals to decide to lie and how this behavior is evaluated by others.

THE SOCIAL FUNCTIONS OF LYING

The primary function of lying is to gain power and tactical advantage in social interaction. Knowledge is a basis of power (e.g., French & Raven, 1959); lies manipulate information in favor of the holder of that information. Therefore, lies enhance the power of an actor by changing the balance of perceived accurate information in the social relationship and diminishing the quality of the target's choice alternatives.[1] Lies do this in several ways:

(1) Lies may *misinform* the opponent so as to obscure some *objective* that was originally desired by the deceived. It is a Friday evening. I come home from work very tired, envisioning a quiet evening with a good book or television. My wife greets me at the door and reminds me that I promised to take her out to dinner. I say that I have a very bad headache and feel feverish (lies); if she buys the story, I can stay at home and relax.

(2) Lies may *eliminate or obscure relevant choice alternatives* for the target person. My wife tells me to take two aspirin and rest a while; I grudgingly agree and decide that I really should take her out to dinner. We then negotiate where to go. I prefer seafood, she prefers Italian. I tell her that the Italian restaurant is closed for vacation, and we set out to go to the seafood place.

(3) Lies may be used to *manipulate the perceived costs and benefits of choice alternatives* for the target. In the above example, my wife calls the Italian restaurant and discovers that it is open. I tell her that I heard that the seafood restaurant has a two-for-one special on lobster tonight (a lie)—her favorite seafood—and that we really ought to go to take advantage of the excellent price. In addition, I tell her that our neighbors dined at her Italian restaurant last week; they said the restaurant had a new cook, and the food was awful (all lies). We go to the seafood restaurant.

(4) Finally, lies *change the degree of uncertainty in the target's choices*—either by increasing or decreasing this uncertainty. Lies decrease uncertainty by making a target more confident in a choice than he or she might be otherwise. When we get to the seafood restaurant, they are out of lobster. My wife is angry and decides to get even with me. I notice that squid is advertised on the menu—something I have never tried—and I ask her whether she has ever tried it. She says, "Yes, I had it once and it was fantastic!" (a lie). Unsuspecting of her motivations, I order the squid. Lies may also *increase* uncertainty

by creating increased discomfort or dissonance over choices already made. The squid is about to be served to me. As I am about to take the first bite, she says, "Well, I liked squid when I had it, but that was at another restaurant. Everyone else I know who has had it here thought it was disgusting." My appetite fades quickly.

A MODEL OF LYING

It has been stated that the primary motivation to lie is to increase the liar's power over the target through manipulation of false or misleading information. As a result of selecting and implementing lying tactics, the liar will experience consequences for that action. These consequences will accrue as a result of the efficacy of the lie and the overall strategy of influence, and they may be positive or negative in nature. Moreover, since lying is a tactic with strong ethical overtones, it is likely to elicit evaluative reactions—from the actor, from the target, and from observers if they are present. The nature of the consequences, and the nature of the evaluation, are likely to have an impact on subsequent lying behavior. This process is diagramed in Figure 4.1.

A negotiator's predisposition to employ deceptive tactics may be influenced by self-evaluation of those actions or by evaluation by the target. (To simplify the current discussion, evaluations by third-party "audiences" shall be excluded.) Consider the situation of a manager and subordinate who have just completed extensive negotiations over a budget cut in the subordinate's department. The manager now discovers that the subordinate extensively "padded" cost projections to assure some slack in operating revenue. Let us examine the situation from the manager's perspective. Those who discover that they have been lied to are typically angry. They experience disappointment and feel manipulated for at least two reasons: They have been "taken in" by the liar, and they have had their choice process falsely manipulated. Discovering that one has been "taken in" is a form of embarrassment. The manager in our example is likely to blame and punish him- or herself for not having been clever enough or "attuned" to the subordinate's verbal and nonverbal cues to detect the deception as it was occurring. This embarrassment may be considered as a form of "face loss" (Goffman, 1969; Brown, 1968, 1971), and it is likely

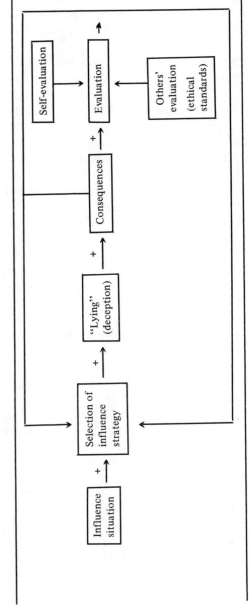

Figure 4.1   A Simple Model of Lying Behavior

that the manager will try to regain or restore face through retaliation or revenge. In addition, the lie has artificially manipulated the manager's choice process. As a result, he or she may have chosen an undesirable alternative—and for reasons that now prove to be spurious. Again, his or her reaction is likely to be anger, disappointment, and resentment.

The impact of discovered lies on the deceived not only produces an emotional reaction but is also likely to alter the deceived's perspectives on future interaction. The manager is likely to become skeptical and suspicious of future interactions, akin to the impact of exploitation in conflict and negotiation (Deutsch, 1958, 1973). The expectation of truth and veracity has been violated. Moreover, since the manager did not detect the earlier lie, can he or she trust his or her own abilities to discern further lies? Will vigilance provide further protection? Doubt has been introduced, and the manager will be wary of future interactions with this subordinate.

From the liar's perspective, the primary motivation to lie is to increase power and control. The "decision" to lie may not have come easily—the subordinate may have wrestled with the decision of whether to make accurate estimates or pad his or her projections and decided that conservative projections could cause problems later. Because most liars are not pathological—i.e., they are aware of both the social and moral responsibilities to tell the truth—the liar is likely to search for "reasons" for a lie. The primary purpose of justification is to "excuse" the lie by providing a legitimate reason for the deception.

It is proposed that the justification process tends to undermine the liar's accurate perception of the costs of lying, both to him- or herself and to society. With regard to the perceived costs to him- or herself, several outcomes are possible. First, the subordinate is aware that he or she has violated his or her own standards of integrity. Moreover, he or she usually knows that the lie, if detected, is likely to undermine his or her credibility and reputation with the boss. The search for justification is intense. Silverman, Rivera, and Tedeschi (1979) report that this search behavior is most likely caused by a need to restore a positive impression to those who may judge the liar's moral conduct. Second, lies may promulgate further lies. The manager's initial deception may require further lies to support it—i.e., how the cost estimates were determined. Moreover, attention must be given to keeping track of the lies—who was told what, when. Failures to keep track may introduce a systematic bias in the manager's judgment over the long term—i.e., the subordinate may be less able to accurately forecast costs without inflating them. As Bok (1978, p. 26) notes,

> Bias skews all judgment, but never more so than in the search for good reasons to deceive. Not only does it combine with ignorance and uncertainty, so that liars are apt to overestimate their own good will, high motives, and chances to escape detection; it leads also to overconfidence in their own imperviousness to the personal entanglements, worries, and loss of integrity which might so easily beset them.

As a result of the frequent repetition of this pattern, the liar is likely to experience a *loss* of power over the long run. While the initial motivation to lie was to obtain power, the subordinate will be less trusted and less credible to his or her boss. As a result, the subordinate will have less informational power (since the veracity of his or her information is likely to be continually questioned) and less reputational and referent power as well (as he or she will be perceived as being less trustable, lower in integrity, and probably less personally attractive than a truth teller).

Therefore, it is proposed that both successful lying and successful justification will be self-serving in the negotiator's protection of reputation and accomplishment of short-term goals but that they are also likely to distort perception, enhance the tendency to lie again, and be damaging to long-term relationships with the opponent. In addition, it is proposed that the initial selection of deception as a negotiation tactic, and subsequent willingness to use the tactic, will also be influenced by two additional groups of factors: (1) the values, personality characteristics, background, and demographic characteristics of the negotiator; and (2) situational factors such as the contingent rewards and punishments associated with lying and truth telling, the relationship between the parties and their relative power and status, and the group or cultural norms that dominate the social context of the negotiation. The additional impact of these elements is represented in Figure 4.2 and will now be reviewed. Once again, given the paucity of research on lying behavior, additional research on deceptive and unethical behavior will be included, with implications drawn for lying behavior per se.

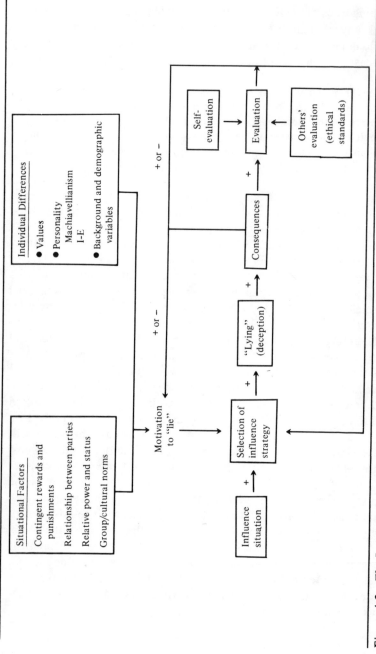

Figure 4.2   The Impact of Individual Differences on Lying Behavior

The Impact of Individual
Differences on Lying

Values. It has frequently been suggested that unethical conduct may be traced to differences in individual values and value systems. Several authors (Rokeach, 1973; England, 1967; Allport, Vernon, & Lindzey, 1960) have proposed broad classifications of human values. However, all of these approaches are limited in that they can be used only to make broad statements about individual values and value sets and not about specific predictions about ethical or unethical conduct in a particular environment (e.g., negotiation).

Moral Development. More promising results are derived from the work of Laurence Kohlberg (1969) on moral development. Following the earlier writings of Piaget, Kohlberg argued that individuals attain various stages or levels of moral development and that attainment of higher levels of moral development should lead to more "moral" actions and fewer unethical actions. Numerous studies have been conducted in this regard (see Rest, 1979, for one review), generally confirming this result. In one study, for example, Leming (1978) administered a test of moral development—Rest's Defining Issues Test—to college undergraduates and then monitored their behavior on a self-scoring test that permitted cheating. Students with higher levels of moral development cheated less. However, the disposition to cheat was also affected by situational variables, as will be reported later. From this research it may be proposed that negotiators who are at higher levels of moral development will be more "principled" in their tactics than will those at lower levels.

While research in human values has tended to be too general and global in its approach, studies on the impact of particular personality variables have yielded more successful results. Several are worth noting in detail:

Machiavellianism. Christie and Geis (1970) created a scale from the writings of Machiavelli and similar political philosophies. Three groups of items were created: predispositions toward the use of certain interpersonal tactics in influence settings (e.g., "The best way to handle people is to tell them what they want to hear"), perspectives on human nature and the human condition (e.g., "It is hard to get ahead without cutting corners here and there"), and views on morality (e.g., "All in all, it is better to be humble and honest than important and dishonest"). The more an individual tended to agree with items in each of these three categories, the higher in Machiavellianism he or she scored. Christie and Geis demonstrated, through subsequent research, that those who scored highly (high Machs) were more willing and able con artists than were low Machs.

Several recent studies (see Geis and Moon, 1981, for a review) have confirmed that high Machs are more likely to lie, deviate further from the truth while sounding less anxious about it (Exline, Thibaut, Hickey, & Gumpert, 1970), and tend to be more persuasive in their lies (Braginsky, 1970). A study of Geis and Moon demonstrates that high Machs are more convincing liars; they were believed to be as truthful as truthful high Machs, while lying low Machs were believed less often than were truthful low Machs. The ability of high Machs to be successful liars seems to relate to their tendency to use a theatrical, "hamming" strategy—exaggerating sentiments of liking or disliking in order to mask their true emotions (DePaulo & Rosenthal, 1979). Thus a Machiavellian predisposition appears to be strongly related to the predisposition to lie, stylistic approach to lying, and success at lying.

Internal-external control. Rotter (1966) proposed that individuals differed in their generalized beliefs regarding the degree to which event outcomes are contingent upon their own ability or effort (internal control) or are largely determined by forces such as fate or chance (external control). Initially, it may not be intuitively clear whether internals or externals might be more predisposed to lie or cheat; more information about the situation, and particularly whether outcomes are largely tied to skill or luck, is necessary. Srull and Karabenick (1975) reviewed the relevant research literature and proposed a test to determine the relationship between locus of control and tendency to cheat, also varying the actor's perception of the situation and the role of skill or luck in influencing outcomes. Srull and Karabenick report that the greatest predisposition to cheat occurred under conditions of personality-situation congruence—i.e., internal controls tended to cheat when they believed that skill determined outcomes (but they couldn't master the skill sufficiently to be successful), and external controls tended to cheat when they believed that luck determined outcomes (and when they weren't lucky enough to be successful in the experimental task). These results explain a related finding by Hegarty and Sims (1978) that externals were more predisposed than internals to cheat by participating in a kickback scheme; the Hegarty and Sims study portrayed the success of the kickback in "probability" terms (an act of luck), rather than as determined by the skill of the actor. In a later study, Karabenick and Srull (1978) demonstrated that internals cheated in order to conform to their self-perceived status on some dimension of ability, while externals cheated in order to conform to some self-perceived status as a lucky individual. Internally controlled negotiators may lie, therefore, in order to obtained desired outcomes and confirm to themselves that they are good negotiators; externally controlled negotiators may lie because the "can't control themselves" or to overcome the perceived negative effects of luck on their outcomes.

Background and Demographic Variables

A number of background and demographic variables have also been empirically related to the tendency to act ethically or unethically. Hassett (1981, 1982), reporting on a large sample of individuals who responded to a survey in the magazine *Psychology Today,* stated that age and religiosity are strongly related to ethical behavior. Older respondents, and those who indicated that they were very religious in their convictions, tended to be much more moral and ethical in their judgments. Similarly, Maier and Lavrakas (1976) reported that individuals with parochial school backgrounds believed that there was a greater incidence of lying behavior in daily life and perceived the act of lying as more reprehensible. Individuals who also claimed a strong religious commitment or that they lead their lives in accordance with a strong personal and moral code rated lying as more reprehensible than did those who were less religious or less committed to a moral code.

Sex and occupational role also appear to have some impact on the perception of lying. Maier and Lavrakas report that women perceived it as less reprehensible for women to lie to women and most reprehensible for men to lie to women; males perceived that it was least reprehensible when men lied to men, and most reprehensible when women lied to men. Finally, lies by politicians tended to be seen as more reprehensible than lies by other occupational groups (see also Klintz, 1977).

SITUATIONAL FACTORS

Contingent Rewards and Punishments

It is proposed that attaining outcomes successfully, or of failing to achieve those outcomes, will have a direct effect on the predisposition to lie in the future. Research by Hegarty and Sims (1978) on unethical conduct may be cited to support this assertion. Hegarty and Sims manipulated the "success" or "failure" in attaining outcomes in a simulated purchasing-kickback scheme. When an unethical decision (a kickback) was likely to increase the probability that a purchasing contract would be signed, subjects tended to make the kickback decision more frequently. Threat of punishment—legal liability and threat of fine if the kickback were discovered—counterbalanced the impact of reward. Successful attainment of outcomes, or threat of punishment for attainment, should also affect the frequency of deceptive behavior. In addition, the higher the level of situationally induced competition—public announcement of each party's relative payoffs, with reward associated with "beating" an opponent—the more unethical the decision making. Finally, the perceived rewards or costs to be borne by the target may affect the frequency of lying behavior. Maier and Lavrakas (1976) reported that lies that are perceived to be more costly to the target—in economic or psychological terms—are perceived as more reprehensible than are those that are less costly.

Relationship Between the Actor and Target

The relationship between negotiators is likely to influence the frequency of lies. Maier and Lavrakas also reported that the act of friends lying to friends is perceived as more reprehensible than that of friends lying to enemies. Conversely, defining the opposing negotiator as an "enemy"—or a liar—both legitimizes and necessitates one's own use of deceptive tactics. The opponent's behavior has created—

or is likely to create—imbalance and injustice in the distribution of rights, privileges, rewards, or punishments. The opponent is believed to have gained, or is likely to gain, at the negotiator's expense, and the negotiator needs to retaliate or preempt the other's strategy. Thus negotiators lie to liars in order to punish them or to restore the balance of equity; negotiators lie to enemies in order to defeat them before they are defeated themselves. In a historical context, Machiavelli (1958) was a prime advocate of preemptive lying in order to ensure the necessary victories in war and politics. In a research context, several negotiation studies have shown that the relationship between the parties affects the use of deceptive tactics. Gruder (1971) demonstrated that negotiators are more likely to make more deceptive arguments, negotiate for a longer period of time, and make less concessions to an exploitive opponent than to a cooperative one. Monteverde, Paschke, and Tedeschi (1974) reported that subjects in a prisoner's dilemma game who experienced an opponent playing a dishonest but cooperative strategy—stating his or her intentions to be competitive but then playing cooperatively—frequently exploited the opponent in order to punish him or her for his or her dishonesty.

Length of the Relationship Between the Parties

The frequency of unethical conduct is also related to the duration of the relationship between the parties. Negotiators who do not anticipate dealing with their opponent again in the future may be tempted to employ power-enhancing tactics. These tactics would not be used in long-term bargaining relationships because the negotiator is aware of the anger and retribution that can be expected from the opponent if such tactics are attempted. While a few research studies have investigated the impact of the duration of the relationship on negotiator conduct (e.g., Lewicki, 1969; Deutsch, 1973), none have directly investigated the use of ethical versus unethical tactics as a function of the length of the relationship.

Power and Status Differences Between Negotiators

The difference in power or status between negotiators may also influence the frequency of deceptive behavior. Crott, Kayser, and

Lamm (1980) studied negotiating behavior in an asymmetrical payoff game from the perspective of the actor. The players in the advantaged negotiating position—receiving better payoff possibilities—bluffed more frequently and communicated less with the opponent than did their disadvantaged opponents. Obligatory verbal communication between the parties decreased the frequency of bluffing, as did the requirement for true communication of intentions. From the perspective of the target, bluffers in this study were liked less than truth tellers.

Group, Organizational, and Cultural Norms

Finally, the norms of the "culture"—be it group or organization—may also influence the predisposition to use deception. For example, in a recent survey of American managers, Posner and Schmidt (1982) found that 80 percent of their sample believed that their organizations were guided by highly ethical principles. Thus it would initially appear that most organizational cultures favor ethical conduct. However, when asked what influences unethical behavior in the organization, "formal organizational policy" (or lack thereof) was rated *least* important, while the specific conduct of one's boss and one's peers in the organization was rated most important—regardless of the age, education, gender or organizational level of the rater. To the degree that one's superior and peers set the "normative tone" for how organizational rules and cultures are interpreted, the behavior of relevant others strongly contributes to the perception of ethical and appropriate conduct.

In a negotiation setting, norms also govern that behavior which is judged to be appropriate or inappropriate. Thibaut and Faucheux (1965) proposed that negotiators develop contractual norms for how to judge the "fairness" of particular outcome distributions between the parties. In addition, it is proposed that similar norms regulate the use of strategy and tactics in negotiation—what is ethical and unethical, appropriate and inappropriate. Individuals differ in their perception of these norms and how they apply, and it is not uncommon for these perceptions to go unstated and untested prior to actual bargaining. As a result, normative rules are often "violated" because one party perceives a tactic to be within the bounds of ethical propriety, while the other judges the tactic to be outside of the bounds. For example, it is common to identify certain social situations as "games" (McDonald, 1963) and thereby legitimize behavior that is sanctioned in games— bluffing, deception, and so on. In the game of poker, the player may bet as though he or she has a winning hand even though he or she does not have the cards to win; the strategy may be designed to drive others out of the game to win by default. Similarly, a negotiator may state his or her demands and threaten to take strong action if the demands are not met; if he or she succeeds, his or her real intention to carry out the threat remains unknown. Carr (1968) sparked phenomenal controversy when he argued that strategy in business should follow the rules of poker rather than the broad ethical principles of society. Reader response (Blodgett, 1968) revealed that Carr had identified a value-laden area of significant disagreement for the business community; it was clear that there was great disparity in the judgments of appropriate ethical business strategy in this area.

CONCLUSIONS AND IMPLICATIONS

This chapter has proposed a model of lying behavior. It has been proposed that lying and deception are intentional, purposive behaviors. The most common function of lies and deception is to increase or maintain power in an influence setting, primarily through the manipulation of information in the actor's favor. The disposition to employ deception as a tactic is influenced by a wide variety of factors. First, values and personality differences among negotiators—such as level of moral development, Machiavellianism, and internal-external control—may predispose an actor to employ deception. Demographic factors such as level of religious training and age may also affect this disposition. Second, the reward and punishment contingencies associated with truth telling and deception in the environment will affect the initial tendency to adopt a deceptive strategy and the likelihood of repeating this strategy in the future. Finally, situational factors such as relative power, quality of the relationship between the parties, length of the negotiating relationship, and situational norms will affect the degree to which lying and deception are viewed as appropriate and necessary influence tactics. It was proposed that while lying and deception may enhance the negotiator's short-term power and competitive advantage, "discovered" lies are likely to have a negative impact on the opponent and contribute to a decline in the actor's power over the longer term. Many of these assertions are drawn from related research or from writing on the moral and ethical implications of lying and need to be tested directly in interpersonal negotiation situations.

Although not specifically addressed in this chapter, the decision to lie and use deception may be a moral decision as well as a tactical one. Individuals differ in their perception and determination of "the moral rules" and the application of these rules to specific situations. How to "draw the line" between ethical and unethical conduct is a common social debate and one amenable to behavioral science research. It is expected that individuals will differ in their determination of ethical versus unethical conduct and in the reasons, excuses, and "justifications" pursued for occasional violations of those standards. Finally, differences in the characteristics of the deceptive tactic itself may affect these perceptions. Lies differ in their adjudged seriousness based on the "magnitude" of the lie, costs and benefits associated with the lie for both the actor and the target person, perceived "purpose" of the lie, and the social context in which the lie occurs. Successful "scaling" of lies along these dimensions will also aid in further understanding of how individuals perceive deceptive tactics and their predisposition to employ them as negotiation strategies.

NOTES

1. In this chapter "actor" and "target" will be used to identify individuals in the broader social context of lying; "negotiator" and "opponent" will be used when a more specific adversarial or competitive relationship between the parties is being characterized.

REFERENCES

Allport, G. W., Vernon, P. E., & Lindzey, G. *The study of values* (3rd ed.). Boston: Houghton Mifflin, 1960.

Augustine, S. On lying. In S. Augustine, *Seventeen short treatises.* London: F. & J. Rivington, 1847.

Blodgett, T. B. Showdown on business bluffing. *Harvard Business Review,* 1968, May-June, 162-170.

Bok, S. *Lying: Moral choice in public and private life.* New York: Pantheon, 1978.

Braginsky, D. D. Machiavellianism and manipulative interpersonal behavior in children. *Journal of Experimental Social Psychology,* 1970, *6,* 77-99.

Brown, B. R. The effects of need to maintain face on interpersonal bargaining. *Journal of Experimental Social Psychology,* 1968, *4,* 107-122.

Brown, B. R., & Garland, H. The effects of incompetency, audience acquaintanceship and anticipated evaluative feedback on face-saving behavior. *Journal of Experimental Social Psychology,* 1971, *7,* 490-502.

Carr, A. Z. Is business bluffing ethical? *Harvard Business Review,* 1968, January-February, 143-153.

Chertkoff, J. M., & Baird, S. L. Applicability of the big lie technique and the last clear chance doctrine in bargaining. *Journal of Personality and Social Psychology,* 1971, *20,* 298-303.

Christie, R., & Geis, F. (Eds.). *Studies in Machiavellianism.* New York: Academic, 1970.

Crott, H., Kayser, E., & Lamm, H. The effects of information exchange and communication in an asymmetrical negotiation situation. *European Journal of Social Psychology,* 1980, *10,* 149-163.

De Paulo, B. M., & Rosenthal, R. Telling lies. *Journal of Personality and Social Psychology,* 1979, *37*(10), 1713-1722.

Deutsch, M. Trust and suspicion. *Journal of Conflict Resolution,* 1958, *2,* 265-279.

Deutsch, M. *The resolution of conflict.* New Haven, CT: Yale University Press, 1973.

England, G. Personal value systems of American managers. *Academy of Management Journal,* 1967, *10,* 53-68.

Exline, R., Thibaut, J., Hickey, C., & Gumpert, P. Visual interaction in relation to Machiavellianism and an unethical act. In R. Christie & F. Geis (Eds.), *Studies in Machiaveillianism.* New York: Academic, 1970.

French, J.R.P., & Raven, B. The bases of social power. In D. Cartwright (Ed.), *Studies in social power.* Ann Arbor: University of Michigan Press, 1959.

Geis, F. L., & Moon, Tae Hyun. Machiavellianism and deception. *Journal of Personality and Social Psychology,* 1981, *41*(4), 766-775.

Goffman, E. *The presentation of self in everyday life.* New York: Doubleday, 1969.

Gruder, L. Relationships with opponent and partner in mixed-motive bargaining. *Journal of Conflict Resolution,* 1971, *15,* 403-416.

Hassett, J. *Correlates of moral values and behavior.* Paper presented at a Symposium on "Current Empirical Perspectives in Business Ethics and Values," Academy of Management meetings, August 1982.

Hassett, J. Is it right? An inquiry into everyday ethics. *Psychology Today,* June 1981, pp. 49-53.

Hassett, J. But that would be wrong. . . *Psychology Today,* November 1981, pp. 34-53.

Hegarty, W. H., & Sims, H. P. Some determinants of unethical decision behavior: An experiment. *Journal of Applied Psychology,* 1978, *63*(4), 451-457.

Karabenick, S. A., & Srull, T. K. Effects of personality and situational variation in locus of control on cheating: Determinants of the "congruence effect." *Journal of Personality,* 1978, *46,* 72-95.

Kelley, H. H. A classroom study of the dilemmas in interpersonal negotiation. In K. Archibald (Ed.), *Strategic interaction and conflict: Original papers and discussion.* Berkeley, CA: Institute of International Studies, 1966.

Kelley, H. H., & Thibaut, J. Group problem solving. In G. Lindzey & E. Aronson (Eds.), *Handbook of social psychology* (2nd ed.), Vol. IV). Reading, MA: Addison-Wesley, 1969.

Klintz, B. L. College student attitudes about telling lies. *Bulletin of the Psychonomic Society,* 1977, 10(6), 490-492.

Kohlberg, L. Stage and sequence: The cognitive-development approach to socialization. In D. Goslin (Ed.), *Handbook of socialization theory and research.* Chicago: Rand McNally, 1969.

Leming, J. S. Cheating behavior, situational influence and moral development. *Journal of Educational Research,* 1978, *71,* 214-217.

Lewicki, R. J. *The effects of exploitative and cooperative behavior on subsequent interpersonal relationships.* Unpublished doctoral dissertation, Columbia University, 1969.

Lewicki, R. J. Ethical concerns in conflict management. In G.B.J. Bomers & R. B. Peterson (Eds.), *Conflict management and industrial relations.* Boston: Kluwer Nijoff, 1982.

Machiavelli, N. *The prince* (W. K. Marriott, trans.). London: J. M. Dent & Sons, 1958.

Maier, R. A., & Lavrakas, P. J. Lying behavior and the evaluation of lies. *Perceptual and Motor Skills,* 1976, *42,* 575-581.

McDonald, J. *Strategy in business, poker and war.* New York: W. W. Norton, 1963.

Monteverde, F. J., Paschke, R., & Tedeschi, J. T. The effectiveness of honesty and deceit as influence tactics. *Sociometry,* 1974, *37,* 583-591.

Oates, W. J. (Ed.). *Basic writing of St. Augustine* (Vol. 1). New York: Random House, 1948.

Posner, B. Z., & Schmidt, W. H. *Managers and ethics.* Paper presented at a Symposium, "Current Empirical Perspectives on Business Ethics and Values," Academy of Management Meetings, August 1982.

Rest, J. R. *Development in judging moral issues.* Minneapolis: University of Minnesota Press, 1979.

Rokeach, M. *The nature of human values.* New York: Free Press, 1973.

Rotter, J. Generalized expectancies for internal versus external control of reinforcement. *Psychological Monographs,* 1966, *80*(Whole 609).

Rubin, J. Z., & Brown, B. R. *The social psychology of bargaining and negotiation.* New York: Academic, 1975.

Silverman, L. J., Rivera, A. N., & Tedeschi, J. T. Transgression-compliance: Guilt, negative affect, or impression management. *Journal of Social Psychology,* 1979, *108,* 57-62.

Srull, T. K., & Karabenick, S. A. Effects of personality-situation locus of control congruence. *Journal of Personality and Social Psychology,* 1975, *32*(4), 617-628.

Thibaut, J., & Faucheux, C. The development of contractual norms in a bargaining situation under two types of stress. *Journal of Experimental Social Psychology,* 1965, *1,* 89-102.

5

VOLUNTARY ADOPTION OF NEGOTIATION PROCESSES

Ronald J. Ebert
James A. Wall

University of Missouri—Columbia

As if it were not already complex enough, why further confound the topic of negotiation with discussions of decision making? Since good questions deserve even better answers, we offer the following: In contemporary organizations, decision makers must undertake negotiations, but few studies have addressed the interaction of the two processes—decisions and negotiation. Our purpose is to examine these decision/negotiation interconnections.

Drawing upon the organizational and management literature, which suggests that the two processes occur together and are frequently interdependent, we will argue that decision makers enter into negotiations to acquire another party's participations. Before mounting that discussion we address several background issues, the first of which contends that decision/negotiation processes—one form of intraorganizational negotiations—merit scientific inquiry.

Authors' Note: this research was funded by the Ponder Faculty Development and Research Fund of the College of Business and Public Administration, University of Missouri—Columbia.

VOLUNTARY NEGOTIATION IN
INDIVIDUAL DECISION FORMULATION

Negotiation is widely studied as a process in international relations, is recognized as a legitimate instrument for maintaining functional relationships among organizations, and is an inherent element in formalized bargaining processes among organizational subunits. While extensive attention to these arenas continues, sparse consideration is given to negotiations, especially to voluntary and nonprescribed negotiations, that evolve among individuals in the daily execution of their organizational responsibilities. Thompson and Tuden (1964), for example, propose bargaining as a decision strategy. However, their paradigm emphasizes organizations as collectives with little attention to either the individual or the situational variations that lead decision makers into relationships with others. In their decision processes, people initiate negotiations as they formulate and solve problems, select courses of action, and otherwise provide direction for accomplishing desired outcomes. Although the pervasiveness of these nonformalized negotiations remains elusive from any precise measure, an abundance of literature suggests, both directly and implicitly, that voluntary negotiations are often an effective method for influencing decisions. Variously referring to "managerial style," "organizational politics," "side payments," and "interpersonal skills," the commentary from diverse sources substantiates the claim that some important nonformalized aspects of decision processes are underplayed in our research (Gore, 1964; Rowe, 1974; Zaleznik, 1970; Heller, 1971).

Having built a short, but it is hoped convincing, case that decision-influencing behavior deserves better understanding, we now proffer a framework for such exploration. This framework concentrates upon the individual and the distinct steps entailed in his or her decision making.

ATTRIBUTES OF INDIVIDUALS AND THEIR
DECISIONS IN ORGANIZATIONAL SETTINGS

Our focus is on individuals and the behavior and processes they voluntarily adopt in their organizational roles. This leads us to draw upon some concepts from individual decision theory, organizational decision theory, and organizational behavior. By doing so, we aim toward a conceptualization that encompasses the diversity of variables that stipulate how decisions really occur in organizations.

In selecting these concepts, we have made some basic assumptions about individuals and their decision environments that form the bounds for our analysis. First, we deal with voluntary participation in contrast to formally specified relationships among individuals. This presumes, accordingly, that organizational members have, in addition to their formally prescribed relationships and responsibilities some reasonable freedom of access to others. Further, the initiation of voluntary relationships is contingent upon the demands of the task, the organizational context, and some characteristics of the others that the individual can potentially engage in such relationships. In considering how one might initiate the participation of others, we assume that each individual is driven by a combination of both personal and organizational motives. Finally, we assume that individuals act with intentions of rationality, albeit imperfectly and selectively because of imperfect information, within the contexts of their personal values.

The simple, yet crucial, implication of these assumptions is that decisions cannot be understood by merely observing a terminal "choice" of one person. Rare indeed is a final decision that emerges cleanly from a process unilaterally executed by an individual. As stated earlier by Simon (1957, p. 221):

> It should be perfectly apparent that almost no decision made in an organization is the task of a single individual. . . . Its various components can be traced through the formal and informal channels . . . to many individuals who have participated in forming its premises.

Since the time of Simon's comments on composite decisions, events have given even further impetus to multiperson rather than unilateral decisions. This added thrust stems from the components of decision making combined with the heightened complexities of contemporary organizations examined below. These conditions compel individuals to seek the assistance of others.

Components of Decision Making

The components comprising individual decision making have been delineated variously by others (MacCrimmon & Taylor, 1976). In organizational settings, at a given point in time, an individual's decision problems each reside in one or more of the following phases (Ebert & Mitchell, 1975):

(a) recognizing the need for a decision;
(b) initiating the decision task;
(c) defining the decision problem and its parameters;
  • for clarification of the alternatives,
  • for establishment of criteria, and
  • for implementation feasibility;
(e) processing information (evaluation);
(f) choosing criteria and feasible alternatives;
(g) choosing one alternative; and
(h) implementing the final choice.

This array of elements raises an important issue for decision makers: The human competencies and informational requirements for effectiveness in any one phase are different from those in the other stages of decision execution (Slovic, Fischhoff, & Lichenstein, 1977). To facilitate effectiveness, organizations establish formalized processes for handling some stages while others remain unstructured. However, even the formalized processes do not preclude nonformalized interactions and sideplay. Furthermore, in the absence of complete information, decision makers have incentives to seek out the assistance of others at various phases because of some complexities found in today's organizations.

Contemporary Organizational Complexities

The metamorphosis of organizations has been dramatic since 1957 when Herbert Simon identified decision making as the pivotal administrative act. Organizations today face highly diverse and demanding environments, utilize more sophisticated product and process technologies, and are more differentiated and functionally specialized internally. All of these introduce complexities and pressures unparalleled in organizational history (Scott & Hart, 1979). These conditions have amplified functional interdependencies— more parties are relevant to complex problem resolution and this has led to intensified concern for integrating their efforts to achieve overall effectiveness (Khandwalla, 1977).

In the contrasting setting of an earlier and simpler age, intraorganizational relationships were fewer and relatively clearly defined. Decisions were made or delegated on primarily authoritarian bases (or at least were thought to be), bounds of discretion were clearly defined, and parameters of decision were effectively controlled hierarchically. The contraposition today reveals many decisions that involve talents and contributions of multiple individuals phasing in and out of the process at different stages. They participate diversely in one another's decisions, contributing and influencing in differing degrees both formally and informally (Gore, 1964; Sigal, 1973; Rowe, 1974). When nonformalized interpersonal exchange relationships are initiated, they affect the integration of organizational activities. Within these voluntary participative processes, personal motives enter importantly in the give-and-take between people as problems are identified, shaped, and molded into manageable form, and alternatives are created and evaluated to arrive at realistic choices for implementation. The contemporary situation is aptly summarized by Harnett and Cummings (1980, p. 2):

> In most of these complex, yet real, environments there exist no completely clear and agreed-upon rules of behavior or standards for decisions. In the pressure of this uncertainty, bargaining has become a socially acceptable, and even encouraged, method of reaching decisions about how, when, and with whom to behave.

As a method of coping with procedural ambiguity in decision making, voluntary influencing transcends the formalized and delegated relationships that have been studied in group processes (Crawford & Haaland, 1972), leader/member decision behavior (Vroom & Yetton, 1973), and superior/subordinate decision relationships (Patchen, 1974; Mowday, 1978, 1979). Although the form of our analysis is consistent with the approach used for leader/member decision behavior (Vroom & Yetton, 1973; Vroom & Jago, 1974), the content extends to other relationships. On a wider scale, the analysis applies to individuals as they initiate upward, downward, and, most significantly, lateral relationships that cut across hierarchical lines.

More recent organizational theories (e.g., Nutt, 1976) recognize interpersonal exchange processes such as negotiation as important mechanisms for integrating diverse, interdependent functional roles. Mostly, however, the art and science of negotiation has received its most extensive research attention apart from the context of individual decision making. Although negotiation is recognized in a general sense as "a frequently used way of reaching decisions" (Harnett & Cummings, 1980, p. 2), and has been the context for more extensive discussions of decision making (Winham, 1977; Zartmen, 1977), voluntary decision/negotiation interplay has not been subjected to scientific inquiry in any specific way. In attempting to do so, it is helpful to distinguish negotiation from other prominent methods of influence that are available for adoption.

Methods of Influencing Participation

In contemporary settings, varying amounts of involvement are sought from others by diverse means. Four alternative methods for gaining influence are considered here: payment, persuasion, power, and negotiation. Payment involves the delivery of a benefit to the recipient in return for an object or service requested by the payer and features the absence of coercion, bargaining, and affective gratification. Persuasion is the appeal to logic or to the values held by the recipient. Power is the actual or potential exercise of comparative advantage to glean the target person's compliance. Negotiation is an exchange process between two or more people who attempt to arrive at a rate of exchange among items or services to be exchanged.

These diverse methods of influence imply qualitatively different behaviors and relationships; each can be expected to be variously suited to the conditions of the decision maker's current situation.

Decision Makers as Initiators and Targets of Influence

From the decision maker's perspective, there exists simultaneously a network of decision-needing issues and prospective assistance from others for handling them. On the other side of this perspective are multiple other individuals, each of whom potentially views the first decision maker as a relevant participant in some stages of one or more of their own decisions. Each person is, consequently, both a potential initiator and a target of participation attempts.

In presenting the model of organizational decision/influence behaviors, we focus upon the individual's initiation of the participation of others and give only minor consideration to the decision maker as a recipient of influence attempts by others. Furthermore, consistent with the theme of this volume, we emphasize negotiation at the expense of extensive consideration of the other three influence methods in the analysis.

The preceding discourse has argued that decision making in current organizations requires substantial interplay between the decision maker and others. We now broach our central argument: Decision makers, in certain conditions, pick negotiation rather than other methods to alter the behavior of others.

THE CONCEPTUALIZATION OF DECISION/NEGOTIATIONS

The proposed conceptualization of decision/negotiation research entails the parameters and relationships portrayed in Figure 5.1. The decision maker (on the right side of the diagram), aware of his or her own as well as the role responsibilities of others, develops decision agendas. Selected items from the agendas become the current focal set that the decision maker alters periodically. This characteristic shifting of the focal set has been noted by March and Olsen (1976, p. 12): "At any point in time, individuals vary in the attention they provide to different decisions; they vary from one time to another. As a result, the pattern of participation is uncertain and changing." The current focal set, then, consists of several dominant problems each residing in one or more phases of the decision process. In attempting to solve each problem, the decision maker evaluates the conceivable methods for making the decision, including the extent to which others should be involved in the process.

Alternative Decision Mixes

The decision maker, in assessing the progress of current problems, finds at times that a unilateral approach is preferred, but on other

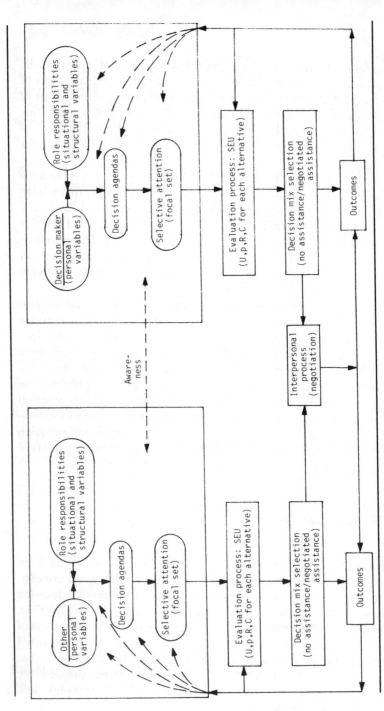

Figure 5.1 Two-Person Decision/Negotiation Processes

occasions concludes that the participation of another would be beneficial. With an awareness of the roles, resources, and skills of others, the decision maker can selectively seek varying amounts of participation from them and can use different methods, including negotiation, to get it. There is also an awareness that this participation of the other entails some costs as well as benefits. The costs, for instance, include the time required to communicate with the other, the anxiety generated by the other's conflicting preferences, and the remuneration demanded for services by the other. Thus in deciding upon the amount and type of participation to seek, consideration is given to the costs, benefits, and probabilities of the costs and benefits inherent to each decision-making style (Payne, 1982). These considerations guide the selection of a "desirable mix" of unilateral and/or participative decision making in various phases of the decision process.

In contemporary organizational settings we posit that several factors—A Factors in Figure 5.2—initially incline the decision maker to seek the participation of others. This need for another's participation requires that the decision maker in some manner gain influence over the other. In doing so, decision makers may adopt any of the influence methods (payment, persuasion, power, negotiation) for intrinsic reasons; but several organizational and environmental factors—B Factors—may compel the instrumental use of negotiation. The conditions in which participation is sought and negotiation is adopted are described more fully after a review of some elements of the individual's evaluation processes.

SEU Evaluation Process

What evaluation process provides the basis for selecting from among the different decision techniques? The proposed conceptualization views decision makers as adopting evaluative decision strategies of the "unaided-analytic variety" (Beach & Mitchell, 1978). More specifically, an amount of participation is sought and a form of influence is adopted such that they yield high subjective expected utility (SEU). Accordingly, for each problem, the decision maker examines the different feasible decision techniques, subjectively identifies for each the probably outcomes (O) it provides, and estimates its total utility (U).

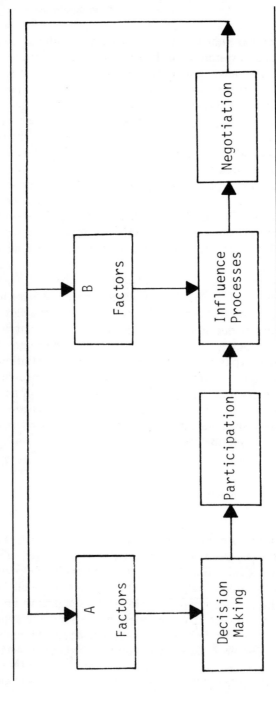

Figure 5.2 Variables Relationships

Consider the components of this SEU process in more detail in the context of a simple two-outcome decision problem where a decision alternative leads either to a correct (c) problem solution or to an incorrect (i) solution. Action alternative (j), then, has outcomes (O_{jc}) or (O_{ji}), each of which is viewed as having its positive payoffs or returns (R_{jc}) and (R_{ji}), and its costs (C_{jc}) and (C_{ji}), so that the net outcome is $O_{jc} = R_{jc} - C_{jc}$ and $O_{ji} = R_{ji} - C_{ji}$. The probability of each outcome, (P_{jc}) and ($P_{ji} = 1 - P_{jc}$), is subjectively determined by the decision maker, and is the utility for each outcome, $U_{jc} = f(O_{jc})$ and $U_{ji} = f(O_{ji})$. Each utility is the net of its positive and negative subcomponent utilities.

For a given decision problem, participation can be a basis for seeking better information, getting assistance in clarifying the problem, garnering support for its implementation, and so on. Each participation possibility enters the evaluation process by the prospects of altering any or all returns, costs, or probabilities. If the other's participation, for example, is seen as an avenue for raising returns or increasing the probability of a desired outcome, there is an incentive to seek it. The benefits, however, are weighed against perceived costs of participation including stress, time, energy expenditures, relinquishment of control over aspects of domain, and expenditures of monetary or other resources, all of which are disincentives to involve the other.

When considering alternative amounts of participation to seek, the decision maker imputes the utility, U_c, for making a correct decision and the utility, U_i, for an incorrect decision. As shown in Figure 5.3, intermediate points (between U_i and U_c) have expected benefits (utilities) determined by the subjective probability of achieving a correct decision, which is a positive function of the level of participation sought from the other.

Using arguments analogous to those of Christensen-Szalanski (1978), we posit that each decision technique lies along the unilateral, participative continuum and has a total cost, U_n (negative utility), that is positively accelerated with the amount of participation. It is assumed that the participative techniques cost more to the decision maker who possesses reasonably accurate perceptions of the costs inherent to each style. Furthermore, for differing techniques that could be used in a given situation, the decision maker imputes a probability, P_c, that each will lead to a correct decision and a probability of $(1 - P_c)$ that will be incorrect. The model assumes that under most conditions, more voluntarily sought participation from another

is accompanied by higher perceived probabilities of a correct decision because the other's participation is expected to bring with it more
information, a diversity of approaches, and added competence. The
decision maker seeks the technique whose probability (P_c) yields the
highest net subjective expected utility, maximizing the difference
between the expected benefit, $[P_c U_c + (1 - P_c) U_i]$, and the expected
cost, U_n, incurred to get the benefit.

The SEU analysis can be applied now to the A Factors and B
Factors (Figure 5.2) to show how the decision maker selects an
appropriate decision mix. This analysis below follows the format of
Figure 5.2, in which the decision to seek the participation of another
precedes the selection of the influence method. Although this
sequential treatment lends clarity to the presentation and may be
representative of the selection process for many situations, it does not
hold universally because of possible interdependencies of the two
choices. An individual's past experiences with a self-initiated method
of influence may precondition the choice of how much participation
to seek in the future. Similarly, a self-imposed limitation (for whatever
reasons) on the amount of participation to seek might condition one's
thoughts about appropriate forms of influence for that situation.
These possible interdependencies are indicated by the feedback
process shown in Figure 5.2 and are considered further in the later
discussion of process dynamics. The emphasis for now is on each of
the two choices.

Factors Affecting the Amount of Participation Sought

Given a decision maker's existing problem situation and the
possibilities for engaging various amounts of participation, what
factors (A Factors in Figure 5.2) modify the benefits and/or costs,
thereby favoring one level of participation over another? Several can
be identified that are indigenous to the individual, some that are
characteristics of the other, and still more that arise from the task, the
decision maker/other relationship, and the environment. The several
factors listed in Table 5.1 are consistent with and extend those
suggested elsewhere as being determinants of the effectiveness of
participation in decision making (Locke & Schweigere, 1979). From
these, three are selected as illustrative examples in the context of the
SEU analysis.

TABLE 5.1   Factors Determining the Amount of Participation
to Be Sought from Other

| | | Source | | |
Decision Maker	Other	Relationship	Problem	Environment
Locus of control	Competence	Interdependence	Risk	Time constraints
Need for consensus	Goals	Conflict	Importance	Norms
Role	Demands	Ease of interaction	Visibility	Acceptance required
Need for affiliation	Time available	Number of contacts	Complexity	Variety
Goals	Past performance		Variety	Uncertainty
Competence	Resources		Uncertainty	Information sources
Resources			Structure	Feedback available
Cognitive limitations			Reversibility	Quality requirement
Dogmatism			Alternatives	Leadership style
Anxiety			Precedents	

Decision maker locus of control. A factor arising from the decision makers themselves is their locus of control, the degree to which they feel that their actions can influence their own outcomes in whatever they do. "Internals" believe that their behavior is very important in determining their fate, whereas "externals" downplay the importance of their behavior, believing chance, luck, and powerful others are decisive factors.

In general, internals are in better control of their behavior and make greater attempts than externals to seek information relevant to their task (Seeman & Evans, 1963; Valecha, 1972; Organ & Green, 1974). The latter observation suggests that internals will more actively seek participation from others than will externals. Internal decision makers, because they feel that their success in making decisions is contingent upon actions they can take (e.g., seek other's participation), are more likely to value and undertake this action.

An internal's perceived higher value (or lower cost) in the more participative styles would be reflected in a lowering of the U_n curve of Figure 5.3. The resulting U_n curve would then lie below and to the right of the external's U_n curve, indicating greater net benefits from a higher amount of participation. In contrast, the external's U_n cost curve would pivot upward (counterclockwise about axis O in Figure 5.3), reflecting his or her belief that the probability of making a correct decision is unrelated to the choice of style. He or she therefore regards the benefits from seeking the other's participation as not being worth the costs of the undertaking.

Problem risk. To illustrate a characteristic of the problem, we note that most organizational decisions involve risks and that the litera-

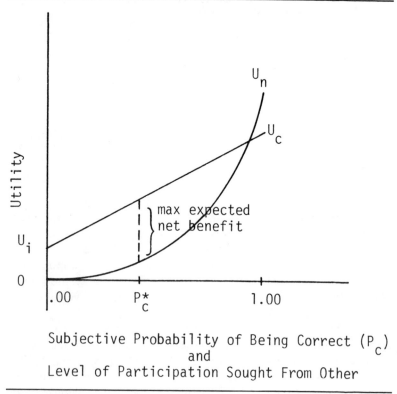

Figure 5.3 Cost-Benefit Representation

ture currently discusses risk in two ways. One approach focuses on the dispersion of probabilities of decision outcomes. The second is concerned with outcome desirability and, specifically, with the severity of the consequences to which the decision maker is exposed. Here we accept both definitions, since they need not be contradictory, and posit that a decision maker is at low risk whenever the probability of a negative outcome(s) is low *and* the negativity of the outcome(s) is of low consequence. Whenever the probability of a negative outcome is high *or* the outcome has high negative consequences, the decision maker is considered to be in a high-risk situation.

In terms of the cost/benefit function, Figure 5.4, high risk lowers the U_i (to U_H) resulting in a rightward shift of P_c and the choice of a more participative decision style; low risk is reflected in a high U_i (U_L) and a more unilateral style. This contention is consistent with other research that observed various methods that are used by

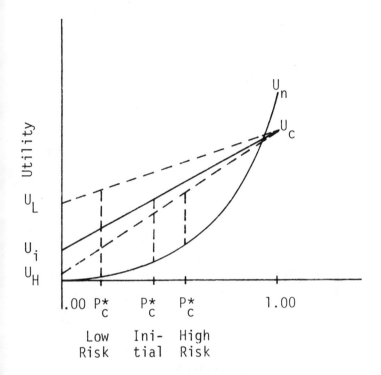

Figure 5.4 Effects of Risk

organizational decision makers to adjust to risk problems (Mac-Crimmon & Wehrung, 1981). Three of the reported adjustment methods—decision avoidance, risk sharing with others, decision delay by information search—are accomplished by adopting more participative (versus unilateral) decision styles.

Time constraint. Turning to an environmental factor (from Table 5.1), the pressure of a time constraint induces the use of more unilateral decision-making styles. As Christensen-Szalanski (1978) notes, the lack of time constraint gives a broader range of feasible participation styles from which the decision maker can pick his or her P_c. In contrast, a tight time constraint narrows the range of feasible options to those involving low participation, near the origin on the graph, thus encouraging more unilateral styles requiring smaller time expenditures.

In the same fashion as above, each of the remaining variables in Table 5.1 can be analyzed to yield testable hypotheses of the amount of participation sought.

Decision Mix Selection: Method Used to Gain Participation

Continuing with the theme in Figure 5.2, the decision to seek another's participation entails choosing the method of influence for doing so. In context of the SEU analysis, the relative costs associated with the different methods must be considered. Generally, persuasion is the least expensive influence form because it requires no resource expenditures beyond the efforts and energies expended during the persuasion process. Payments and power are more expensive than persuasion, but the payment versus power cost is problematic, depending upon the amounts of payment given and power lost. Since the use of power might involve some power relinquishment through alienation of the other, the amount of lost power becomes relevant. Their costs hinge upon the relative values of the power loss versus the payment to the other. Finally, negotiation is the most costly method of influence because it entails payment, loss of time, and a demonstration of decision maker weakness (Wall, 1982).

The potential benefits and probabilities of success for each method as assessed by the decision maker are determined by four variables (B Factors in Figure 5.2): the decision maker's command of resources, the decision maker/other's agreement on exchange rate, the decision maker/other's power relationship, and goal congruence. These factors dictate the methods that are used to gain another's participation.

Decision maker's resources and agreement on exchange rate. A direct manner of attaining the other's participation is by payment of goods or services for that participation. In adopting this play, the decision maker can utilize his or her resources by offering payments for the other's participation, by reinforcing the other's participation, or by combining these offers and reinforcements. But there are two requisites for the use of such payments: (a) control over resources desired by the other and (b) agreement on the participation/resource exchange rate.

Without command of some resources, the decision maker cannot use them as payments. In such a case negotiation also becomes quite difficult because the decision maker has nothing to trade; he or she must therefore depend heavily on threat or coercive tactics.

In contrast, if the decision maker has or can garner control over some resources that are of value to the other, they can be used as payments for the other's participation. When the decision maker does have resources—which is the case in most organizational roles—the question of an exchange rate assumes high relevance. If the other tacitly or explicitly accepts the decision maker's offer and payment, the participation is obtained without recourse to power, persuasion, or negotiation. On the other hand, if there is a disagreement as to the amount of payment (i.e., exchange rate), the decision maker must fall back on these other techniques. The choice from among the remaining techniques is determined in part by two additional factors operating within the organization: the power relationship and the goal congruence of the decision maker and the other person.

Power relationship. The decision maker's high power, rather than alternative types of influence, can be used to gain the other's participation. However, the viability of power in gaining participation depends on the relative power positions of both parties in the influence process. Whenever equal power exists, the decision maker may wish to exercise it but cannot; the other has sufficient power relative to the decision maker to thwart any power move. So here the decision maker should utilize different ploys to gain participation. When the decision maker has the power advantage, it can be exploited. In a relatively weak power position, the decision maker will have to adopt a conciliatory negotiation style.

Goal congruence. Whenever their goals are incongruent, the decision maker's attempts to gain participation will be resisted by the other. In such a case, persuasion proves ineffective as an influence attempt because there is no logical basis for the other's cooperation; therefore, payments, power, or negotiation must be utilized. On the other hand, whenever the two parties share a common goal, persuasion proves to be of high utility in attaining the participation.

Combined effects. The preceding arguments are combined into a tree structure (Figure 5.5) delineating the influence processes to be utilized under specific organizational conditions. By moving from left to right along the tree, addressing each question at the top of the figure, and then following the appropriate branch, one can close upon the influence technique (a–j) appropriate for designated contingencies.

At some of the branch termini, more than one influence technique is admissible, but one is more appropriate than others. Persuasion— explanation and logic—is the dominant influence method in situation (a), even though all forms are viable. In (b), payment is dominant, with power as the backup if payment becomes too costly. In the other situations, persuasion is dominated by the other form because of incongruent goals. The hypothesized dominant forms of influence for situations a through j are summarized in Table 5.2.

The tree synthesizes a complex set of hypotheses for main and interactive effects manifested by goals, power, and resources. By joining this tree with the A Factors that were considered earlier, we gain new and useful insights as to how organizational decision makers operate under different conditions. For example, a decision maker facing (1) a complex task, (2) another with whom goals are incongruent, (3) an equal power position, (4) control of resources, but (5) disagreement over the exchange rate should seek the other's participation and negotiate to get it (terminus f, Figure 5.5). In contrast, if the task is complex and the goals are congruent with the other's, the decision maker should seek the other's participation and use persuasion to glean it (terminus a). Moreover, if the task is simple, the decision maker should handle it unilaterally.

Extensions to Dynamic Processes and Decision/Negotiation Strategies

Although the proposed conceptualization provides guidance along specific avenues of initial inquiry, it requires further development into the dynamics of decision/negotiation processes. This unexplored area is fraught with conceptual and operational difficulties, yet it is highly significant in contemporary organizations.

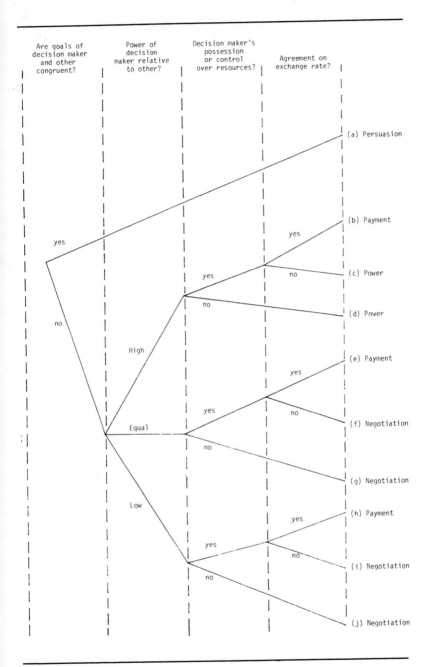

Figure 5.5 Appropriate Influence Attempts

TABLE 5.2   Appropriate Influence Attempts

Situation	Technique	Reasoning
a	Persuasion	It is the least expensive.
b	Payment	Persuasion eliminated by incongruent goals. Power is backup.
c	Power	Disagreement on exchange rate eliminates payment. Power is cheaper than negotiation.
d	Power	No resources eliminates payment. Power is cheaper than negotiation.
e	Payment	Payment is cheaper than negotiation. Equal-power position eliminates power.
f	Negotiation	Disagreement over exchange rate eliminates payment. Equal-power position eliminates power.
g	Negotiation	No resources eliminates payment. Equal-power position eliminates power.
h	Payment	Payment cheaper than negotiation. Low-power position eliminates power.
i	Negotiation	Disagreement on exchange rate eliminates payment. Low-power position eliminates power.
j	Negotiation	No resources eliminates payment. Low-power position eliminates power.

When our conceptualizations refocus from static to dynamic situations, the current model suggests that some additional variables become relevant. With ongoing role responsibilities, under the pressure of time and resource constraints, and in the face of multidecision agendas, decisions become linked, temporally and contextually, with other decisions. These interdecisional relationships combine with the process and outcomes of negotiation, resulting in revised organizational conditions and decision processes that set the tone for further, ongoing decision activity.

In dynamic processes, linkages develop among the decisions of the individual and among decisions across individuals. As a result of new information gained from recent exchange relationships with others, for example, the decision maker's attention may voluntarily shift from a previously unattended problem. Similarly, new decision tasks may be initiated or criteria changed for an existing decision as part of the exchange agreements from negotiations with others. On other occasions, negotiation may be initiated in the midst of ambiguity as an action for clarifying outcome preferences prior to the moment of choice. As stated by Cohen et al. (1976, p. 25), "Preferences are discovered through action as much as being a basis of action." These behaviors typify the kinds of important issues that arise in dynamic, ongoing decision situations and may not be visible in static, one-time decision situations. The process dynamics, in the context of Figure 5.1, can change personal variables, role responsibilities, decision agendas, focal sets, and elements of the individual's evaluation process.

Amidst changing organizational conditions, our concern with decision/influence styles shifts from the level of tactics to one of strategies; individuals adopt time-phased combinations of decision/influence methods forming patterns of decision styles. Consequently, there evolves a two-way adaptation; decision style adapts to organizational conditions, which, in turn, are modified by decision processes. The amounts of turbulence in the oscillatory adjustments between decision style and organizational conditions may vary systematically across different types of organizations and their environments. These oscillatory adjustments deserve investigation because they can be costly or beneficial to both the organization and the individual.

CONCLUSION

The purpose of the decision/negotiations conceptualization is to guide research toward a better understanding of decision processes by accounting for organizational and behavioral factors that affect decision making. More specifically, we seek a significant beginning for showing how voluntarily initiated interpersonal influence processes and particularly negotiation are important, where they enter the decision process, and which conditions foster their use in decision making. Toward these ends we presented a structure and some concepts that have proven valuable for guiding our current research and which offer even further promise for future inquiry. The concepts and model will continue to evolve as these negotiation/decision processes are subjected to empirical testing.

REFERENCES

Beach, L. R., & Mitchell, T. R. A contingency model for the selection of decision strategies. *Academy of Management Review,* 1978, *3,* 439-449.

Christensen-Szalanski, J.J.J. Problem solving strategies: A selection mechanism, some implications, and some data. *Organizational Behavior and Human Performance,* 1978, *22,* 307-323.

Cohen, M. D., March, J. G., & Olsen, J. P. People, problems, solutions, and the ambiguity of relevance. In J. G. March & J. P. Olsen (Eds.), *Ambiguity and choice in organizations.* Bergen, Norway: Universitetsforlaget, 1976.

Crawford, J. L., & Haaland, G. A. Predecisional information seeking and subsequent conformity in the social influence process. *Journal of Personality and Social Psychology,* 1972, *23,* 112-119.

Ebert, R. J., & Mitchell, T. R. *Organizational decision processes: Concepts and analysis.* New York: Crane, Russak & Company, 1975.

Gore, W. J. *Administrative decision-making: A heuristic model.* New York: John Wiley, 1964.

Harnett, D. L., & Cummings, L. L. *Bargaining behavior: An international study.* Houston: Dame, 1980.

Heller, F. A. *Managerial decision-making.* London: Tavistock, 1971.

Khandwalla, P. N. *The design of organizations.* New York: Harcourt Brace Jovanovich, 1977.

Locke, D. A., & Schweiger, D. M. Participation in decision-making: One more look. In B. M. Staw (Ed.), *Research in Organizational Behavior,* 1979, *1,* 265-339.

MacCrimmon, K. R., & Taylor, R. N. Decision making and problem solving. In M. D. Dunnette (Ed.), *Handbook of organizational and industrial psychology.* Chicago: Rand McNally, 1976.

MacCrimmon, K. R., & Wehrung, D. A. *Risk in-basket.* Unpublished.

March, J. G., & Olsen, J. P. *Ambiguity and choice in organizations.* Bergen, Norway: Universitetsforlaget, 1976.

Mowday, R. T. The exercise of upward influence in organizations. *Administrative Science Quarterly,* 1978, *23,* 137-156.

Mowday, R. T. Leader characteritics, self-confidence, and methods of upward influence in organizational decision situations. *Academy of Management Journal,* 1979, *22,* 709-725.

Nutt, P. C. Models for decision making in organizations and some contextual variables which stipulate optimal use. *Academy of Management Review,* 1976, *1,* 84-98.

Organ, D. W., & Greene, C. N. Role ambiguity, locus of control, and work satisfaction. *Journal of Applied Psychology,* 1974, *59,* 101-102.

Patchen, M. The locus and basis of influence on organizational decisions. *Organizational Behavior and Human Performance,* 1974, *11,* 195-221.

Payne, J. W. Contingent decision behavior. *Psychological Bulletin,* 1982, *92,* 382-402.

Rowe, A. J. The myth of the rational decision maker. *International Management,* 1974, *29,* 38-40.

Scott, W. G., & Hart, D. K. *Organizational America.* Boston: Houghton Mifflin, 1979.

Seeman, M., & Evans, J. W. Alienation and learning in a hospital setting. *American Sociological Review,* 1963, *27,* 772-783.

Sigal, L. V. *Reporters and officials: The organization and politics of newsmaking.* Lexington, MA: D. C. Heath, 1973.

Simon, H. A. *Administrative behavior* (2nd ed.). New York: Macmillan, 1957.

Slovic, P., Fischhoff, B., & Lichtenstein, S. Behavioral decision theory. *Annual Review of Psychology,* 1977, *28,* 1-39.

Thompson, J. D., & Tuden, A. Strategies, structures and processes of organizational decisions. In H. J. Leavitt & L. R. Pondy (Eds.), *Readings in managerial psychology.* Chicago: University of Chicago Press, 1964.

Valecha, G. K. Construct validation of internal-external locus of reinforcement related to work-related variables. *Proceedings of the 80th Annual Convention of the American Psychological Association,* 1972, *7,* 455-456.

Vroom, V. H., & Jago, A. G. Decision making as a social process: Normative and descriptive models of leader behavior. *Decision Sciences,* 1974, *5,* 743-769.

Vroom, V. H., & Yetton, P. W. *Leadership and decision-making.* Pittsburgh: University of Pittsburgh Press, 1973.

Wall, J. A. *Negotiation: Theory and practice.* Glenview, IL: Scott-Foresman, 1982.

Winham, G. R. Negotiation as a management process. *World Politics,* 1977, *30,* 87-114.

Zaleznik, A. Power and politics in organizational life. *Harvard Business Review,* 1970, *48,* 47-60.

Zartman, I. W. Negotiation as a joing decision-making process. *Journal of Conflict Resolution,* 1977, *21,* 619-638.

—6—

DETERMINING OUTCOMES OF NEGOTIATIONS
An Empirical Assessment

Leonard Greenhalgh
Scott A. Neslin

Dartmouth College

Negotiation is a central process in many, if not most, organizational settings. Sales transactions and collective bargaining are obvious examples. Less obvious examples span the range from a new low-level employee's working out the terms of a psychological contract (Schein, 1981) to the top-level policymaking process (Allison, 1971). Despite its pervasiveness and importance, negotiation in organizational settings has received surprisingly little empirical research attention.

One reason for the lack of empirical research is that negotiations in organizational settings are typically not amenable to field study. Three major problems confront the researcher. First, the negotiations are often private and involve understood but unstated issues. They are thus not suited to classic observational study. Second, negotiations tend to be complex, involving several interrelated issues. It is important but difficult for the field researcher to discover the relative importance of issues to negotiators. Third, negotiation is a power process, and situational power advantages are difficult to assess in a field study. This is because situational power is often confounded with other variables, particularly negotiator skill and idiosyncratic preferences.

The use of laboratory role-playing simulation can directly address the above problems. Confining the transaction to the laboratory increases the chances of capturing a process that is for the most part inaccessible to the field researcher. At the same time, principles of classical experimental design can be used to manipulate and measure the effects of situational power advantages. For example, in order to separate situational power advantages from differences in individual bargaining skill, the researcher can make sure that over a series of simulations, each role gets its turn to be represented by the more skilled negotiator. This permits unconfounded estimation of the power inherent in each role. Simulation also has a major advantage over field research in that it permits replication. In testing any theory, replication of the test is important if one is to be confident that confirmation (or disconfirmation) of the theory is not spurious. Furthermore, the more uncontrolled elements in the test, the greater the number of replications desirable. Replication of field research is imprecise and inefficient in comparison to simulation.

The disadvantages of laboratory research have been elaborated elsewhere (see, e.g., Berkowitz & Donnerstein, 1982). The most serious problem with using laboratory studies to investigate negotiations in organizational settings is the limitation on external validity (i.e., the degree to which findings valid for laboratory situations can be generalized to organizational situations). Thus the researcher is faced with a tradeoff whereby laboratory control and external validity need to be jointly optimized. Achieving joint optimization—through rich-context simulation, as described below—is unsatisfying to purists of both the laboratory and field research traditions, but may produce the most promising research on negotiation in organizational settings.

This chapter proposes a paradigm to test theories of bargaining by using rich-context simulation in conjunction with a sophisticated procedure of preference measurement and classical experimental design. This research is innovative in three respects. First, it develops highly realistic simulations of organizational situations and then uses measurement techniques that avoid the need to oversimplify complex situations in order to make them amenable to analysis. Second, it does not assume that simulation participants react the same way to the simulated situation but rather measures their reactions individually. In particular, it is not assumed that individuals form the same preferences regarding each bargaining issue, but their idiosyncratic preferences are measured using conjoint analysis. Third, it does not assume that participants are homogeneous on salient dimensions such as bargaining skill, but rather measures these traits directly and incorporates them in the experimental design.

This research organizes the principal determinants of the outcomes of negotiations under three headings: negotiators' *preference* structures, situational *power,* and *individual differences* in negotiators' aptitudes and skills. The relationships between negotiated outcomes and each of the hypothesized determinants listed above have considerable theoretical support. (See, for example, the classic papers by Nash, 1950, 1953, for the importance of preference; see Emerson, 1962, for the importance of situational power; see Rubin and Brown, 1975, for a summary of the research on individual differences and bargaining; see also Bacharach and Lawler, 1981, for an explanation of the role of bargaining skill.) Our goal is to assess these relationships empirically.

METHOD

Development of Rich-Context Simulations

The classical approach of experimental social psychology consists of: (1) derivation of testable hypotheses from theory; then, (2) creation of the simplest labortory situation that involves those (and only those) variables that constitute the hypotheses. Traditional field research, but contrast, also begins with the derivation of hypotheses from theory, but the hypotheses are tested in a field setting that is representative of the class of settings to which the researcher wishes to generalize. As a blending of the classical experimental approach and traditional field research, rich-context simulations recreate representative settings in the laboratory. The emphasis is not on the bare-bones simplicity for which the experimental social psychologist strives, but rather on faithfulness to the real-world situation. The latter is, of course, subject to constraints, such as the need to define an infinite environment in finite terms, biases resulting from the researcher's selective perception, and the cognitive limits of experimental subjects. Nevertheless, the rich-context simulation does produce a laboratory experience that is quite different from what is typically created by experimental social psychologists.

Two such simulations are described next. The media advertising purchase simulation involves a two-person sales transaction. The collective bargaining simulation involves a two-party contract negotiation wherein each party consists of four to five individuals.

(1) Media advertising purchase simulation. This simulation was based on an actual contract that had been negotiated between an advertiser and a television network. The dynamics and context of the negotiation were recreated from documents and interviews. The external validity of the simulated case was positively evaluated by industry experts.

The simulation involved an "opportunistic buy" of a number of 30-second spots ("units") on the television show *M*A*S*H*. CBS Television was the seller and "National Products" the buyer. The scenario depicts National Products needing the television time to help launch a new breakfast cereal targeted toward young, athletic people. *M*A*S*H* is especially well-suited for this market segment. *M*A*S*H* is one of CBS's most highly rated programs, but there exist rumors that Alan Alda, the star, may be leaving the show. Both parties had a strong interest in completing a deal but were not compelled to come to a settlement at any cost. CBS valued National Products as an important customer yet realized that commercial time on *M*A*S*H* could certainly be sold to someone else if the two companies were unable to reach agreement. National Products had a particular interest in *M*A*S*H* because of the match between its audience and National Products' target market. However, other suitable programs were available from other networks if agreement could not be reached on *M*A*S*H*.

Three issues needed to be negotiated. First was the number of units to be purchased. Given the availability of spots as well as National

Products' media schedule requirements, this could range between 8 and 12. Second was a rating guarantee provision. A rating guarantee provided by CBS would state that in the event that $M*A*S*H$ did not achieve its usual 20 rating, CBS would make up the difference in free additional spots. A guarantee of between 15 and 20 rating points was possible, while a guarantee of less than 15 was viewed as no guarantee. The guarantee became a salient issue because of the threatened departure of Alan Alda, which could severely depress $M*A*S*H$'s future ratings. The third issue for negotiation was the price. Given the time of year, a price per thousand anticipated viewers of between $6.25 and $6.75 was reasonable. This reflects the then currently prevailing prices for opportunistic buys.

All factorial combinations of the above three attributes were feasible settlements. National Products, the buyer, naturally preferred a 20 guarantee, a $6.25 price, and 10 units to match its media schedule requirements. CBS naturally preferred no guarantee, a $6.75 price, and sale of all 12 units it currently had available.

Subjects were assigned the role of principal negotiator for either National Products or CBS. Each read a common background statement as well as a separate memo written to each negotiator by his or her superior. The memo from the superior outlined the issues from the buyer's or seller's viewpoint, respectively. These materials gave the negotiators a general idea of the relative importance of the bargaining issues from the viewpoint of the constituencies they represented. However, based on past experience, it was expected that each negotiator would develop a somewhat idiosyncratic viewpoint of these issues. After reading the case material, each participant's utility function for alternative settlements was measured using conjoint analysis (described below). Subjects then conducted the actual negotiations and reached a settlement.

(2) Collective bargaining simulation. This simulation—like the media advertising purchase simulation—was based on an actual contract. Each individual who was to participate in the study was supplied with a copy of the 1975-1977 plant-level agreement between a Fortunc 500 manufacturing company and a large AFL-CIO union, plus a statement of the union's initial demands and mangement's initial response to them. Each package also contained background

information detailing the context of the negotiation as it would be experienced by each party.

The union's demands and management's response involved more than twenty issues, but only five of these were really important to the parties:

(a) *Wages:* The union wanted a substantial increase in real wages; management wanted to hold the adjustment to cover cost-of-living increases only.

(b) *Pay differential:* For political reasons, the union wanted a flat cents-per-pound increase for all job categories; management wanted to reverse the effects of a history of pay compression and widen the pay differential between skilled and unskilled workers.

(c) *Benefits:* The union wanted additional fringe benefits, including Sunday double-time, more holidays, more generous shift differentials, longer vacations, and improved health care insurance; management was opposed to making any changes in the benefits package.

(d) *Work rules:* The union wanted to maintain tight constraints on the range of job duties required of maintenance workers; management was pushing for more flexibility in assigning maintenance workers to tasks.

(e) *Union shop:* The union wanted a union security provision that would require all employees to become union members within 30 days of hiring; management resisted this.

The five attributes were essentialy bipolar; all factorial combinations were feasible settlements. As in the case of the media advertising purchase simulation, individuals' preferences were assessed using the conjoint analysis technique. However, the collective bargaining exercise was an intergroup negotiation; therefore, intragroup preference discrepancies needed to be reconciled in a prenegotiation meeting and the group-level preference structure assessed.

Conjoint Analysis

Conjoint analysis analyzes preference judgments for outcomes in terms of the attributes that compose those outcomes. For this program of research, the outcomes are alternative negotiation settlements and the attributes are the issues that are being negotiated. The conjoint analysis methodology requires that subjects rate a collection of possible settlements in terms of their preferences for achieving each settlement. Each settlement differs in terms of the combination of outcomes on each attribute. For example, in the media advertising purchase simulation, the CBS negotiator would tend to rate higher those settlements that involved a high price, a large number of units, and no rating guarantee. More specifically, the primary outputs are a set of intervally scaled "part-worths" (analogous to "utilities") for each level of each attribute and a rule for combining these utilities so as to obtain preference predictions for new items composed of varying levels of each attribute.

The steps in implementing a conjoint analysis study include (1) definition of attributes, (2) construction of the conjoint measurement exercise, (3) data collection, (4) estimation, and (5) analysis. Each step is briefly described (see Greenhalgh and Neslin, 1981, for further detail on applying conjoint analysis in bargaining situations).

(1) Definition of attributes. Conjoint analysis begins with the equivalent of Zartman's (1977) formula-definition stage: generating and selecting attributes. In most applications, it is possible to generate a large number of attributes, but only a limited set can be meaningfully evaluated. This is due to cognitive limits on the respondent's ability to evaluate complex multidimensional stimuli: Most applications involve fewer than seven attributes.

Attributes are given a generic name or label, and then each of the more specific "levels" of the attributes must be defined. In general, conjoint analysis required that the attributes be dichotomized or polychotomized into definite levels. The levels may be simply nominal classifications (as with the presence or absence of a guarantee) or reflect some metric (as in the case of price).

(2) Construction of the conjoint measurement exercise. Once the levels of each attribute have been defined, hypothetical outcomes can be constructed as factorial combinations of attributes. As noted above, conjoint analysis derives part-worths and hence preferences based upon a subject's rank ordering of these hypothetical outcomes. A problem is that the number of potential outcomes can rapidly

become quite large. This problem can be addressed using principles of experimental design (see Greenhalgh & Neslin, 1981; pp. 309-310).

(3) Data collection. Several methods are available for collecting preference data for potential outcomes. The differences between alternative methods are evaluated in Green and Srinivasan (1978). The method found useful in research on negotiations is simple rank ordering. Negotiators are presented with a set of outcome "packages," which they must rank order. The tradeoffs they make among the attributes in rank-ordering the packages evidence the utility of each attribute.

(4) Estimation. Once data have been collected, a model must be estimated that relates attribute levels to preference. The most common model form used in conjoint analysis is the *additive compensatory model.* This model is analogous to a main-effects-only analysis of variance model. Despite its simplicity, the model has proven to be a good predictor (Green & Srinivasan, 1978) and the utility part-worths are easy to interpret and can be readily examined for face validity. More complex interaction effects can be included in the model, but when rigorously tested using analysis of variance, many interactions turn out not to be statistically significant (Neslin, 1978).

A variety of techniques are available for estimating the part-worths, depending on the data collection procedure employed. If rank ordering has been used, as in this program of research, monotone analysis of variance (MONANOVA) is the appropriate procedure (Kruskal, 1965; Kruskal & Carmone, 1968). The MONANOVA algorithm finds the set of part-worths that best recover the original rank-order data.

(5) Analysis. Part-worth values can be interpreted as a measure of the relative utility of the various attributes being negotiated. The part-worths for each component of an alternative settlement package (i.e., combination of attributes) can be added to predict the utility of each package. Comparison of actual and predicted rank-ordered preferences of alternative outcome packages provides a means of evaluating the accuracy of the part-worths.

The part-worths obtained by conjoint analysis can thus be used to calculate a negotiator's utility for any possible outcome. This utility can then serve as input to test theories relating negotiator preferences to outcomes. For example, one theory is Nash's theory of cooperative games. Given each party's utilities for all possible settlements, Nash identifies the unique settlement (the Nash "solution") that satisfies four desirable properties: (1) independence of utility function scale, (2) Pareto optimality, (3) independence of irrelevant alternatives, and (4) symmetry of utility functions (for further details, see Nash, 1950; Luce & Raiffa, 1957; Davis, 1970).

The Nash solution is the only settlement that satisfies all four of the above conditions. It is calculated by rescaling each negotiator's utilities with respect to the utility of the point at which the negotiator would prefer no settlement at all to lower-ranked outcome packages (this is also sometimes referred to as the "resistance point"). Thus rescaling involves subtracting the no-settlement utility from the utility for each outcome package. The Nash solution can at this point be identified; it is the outcome package that maximizes the product of the two negotiators' utilities. In summary, let

U_{ij} = utility of player i for settlement j
U_{io} = utility of player i for no settlement

The Nash solution is the settlement that maximizes the product

$$(U_{1j} - U_{1o}) (U_{2j} - U_{2o})$$

Figure 6.1 provides a useful vehicle for understanding the concepts outlined above. The points on this graph represent a sampling of possible settlements. The location of each point is determined by the utility of the party I (e.g., the union negotiators) for that settlement (x-axis) and the utility of party II (e.g., the management negotiators) for that settlement (y-axis). Utilities are calculated using the conjoint analysis technique and are scaled relative to the no settlement outcome.

Since the points plotted on the graphs represent settlements that have positive utilities for both negotiators, they all represent feasible settlements in that each one would leave both negotiators better off than they would be if no settlement were reached. Some settlements are obviously inferior because there exist settlements that offer both

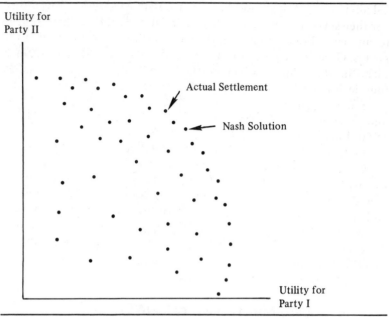

Figure 6.1   Party Utilities, Actual Settlements, and Nash Solutions

negotiators higher utility. The settlements that lie on the outermost boundary are "Pareto optimal" in that no other settlement offers higher utilities to *both* negotiators. The Nash solution is such a point, but it also satisfies the criterion of maximizing the product of the parties' rescaled utilities. The particular situation depicted in Figure 6.1 is one in which the Nash solution is close to the actual but differs in that Party II was able to achieve a better outcome at the expense of Party I.

Experimental Design

The program of research outlined above has been used to investigate different facets of the relationship between negotiated outcomes and their hypothesized determinants. Different experimental designs are appropriate depending on which facet is being investigated. For example, in using the media purchase simulation, it was important to be able to separate the effects of situational power from effects of individual differences in negotiators. Subjects were thus "seeded" in terms of peer-assessed overall bargaining ability. Subjects were then paired and assigned to roles so that each role (buyer or seller) was assigned a balanced share of relative individual skill advantage. Similar steps were taken with the collective bargaining simulation. The effects of bargaining skill and situational power inherent in each role could thus be estimated on an unconfounded basis.

A later study of the media advertising purchase negotiations was designed to assess the effect of the situational power on negotiated outcome. Subjects were randomly assigned to roles, and preferences were measured rather than assumed to be identical with the specifications of the simulated roles (as is typically the case in laboratory studies). In addition, situational power was experimentally manipulated by randomly assigning buyers and sellers to high and low power conditions.

EMPIRICAL FINDINGS

Linking Negotiator Preferences to Outcomes: Testing Nash's Theory

As described previously, Nash's theory of cooperative games provides a mechanism for translating negotiator preferences into negotiated outcomes. The only data needed for this translation are the utilities of each negotiator for each of the possible outcomes. These data can be provided by conjoint analysis. Once the Nash solution has been calculated, it can be compared to the actual outcome. This provides a test of Nash's theory as a predictor of the actual outcomes of negotiations.

Before comparing actual outcomes with the outcomes predicted by Nash's theory, it is interesting to observe the average preferences of participants. Figure 6.1 depicts these preferences for the collective bargaining simulation. The slopes in these graphs can be interpreted as the relative importances of each of the issues. For example, the average union negotiator is quite concerned about wages, but less concerned about work rules. Management is very concerned about the union shop issue, but less concerned about benefits. The graphs also provide a pictorial means of assessing the conflict in negotiator interests. For example, Figure 6.2 indicates that, in general, there is more conflict on the pay differential issue than on the work rules issue, because both parties tend to be more concerned about pay differential.

The collective bargaining simulation was later updated and rerun using a slightly revised scenario: A no-layoff guarantee rose in priority to replace the benefits package, a specific job jurisdiction issue (creation of a multiskill "premium mechanic" position) replaced the general issue of work rules, and wages were operationalized to three levels (8 percent, 12 percent, and 16 percent "across-the-board" wage increases). Since the collective bargaining involved two multi-person groups, each group performed the conjoint analysis exercise as a group. In addition, utility for the no-settlement outcome was measured (see Greenhalgh & Neslin, 1981, p. 318 for details). This last adjustment enabled the calculation of Nash settlements (Nash, 1950, 1953), which could be compared with actual simulated outcomes. The results of this comparison for three negotiations are depicted in Table 6.1.

Table 6.1 indicates that although each group reached a somewhat different settlement, there is good correspondence between Nash solutions and the actual settlements. For team pairings A and B, the Nash and actual settlements correspond exactly on three of the five issues. For team pairing C, they correspond on three of the five issues. While the results displayed in Table 6.2 are encouraging, they cannot be tested for statistical significance: There are only three observations. The media advertising purchase simulation was subsequently run with 27 dyads. A regression equation was calibrated that related the Nash predicted negotiator utility to the actual utility. Results indicated that the actual utilities were not statistically different from those predicted by Nash's theory (see Neslin & Greenhalgh, 1982, for details).

In summary, empirical work has revealed evidence that Nash solutions correspond well to actual settlements as obtained in a role-playing simulation. While Nash's theory is the predominant approach

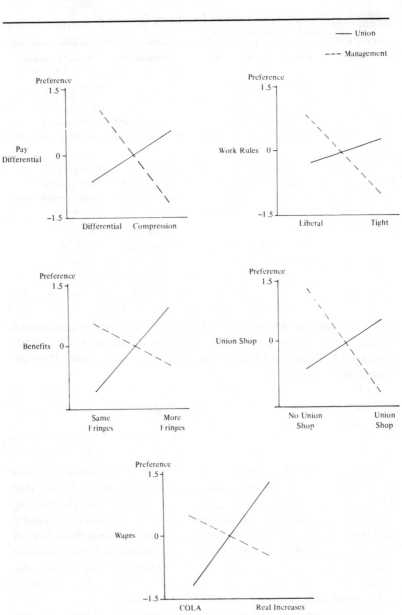

Figure 6.2 Party Preferences for Issue Resolution: Collective Bargaining Simulation

TABLE 6.1   Comparison of Actual Bargaining Outcomes and Nash Settlements

Pair of Teams	Issue	Nash Solution	Actual Solution
A	Wages	16%	12%
	Union shop	Not granted	Not granted
	Premium mechanic	Granted	Granted
	No layoff provision	Not granted	Not granted
	Skilled wage differential	Granted	Granted
B	Wages	16%	14.5%
	Union shop	Granted	Granted
	Premium mechanic	Not granted	Not granted
	No layoff provision	Not granted	Not granted
	Skilled wage differential	Granted	Granted
C	Wages	16%	14%
	Union shop	Not granted	Granted
	Premium mechanic	Granted	Granted
	No layoff provision	Not granted	Not granted
	Skilled wage differential	Granted	Granted

to incorporating perferences into the analysis of bargaining outcomes (Bacharach & Lawler, 1981), it is only one such theory. The promising results obtained here encourage the testing of other theories using conjoint analysis and simulation.

Situational Power

The results of the media advertising purchase simulation also suggested a possible situational power advantage, although this finding was not statistically significant. Specifically, the finding suggested that the average buyer was able to achieve a utility slightly higher than that predicted by Nash's theory, while the seller achieved a slightly lower utility than predicted. This suggested a slight power advantage for the buyer. Although the effect was not statistically significant, it encouraged further research involving experimentation in which situational power might be manipulated.

Such research was undertaken, using another set of subjects and a revised simulation. In the new simulation, situational power was

TABLE 6.2   An Experiment Manipulating Situational Power

		Seller	
		Low Power	High Power
Buyer	Low Power	(1) Balanced low power	(2) Unbalanced "seller's market"
	High Power	(3) Unbalanced "buyer's market"	(4) Balanced high power

manipulated according to the plan summarized in Table 6.2. The manipulation was achieved by changing the background descriptions provided to subjects to reflect different degrees of dependence (Emerson, 1962; Bacharach & Lawler, 1981). In short, a "high-power" condition meant that the buyer (seller) was the only customer (television network) available. The "low-power" conditions meant that several buyers (sellers) were available. It was thus possible to create the four experimental conditions displayed in Table 6.2.

The experiment described in Table 6.2 was conducted using 80 MBA student subjects and hence 40 dyads; 10 dyads were randomly assigned to each cell. The first step was to check whether the experimental manipulation was perceived by the subjects as desired by the researchers. A questionnaire was administered to subjects both before and after each bargaining session. The questionnaire measured perceptions of which role had the better bargaining position. The results indicate that the power position was perceived as desired, both before and after the actual negotiation.

As a further check on the validity of the experiment, one-way analyses of variance showed that mean preferences were equal across the four experimental cells: None of the F statistics was significant at the .10 level. In summary the participants in this experiment perceived the power situations as desired, yet the pattern of preferences remained the same in all four treatment cells.

Table 6.3 provides information on the value the average participant in each treatment condition placed on the no-settlement outcome. As expected, there are significant differences in this value, with

TABLE 6.3   Buyer-Seller Utility Values for No Settlement

Cell	Buyer[a]		Seller[b]	
	Power	Mean Utility	Power	Mean Utility
1	Low	−2.23	Low	−1.82
2	Low	−1.54	High	−1.22
3	High	−.75	Low	−2.03
4	High	−.30	High	−1.03

a. $F(3,36) = 8.84$ ($p < .005$).
b. $F(3,36) = 2.75$ ($p < .005$).

participants in low-power situations having significantly lower preferences for the no-settlement outcome (in other words, people feeling highly dependent on the other party will accept a worse deal than will their less dependent counterparts). The results of Table 6.3 can be viewed as a further check that verifies the validity of the experimental manipulation depicted in Table 6.2. Table 6.4, however, shows virtually no significant differences in the participants' utilities for the actual outcomes of their bargaining.

In summary, no difference was detected in outcomes even though the power manipulation was clearly perceived, the underlying preference structure was unaffected, and preferences for the no-settlement outcome were affected in the predicted direction. Participants in relatively more powerful bargaining positions did not achieve more favorable outcomes.

There are two possible reasons for the result in Table 6.4. First, the experiment might not have been powerful enough to detect significant effects. Second, the observed result may simply be accurate, indicating that in the particular role-playing simulation examined, and using that particular group of subjects, situational power did not affect outcomes. The first reason is plausible, since the sample size is only ten per cell. However, other significant effects, regarding perceptions and preferences for the no-settlement outcome, were detected. The second reason may very well hold. One explanation might be that the simulation made clear to participants the realistic assumption that the particular bargaining situation they were in was part of an ongoing relationship between buyer and seller (Caplow, 1968, explains the different dynamics of episodic and continuous interactions); this may have dissuaded participants from pressing their advantage when they were in a favorable power situation, fearing later repercussions.

TABLE 6.4   Buyer-Seller Utilities for Actual Outcomes

Cell	Buyer[a]		Seller[b]	
	Power	Mean Utility	Power	Mean Utility
1	Low	.94	Low	.62
2	Low	.71	High	.00
3	High	.91	Low	.34
4	High	.73	High	1.03

a. $F(3,36) = .37$ (n.s.).
b. $F(3,36) = 2.30$ ($p < .10$).

Individual Differences

In the earlier media purchase simulation, the strong correspondence between actual and Nash solutions indicated that the relative skill advantage as perceived by the participants did not account for much variation in outcomes. The failure of this variable to explain results suggests that more in-depth measures might be required to link individual differences to bargaining outcomes. As part of the followup experiment, which manipulated situational power in the revised media advertising purchase simulation, such measures were collected. The individual difference measures were then correlated with two variables: preference for the no-settlement outcome (a determinant of Nash solutions) and utility for the actual outcome. These correlations appear in Table 6.5.

Table 6.5 must obviously be viewed as purely exploratory: Further analysis is needed to both better structure the set of personality measures and relate them to the two dependent variables. However, the results in Table 6.5 demonstrate some interesting linkages and suggest that individual differences may indeed explain some of the variation in bargaining outcomes. It appears that these variables affect both the negotiators' preference for achieving some sort of settlement rather than an impasse, and the actual utility achieved by the negotiator.

These preliminary data show that the initiating structure dimension of leadership (Fleishman, 1957) correlates most highly with

TABLE 6.5   Correlations of Individual Difference Variables
with Preferences for No Settlement Outcome
and Utility for Actual Outcome

Variable	Correlation with No Settlement Preference[a]	Correlation with Utility for Actual Outcome[a]
(1) Leadership-Structure (Fleishman, 1957)	.12 (n.s.)	.25 (.02)
(2) Masculinity (Bem, 1974)	−.26 (.01)	−.03 (n.s.)
(3) Femininity (Bem, 1974)	−.21 (.04)	−.03 (n.s.)
(4) Machiavellianism (Christie & Geis, 1970)	.17 (.08)	−.20 (.05)
(5) Perspective-taking ability (Davis, 1980)	−.13 (n.s.)	.05 (n.s.)
(6) Thinking versus feeling (Myers, 1962)	.01 (n.s.)	.15 (.10)
(7) Extroverted/introverted (Myers, 1962)	.17 (.08)	−.05 (n.s.)
(8) Locus of control (Rotter, 1966)	.17 (.08)	.03 (n.s.)

a. Numbers in parentheses are two-tailed significance levels for comparing the correlation to zero.

achieved outcome utility. It appears that those who have the ability or tendency to take charge and guide the negotiation achieve more favorable results. This is consistent with the finding that negotiators who are predominantly the "thinking" rather than the "feeling" type (Myers, 1962) achieve higher outcomes. The task-oriented approach has its limitations, however, Machiavellians, who are task oriented at the expense of people oriented, achieve worse results. Their proper outcomes are not consistent with much of the research reported in the experimental social psychology literature and at first seem counterintuitive. However, most social psychological bargaining experiments involve episodic interactions, in sterile contexts, using negotiators who are usually unknown to each other prior to the negotiation. In real-life organizational settings, there is context and history, and trust and credibility play a large role in determining outcomes. In such circumstances, Machiavellians may well be at a disadvantage.

Several variables are correlated with preference for the no-settlement outcome. (This preference is simply the desire to achieve only relative worthwhile settlements.) Individuals who would prefer an impasse to a relatively favorable settlement tend to be neither very masculine nor very feminine, but Machiavellian and extroverted.

In summary, individual differences influence the preference structure by affecting preferences for the no settlement outcome, and also influence the bargainer's ability to achieve favorable outcomes. The fact that some individual differences affect one factor and not the other suggests the following causal model:

Individual
Differences

↓

Preference
Structure

↓

Outcome

That is, individual differences affect outcomes both directly and through preference structure.

CONCLUSION

This chapter has reviewed a methodological paradigm for examining the determinants of bargaining outcomes. This paradigm is conceived as an integration of classical laboratory experimentation in social psychology and traditional field experiments. The most significant aspects of this paradigm are (1) the use of rich-context role-playing simulation, (2) conjoint measurement of negotiator preferences, and (3) principles of experimental design.

The advantage of using role-playing simulations is that they can recreate the rich context that characterizes negotiations. For example, the nature of buyer/seller negotiations as ongoing relationships can be put in proper perspective to simulation participants. Realistic situational power contexts can also be created. The conjoint analysis

allows for reliable and valid measurement of idiosyncratic preferences. The researcher thus need not assume that all simulation
participants respond the same to the simulation context. The conjoint
analysis thus balances the use of role-playing simulation, because in
the effort to create rich-context simulations, one would expect significant differences in participant interpretation of the issues. The use of
classical experimental design allows for the manipulation of conditions and hence an improvement in internal validity. For example,
this chapter described the manipulation of situational power.

In summary, the methodological paradigm proposed in this research
attempts to capture the external validity that characterizes field
research while retaining the internal validity that can be achieved in
the laboratory. The rich-context simulation addresses external
validity, while the conjoint analysis and experimental design address
internal validity.

The results presented in this chapter indicate that this program of
research can be fruitful for measuring the determinants of negotiated
outcomes. For example, we have established the ability of Nash's
theory of cooperative games to predict the outcomes of negotiations.
We have also found important linkages between individual difference
measures and bargaining outcomes.

Despite the progress made to date, much work remains. This work
includes (1) examining the *joint* effects of preferences, power, and
bargaining ability (e.g., to what extent can aggressive personalities
overcome power disadvantages, or whether certain power situations
promote the effectiveness of individual bargaining skill), and (2)
testing other theories of conflict resolution (e.g., see Bartos, 1974).

REFERENCES

Allison, G. T. *Essence of decision.* Boston: Little, Brown, 1971.

Bacharach, S. B., & Lawler, E. J. *Bargaining.* San Francisco, Jossey-Bass, 1981.

Bartos, D. J. *Process and outcome of negotiations.* New York: Columbia University
Press, 1974.

Bem, S. L. The measurement of psychological androgyny. *Journal of Counsulting and
Clinical Psychology,* 1974, *42,* 155-162.

Berkowitz, L., & Donnerstein, E. External validity is more than skin deep: Some
answers to criticisms of laboratory experiments. *American Psychologist,* 1982,
37, 245-257.

Caplow, T. *Two against one: Coalitions in triads.* Englewood Cliffs, NJ: Prentice-
Hall, 1968.

Christie, R., & Geis, F. L. *Studies in Machiavellianism.* New York: Academic, 1970.

Davis, M. *A multidimensional approach to individual differences in empathy.* Unpublished doctoral dissertation, University of Texas, 1980.

Davis, M. D. *Game theory: A nontechnical introduction.* New York: Basic Books, 1970.

Emerson, R. M. Power-dependence relations. *American Sociological Review,* 1962, *27,* 47-52.

Fleishman, E. A. The leadership opinion questionnaire. In R. M. Stogdill & A. E. Coons (Eds.), *Leader behavior: Its description and measurement.* Columbus: Ohio State University, Bureau of Business Research, 1957.

Greenhalgh, L., & Neslin, S. A. Conjoint analysis of negotiator preferences. *Journal of Conflict Resolution,* 1981, *25,* 301-327.

Green, P. E., & Srinivasan, V. Conjoint analysis in consumer research—issues and outlook. *Journal of Consumer Research,* 1978, *5,* 103-123.

Kruskal, J. B. Analysis of factorial experiments be estimating monotone transformations of the data. *Journal of the Royal Statistical Society, Series B,* 1965, *27,* 251-263.

Kruskal, J. B., & Carmone, F. J. *MONANOVA four (4) character version: Nonmetric analysis of factorial design.* Philadelphia: Marketing Science Institute, 1968.

Luce, R. D., & Raiffa, H. *Games and decisions.* New York: John Wiley, 1957.

Luce, R. D., & Tukey, J. W. Simultaneous conjoint measurement: A new type of fundamental measurement. *Journal of Mathematical Psychology,* 1964, *1,* 1-27.

Myers, I. B. *Manual for the Myers-Briggs type indicator.* Princeton, NJ: Educational Testing Service, 1962.

Nash, J. F. The bargaining problem. *Econometrica,* 1950, *18,* 155-162.

Nash, J. F. Two-person cooperative games. *Econometrica,* 1953, *21,* 128-140.

Neslin, S. A. Linking product features to perceptions: Application of graded paired comparisons. In S. Jain (Ed.) *Educators' conference proceedings.* Chicago: American Marketing Association, 1978.

Neslin, S. A., & Greenhalgh, L. *Nash's theory of cooperative games as a predictor of the outcomes of buyer-seller negotiations: An experiment in media purchasing* (Working paper 113). Hanover, NH: Amos Tuck School of Business Administration, Dartmouth College, November 1982.

Rotter, J. B. Generalized expectancies for internal versus external control of reinforcement. *Psychological Monographs,* 1966, *80,* 1-28.

Rubin, J. Z., & Brown, B. R. *The social psychology of bargaining and negotiation.* New York: Academic, 1975.

Schein, E. *Organizational psychology.* Englewood Cliffs, NJ: Prentice-Hall, 1980.

Zartman, I. W. Negotiation as a joint decision-making process. *Journal of Conflict Resolution,* 1977, *21,* 619-638.

CONFLICT EPISODES

Gerrit Wolf

University of Arizona

Bargaining behavior within organizations assumes that there are conflict episodes—interactions between employees with differing interests. Conflict episodes can be contrasted to problem-solving situations, which are characterized by uncertainty and disagreement about how to find a solution, not about solutions themselves (Thompson & Tuden, 1959). An episode, either problem solving or conflict, is a sequential process of social interaction between two or more people (Barker & Wright, 1954). In the conflict episode, the social interaction involves understanding the differing interests of the participants and finding solutions to the conflict of interests.

Where do conflict of interests arise in organizations? Is there a structure to the conflict episode? Are conflict episodes dependent upon each other? To answer these, we drew on some of the chapters in this volume and on previous work on exchange theory (Wolf & Zahn, 1972). These articles become central to understanding organizations when one assumes that conflict and its resolution is a recurring and sometimes useful event in organizations. The field of organizational behavior has relatively recently become interested in bargaining and conflict beyond labor/management differences in the name of organizational politics, boundary-spanning roles, and organizaitonal power views of organizations (Pfeffer, 1981). These areas focus on interdependent strategies and outcomes, not just on the behavior of a single individual in a given environment. The analysis of strategic interdependencies within organizations becomes the center of attention.

WHERE DO CONFLICT EPISODES ARISE?

A necessary condition is the presence of strategy alternatives. Viewing an organization as having strategies is the essence of studying modern business policy, but conceiving of individuals or groups within organizations as having strategies is antithetical to traditional management thought (Flippo, 1981) as well as to contemporary organizational behavior teaching (Porter, Lawler, & Hackman, 1976). The reasons for not seeing an employee as strategic stems from viewing organizations as unitary, goal-oriented units; an anti-Marxist view of an alienated employee's relationship to the firm; a psychologist's bias of seeing only the behavior of the individual and not the interdependence of people; and the field's lack of understanding of game theory as a meta-theory for understanding strategy and conflict. Strategic alternatives are commonly perceived for the manager in the allocation of resources, choice of information management, and interpersonal roles (Minzberg, 1973): for example, performance appraisal by the supervisor or boundary negotiations by the purchasing agent, financial manager, or personnel department. However, within a work unit the employee's strategic alternatives are often ignored or overlooked. These options relate to attendance, participation, quality of work, and turnover. While expectancy theory has recognized these as choices by the employee, it has not seen these choices as strategic options linked to a second set of strategic alternatives that are available to the supervisor or manager. Conflict episodes emerge with the consideration of the joint strategic alternatives of both the employee and the supervisor (Zahn & Wolf, 1981). Whether both participants need to be aware of strategic alternatives for the episode to emerge is a good research question. Both need to be aware in order to solve the conflict.

While the essays in this volume recognize managerial strategies, they usually fall short of analyzing what happens if all employees have strategic alternatives. For example, Bazerman and Neale point out cognitive biases such as overconfidence, perspective taking, and the perception of gains and losses through the concept of framing for one person, but not for both; Wall and Ebert suggest negotiation as a managerial strategy and ignore the subordinate's strategy; Lewicki explores the ins and outs of lying strategies by one party but not by both; Pruitt explores integrative strategies that assume both parties are cooperative problem solvers. Only Greenhalgh and Neslin look at what happens if both employees in a conflict episode follow the suggested strategies. However, their game-theoretic approach is static and tells us little about the dynamics of the conflict episode.

The bargaining dilemma, noted by Bartos (1967), highlights the issue. It says that if both parties are knowledgeable and of good will, bargaining leads to successful outcomes. Otherwise, the bargainer who has read this volume while his or her opponent has not will receive smaller outcomes than his or her opponent, who will most likely use a competitive strategy. This is what Kelley and Stahleski (1970) found empirically when they pitted different types of bargainers against each other. The competitive bargainer teaches the cooperative bargainer to be competitive, yielding losses to both of them. What is apparent is that one needs a third-party mediator or organizational climate to help out the bargainers. There is no unilateral strategy that works against all types of opponents in partial conflict situations. The solution strategy must teach the other dynamically how to cooperate or one must get help in changing the structure of the interests in the conflict episode.

THE STRUCTURE OF INTERESTS

Strategic alternatives are choices relative to outcomes recognized by the employee. For example, assume that the outcome is a raise of at least some particular amount and the manager is constrained to offer a raise of no more than another amount. The strategic alternatives depend upon, in part, the range of the raise difference between the employee and manager (the contract zone). In this example, the outcome is defined as a single issue concerning a tangible resource that is evaluated as winning and losing. The conflict of interest episode has a different definition if one changes the anchor for defining winning and losing (Bazerman & Neale) or finding other outcome dimensions (Pruitt). For example, a redefinition of winning would be a raise that is higher than the current pay, rather than a loss as anything less than the maximum. The raise may only be symbolic of the respect desired, and this could be signified by a new office, added support personnel, or public recognition, which might take less money but satisfy the objective. In other words, conflict episodes in organizations often center on the psychological, information, or social relations. The ability to restructure the issues in the outcome package can be critical to finding a solution according to Pruitt. Also, the perception of the outcomes can be important (Bazerman & Neale).

There is another level at which to work on the conflict episode. For each outcome there is an evaluation by each person involved. This evaluation can be decomposed into the values of the attributes that compose the outcome using information integration theory (Anderson, 1982) or into the values of the outcomes' component that are unilaterally and mutually valued by the participants (Wolf, 1972). These decomposition techniques provide a means for understanding divergent and convergent interests. Without specific techniques, the restructuring of the conflict interest by Bazerman and Neale, Pruitt, and Lewicki is more an art than a usable procedure.

CONFLICT EPISODE DEPENDENCE

Several of these chapters argue that a conflict episode depends on the situation (Greenhalgh & Neslin), particularly as perceived by the manager, who has the discretion to define the situation as requiring bargaining (Wall & Ebert). Wall and Ebert do not give strategies for bargaining but give conditions under which the manager would rather bargain than consult or make the decision unilaterally. The conditions are similar to those of Vroom and Yetton (1973) for deciding when to participate. Greenhalgh and Neslin suggest that bargainers use a solution with some variation from the optimal due to situational and personal variables. These studies see bargaining as a managerial option that is task dependent.

While these studies begin to look for organizational conditions for bargaining, they raise some questions. First, bargaining takes two participants, not just the manager. Both parties have to see the situation as calling for bargaining because of relatively equal power in the situation. What are the conditions in which a superior and a subordinate, or managers from different departments, see the situation as one of bargaining? Second, are the conditions for bargaining mostly task dependent or are they role dependent? The conflict episode may be a function of the task situation and the role relationship of the two.

This possibility is the basis for developing a model of leadership/ followership (Zahn & Wolf, 1981). The model proposes that the incentives in these roles form a non-zero-sum prisoner's dilemma conflict structure. Manager and subordinate have the strategic choice of cooperating to various degrees. What choice is made depends on the results of previous conflict episodes between them. Further work suggests that choice also depends on the kind of relationship that develops over successive conflict episodes (Wolf & Zahn, 1983). This model may be useful, also, for understanding boundary-spanning roles such as those between the firm and customers or suppliers.

CONCLUSION

The papers of Bazerman and Neale, Lewicki, and Wall and Ebert focus on the individual's strategies and conceptions, while Greenhalgh and Neslin, Pruitt, and I use the dyad as the unit of analysis. The two individuals must be analyzed jointly for strategies and outcomes; the analysis of the individual is necessary but far from sufficient. One must consider that each party is following differing strategies and goals that change over time as a function of the social interaction. The dynamic approach is missing from all the chapters, but there is the evidence that episodes are dynamic and not independent (Rapoport & Chammah, 1965). The challenge is to test a dynamic model in natural and realistic conditions.

REFERENCES

Anderson, N. *Information integration theory.* New York: John Wiley, 1982.

Barker, R., & Wright, W. *Midwest and its children.* New York: John Wiley, 1954.

Bartos, O. *Simple models of group behavior.* New York: Columbia University Press, 1967.

Flippo, E. *Management.* Englewood Cliffs, NJ: Prentice-Hall, 1981.

Kelley, H. H., & Stahelski, A. J. The social interactions basis of cooperators' and competitors' beliefs about others. *Journal of Personality and Social Psychology,* 1970, *60,* 66-91.

Minzberg, H. *The nature of managerial work.* New York: Haper & Row, 1973.

Pfeffer, J. *Power in organizations.* Marshfield, MA: Pitman, 1981.

Porter, L., Lawler, E. E., & Hackman, J. R. *Organizational behavior.* Englewood Cliffs, NJ: Prentice-Hall, 1976.

Rapoport, A., & Chammah, A. *Prisoners' dilemma.* Ann Arbor: University of Michigan Press, 1965.

Thompson, J., & Tuden, A. Strategies, structures and processes of organizational decision. In J. D. Thompson, P. B. Hammond, R. W. Hawkes, B. H. Bunker, & A. Tuden, *Comparative studies in administration.* Pittsburgh: University of Pittsburgh, 1959.

Vroom, V., & Yetton, P. *Leadership and decision making.* Pittsburgh: University of Pittsburgh Press, 1973.

Wolf, G. Evalution within interpersonal systems. *General Systems,* 1972, *17,* 43-51.

Wolf, G., & Zahn, L. Exchange in games and communication. *Organizational Behavior and Human Performance,* 1972, *7,* 142-187.

Wolf, G., & Zahn, L. A model of superior and subordinate cooperation. Unpublished manuscript, Department of Management, University of Arizona, 1983.

Zahn, L., & Wolf, G. Leadership and the art of cycle maintenance. *Organizational Behavior and Human Performance,* 1981, *28,* 26-49.

—III—

THE USE OF
THIRD PARTIES IN
ORGANIZATIONAL DISPUTES

—8—

THE MANAGER AS ARBITRATOR
Conflicts Over Scarce Resources

William W. Notz
Frederick A. Starke
John Atwell

University of Manitoba

The United States emerged in 1945 as the world's supreme economic and military power. Although the devastation of a total war that its rivals had suffered was part of the cause, a major reason was the rise to international dominance of a number of key industries: oil, electronics, aircraft, automobiles, agricultural products, and finance. By the late 1970s, however, these same industries were having difficulty coping with the revitalized economies of Western Europe, Japan, and the Third World.

At the macro level, the United States must cope with declining productivity, permanently higher oil prices, and increased international competition. Each of these problems has the potential to cause a substantial restructuring of the economy. As the reallocation of resources takes place, there will be major conflicts between various sectors of the economy.

From the perspective of the individual organization, the problems noted above manifest themselves in a wide variety of ways including rising unit costs, declining sales, and falling profits. When organizations attempt to deal with these problems, there is invariably pressure to change direction and reallocate resources in response to a changed competitive environment.

In order to assess the implications of scarce resources for organizations, this chapter

(1) examines the impact of resource scarcity on three important organizational activities (goal setting, resource allocation, and measuring organizational effectiveness);

(2) discusses the procedure normally used to allocate resources in organizations and analyzes the implications of this procedure for conflict over budgets; and

(3) speculates on ways to improve the effectiveness of the budgeting process in organizations.

RESOURCE SCARCITY AND ORGANIZATIONAL ACTIVITY

Three time-sequenced organizational activities are influenced by resource scarcity: goal setting, resource allocation, and the assessment of organizational effectiveness. Each of these is examined below from both the rational model and political model perspectives (Pfeffer & Salancik, 1974). Before we consider these three organizational activities, let us examine the basic elements of these two models.

A fundamental difference between the rational and political models is the way they approach organizational decision making. The rational model is comparable to Lindblom's (1965) synoptic method of decision making. The decision maker identifies the objectives and values that will be used as the criteria for choosing, searches for alternatives and analyzes their consequences, and finally picks the alternative that best meets the criteria. Thus the rational model emphasizes the logical analysis of alternatives within a previously determined framework of values. Moreover, the decision maker gains closure for decisions simply by announcing them to subordinates. Acceptance of the decision is not an issue since it flows automatically from the superior authority of the decision maker.

The political model assumes that organizational decision making is far more complex and that negotiation over conflicting goals and values is the primary method of problem solving. In the political model, the search for accommodation can occur even in the absence of prior agreement on criteria. This element contrasts sharply with the rational model, in which the search for alternatives cannot begin until criteria have been specified. Similarly, the two models differ substantially in their methods of closure. As opposed to the authority basis of the rational model, decision closure in the political model occurs through a process of mutual adjustment.

With these basic features of the rational and political models in mind, let us consider goal setting, resource allocation, and the assessment of organizational effectiveness in an environment of resource scarcity.

Goal Setting

From the rational model perspective, the establishment of goals is the first step in organizational activity, since goals are necessary to define what constitutes rationality (Friedland, 1974). Once goals have been established, alternatives can be pursued that will achieve these goals. In the rational model, little emphasis is placed on disagreements about goals. Instead, it is assumed that the reward structure and the employment contract will overcome problems of diverse individual goals (March & Simon, 1958). The employment contract conveys to employees the fact that in exchange for money they will pursue organizational objectives.

By contrast, the political model recognizes that conflict over goals is often observed in organizations. Hannan and Freeman (1977) contend that both the multiplicity of goals and the divergence between official and operative goals reflect conflict between individuals and groups. Pfeffer (1977) argues that organizational goals are multiple and contradictory, that organizations are coalitions, and that power and political processes are the means by which action is determined. Pennings and Goodman (1977, p. 148) endorse the idea that organizations are political arenas in which different groups attempt to promote their own goals—often at the expense of the total organization.

Why should this be the case? First, even if we make the unrealistic assumption that resources are unlimited, goal conflict exists because of the increasing heterogeneity of the workforce and the diversity of values held by individuals (Pfeffer, 1981). With this diversity, there are bound to be major disagreements about which organizational goals are desirable.

Second, when coupled with two basic characteristics of organizations—interdependence of work activity and scarce resources—this diversity inevitably leads to goal conflict. Interdependence of activities can cause conflict that initially has nothing to do with resource allocation, but it may influence the budgeting process because of the animosity it creates between individuals and subunits. The interdependence of work activities therefore allows individuals or groups to interfere with each other's goal attainment (Schmidt & Kochan, 1972).

Resource Allocation (Budgeting)

Budgeting is the process of committing financial resources to organizational purposes. The budget is a series of organizational goals with price tags attached, and budgeting is a process of making choices between organizational goals. As such, it is a means of reconciling conflicts between the various elements making up an organization, thus permitting the organization to move in a coordinated and integrated way to achieve its overall objective.

Assembling a budget for a large organization is a substantial endeavor, and those engaged in this process are inevitably driven to employ strategies that reduce the burden of calculation. Budget officials view budgeting as incremental, not comprehensive. Given this, the main determinant of this year's budget is last year's budget. Since much of the budget is the product of previous decisions anyway, it is not difficult to predict that a strategy of incrementalism will be used. Thus satisficing rather than maximizing becomes evident (March & Simon, 1958).

If goals are rationally established in some preferential relationship and organizational actors are committed to the established goal hierarchy, there should be few conflicts in the resource allocation process. As well, organizations operating in favorable resource environments may experience little resource allocation conflict because they can reach their objectives without expending all their "energy" (March & Simon, 1958, p. 126). This excess energy, or slack (Cyert & March, 1963), reduces the motivation of various parties to interfere with each other.

When resources are relatively unlimited, the organization need not resolve the relative merits of subgroup claims—each area is given what it wants. Because each subgroup is given the resources it needs to pursue its own interests, slack also encourages differentiation of goals. Increased differentiation of goals may become a source of conflict if, at a later time, the organization encounters a less favorable environment and retrenchment becomes necessary. This retrenchment, and the accompanying reduction of aspirations it imposes, creates the potential for severe conflict (Pfeffer, 1981; Cyert & March, 1963). Individuals and groups are quick to accept increased resources in favorable environments; unfortunately, these increased resources quickly come to be viewed as "normal." If future budgeting exercises threaten to reduce these additional resources, the individuals and subunits act as if they had always had the increased resources. Conflict then develops as each unit attempts to protect itself against budget cuts.

While these two circumstances (rational criteria and a favorable environment) do occasionally exist, the budgeting process is usually conducted in much more complicated circumstances. It is political in the sense that it deals with conflict over whose preferences will prevail in the determination of organizational policy (Wildavsky, 1968, 1979; Cyert & March, 1963; Pfeffer, 1981; Pfeffer & Salancik, 1974; Hills & Mahoney, 1978; Pfeffer & Leong, 1977). Conflict over the allocation of resources is often a manifestation of unresolved goal conflict. Those areas in the organization that have historically received less than what they consider to be their fair share of resources will use the budgeting process to press for a more equitable allocation, while those areas that wish to retain their historical share will use the previously established goal hierarchy to justify their claims.

If the various budget demands are compatible with each other, the final budget can be determined by a process of analysis and computation, and one would think of budgeting as a precise and purely technical activity. However, arising as they do from heterogeneous individuals and groups within the organization, there is a high probability that some budget demands will be incompatible, i.e., they cannot all be met within the time and resource constraints of the organization. With no resource constraints, potentially competing demands can be accommodated simultaneously. With no time constraints, some conflicting demands can be accommodated sequentially. However, where there are time constraints or limited resources, and where managerial commitment to budget demands is high, the potential for conflict is enhanced. Such conflict is likely to be heightened by limited social interaction and by reliance on different sources of information (Hopwood, 1974).

In practice, therefore, a budget demand may be many things and not simply a resource claim based on rational pursuit of predetermined and agreed upon goals. It may be an aspiration, expectation, strategy, or communication device. As participants act in the budgeting process, they receive information on the preferences of others and communicate their own desires through the choices they make. Since in the final budgetary determination the amounts received are related to the amounts requested, the requests are themselves strategies for influencing the budget outcomes. Budgeting therefore becomes a bargaining process. The issues transcend the immediate state of the organizational economy to include personal motives for status, recognition, or advancement. As a result, the process involves advocacy, consultation, negotiation, and bargaining.

Thus budgeting is (1) an important part of the larger process by which individual and group aspirations evolve within organizations and (2) an attempt to deal periodically with some of the conflicts that result from these aspirations. The outcome of the budgeting process is a temporary (but influential) map of the emergent position, expressed in terms of a current operating plan and proposed allocation of resources.

Organizational Effectiveness

In the rational model, the assessment of organizational effectiveness (OE) is straightforward. Organizational performance is compared to organizational goals, deviations are noted, and corrective action is taken. The cycle of goal setting, resource allocation, and OE assessment is then repeated on a regular basis. In this model there is no dispute about the criteria that should be used to measure OE (unless there are two or more equally good ways to reach goals) because these criteria flow naturally from the goals that have previously been agreed upon.

To what extent does this describe what happens in practice? An analysis of the OE literature (Miles, 1981) reveals major disagreements about what OE is and the criteria that should be used to measure it. Conflict over OE criteria is yet another manifestation of unresolved goal conflict. Those areas of the organization that have been unsuccessful at the goal setting and resource allocation stage of the process can be expected to try again at this stage to legitimize their demands by stressing OE criteria that make them look good.

As before, increasing resource scarcity increases the vigor with which different parts of the organization conflict with each other. As the area of discretion narrows, different parts of the organization find themselves doing more sharing of resources and perceiving a greater need and/or opportunity to interfere with one another. Conflict potential therefore increases.

THE VALUE OF CONFLICT

It might be inferred from the preceding analysis that conflict within organizations is "bad" and that increasing conflict is even worse. Decision makers seem particularly prone to such an inference because of their desire to preserve existing organizational arrangements (Coser, 1956). Since executives exercise power and influence through the organization's structure, conflict within those structures is likely to be viewed as disruptive and dysfunctional. In addition, decision makers are probably more likely to attend to the dysfunctions of conflict for the total organization while ignoring the benefits of conflict for particular subunits or groups. Finally, although conflict produces both positive and negative effects (Mack & Snyder, 1957), they may not be perceptually equivalent because the negative effects may appear first.

What are the positive functions of conflict that are usually over-looked? One is closely linked to an experience that nearly everyone has had: the enhanced feelings of "we-ness" versus "they-ness" that follows from intergroup conflict. Such feelings are a clear indicator of how conflict functions positively to establish and maintain the identity and boundaries of groups (Coser, 1956). As a corollary, conflict encourages the clarification of group objectives and heightens consciousness of group purpose (Kornhauser, Dubin, & Ross, 1954). These responses to conflict tend to increase the internal coherence and stability of groups, which, in turn, makes it easier to regulate conflict between them. A heightened consciousness of group purpose also encourages collaboration and a more efficient division of labor between parties (Mack & Synder, 1957).

Groups tend to guard values they believe will be neglected by other groups. They therefore become more sensitive and alert to certain lines of consequences and more competent at explaining them than are others to whom the particular consequences are less significant or are subordinate to other values or objectives (Lindblom, 1965). In conflict circumstances groups are also powerfully motivated to mobilize information and analysis on the possible consequences of decisions and on the possible relations among decisions (Lindblom, 1965). Finally, conflict can contribute to an organization's overall ability to adapt to a changing environment by stimulating adjustment processes aimed at creating and modifying norms and altering the distribution of power within the organization (Brown & Brown, 1982; Coser, 1956).

From the perspective of the total organization, there are obviously limits within which the effects of conflict will be positive. Within these limits, however, conflict can benefit both subunits and the entire organization. Thus the issue is not how to prevent conflict but how to manage it so that the positive effects are realized or at least not dominated by the dysfunctional consequences. Deutsch (1965) has conceptualized this problem most usefully as one involving coopera-tion versus competition. Most conflict situations permit either cooperation or competition; the conditions must therefore be found that will enable the participants to evolve a relationship that is pre-dominantly cooperative. Moreover, the evolution of a predominantly cooperative or competitive relationship will be manifested in the *processes* as well as the *outcomes* that develop. Thus a cooperative relationship is characterized by open and honest communication, increased perceptual sensitivity to common interests, and a trusting attitude that the conflict be viewed as a mutual problem. Competitive processes reverse these characteristics—communication is minimal or misleading, perceptual processes maximize differences and minimize common interests, suspicious and hostile attitudes are produced, the scope of the conflict expands, and the legitimacy of the other side's interest in the situation is minimized (Deutsch, 1965).

Deutsch's analysis focuses attention on the mangement process of conflict resolution as the mechanism by which the functional values of conflict are maximized. Several conditions increase the likelihood that conflict will move in the direction of a cooperative process. Of particular relevance to this analysis are the following:

(1) A cooperative process is more likely when the conflict is realistic (directed at a specific issue within the relationship) than when it is nonrealistic (derived from a need for tension release such that the conflict is an end in itself; Coser, 1956).

(2) A cooperative process is more likely when conflict is institutionalized and regulated (e.g., collective bargaining). This condition is enhanced when rules are known, unambiguous, consistent, and unbiased; when violations are quickly known by significant others; and when there is significant social approval for compliance with the rules and disapproval for violation (Deutsch, 1965).

(3) Cooperative processes are more likely when the consequences of competitive behavior are costly or potentially so (risky). This condition is facilitated when the distribution of power between the parties is relatively equal so that no one of them can force a resolution on the others. A related factor would seem to be that the parties should expect to resolve the conflict themselves, i.e., that resort to a third party should be seen as costly or risky.

Clearly, increasing conflict within organizations can lead to either destructive or positive outcomes depending on how the conflict is managed. Let us return to the arena of organizational budgeting and examine conflict management within that context in more detail.

BUDGETING AND CONFLICT MANAGEMENT

As indicated earlier, increasingly scarce resources increase the potential for conflict, and that potential is likely to be realized in the budgeting process. Budgets normally represent the outcome of bargaining processes over the setting of action priorities (Cyert & March, 1963; Wildavsky, 1979), and increasing conflict is likely to increase the frequency and intensity of bargaining. However, such bargaining processes are not always successful, and there are few mechanisms within the typical organization for *directly* resolving budget conflicts among individuals or departments at the same level in the hierarchy. Instead. the hierarchy itself tends to be used as a device for coordination and conflict resolution (Lawrence & Lorsch, 1967). Thus when the less formal bargaining that lies behind the rational facade is not successful, a third party in the organizational hierarchy—generally a common superior—is either implicitly or explicitly called upon to resolve the conflict.

We have then, in the budgetary process, a mixed system of decision making. We have a system of mutual adjustment by decision makers acting as partisans embedded in a centralized decision process where the final power with reference to the coordination and reconciliation of decisions lies with the central authority. This central authority has the power to make the demands of a certain group effective by ruling in its favor.

When a subordinate decision maker acts as a partisan in mutual adjustment, he or she is dependent on any allies that can be mobilized to make his or her demand effective, and effort and time must be expended in order to achieve success. The partisan must anticipate the possible reactions of other participants when framing his or her own demands.

By contrast, in a purely centralized decision-making process, each group of participants can make demands that impinge on the interests or aspirations of other decision makers with little cost to itself. It is the responsibility of the central decision maker to consider the implications for others. Lindblom characterizes as *integrative solutions* those that are worked out in partisan adjustment because each participant is motivated by self-interest. He characterizes as *compromise solutions* those that are worked out by a central decision maker because such a decision maker may see him- or herself as a judge or arbitrator with the responsibility for equitably resolving the conflicting desires of the various parties.

In order to illustrate these processes at a very high level, consider the recent negotiations within the White House over the size of the defense budget. The issue emerged because of President Reagan's commitment to balance the budget by fiscal 1984. David Stockman, Director of the Office of Management and Budget, became the administration's "budget-cutting powerhouse"; as part of that role, Stockman also became the chief advocate of a substantial cut in the defense budget. Casper Weinberger, secretary of defense, quite naturally assumed the role of chief apologist for only a minimal reduction in military spending. After several weeks of negotiations, the two men squared off for a two-and-one-half-hour "showdown session" with President Reagan in the cabinet room of the White House. *Time* reported that meeting as follows (September 21, 1981, p. 15):

> Stockman argued for 45 minutes in favor of a $30 billion reduction in 1983-84 defense authorizations. Weinberger, strongly supported by Haig, argued for a following 45 minutes that any rollback beyond about $7 billion or $8 billion would undermine the Administrator's foreign policy commitments. . . . Under questioning from Reagan, Stockman, whose presentation was the smoother of the two, came down to a $26 billion cut, and Weinberger stood firm at $7 billion or $8 billion. Reagan ordered them to "split the difference" and produce a compromise figure; at week's end they had a one-hour meeting with Reagan and agreed on the $11 billion figure.

The report clearly illustrates how President Reagan behaved like an arbitrator when subordinates Stockman and Weinberger failed to negotiate an agreement on their own. His order to "split the difference" is also a nice illustration of a popular kind of conflict resolution— conventional arbitration—wherein a binding compromise is imposed on both parties. Yet there is considerable evidence that this form of intervention may have several dysfunctional effects, including an exacerbation of the competitive process that it is supposed to remedy. Thus in the above instance, if Stockman and Weinberger anticipated that President Reagan would "split the difference," they may have developed and maintained extreme positions in order to offset the effects of the imposed compromise.

In some ways, the Stockman/Weinberger debate resembles labor/management negotiations. Before we examine the implications of managers acting in the role of arbitrators, let us consider another resource problem commonly found in organizations. How, for example, might a resource allocation dispute between managers of three widely scattered manufacturing plants be resolved? Probably not by face-to-face negotiations between the conflicting managers. Rather, it would seem more likely that the managers would make known their concerns to their common superior, who would in turn consider each of their arguments and then make a decision to which the three of them would have to adhere. Communication and negotiation between the three individuals in such situations would be *indirect,* at best. Indeed, it seems quite possible that any bargaining relationship between the parties in most instances like these would be tacit rather than explicit (Schelling, 1960; Bacharach & Lawler, 1980); therefore, the bargaining would not be publicly acknowledged and would involve extensive use of political tactics instead of explicit offers and counteroffers by the parties (concession behavior). Where resources are scarce, one manifestation of this process is likely to be that each manager will ask for a larger amount than is really needed in an effort to protect him- or herself from the similar demands of the other managers and the anticipated compromise of top management (everyone receives less than they asked for).

Although there are undoubtedly other mechanisms used to resolve conflicts over scarce resources, we suspect that the two cases described above (the Stockman/Weinberger debate and the plant manager example) contain certain fundamental elements that are likely to be found in most resource allocation problems. First, we posit that increasingly scarce resources will evoke bargaining processes, and, given the common managerial reluctance to acknowledge bargaining (March & Simon, 1958; Pfeffer, 1981), those processes will tend to be tacit instead of explicit. Second, we suspect that when those bargaining processes are unsuccessful, the ultimate resolution will be achieved through some form of compromise imposed upon the parties by a common superior. This last point is partially supported by Sheppard's (this volume) finding that the predominant conflict resolution strategy employed by managers is one that involves making a decision and then enforcing it.

Several observations can be made about methods of conflict resolution that involve these features. First, the intergroup conflict that is fundamental to the informal bargaining process undoubtedly strengthens subunit identification. While such outcomes are positive in terms of strengthening the boundaries and identity of units, they are obviously negative if they occur at the expense of other units or the entire organization. Furthermore, excessive subunit identification undoubtedly feeds back to reinforce and extend the competitive processes of which it is a result. Second, the conflict resolution processes described above are predominantly informal without clearly defined procedures and criteria. As noted earlier, noninstitutionalized and unregulated conflict is likely to evoke competitive processes, to be characterized by little direct communication between parties, and to generate little concession behavior. Unregulated conflict is also more likely to be nonrealistic and therefore more likely to produce unstable agreements. Finally, the key person in the resolution of such conflicts—the disputants' common superior—acts much like an arbitrator. Research from the labor/management area suggests that the manager's behavior may have a substantial effect on the process as well as on the outcomes of the conflict.

ARBITRATION AND ITS EFFECTS ON LABOR/MANAGEMENT CONFLICT

The most commonly used device to resolve impasses in interest disputes between labor and mangement—conventional arbitration— provides for a third party to resolve disputes such that the final outcomes balance the political and organizational needs of each party (Kochan, 1980). However, critics have argued that conventional arbitrators tend to "split-the-difference" between the parties' final positions (Northrup, 1966; Stevens, 1966; Starke & Notz, 1981) and that this expectation reduces the parties' motivation to concede during bargaining.

This "chilling effect" occurs because the parties attempt to offset the negative effects of the arbitrator's expected compromise by maintaining extreme positions. Thus the probability that the parties will resolve their own dispute is also decreased (Anderson & Kochan, 1977; Notz & Starke, 1978; Starke & Notz, 1981). As well, the parties may feel little responsibility for the bargaining outcomes and may become increasingly reliant upon arbitration to resolve conflicts— the "narcotic" effect (Wheeler, 1974).

These effects of conventional arbitration (CA) have been judged to be so dysfunctional by some researchers that final offer arbitration (FOA) has been proposed as an alternative (Stevens, 1966; Fueille, 1975). Arbitrators in FOA cannot compromise; instead, they must choose one of the disputing parties' final offers in its entirety. The risk of such an all-or-nothing decision rule presumably increases the parties' motivation to settle their dispute by themselves and thereby avoids the limitations of CA. Empirically, these predictions have generally been supported; FOA has been found to induce more negotiator compromise than CA (Long & Feuille, 1974; Feuille, 1975; Kochan, Ehrenberg, Baderschneider, Jick, & Mironi, 1977; Starke & Notz, 1981; DeNisi & Dworkin, 1981; Grigsby & Bigoness, 1982; Neale & Bazerman, in press).

These findings regarding the differential effects of CA and FOA in labor/management conflicts may have application to intra-organizational conflicts over resource allocations. Although there are differences between the contexts, there are two fundamental similarities: Both involve interest disputes and both may require the intervention of a third party for ultimate resolution. Since the dominant mechanism for resolving budgetary conflicts (compromise) appears to be analogous to that used in CA, the dysfunctional aspects of CA that have been observed in labor/management conflicts may well generalize to a budgetary context as well. Similarly, FOA might be profitably used to resolve intraorganizational budgetary conflicts.

To the best of our knowledge, there are no organizations that explicitly use either CA or FOA systematically to resolve budget conflicts (although, for the reasons stated earlier, we suspect that the informal use of CA is common). Thus there are no field data that bear directly on the above issues. However, some data on these matters are available from a recent laboratory experiment (Notz, Starke, Sproule, & Gibbs, 1982).

The study focused on only a few of the issues that were either raised or implied in the preceding analysis. First, in a very practical sense, any explicit application of CA or FOA to budgeting conflicts would probably involve more than two parties, whereas in labor/management negotiations there are only two. When more than two parties are involved, the possibility exists that coalitions could form so as to modify substantially the differential effects of CA and FOA that have generally been found in the labor/management context. A second and related issue concerns the effectiveness of CA and FOA in the presence of different power distributions.

The experiment used a 2×2 design where the independent variables were the form of third-party intervention (FOA or CA) and the distribution of power among the negotiators (equal or unequal). Ninety-three subjects were assigned the role of dean of a university faculty. As part of a three-person group, each dean's task was to negotiate next year's budget allocation for his faculty. If the three deans failed to reach an agreement, one of the two forms of arbitration was imposed upon them by the (fictitious) university president.

The independent variables were analyzed for their impact on prenegotiation aspiration levels, actual bargaining behavior, and postnegotiation commitment. Although there were no effects of power, FOA triads were significantly closer together than CA triads on four measures of *prenegotiation aspiration levels:* (1) subject opinions on what constituted the most reasonable settlement, (2) the extent to which the shares of the budget of other members of the triad should be increased or decreased, (3) opening offers of each member of the triad, and (4) subject opinions on what constituted the optimal allocation of resources.

The *bargaining behavior* of the triads was similarly affected by the form of intervention. FOA triads were significantly closer to agreement at the conclusion of negotiations than were the CA triads. An analysis of bargaining behavior for coalition development indicated no effects of either the form of intervention or distribution of power within the triad.

The *postnegotiation commitment* of the subjects was similarly affected by the form of intervention. Analysis of several variables at both the individual and group level showed FOAs to be significantly more committed to the settlement than CAs. These analyses extended over both attitudinal variables (e.g., the extent to which the subjects felt the settlement was in the best interest of the university as a whole) and behavioral variables (e.g., whether or not subjects appealed the arbitrator's decision).

SOME REFLECTIONS ON ARBITRATION
AND THE BUDGETARY PROCESS

Notwithstanding the supporting nature of these exploratory findings, there are at least three major issues that must be dealt with before FOA might become a regular part of the budgeting process in organizations: (1) The tacit bargaining that is evident in organizations must be made more explicit, (2) problems will probably arise when attempts are made to do so, and (3) FOA will have to be revised somewhat to take into account certain characteristics of administrative structures.

The Faculty of Administrative Studies at the University of Manitoba has some recent experience with points 1 and 2. Some difficult budgetary decisions needed to be made in an environment of declining resources, so the dean of the faculty decided that the five department heads and the associate dean would meet regularly in an attempt to decide collectively how to deal with these issues. At these meetings, a variety of budget-related issues were openly discussed, and with the consent of the members of each department, various allocation decisions were made by this group. We use examples from this experience to illustrate some of the issues that are raised in the following paragraphs.

Making Tacit Bargaining More Explicit

It must be recognized that the final offer mechanism is merely the capstone of a formalized system of conflict management. If our assumption is correct that bargaining processes in most organizations are predominantely tacit (i.e., there are no clearly defined procedures and criteria), the first requirement would be to move those processes gradually in the direction of greater formality. This would involve more open acknowledgment of conflict, more direct communication between parties, and more explicit bargaining. Such efforts should enable the participants gradually to develop the experience and negotiation skills that are required in a formalized system. Moreover, any movement toward more open and explicit negotiation should evoke from participants more consideration and discussion of resource allocation criteria and their relationship to organizational goals. Our recent experience of making the bargaining over departmental budgets more explicit supports this last point. It is important that criteria are understood and accepted because mutual accommodation is facilitated and excessive subunit identification is avoided.

Some Potential Problems in Making Bargaining More Explicit

There will probably be resistance to any attempts to make bargaining more explicit. This resistance will come from those individuals who have in the past received disproportionately large budget allocations because of their ability to engage in effective tacit bargaining and other political behaviors. How might this resistance be overcome? From our own experience, one feasible way is by peer pressure. For example, it was difficult for a given department head to refuse to participate in budget negotiations because all other heads had agreed that it was a good thing to do. The reluctant department head feared that he would be accused of not being a team player or that the other heads would decide something that would be detrimental to the interests of his department.

Resistance may also come from managers who, for a variety of reasons, feel that subordinates should not have any voice in budget allocation decisions. For example, the manager of a group of department heads may not be interested in involving them in the budgeting process simply because the manager perceives no resource allocation dilemma. If this were the case, the rational model would probably be a reasonably accurate description of the decision process. In effect, decision quality and acceptance would not be issues and thus negotiations would be unnecessary. On the other hand, even if the manager views subordinate involvement in resource allocation decisions favorably, the proposed system requires the manager to accept the possibility that resources might be allocated in a way that is different from what the manager would have done. The manager may interpret this as a lack of confidence in his or her past judgment. This type of resistance may be difficult to overcome because it requires changing strongly held beliefs about how resources should be allocated. One way to overcome this problem is to have the manager's superior indicate that a more participative system is desirable. This tactic was used successfully at the University of Manitoba.

Accommodating FOA to Administrative Structures

In collective bargaining, the disputing parties submit their offers to the arbitrator and agree to be bound by his or her decision. The arbitrator is therefore a person who (a) is chosen and (b) derives the power to judge by the *mutual consent* of the parties involved. The parties may place restrictions on the process of arbitration, the method of arbitrator selection, the subject matter with which the arbitrator must deal, and so on. Administration processes, however, are somewhat different. Here, subordinates exercise delegated authority, but superiors in the hierarchy retain the power to overrule. There are no contractural transactions possible between subordinates since ultimate responsibility and authority rest with a common superior. Thus there is a contrast between the labor relations and administrative contexts: In the former, the disputants agree to be bound by an arbitrator's decision, while in the latter, the boss agrees to be bound by the subordinates' decisions. Because of this difference, final offer arbitration will likely have to be adapted to the special requirements of administrative structures.

What form might this adaptation take? First, an FOA system embedded in an administrative structure must recognize the fact that the interests of the parties in a budgetary impasse may not necessarily be consistent with the global interests of the organization. Unless the various subunits have access to information bearing on these global interests, they are unlikely to take them properly into account when fashioning their final offers. This would appear to be true even if the positive effects of the FOA process on subunit identification are as robust as the exploratory evidence indicates.

Second, the revised system must also leave room for the judgment of superiors or for the correction of error or miscalculation. This could be done by allowing the superior to reject all offers if none are satisfactory. It could also involve further clarifying the criteria in each situation so that the disputing parties could make well-informed offers. These types of procedures are important since management is confronted by a variety of groups wanting to fulfill their aspirations through the medium of the enterprise: workers, functional groups within the management hierarchy, suppliers, customers, shareholders, and lenders. Yet only one decision can be made with respect to any issue and that decision should ideally be seen as best in a system sense. The superior must, however, retain ultimate authority and responsibility.

Finally, unlike an arbitrator, the manager-arbitrator is not independent of the decision. Instead, he or she is one of the key parties in the sense that (1) the decision is being fashioned on his or her behalf, and (2) the manager-arbitrator is continuously aware of the negotiations. What the organization wants from the manager-arbitrator (knowledge and involvement) is quite different from what bargainers in a labor/management dispute want from an arbitrator (independence). Within this context of ultimate authority, the superior has a responsibility to be well informed about dispute situations in general, and about the disputing parties' final offers in particular. When final offers are submitted, the manager-arbitrator is in a position to consider in detail the implications of each offer for the organization as a whole. If the process involves the administrator from the start, in the role of say, mediator, then final offers that converge with the overall needs of the organization should be evident (Grigsby & Bigoness, 1982).

SUMMARY

Let us reiterate the major points that we have attempted to make in this chapter. First, most organizations in North America are confronted by an environment of increasingly scarce resources. Such an environment, when it is coupled with goal heterogeneity and activity interdependence, will lead to increasing conflict that will be manifest in the budgeting process. While increasing conflict over resources is not necessarily dysfunctional if it is properly managed, we posit that organizational bargaining processes are usually informal, indirect, and tacit. Furthermore, we suspect that when these bargaining processes are unsuccessful, the ultimate resolution is achieved through some form of informal compromise (analogous to conventional arbitration) that is imposed upon the parties by a common superior.

These two factors—tacit bargaining and ultimate resolution via the compromise of a superior—make several dysfunctional aspects of conflict likely (e.g., processes dominated by competition, little concessionary behavior, excessive subunit identification, and so on). We believe that these dysfunctional features of conflict can be minimized by moving the bargaining process in the direction of institutionalization with known and unambiguous rules. Such regulated bargaining, however, would also require a more explicit mechanism for ultimate resolution, either a more formal version of superior compromise (CA) or some form of final offer selection.

We concluded this essay by speculating about some of the additional issues and questions involved in using a final mechanism in order to manage intraorganizational budget conflicts explicitly.

REFERENCES

Anderson, J. C., & Kochan, T. Impasse procedures in the Canadian Federal Service. *Industrial and Labor Relations Review, 1977, 30,* 283-301.

Bacharach, S., & Lawler, E. *Power and politics in organizations.* San Francisco: Jossey-Bass, 1980.

Brown, L. D., & Brown, J. C. *Organizational microcosms and ideological negotiation.* Paper presented at the symposium on New Perspectives on Negotiations in Organization Settings, Boston, 1982.

Coser, L. *The functions of social conflict.* New York: Free Press, 1956.

Cyert, R. M., & March, J. G. *A behavioral theory of the firm.* Englewood Cliffs, NJ: Prentice-Hall, 1963.

DeNisi, A., & Dworkin, J. B. Final offer arbitration and the naive negotiator. *Industrial and Labor Relations Review, 1981, 35,* 78-87.

Deutsch, M. *Conflict and its resolution.* Paper presented at the American Psychological Association, 1965.

Feuille, P. Final offer arbitration and the chilling effect. *Industrial Relations, 1975, 14,* 302-310.

Friedland, E. *Introduction to the concept of rationality in political science.* Morristown, NJ: General Learning Press, 1974.

Gamson, W. A. A theory of coalition formation. *American Sociological Review, 1961, 26,* 565-573.

Gamson, W. A. Experimental studies of coalition formation. In L. Berkowitz (Ed.), *Advances in experimental social psychology,* Vol. 1. New York: Academic, 1964.

Grisby, D. M., & Bigoness, W. J. Effects of mediation and alternative forms of arbitration on bargaining behavior: A laboratory study. *Journal of Applied Psychology, 1982, 67,* 549-554.

Hannan, M. T., & Freeman, J. H. The population ecology of organizations. *American Journal of Sociology, 1977, 82,* 929-964.

Hills, F. S., & Mahoney, T. A. University budgets and organizational decision making. *Administrative Science Quarterly, 1978, 23,* 454-465.

Hopwood, A. Accounting and human behavior. Englewood Cliffs, NJ: Prentice-Hall, 1974.

Kochan, T. Collective bargaining and organizational behavior research. *Research in Organizational Behavior,* 1980, *2,* 129-176.

Kochan, T., & Baderschneider, J. Determinants of the reliance on impasse procedures: Police and firefighters in New York State. *Industrial and Labor Relations Review,* 1978, *31,* 431-440.

Kochan, T., Ehrenberg, R. G., Baderschneider, J., Jick, T., & Mironi, M. *An evaluation of impasse procedures for police and firefighters in the state of New York:* Final Report submitted to the National Sciences Foundation, 1977.

Kornhauser, A., Dubin, R., & Ross, A. M. *Industrial conflict.* New York: McGraw-Hill, 1954.

Lawrence, P., & Lorsch, J. *Organization and environment.* Cambridge, MA: Harvard University Press, 1967.

Lieberman, S. The effects of changes in roles on the attitudes of the occupants. *Human Relations,* 1956, *9,* 385-402.

Lindblom, C. E. *The intelligence of democracy.* New York: Free Press, 1965.

Long, G., & Feuille, P. Final offer arbitration: Sudden death in Eugene. *Industrial and Labor Relations Review,* 1974, *27,* 186-203.

Mack, R., & Snyder, R. C. The analysis of social conflict: Toward and overview and synthesis. *Journal of Conflict Resolution,* 1957, *1,* 212-248.

March, J. G., & Simon, H. A. *Organizations.* New York: John Wiley, 1958.

Miles, R. *Macro organization behavior.* Santa Monica, CA: Goodyear, 1981.

Neale, M., & Bazerman, M. The impact of perspective taking ability on the negotiation process under alternative forms of arbitration. *Industrial and Labor Relations Review,* in press.

Northrup, H. R. *Compulsory arbitration and government intervention in labor disputes.* Washington, DC: Labor Policy Association, 1966.

Notz, W., & Starke, F. A. Final offer vs. conventional arbitration as means of conflict management. *Administrative Science Quarterly,* 1978, *23,* 189-203.

Notz, W., Starke, F. A., Sproule, R., & Gibbs, B. *The manager as arbitrator: Budgets, bargaining, and power.* Presented at the National AIDS meetings, November 22-24, 1982.

Pennings, J. M., & Goodman, P. S. Toward a workable framework. In P. S. Goodman & J. M. Pennings (Eds.), *New perspectives in organizational effectiveness.* San Francisco: Jossey-Bass, 1977.

Pfeffer, J. Power and resource allocation in organizations. In B. M. Staw & J. M. Pennings (Eds.), *New perspectives in organizational behavior.* Chicago: St. Clair Press, 1977.

Pfeffer, J. *Power in organizations.* Boston: Pitman, 1981.

Pfeffer, J., & Leong, A. Resource allocations in united funds: Examination of power and dependence. *Social Forces,* 1977, *55,* 775-790.

Pfeffer, J., & Salancik, G. R. Organizational decision making as a political process. *Administrative Science Quarterly,* 1974, *19,* 135-151.

Riker, W. H. *The theory of political coalitions.* New Haven, CT: Yale University Press, 1962.

Rolling back on defense. *Time,* September 21, 1981, pp. 14-16.

Schelling, T. C. *The strategy of conflict.* New York: Oxford University Press, 1960.

Schmidt, S. M., & Kochan, T. Conflict: Toward conceptual clarity. *Administrative Science Quarterly,* 1972, *17,* 359-370.

Starke, F. A., & Notz, W. W. Pre- and post-intervention effects of conventional vs. final offer arbitration. *Academy of Management Journal,* 1981, *24,* 832-850.

Stevens, C. Is compulsory arbitration compatible with bargaining? *Industrial Relations,* 1966, *5,* 38-52.

Thompson, J. D. *Organizations in action.* New York: McGraw-Hill, 1967.

Vinacke, W. E., & Arkoff, A. An experimental study of coalitions in the triad. *American Sociological Review,* 1957, *22,* 406-414.

Weick, K. *The social psychology of organizing.* Reading, MA: Addison-Wesley, 1969.

Wheeler, H. N. Is compromise the rule in firefighter arbitration? *Arbitration Journal,* 1974, *29,* 176-184.

Wildavsky, A. Budgeting as a political process. In D. L. Sills (Ed.), *The international encyclopedia of the social sciences,* Vol. 2. New York: Crowell, Collier, & Macmillan, 1968.

Wildavsky, A. *The politics of the budgeting process.* Boston: Little, Brown, 1979.

—9—

MEDIATOR-ADVISERS
A New Third-Party Role

Jeanne M. Brett
Stephen B. Goldberg

Northwestern University

Traditionally, there have been two different third-party models in conflict resolution: that of the facilitator or counselor who tries to stimulate the parties to resolve their own dispute by directing the manner in which the parties interact about the issue in conflict and/or the content of that interaction; and that of the adjudicator who, after listening (more or less) to both sides, decides the dispute. This chapter discusses a new third-party role, one that combines aspects of facilitation and adjudication. We call this third-party a *mediator-adviser*. He or she has all the tasks and skills of a facilitator, plus sufficient expertise to predict the outcome of the dispute, if it were adjudicated. The mediator-adviser's prediction may be made publicly to both parties or privately to one or both parties. It is nonbinding and cannot be introduced as evidence if the dispute is subsequently adjudicated.

The mediator-adviser model has significant theoretical benefits over both the facilitator and the adjudicator models when conflict resolution ultimately leads to adjudication. Compared to a procedure in which the parties resolve disputes on their own, adjudication is slow, expensive, and probably perceived as less procedurally just because disputants must turn control over the process and outcome to a third party.[1] Adjudication does, however, resolve disputes if not solve the problems underlying them. Compared to adjudication, facilitation may be quicker, less expensive, and perceived as more procedurally just because the disputants turn only control over the process, and not the outcome, of disputing to the third party. Facilitation, when it is successful, may also resolve the problem underlying the dispute, but there is no guarantee. The major advantages of the mediator-adviser model, if it is effective in resolving disputes, are that it should facilitate the resolution of the problem underlying a particular dispute and preserve procedural justice because no outcome control is given to the third party. It should also be designed to be quicker and faster than the adjudicatory model.

The mediator-adviser model has been used in two settings. Eric Green (1982a, 1982b) describes the minitrial, initially developed to resolve large intercorporate disputes outside the judicial system. Lawyers for both sides "make informal and abbreviated presentations of each party's 'best' case before principles of the parties with settling authority" and a neutral third party. The presentations are designed to give each party's principals a clear, balanced conception of the strengths and weaknesses of the positions on both sides as preparation for settlement negotiations, which begin immediately upon conclusion of the presentations (1982, pp. 9-41). While Green does not describe the third party's role as that of facilitating the negotiations, the third party may, "if necessary," provide an opinion as to how the case would be resolved if it went to trial. According to Green, "from all reports, in most cases in which they have been applied, mini-trials have successfully resolved the dispute" (1982a, pp. 9-43). No other evaluation data are available.

We have been experimenting with the mediator-adviser model in the unionized sector of the bituminous coal industry to resolve grievances during the term of the collective bargaining agreement (Brett & Goldberg, forthcoming). In this experiment, the parties agree to extend step 3 of their grievance procedure[2] and meet with a mediator-adviser. The purpose of the meeting, called a mediation conference, is to assist the parties in settling grievances in a mutually satisfactory way. The mediator-advisers conduct the conferences in an informal manner and elicit relevant facts in a narrative fashion rather than through examination and cross-examination of witnesses. The rules of evidence do not apply, and no record of the proceeding is made. Grievants are encouraged to participate fully in the proceedings both by stating their views and by asking questions of others attending the conference. The mediator-adviser primarily assists the parties in searching for a mutually satisfactory solution to the grievance. If no such solution is forthcoming, the mediator-adviser gives an oral advisory opinion, based on the collective bargaining agreement, as to how the grievance is likely to be decided if it is arbitrated. The advisory opinion, while not binding, is intended to serve as a basis for further settlement discussions or for granting or withdrawing the grievance. If the grievance is not resolved in any of these fashions, the parties are free to arbitrate. If they do so, no mediator-adviser participating in the experiment may serve as arbitrator, and nothing said or done by the parties or the mediator during mediation may be used against a party at arbitration.

We have substantial evaluation data from the experiment in coal that allow us to compare the adjudicatory model, which in this setting is arbitration, with the mediator-adviser model.

The mediator-adviser model does resolve disputes. Of the 153 grievances considered so far by mediator-advisers, 89 percent settled short of arbitration. Figure 9.1 shows four different types of settlements were achieved. In 51 percent of the cases, a compromise was reached; in 7 percent, the company granted the grievance at the conference; in 15 percent, the union withdrew the grievance at the conference; and in 16 percent, the grievance was settled subsequent to the conference. When the conference did not end in a settlement, the mediator-adviser was obliged by the rules to give a formal advisory decision, unless both parties requested that an advisory decision not be given.[3] Formal advisory decisions were given at the end of 20 percent of the conferences. Seven percent of the conferences ended without a settlement or an advisory decision. In those cases in which the mediator-adviser gave an advisory decision and the grievance did not settle prior to arbitration, there was a 75 percent congruence between the advisory decision and the arbitrator's subsequent decision.

Grievants who had experience in both the mediator-adviser procedure and the coal arbitration procedure preferred the former procedure over the latter 51 percent to 25 percent. Figure 9.2 shows the proportion of all participants who had experience with mediation and arbitration who preferred each procedure.[4] The preference for the mediator-adviser model is particularly strong among those who

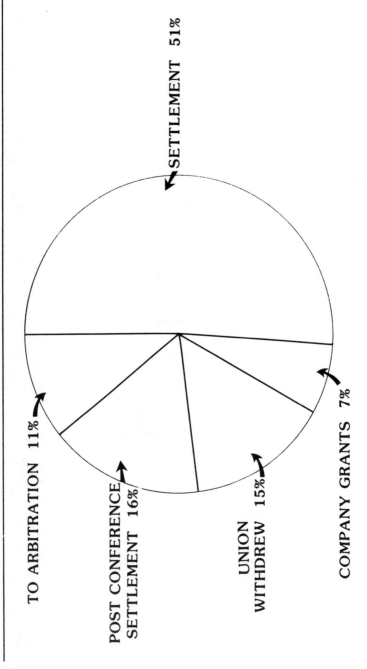

Figure 9.1   Type of Resolution of Grievances Taken to Mediation

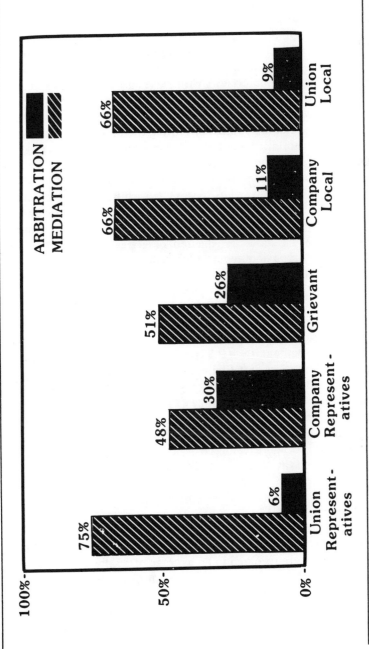

Figure 9.2 Proportion of Participants Who Had Experience With Both Mediation and Arbitration Who Preferred Each Procedure

present grievants' cases to the mediator-adviser or arbitrator, local union officials, and local company operating personnel. Representatives who present the companies' cases at mediation conferences or arbitration hearings preferred the mediator-adviser model over arbitration by a much smaller margin than did other participants. Qualitative data from interviews with these participants suggest that those who perceive themselves to be more skilled at presenting cases to an arbitrator than they perceive their union counterparts to be perceive more outcome control in turning the case over to an arbitrator than in negotiating a settlement at mediation, where an a priori expectation of compromise exists.

Further data from interviews with grievants attending mediation conferences and grievants whose cases were arbitrated, not mediated, support the proposition that the mediator-adviser model results in greater perceptions of procedural justice than does the arbitration model.[5] Figure 9.3 shows satisfaction of grievants with procedure and outcome by type of outcome. Grievants at mediation were more satisfied with the mediator-adviser procedure than were grievants at arbitration with the arbitration procedure ($F = 13.18$; $p < .01$). Among the grievants who participated in mediation conferences,[6] there were no significant differences in satisfaction with the procedure by outcome, but as one would expect, significant differences in satisfaction with the outcome ($F = 9.77$ p $p < .01$). Grievants at arbitration were significantly less satisfied with the procedure ($F = 4.56$; $p < .05$) and the outcome ($F = 123.64$; $p < .01$) when their grievance was sustained than when their grievance was denied. However, partialing on satisfaction with the outcome makes the correlation between outcome and satisfaction with procedure go to zero, suggesting that in the arbitration procedure feelings of procedural justice may be affected by feelings about the outcome. The finding that this spillover occurs with the arbitration procedure and not with the mediator-adviser procedure may also be due to the vastly different degree of outcome control grievants have in the two procedures.

The mediator-adviser model was also superior to the arbitration model with respect to time delay and cost. Grievances in the mediator-adviser model were resolved in an average of 15 days from the call requesting a case be scheduled for a mediation conference. Arbitration of nondischarge grievances during the experimental period in the participating union districts averaged 109 days from the request for an arbitrator to the receipt of the arbitrator's written decision. Much of the time saving in mediation was due to the absence of any third-

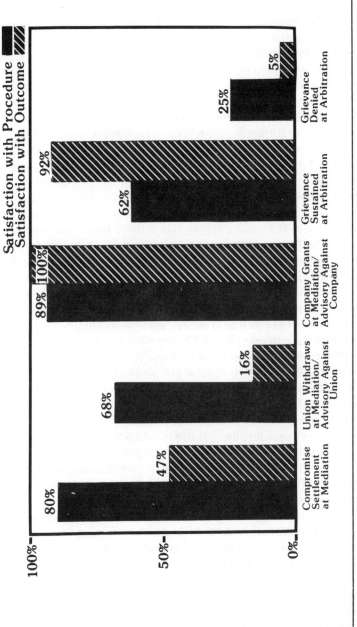

Satisfaction with Procedure ■
Satisfaction with Outcome ▨

100%—

50%—

0%—

| Compromise Settlement at Mediation | Union Withdraws at Mediation/ Advisory Against Union | Company Grants at Mediation/ Advisory Against Company | Grievance Sustained at Arbitration | Grievance Denied at Arbitration |

80% 47%   68% 16%   89% 100%   62% 92%   25% 5%

Figure 9.3 Proportion of Grievants in Mediation and Arbitration Who Were Satisfied With the Procedure and the Outcome by Type of Outcome

party decision, written or oral. Some of these time savings are also due to the fact that a regular monthly schedule of mediation conferences was set and mediator-advisers were engaged in each participating district. No such schedule exists for arbitration.

The average cost (fee plus expenses) in the mediator-adviser model was $295 per case; the average cost in the arbitration model for nondischarge grievances during the same time period and in the same districts was $1034. Thus the mediator-adviser model results in substantial cost savings even though the mediator-adviser's per diem rate of $600 is probably twice the average per diem of arbitrators working in the coal industry. The cost savings are primarily due to the absence of a written decision and the ability of the mediator-advisers to resolve three cases per day.[7]

In sum, these results show that the mediator-adviser procedure resolves disputes and is superior to the arbitration procedure with respect to perceptions of procedural justice, time, and cost. Two questions relevant to the internal validity of these findings remain: Whether or not the mediator-adviser model has any negative impact on the larger grievance resolution procedure in which it is embedded and whether the mediator-adviser model is the key, or whether any nonadjudicatory, third-party model would be successful in bringing about final resolution of grievances and procedural justice.

The major threat that the mediator-adviser model poses for the grievance system in which it is embedded is that disputants will learn quickly to push the dispute on to the third-party stage when the third-party stage provides quick, inexpensive, and procedurally fair resolution of the disputes rather than resolve the dispute between themselves. Time series data suggest that this has occurred only in one of four union districts during that district's second six-month experiment with the mediator-adviser model when all grievances except discharges not settled by the disputants went automatically to a mediation conference. In this district the disputant's settlement rate without resort to third-party intervention declined 10 percent from the previous 18-month average. No such decline was evident in other districts where mutual consent or the request of union or company is necessary to send a grievance to a mediation conference.

The major alternative explanation for the results is that any third-party procedure, even a purely facilitative model, would resolve grievances and be perceived as more procedurally just than arbitration. We did not test a purely facilitative model. Though mediator-advisers got settlements without giving formal advisory opinions in 80 percent of the cases, they gave private advice, predicting the case's outcome at arbitration, to one or both parties in 79 percent of the conferences. The mediators' behavior demonstrates their belief that private advice is a useful tactic, and the situation, i.e., a dispute resolution procedure in which an adjudicatory process is the final step, lends itself to such advice. It seems unlikely that a purely facilitative model would be as effective in bringing about the final resolution of grievances. It is unclear what differences there would be between a facilitator model and the mediator-adviser model with respect to procedural justice.

Successful experiments tell the researcher little about the boundaries to the generalizability of the experimental procedure. Several boundary conditions are worth consideration. The first limit of the mediator-adviser model is that it must be embedded in a dispute resolution procedure in which adjudication is the ultimate step. Beyond this, there are few obvious limits. It is not clear, for example, that an ongoing relationship between the parties or low-stakes issues are boundaries of the mediator-adviser model. While these are both characteristic of the experiment with grievances, they are not characteristic of situations in which the minitrial has been used. In ongoing relationships, the relationship itself is frequently more important than the stakes associated with any particular issue. Skillful third-party facilitators can get the parties to put the dispute in the context of the ongoing relationship and get compromise settlements. When the relationship is not ongoing but the stakes are high, the advisory decision offered publicly or privately may play a large role in settlements.[8]

In sum, the mediator-adviser model appears to be applicable to a broad range of disputes. While it is not likely to supplant bench decisions, jury trials, or arbitration, it does offer an alternative dispute resolution procedure that is effective in finally resolving disputes with procedural justice, low cost, and reduced time delay.

The mediator-adviser model may also be useful for resolving intra-organizational disputes. Blair Sheppard (this volume) describes managers' conflict intervention behavior in adjudicatory terms, which suggests that the one clear boundary condition for the mediator-adviser model is met. Sheppard points out that managers' adjudicatory behavior is understandable given that decision making not counseling is managers' habitual mode of behavior but that there are real difficulties with this model of third-party intervention: "decisions that did not really resolve the conflict or that created new conflict between the disputants, often involving additional actors." The manager who plays a mediator-adviser role should be able to help the disputants resolve their own conflict in a way that is responsive to the problems underlying the dispute. In playing a mediator-adviser role, the manager may spend a little more time with the dispute than he or she would if playing an adjudicatory role. But time spent resolving the underlying issue may actually be time gained if issues underlying adjudicated disputes reappear. Another benefit of the manager playing the mediator-adviser role is that he or she provides disputants with a model of conflict resolution skills. Disputants are unlikely to learn much from a manager-adjudicator. They may not even be able to determine the basis on which he or she decided the dispute. In contrast, when a mediator-adviser manager works with the parties to get settlements, his or her behavior is observable, and a good settlement should reinforce both the manager's continuing to play the mediator-adviser role and the disputants' modeling the manager's behaviors.

The major drawbacks of this proposal that managers play a mediator-adviser role are the lack of distinction between the person playing the mediator-adviser and the ultimate adjudicator, the lack of dispute resolution skills among managers, and the curious perception that "real men don't meditate" (Feirstein, 1982).

In the mediation of grievances experiment and the minitrials the mediator-adviser is not the ultimate adjudicator. In the mediation of grievances experiment, it was decided that mediator-advisers could not arbitrate a mediation case. The following concerns underlay that decision. It was felt that disputants would not be as open with a third party who ultimately had outcome control as with a third party who had only procedural control, hence reducing the potential for settlements. It was felt that a system in which the third party could act as facilitator, adviser, and adjudicator would be perceived as less procedurally just than the mediator-adviser model. For example, when the third party suggests a disputant should accept a particular settlement, the disputant does not accept, and the third party decides the issue against the disputant, it may not be clear to the disputant whether or not he or she lost on the merits or because of failing to take the third party's advice. For these reasons, in designing a mediator-adviser role in a formal dispute resolution procedure, we separated the mediator-adviser role from the adjudicatory role. Our reasons are untested assumptions, and there are many third-party adjudicators who do not believe these roles need to be separated.[9] In an informal dispute resolution procedure such as managers use on a day-to-day basis, the separation of roles seems less necessary. What is more important is that the managers use mediation skills and private advice to help disputants to resolve their own conflict.

This brings us to the major issue of whether or not managers have the dispute resolution skills to play the mediator-adviser role. If the number of weeks Herbs Cohen's book, *You Can Negotiate Anything,* has been on the best seller list is a valid indicator, managers are interested in acquiring negotiating skills. While reading Cohen's book may not be the best way to acquire such skills, it may be a first step. If managers take advantage of the burgeoning opportunities to take skills-oriented courses in dispute resolution, and those courses work, skills should improve. The "real men don't mediate" image is a problem that can only be dealt with by successful experiences with nonadjudicatory third parties.

In conclusion, the mediator-adviser model has the potential to be used in a wide variety of dispute settings where the ultimate step in dispute resolution is adjudicatory. How widely the procedure will be used depends upon the publicity attendant to its successes and failures, the continued poor economy that helps stimulate cost savings innovations, the degree to which disputants wish to retain control over the outcome of their dispute and are willing to use a third party to control the emotional aspect of the dispute and help them see the costs and benefits of settlement versus adjudication.

NOTES

1. Brett (1983) argues that Thibaut and Walker's (1975, p. 2) conclusion about procedural justice that "a procedure that entrusts much control over the process to the disputants themselves and relatively little control to the decision maker" may be wrong. She proposes that a just procedure is one that entrusts much control over the outcome to the disputants themselves. The data presented in Brett (1983) and in this chapter confirm her proposition.

2. Article XXIII, Section (c) of the Bituminous Coal Wage Agreement provides that in step 1 of the grievance procedure the employee will make this complaint to his immediate foreman; that if no agreement is reached, the complaint shall be taken up by the mine committee and mine management (step 2) and if no agreement is reached, the grievance shall be referred to a union district representative and a representative of the employer (step 3); and if no agreement is reached, the grievance is referred to an arbitrator who decides the case (step 4).

3. As will be discussed subsequently, mediators often gave either or both parties private advisory decisions during negotiations.

4. All local participants in the mediation conferences—grievants, local company operating personnel, and local union leaders—were interviewed by telephone shortly after the conference. Union and company representatives were interviewed six months into the experiment.

5. Arbitration grievants interviewed were from the same union districts as the mediation conference grievants, had taken a nondischarge grievance to arbitration

during the period of the experiment (no discharge grievances were heard by mediator-advisers), and had active telephone numbers.

6. Mediation conference grievances had to be analyzed separately because there are three possible outcomes of mediation conferences (win, lose, compromise) and only two outcomes (win, lose) of arbitration hearings.

7. These cost figures are not properly compared to expedited arbitration which, while substantially cheaper than conventional arbitration, does not in coal or other industries handle the range of cases taken to mediation conferences and conventional arbitration.

8. Based on Steve Goldberg's limited experience mediating civil cases, we have doubts about the utility of a private advisory in that context. When he has used the private advisory, the lawyers have a tendency to react by changing the focus of the discussion from settlement to arguing with the third party about the strength of their case. We have subsequently asked the coal mediators for their recollections as to the frequency of a similar response to one of their private advisory decisions. They were able to recall no instances of this. At least one reason for this difference is the presence of lawyers in the former context. Another is the coal mediators' reputations as arbitrators in the coal industry, a reputation that Steve does not have in the world of civil litigation.

9. See Wall and Schiller's description of judges' behavior (this volume) and Stephen Goldberg's (1982) description of grievance arbitration.

REFERENCES

Brett, J. M. *Procedural justice.* Paper prepared for the Academy of Management Meeting Annual Meeting, 1983.

Brett, J. M., & Goldberg, S. B. Mediation of grievances in the coal industry: a field experiment. *Industrial and Labor Relations Review,* forthcoming.

Feirstein, B. *Real men don't eat quiche.* Pocket Books, 1982.

Goldberg, S. B. The mediation of grievances under a collective bargaining contract: An alternative to arbitration. *Northwestern University Law Review,* 1982, 77, 270-315.

Green, E. D. *Reducing and mitigating organizational disputes: The causes and effects of corporate and private institution disputes.* Prepared for the National Conference on The Lawyer's Changing Role in Resolving Disputes, Harvard Law School, Cambridge, Mass. October 14-16, 1982.

Green, E. D. *Center for Public Resources, Mini-Trial Handbook.* New York: Matthew Bender, 1982.

Thibaut, J., & Walker, L. *Procedural justice: A psychological analysis.* Hillsdale, NJ: Lawrence Erlbaum, 1975.

THE JUDGE OFF THE BENCH
A Mediator in Civil Settlement Negotiations

James A. Wall, Jr.

University of Missouri

Lawrence F. Schiller

Smith, Hirsch, Brady & Weingarden

The studies reported here deal with the use of third parties within the civil court system. In the United States, approximately 5 million civil cases are filed each year and they are quickly overloading the judicial processes. To cope with the overload and to administer quick, afford-

Authors' Note: Support for this research was provided by the Graduate School of the University of Missouri and the Ponder Fund from the College of Business and Public Administration.

able justice, many judges are attempting to mediate out-of-court settlement negotiations, and the Chief Justice is prescribing the use of arbitration and administrative panels to remove some cases from the courts. Unfortunately, legislation to support the Chief Justice's prescriptions lies well beyond the horizon, leaving the burden of expediation upon the practicing judges' shoulders. While faced with this task they are guided for the most part by intuition and past experience, with no theory or data to steer them. The works reported here are initial efforts to provide some guidance.

As an overview, our research entails two complementary objectives: Our first goal is to close upon a set of judicial mediary techniques that are frequently utilized and rated as highly effective. In future studies, the techniques within this set will be studied intensively to determine the effectiveness of each as well as the manner in which the techniques should be combined and sequenced so as to expediate out-of-court agreements.

Our second objective is to determine which factors account for the utilization of various mediation techniques. Is it their effectiveness? The costs in using them? Overload of the court? The answers as well as the questions are quite interesting; before broaching them, however, we need to address some basics.

SETTLEMENT: A NEGOTIATION IN THE LEGAL SETTING

Settlement is a negotiation process in which the plaintiff and defendant, or their attorneys, attempt to reach an agreement outside of the courtroom. In most cases, the plaintiff initiates the process by contacting a lawyer who files a complaint against the defendant; however, prior to the filing, the plaintiff's attorney may negotiate directly with the defendant or the defendant's attorney. If there is no agreement—the complaint is filed—the plaintiff's and defendant's attorneys can, and will generally, enter into negotiations in an attempt to settle out of court. If they do not reach an agreement, the case is scheduled for a pretrial conference with a judge. Here, the judge reviews the case with the attorneys, rules on procedural points such as the number of expert witnesses, delineates which points are at issue and which under agreement, orders discovery (dictates which information possessed by one attorney must be given to the other), schedules the case for trial, and possibly attempts to facilitate a settlement. If the judge, the attorneys, or the court rules call for a settlement conference, the judge will schedule one; here the attorneys will engage in active negotiation, with the judge playing whatever role he or she chooses.

If there is no agreement prior to trial, the case comes before the bench and here the judge can initiate or continue mediary efforts. In addition, he or she can be quite active in the period between the conferences and the trial. Mediation efforts may continue up to the point that the judge or jury brings in a verdict, and beyond. Immediately after the verdict, the judge can attempt to strike a different agreement between the two sides (Mack, 1975).

VALUE OF A NEGOTIATED SETTLEMENT

As for the value of a negotiated agreement, the process and resultant agreement benefit the clients as well as the judicial system. The consensus of opinion from lawyers and judges (e.g., Lincoln, Learned Hand, and Chief Justice Burger) is that the freely negotiated, "give a little, take a little" settlement in most cases results in a higher quality of justice to the clients than does an absolute trial (Will, Merhige, & Rubin, 1978). The settlement saves money for both sides because costly trials and appeals are avoided; likewise, the settlement gives the parties control of the case (Avakian, 1978). They can settle before the case goes to trial, before the verdict, or even after the verdict is rendered. Settlement also yields certainty because it cannot be appealed; it offers confidentiality—the results do not have to be made part of a public record—and it is expedient.

For the judicial system, the process proffers many advantages. First, it is a final disposition of a case. It reduces the court's load because only those cases that could not be settled come to trial. Determination by settlement reduces the time between filing and disposition; this advantage, in addition to aiding the judge, also improves the public's evaluation of the efficiency of judicial administration (Fox, 1972).

JUDGE'S ROLE IN SETTLEMENT

In brief, the judge's role is whatever he or she wants it to be. Opinions vary; one judge replied to the authors, "I don't interfere in the lawyers' business" and another noted "I get agreements." The variety in the judges' approaches results from three phenomena: first, the judge is a very powerful party; unlike most mediators, he or she has more power than do the two opposing parties. Second, almost all mediary activities are off the record: neither stenographers nor recording devices are used in the pretrial and settlement conferences. Likewise, judges seldom allow their overtures to become part of the court record. Finally, while the judge can undertake a wide range of mediary endeavors, he or she cannot dictate the agreement because either side can take the case to trial.

The judge's freedom to do or not to do whatever he or she wishes vis-a-vis the attorney's negotiations is also underpinned by an absence of guidance from formal procedures. The *Handbook for Effective Pre-Trial Procedure* (1965) states that the discussion of settlement at pretrial should not be avoided; likewise, many scholars feel that settlement is a product of a good pretrial procedure.

For the federal courts, Rule 16 of the Federal Rules of Civil Procedure lays out the procedures for the pretrial conferences. Within this Rule, no mention is made of settlement as a purpose of the conference. Yet most judges interpret subsection 6 of the Rule— which permits as a topic of consideration at the conference "such other matters as may aid in the disposition of the action"—as a license to become involved in settlement negotiations.

Some state rules seem to encourage the judge to mediate. For example, some states' rules specifically permit the judge to inquire into the possibility of settlement at pretrial conferences. And in California a pretrial conference for the sole purpose of encouraging settlement is mandatory if either party accepts a settlement conference invitation sent to them by the court clerk; in a similar vein, Ohio's pretrial procedure rule lists settlement as the major objective of the pretrial conference.

PRIOR RESEARCH

Given that settlement negotiations proffer benefits to the parties involved and that judges are allowed, or encouraged, to facilitate settlement, what steps do judges take, under what conditions do they participate, and how effective are their techniques?

In order to address these questions, we initially interviewed 50 lawyers and judges to determine which techniques they had observed and utilized in civil cases. The 71 techniques unearthed were found to be applied to multiple leverage points: (a) the interlawyer relationship, (b) the lawyers themselves, (c) the lawyer/client relationship, and (d) the clients themselves. Of the techniques, many were parallel to those applied in other negotiation arenas (Wall, 1981; for example, asking the attorneys to split the difference), while some were more legally specific (for example, threatening to declare a mistrial if the attorneys did not settle). Some were simple (for example, offers advice to a lawyer); other, strikingly complex (for example, transferral of the case to another district on the day of trial in order to force settlement rather than to have the trial far away).

STUDY 1

The variety in the techniques raised questions as to which were most often used and the conditions under which techniques were employed. Determination of the frequencies with which the techniques were employed seemed a rather straightforward affair; yet our interests were heightened by the responses encountered during and subsequent to the first study. First, there were strong differences of opinions regarding the frequency with which the various techniques were used. For example, several lawyers who practiced before the same court noted that a certain technique was employed quite often by judges. Other lawyers expressed disbelief that we had uncovered any instances in which the technique was used. With regards to a different technique—which was frequently mentioned during our interviews—the editor of a leading law journal questioned our findings, stating that a judge would never use such a technique because if he or she did "the opposing party could obtain a writ against (the judge) so fast that the judge's head would spin."

As for the conditions under which the 71 techniques were used, we developed several hypotheses. The first was that courts serving highly populated areas would have the most crowded dockets and thereby in these courts the judges would be more active—use more settlement techniques—than would those in less populated, less crowded court systems.

The second set of hypotheses focused upon the effect of requiring pretrial and settlement conference. From locale to locale there is variance in the state, local state court, and local federal court rules; any or all of the three rules can require a pretrial conference and/or a settlement conference. It was posited that the requirement for settlement conferences likewise would result in more judicial mediation. It was felt that the settlement conferences would give the judge opportunities to facilitate the disputes and that he or she would take advantage of this opportunity.

Method

One thousand attorneys randomly selected from the current membership lists of the Association of Trial Lawyers of America and the Defense Research Institute were presented with the 71 techniques identified in the aforementioned study and asked to indicate whether or not they had observed the techniques.

Also the respondents were asked to indicate the population served by the state court before which they primarily practiced by checking one of ten categories (< 25,000; 25,000-50,000; 50,000-75,000; 75,000-100,000; 100,000-200,000; 200,000-300,000; 300,000-400,000; 400,000-500,000; 500,000-1,000,000; and > 1,000,000) and to judge the congestion of their court docket on a seven-point, bipolar, extremely crowded/not at all crowded scale. In order to test the second set of hypotheses, the lawyers were asked to indicate whether or not their state, local, and federal court rules required pretrial and settlement conferences.

Results

Of the 1000 questionnaires, 361 were returned and corroborated seemingly common knowledge that cases take too long to come to trial; 18 months transpire between the date a complaint is filed and the first day in court. Given that there is an established need to expedite the judicial process, to what extent are the judges facilitating the settlement process?

Our findings reveal that the judges are participating significantly in 34 percent of the settlement proceedings. Is this a high percentage? That is, are judges quite active in the settlement process? Many judges and lawyers contacted feel this is a high percentage, and perhaps it is, if we consider that some cases are settled prior to the pretrial conference. On the other hand, this percentage does seem to indicate that there is ample opportunity for increased judicial efforts; more will be said about this later.

As for the technique that the judges are employing, Table 10.1 provides our results, listing the 30 most commonly utilized techniques. An initial examination of Table 10.1 indicates that most of the frequently utilized techniques concentrate upon the attorneys and their relationship. Such a finding is consonant with observations in other mediary climates such as labor management negotiations. Also, many of the techniques reported here are procedural and nonassertive. On the other hand, some of the techniques—such as telling the lawyer to call his or her client immediately to get a response—are considered by legal practitioners to be quite assertive.

As for our hypotheses, the data generally supported the first one: Attorneys practicing in the larger population areas rated the docket in these courts as being more crowded than did those practicing in smaller areas. Specifically, as the categories of population served by the lawyer's court rose from less than 25,000 to over 1,000,000, the docket was evaluated as more and more crowded (from 4.6 to 2.4, respectively, with 1 = extremely crowded and 7 = not at all crowded; $F(9,342) = 8.38$, $p < .001$). Similarly, as can be seen in Table 10.2, attorneys practicing in high population areas observed more techniques in use than did those practicing in less populated areas [$F(9,344) = 6.73$, $p < .001$].

Turning to our second set of hypotheses—effects of required pretrial and settlement conferences—we find the data revealing that only the requirement for settlement conferences altered the level of judicial participation. When the state court rules required a settlement conference, more techniques were observed than when a settlement conference was not required: means = 41 versus 32, respectively; $F(1,300) = 13.71$, $p < .001$; when local court rules required a settlement conference, more techniques were observed: mean = 40 versus 32 when none was required; $F(1,306) = 12.53$, $p < .001$; and when local federal courts rules required a settlement conference, again more techniques were observed: mean = 37 versus 30 when none was required; $F(1,293) = 10.55$, $p < .001$.

**TABLE 10.1   Mediation Techniques Most Frequently Observed
by Lawyers**

Technique
(1) Meets with lawyers in his or her chambers for a settlement conference.
(2) Talks with both lawyers together about the settlement.
(3) Raises the settlement issue but no more.
(4) Asks both lawyers to compromise.
(5) Analyzes the case for a lawyer.
(6) Sets a settlement conference upon request.
(7) Requires settlement talks.
(8) Says split the difference.
(9) Pressures the ill-prepared attorney.
(10) Argues logically for concessions.
(11) Has the lawyer immediately call his or her client to get his or her response.
(12) Notes, to the lawyer, the high risk of going trial.
(13) Tells attorneys to concentrate on the relevant issues.
(14) Evaluates one or both cases for the attorneys.
(15) Calls a certain figure reasonable.
(16) Leaves the lawyers together and exits him- or herself.
(17) Channels discussion to areas that have the highest probability of settlement.
(18) Suggests settlement figure *after* asking for lawyer's inputs.
(19) Informs the attorneys as to how similar cases have been settled.
(20) Asks amount each attorney would concede, going back and forth to break settlement into small steps.
(21) Continues to bring up settlement during trial recesses.
(22) Argues one attorney's case to the other.
(23) Offers alternative proposal not thought of by the lawyers.
(24) Notes, to the client, the rewards of pretrial settlement.
(25) Offers advice to a lawyer.
(26) Brings client to the conference.
(27) Interprets the issues for the lawyers.
(28) Talks to each lawyer separately about settlement.
(29) Tells attorneys not to stall.
(30) Requires settlement conference even though not mandated by court rules.

Why did judges in courts required to hold a pretrial conference engage in settlement activities no more frequently than did those judges in courts not requiring a pretrial conference? The answer

TABLE 10.2 Population Served by the Court and Number of Techniques Observed

Population Served	Number of Techniques Observed
Less than 25,000	23
25,000-50,000	24
50,000-75,000	30
75,000-100,000	31
100,000-200,000	31
200,000-300,000	32
300,000-400,000	27
400,000-500,000	33
500,000-1,000,000	38
Over 1,000,000	42

probably is that most judges currently hold pretrial conferences even when they are not required; therefore, the extent to which pretrial conferences are actually held does not vary significantly between courts requiring them and those not requiring them.

Discussion

In sum, our results show that civil courts currently are overcrowded even though some judges are actively mediating to facilitate out-of-court negotiated settlements. A few steps, it seems, could be undertaken to improve the current predicament. One is to increase the extent of judicial involvement in the pretrial settlement process. Second, the effectiveness of this involvement can be improved. And finally, third-party procedures can be utilized to decide many cases outside of the courts.

Of these steps, the first depends principally upon educating judges as to the variety of mediation techniques available to them and informing them that these techniques are being utilized by many courts. In addition, some instruction in the utilization of the available mediation techniques no doubt would prove useful. This brings us to the second step—improving the effectiveness of judicial involvement. Pursuit of this goal requires determination as to which of currently utilized mediary techniques are most effective. Prior to our studies, the legal community had no knowledge as to the mediary techniques being employed by judges. Now we know that approximately 71 techniques are being utilized, and we have information as to which are most frequently employed. Next we must close upon the most effective techniques: this is the goal of the subsequent study.

Prior to reporting on that study, we need to address the final step for the expedition of civil cases—the implementation of third-party procedures that remove many cases from the court system. On January 24, 1982, Chief Justice Burger (1982) in a speech to the American Bar Association decried the delay and lack of finality of the civil justice system and advocated three measures to alleviate the problem: (a) some civil cases (e.g., divorce, child custody, personal injury) should be removed from the courts to private, binding aribtration; (b) some cases should be moved to administrative panels; and (c) some should be handled with court-supervised, nonbinding arbitration. We felt these suggestions deserved formal investigation.

STUDY 2

The major purpose of this study was to determine which of the mediation techniques were considered by judges and lawyers to be most effective in facilitating settlements in civil cases. This information in combination with that of the previous studies will allow us to select the techniques (for instance, the top 10) that are most frequently utilized, as well as most effective and thereby deemed effective for future research.

A second goal was to measure the legal community's reaction to the Chief Justice's proposal. Mr. Burger predicted some resistance to these ideas, and it seemed worthwhile to tap the judges' and lawyers' reactions.

We also wished to test three hypotheses, the first being that the techniques most often observed by practicing lawyers will be rated higher in effectiveness than will the techniques that are less often observed. Underpinning this hypothesis is the rather general deduction that judges have, over the years, retained the techniques that have proved useful and abandoned those that were less effective. More specifically, this hypothesis can be defended from the operant conditioning standpoint (Skinner, 1969) with the argument that the judges have been reinforced for using the effective techniques and thus have continued their employment. On the other hand, the ineffective techniques do not yield such rewards (i.e., quick and frequent settlements) and thus are no longer employed.

The second hypothesis posits that one of the techniques reported as frequently utilized by judges—asking the attorneys to "split the difference"—will be reported as highly effective. This latter proposition sits astride the premise that such a suggestion has both prominence and acceptability for the attorneys (Schelling, 1960) and thereby is effective. Further strengthening this argument is the observation that the 50-50 split is a mediation technique commonly found to be effective in labor/management negotiations (Young, 1972).

A third hypothesis posits that the frequently observed technique, "suggests a settlement figure *after* asking for the lawyers' input," will be reported as highly effective. Such a proposal facilitates the attorneys' agreement because it saves face for the attorneys (Pruitt & Johnson, 1970). Likewise, the proposal reduces the attorneys' aspirations (Siegel & Fouraker, 1960) and gives them a prominent point (Schelling 1960) toward which they will concede (Wall, 1979).

Method

For the present study questionnaires were sent to 100 federal judges and 100 lawyers; the larger study will include 500 federal judges, 500 state judges, and 500 lawyers. These 200 legal practitioners were asked to evaluate the effectiveness of 40 judicial mediation techniques on a seven-point, bipolar scale (extremely effective/not at all effective). As for the techniques offered, they included the twenty most frequently observed by lawyers in the previous survey and twenty randomly selected from the 51 less frequently observed.

In order to measure the judges' and lawyers' evaluations of the Chief Justice's proposals, the parties were asked to record their argeement with each on a seven-point bipolar scale (strongly agree/ strongly disagree). Also, they were asked to respond on a seven-point (extremely effective/not at all effective) scale indicating how effective they thought the measures would be in reducing the delay in civil cases.

TABLE 10.3   Mediation Techniques Judged Most Effective

Techniques in Order of Effectiveness	Rank on Table 10.1
(1) Channels discussion to areas that have highest probability of settlement.	17
(2) Meets with the lawyers in his or her chambers for a settlement conference.	1
(3) Talks with both lawyers together about the settlement.	*
(4) Calls a certain figure reasonable.	15
(5) Argues logically for concessions.	10
(6) Requires a settlement conference even though not mandated by court rules.	*
(7) Suggests a settlement figure *after* asking for lawyers' inputs.	18
(8) Tells attorneys to concentrate on the relevant issues.	13
(9) Gets a settlement conference upon request.	6
(10) Requires settlement talks.	7
(11) Asks amount each attorney would concede, going back and forth to break settlement into small steps.	20
(12) Evaluates one or both cases for the attorneys.	14
(13) Requires pretrial conference even though not mandated by court rules.	*
(14) Asks both lawyers to compromise.	4
(15) Informs the attorneys as to how similar cases have been settled.	19
(16) Notes, for the client, the rewards of pretrial settlement.	*
(17) Analyzes the case for a lawyer.	5
(18) Has the lawyer immediately call his or her client to get his or her responses.	11
(19) Notes, to the lawyer, the high risk of going to trial.	12
(20) Speaks personally with the client to persuade him or her to accept.	*

*Not included in 20 techniques most frequently observed.

Results

Table 10.3 lists the twenty techniques judged most effective in facilitating settlement in civil cases. As the reader can note, the techniques included in this "top-twenty" category are not identical to those twenty most frequently observed (Table 10.1); nor is the ordering the same. However, as hypothesized, the twenty most frequently utilized techniques were judged, in sum, as more effective than those less frequently employed, $t(43) = 5.37$, $p < .0001$.

With regards to the other two hypotheses under study, only one was supported. The "split-the-difference technique," in contrast to our hypothesis, was not ranked in the top twenty most effective techiques. On the evaluation scale (1 = extremely effective; 7 = not at all effective), it posted an average of 4.39, above the midpoint on the ineffective side.

The suggested settlement point fared better, with the data supporting our hypothesis. This technique was scored as the seventh most effective technique and its mean score of 3.26 was significantly different than the mean on the extremely effective/not at all effective scale, $t(48) = 3.21$, $p < .001$.

As for the reactions to the Chief Justice's proposed use of third parties, the overall figures are somewhat misleading: in general the respondents disagreed with moving some cases to binding arbitration (Mean = 5.17 on a seven-point scale with 1 = strongly agree and 7 = strongly disagree), transferring some to administrative panels (Mean = 4.91), and shifting some to court-supervised, nonbinding arbitration (Mean = 4.95).

With regards to the predicted effectiveness of these techniques, each was unenthusiastically condemned. On a seven-point bipolar scale (with extremes tagged as 1 = extremely effective and 7 = not at all effective), the binding arbitration scored a 4.54, the administrative panels received a 4.54 rating, and the nonbinding arbitration rated a 4.23.

A more valid representation of the opinions surfaces whenever we compare the lawyers' and judges' responses (Table 10.4). As can be seen, the lawyers strongly opposed the measures, whereas the judges were more fondly disposed toward them. The differences in opinions on the first four questions were all significant ($p < .002$, $p < .008$, $p < .0001$, and $p < .005$, respectively). On the other hand, lackluster nonsupport for the nonbinding arbitration emerged from both camps, the differences for the last two questions being nonsignificant.

Discussion

In reviewing the data from these two studies, the emergent conclusions seem rather straightforward. Civil courts currently are overly crowded: Our survey noted this, the practicing attorney

TABLE 10.4 Lawyers' and Justices' Reactions to
the Chief Justice's Proposal

Question	Mean of Lawyers' Responses	Mean of Judges' Responses
To what extent do you agree with moving some civil cases to private binding arbitration?[a]	5.8	3.9
How effective do you think binding arbitration will bill in reducing the delay in civil cases?[b]	5.0	3.4
To what extent to you agree with moving some civil cases to administrative panels?[a]	5.6	3.4
How effective do you think administrative panels will be in reducing the delay in civil cases?[b]	5.1	3.4
To what extent do you agree with handling some cases with court-supervised, nonbinding arbitration?[a]	4.6	4.0
How effective do you think nonbinding arbitration will be in reducing the delay in civil cases?[b]	4.5	3.8

a. 1 = strongly agree; 7 = strongly disagree.
b. 1 = extremely effective; 7 = not at all effective.

observed the phenomenon, and the Chief Justice has quite specifically targeted it as a central judicial problem. As a result, quick, affordable justice is less than readily available to the average person. There are several third-party techniques for speeding up the judicial process: mediation by a judge, binding arbitration, administrative panels, and court supervised, nonbinding arbitration. Of these four, the latter three must be instituted via legislation, and our results suggest that such legislation will not be immediately forthcoming. Even though the judges favor the measures, lawyers do not. And since (a) there are more lawyers than judges, (b) the lawyers are highly organized and communicate effectively with legislators, and (c) many legislators are attorneys, the deck appears strongly stacked against legislation providing extracourt dispute resolution. Therefore, the burden of affording expedient civil justice falls somewhat heavily upon judicial mediation.

We hope that our research proffers some guidance for the improvement of this process. From our data, we have gleaned a manageable set of judicial mediary techniques that are frequently utilized and rates as highly effective. We can test the effectiveness of each in field studies, determine the combinations that prove effective, and ascertain the optimal sequencing for the techniques. Presently, the best strategic approach toward these research goals appears to be lawyers interviews. In these, the lawyers will be asked to recall a case that recently has been filed or settled and to report which of the enumerated techniques (e.g., techniques 1-20 from Table 10.1 and techniques 3, 6, 13, 16, and 20 from Table 10.3) the judge used to facilitate a settlement. Having responded to these queries, the lawyer will be asked to recall the sequence in which the judge applied the techniques and queried as to whether or not the case was settled. Data obtained in this manner will allow us to correlate settlement (versus no settlement) with the techniques, sequences, and combinations utilized by the judge and, as a first cut, will give us some indication as to which of these are most effective.

Turning now to the second objective in our undertaking—determination of which factors affect the utilization of mediation techniques—we note that the strong overlap of Tables 10.1 and 10.2 indicates that the utilization of a technique appears to be highly dependent upon its effectiveness. However, other factors seem to be entering the picture. One factor—suggested at the conference—is the cost of utilization; specifically, it seems reasonable to assert that *creteris paribus,* a judge is more likely to use a low-cost technique (e.g., time, effort) than a high-cost one. Ethical techniques probably will also be utilized more often than will those deemed unethical. Weaving these rough initial threads into a fabric yields the following formula:

Technique   = f (effectiveness, cost, and ethicalness of the
Utilization   technique)

This also should be tested in a field setting.

In terms of practical value, the determination of the effectiveness of each technique perhaps offers more payoff to the individual judge than does a clarification as to why a technique is used or not used. Yet for one interested in improving mediation within the civil court system, the "utilization" formula above is of equal importance. Investigations of this latter relationship might reveal if and why effective techniques are not being used, or why they are underutilized. Such findings, in turn, could prove to be of assistance in developing procedures for the implementation of effective techniques.

For instance, research guided by the above formula might reveal that a technique (e.g., requiring a settlement conference even though it is not mandated by court rules is highly effective but seldom utilized because it entails such a high cost to the judge. Armed with such data, the appropriate officials could take steps (e.g., have a magistrate conduct the settlement conference after the judge calls it) to reduce the costs of this technique and thereby facilitate more frequent utilization of the technique.

In closing, our data indicate that the civil court system is overloaded and that some judges, in an attempt to deal with the problem, are utilizing mediation. We have found which techniques are being utilized and which are effective. Additionally, our data provide underpinnings for further investigations that will guide judges in their mediations and legislators in their endeavors to facilitate the judges' mediary ventures.

REFERENCES

Avakian, R. How one trial judge settles cases. *Guild Practitioner*, 1978, *35*, 16-21.

Burger, W. E. Isn't there a better way. *American Bar Association Journal*, 1982, *68*, 274-277.

Fox, R. Settlement: Helping the lawyers to fulfill their responsibility. *F.R.D.*, 1972, *53*, 129-142.

Handbook for effective pre-trial procedure, reprinted in *F.R.D.*, 1965, *37*, 263-271.

Mack, J. Settlement procedures in the U.S. Courts of Appeal, a proposal. *Justice System*, 1975, *17*.

Pruitt, D. G., & Johnson, P. W. Mediation as an aid to face-saving in negotiation. *Journal of Personality and Social Psychology*, 1975, *31*, 621-633.

Schelling, T. C. *The strategy of conflict*. Cambridge, MA: Harvard University Press, 1960.

Siegel, S., & Fouraker, L. *Bargaining and group decision making*, New York: McGraw-Hill, 1960.

Skinner, B. F. *Contingencies of reinforcement: A theoretical analysis*. Englewood Cliffs, NJ: Prentice-Hall, 1969.

Wall, J. A. The effects of mediator rework and suggestions upon negotiations. *Journal of Personality and Social Psychology*, 1979, *37*, 1554-1560.

Wall, J. A. Mediation: An analysis, review and proposed research. *Journal of Conflict Resolution*, 1981, *25*, 157-180.

Will, J., Merhige, J., & Rubin, J. The role of the judge in the settlement. *F.D.R.*, 1978, *75*, 203-223.

Young, O. R. Intermediaries: Additional thoughts on third parties. *Journal of Conflict Resolution*, 1972, *16*, 51-65.

—11—

MANAGERS AS INQUISITORS
Some Lessons From the Law

Blair H. Sheppard

Duke University

One theme of this book is that the research and theory concerning negotiation in labor relations are relevant to the study of negotiation in many other organizational settings. On several occasions (Sheppard, 1982a, in press; Sheppard, Lesser, Li, & Mace, 1982), I have made a similar but more general argument with regard to third-party dispute intervention, an important part of research in labor relations. Specifically, I have suggested that research on the procedures in many diverse areas of dispute intervention (e.g., arbitration and mediation in labor relations, adjudicatory intervention, police crisis intervention, international conflict intervention, and managerial conflict intervention) is largely ignored but extremely relevant to the other areas of conflict intervention. In response to this problem, I have proposed a generic framework for describing conflict intervention procedures across these diverse settings (Sheppard, in press). Portions of this framework have been validated using data collected in police crisis intervention as well as in trial settings (Sheppard et al., 1982). The purpose of this chapter is to report the preliminary results of a study aimed at using this framework to describe how managers intervene in conflict. Further, this study provides an illustration of how the literature in one conflict setting (i.e., the law) is highly relevant to another conflict setting (i.e., managerial conflict intervention).

MANAGERIAL CONFLICT INTERVENTION

Research on Conflict Intervention in Organizations

Evidence from several sources suggests that conflict intervention is a central aspect of the jobs of most managers. For example, observations of how managers spend their time (e.g., Mintzberg, 1975) indicates that a great deal of managerial time is spent in disturbance handling. When managers are asked to describe the major elements of their job, handling of conflicts or disagreements usually is mentioned (e.g., Tornow & Pinto, 1976). Finally, it is easy for researchers interested in conflict management in organizations to find (e.g., Blake, Shepard, & Mouton, 1964). Moreover, from my own research (Lissak & Sheppard, in press) managers appear to be called upon to intervene in a wide array of conflicts. Table 11.1 includes a list of the wide range of conflict issues in which managers appear to become embroiled as a third party (i.e., an initially uninvolved party who later intervenes to help manage the dispute). Some of these conflicts are between individuals, some between groups; some are serious, some not so serious; some are frequent and recurring, others infrequent and nonrecurring; finally, some are between individuals who have known each other for a long time, while others are between relative strangers.

Surprisingly, however, very little research exists regarding how managers actually intervene in conflict within organizations (Thomas, 1976). Most of the research that has been conducted on managerial conflict intervention has focused upon the aims of the intervention, for example, to induce compromise, smooth over differences, or force issues (Blake, Shepard, & Mouton, 1964), or to reduce conflict, or facilitate change in the disputants' relationship (Walton, 1969). This research has not been concerned with how managers intervene in terms of the actual strategies, processes, or procedures used. (Two notable exceptions are Scott [1965] and some of the research reviewed in Walton and Dutton [1969]). In other

TABLE 11.1 Fifteen Types of Conflicts Within Organizations Identified in Interviews

Type of Conflict	Frequency of Occurrence in Interviews
Poor job performance or failure to perform specified duties.	41
Disagreement over a company policy.	17
Excessive work-related demands placed upon or made by one of the disputants.	12
Result of a discriminatory act against or by one of the disputants.	11
Disagreement over pay or salary.	11
Result of one disputant's unauthorized involvement in the other's duties.	10
Result of an infringement upon the property of personal rights of one of the disputants.	9
Disagreement over a contract or breach of a contract.	9
Result of a dishonest act committed by one of the disputants.	9
Denial of responsibility desired by one of the disputants.	8
Disagreement over the priorities or future policy of the company.	8
Result of one party not supplying or delivering materials that were promised.	6
Part of a long-lasting feud or disagreement between two parties.	6
Result of a poorly defined instruction, expectation, or order to one of the disputants.	3
Arose when one of the disputants became involved in an already existing dispute.	3

words, we know more about the types of solutions generated by managerial conflict resolution than we do about how conflict intervention is actually done.

On the other hand, a great deal of literature exists describing how professional third parties intervene in disputes within organizations. Mediation (Wall, 1981), organizational development (Beer, 1976), process consultation (Walton, 1969), arbitration (Anderson, 1981), and fact finding (Newman, 1979) have generally been thoroughly reviewed and researched. More than once, it has been suggested that the technique and research findings developed about professional intervention can be applied to managerial conflict intervention. In fact, this presumption is one of the principle underpinnings of this book and forms the basis of a plethora of training programs throughout the country on conflict management (for a dissenting opinion, see Thomas, 1982). However, since we presently do not know how managers actually intervene in conflict, the proposed correspondence between professional and managerial conflict intervention is taken on faith, not convincing evidence.

One possible reason why we do not have more research as to how managers intervene in conflicts may be that no simple means exists for describing or coding observed or described interventions. The professional intervention procedures identified above provide an inadequate basis for describing how managers intervene in conflict, because they do not represent exhaustive or exclusive procedural categories or types. Therefore, development of a reasonably comprehensive taxonomy that disentangles the various procedures available to third parties is a necessary first step in the study of how managers intervene in conflict.

In summary, in spite of the amount of time managers appear to spend on conflict intervention a good description of how managers intervene in conflict does not presently exist. One reason for the absence of such important descriptive research may be that no means for coding intervention attempts previously existed. The next section of this chapter, then, will describe a preliminary study to identify how managers intervene in conflict based upon a procedural taxonomy of conflict intervention developed in my earlier work (Sheppard, in press). The chapter will then conclude with a discussion of the interesting correspondence between two of the most frequently used managerial procedures found in this study and legal procedure.

A PROPOSED TAXONOMY OF MANAGERIAL CONFLICT INTERVENTION

The study of how managers intervene in conflict occurred in two stages. Only the first stage has been completed and will be reported here. In this first stage, thirty managers were asked to describe the last conflict in which they intervened as a third party, to explain how they intervened in that conflict, and to indicate how successful they felt their intervention has been. In addition, thirty other managers were asked the same questions, but were directed to take the perspective of a disputant involved in an intervention by some other manager. The second portion of this research, now underway, utilized the results of these preliminary interviews to develop a standard questionnaire addressing similar questions that will be sent to a national sample of managers. Descriptions of the interventions in which managers were involved were coded in terms of a taxonomy previously developed for describing conflict intervention across a range of dispute settings (Sheppard, in press). Before describing the results of these preliminary interviews with the managers, it is necessary to familiarize the reader with this taxonomy.

The taxonomy was developed as part of a large framework intended to integrate the variety of research on conflict intervention. In addition to the taxonomy, this framework also includes a relatively comprehensive list of the criteria for choosing and evaluating conflict intervention procedures utilized in various dispute arenas, as well as a discussion of some of the features of conflict, disputants, and conflict settings that are relevant to the study of conflict intervention. (For an in-depth discussion of these two additional features of the framework, as well as a detailed treatment and discussion of the logic underlying the taxonomy, see Sheppard, in press.)

Timing of Intervention

In its simplest form, dispute intervention involves three parties: two disputants and a third, or intervening, party. Further, dispute resolution can be conceived of as proceeding through four sequential stages, including

(1) *definition,* during which parties feel each other out and identify what is in dispute, relevant information, a procedure for resolving the dispute, and alternatives for managing the dispute;

(2) *discussion,* during which opposing views, information, and clarification of points are presented to the party(ies) deciding the disposition of the conflict;

(3) *alternative selection,* during which information is sifted to decide its relevance to the decision maker and an alternative for solving the conflict is chosen; and

(4) *reconciliation,* during which parties are reconciled with the decision and, if necessary, appeals are heard and the decision is enforced.

For similar stage descriptions of dispute resolution see Douglas (1957), Filley (1975), Deutsch (1973), Gottman (1978), Pondy (1967), Walton (1969), and Young (1967).

In the proposed taxonomy, procedures are identified in terms of the type of control assumed by the third party in each of these stages of conflict management (see Thibaut & Walker, 1975). Thus procedure is described in the form of a matrix in which the rows of the matrix represent *when* a third party can intervene in conflict resolution (i.e., a timing of conflict intervention) and the columns of the matrix represent *how* a third party can intervene in conflict resolution (i.e., the form of conflict intervention).

Forms of Intervention

To complete the matrix, it is thus necessary to identify the forms of control a third party can exhibit during the resolution process. Table 11.2 presents a summary of the forms of control potentially available to a third party when intervening in conflict. This summary is based on an extensive review of several conflict literatures (Sheppard, in press) as well as on my own research with managers, lawyers, and the police. This table is intended as a relatively thorough and self-explanatory description of these forms of control. Not included in this table are the features of third-party intervention discussed in the conflict literature that describe the objective of the third party's control attempt (e.g., reduce the level of tension). Instead, Table 11.2 includes only control forms describing the strategies and actions a third party can actually attempt during intervention.

The types of control identified in Table 11.2 also have been classified into four general categories that appear to capture well the general sorts of control available to a third party. These inlcude:

(1) *Process Control:* This refers to any attempts by the intervening party to direct how the disputants and other parties interact during resolution but not what the topics or other substantive aspects of the interaction should be.

TABLE 11.2 **Forms of Control Available to Third Parties in Conflict Intervention**

I. Process Control

   A. General Controls

     (1) Control location of disputants, e.g., separated or together.

     (2) Control general communication process: request written briefs, forces disputants to talk, request eye contact, require reflective listening, establish an agenda, request role reversal, censure interruptions, encourage open discussion or close communication channels.

     (3) Act as an advocate of a position, devil's advocate, or sounding board.

     (4) Counsel one party.

     (5) Act as a go-between.

     (6) Control access to other parties or information.

     (7) Establish time limit on process.

   B. Specific Controls

     (1) Suggest or require a specific process mechanism, e.g., require disputants to vote.

     (2) Limit or disallow particular process mechanism, e.g., disputants are not permitted to argue.

     (3) Audit process, e.g., look for process problems and flag them with disputants.

     (4) Establish particular rules of order.

II. Content Control

   A. General Controls

     (1) Control general communication content: avoid sidetracking, limit discussion to a single item, expand discussion, censor "guilting" other party, censor affect statement, censor ultimatums, censor use of "always" or "never," censor use of trait names, encourage giving praise, encourage expressions of likes or dislikes.

     (2) Establish an agenda.

     (3) Establish rules of evidence or content for consideration.

   B. Specific Controls

     (1) Refute or attack particular point.

     (2) Present own content, e.g., state the nature of the dispute.

     (3) Disallow or discouage particular content.

     (4) Audit content.

     (5) Interpret or clarify content.

     (6) Edit content.

     (7) Withhold content from some or all parties.

(continued)

TABLE 11.2 Continued

III. Motivational Control

    (1) Can provide an incentive to perform desired action, e.g., a parent offers to take children to the fair only if they settle their argument.

    (2) Can provide a disincentive to performing an undesired action, e.g., a boss threatens to fire an employee unwilling to negotiate with a fellow employee.

    (3) Has legitimate authority over some facet of dispute resolution.

    (4) Voluntary agreement to control by some or all of the parties.

    (5) Can change the nature of the power distribution between disputants.

    (6) Has the ear of some figure having one of the controls described above, e.g., a mediator has access to the media and therefore public or stockholder opinion.

    (7) Has threat of control in later stage of the resolution process.

    (8) Persuasive capability.

    (9) Physical force.

IV. Control by Request

The use of any of the controls listed in sections I-III above after some party has explicitly requested such an intervention, e.g., a judge can decide on a rule of evidence after an objection by one of the attorneys.

---

    (2) *Content Control:* The intervening party attempts to determine *what* is to be discussed, considered, and so on but not *how* it should be considered.

    (3) *Motivational Control:* The intervening party has the capacity to provide motivation to perform some desired action. Thus control in this form represents the nature of the power available to the third party to induce compliance with one of the three other control forms.

    (4) *Control by Request:* The third party decides only on a specific process or content question when asked to do so by one or more of the disputants. In this form of control the third party permits the disputants to work through their own resolution until they meet a particular snag and then intervenes only to manage that snag. One example of this is a trial judge who decides on an objection raised by an attorney and then returns to listening passively to testimony and arguments.

It is possible for most of the specific control forms identified in Table 11.2 to cooccur with other specific forms of control. Thus, for example, it is possible for a third party to act as a go-between (i.e., process control) and to establish an agenda (i.e., content control) in the same phase or stage of dispute resolution. Clearly, some of these specific control mechanisms will cooccur more than others. For example, a third party is more likely to act as an intermediary after having separated the disputants than when the disputants are kept together. However, it is conceivable for any combination of control forms to coexist.

Combining the Timing and Form of Third-Party Control

When combined together, these two general features of control, i.e., when and how control is assumed, combine to form a 4 × 4 matrix. (In those instances in which a very precise description is desired 13 × 4, 4 × 13, and 13 × 31 matrices can be constructed, if the specific phase of dispute resolution and type of control are considered.) A procedure would be identified, then, by making an entry in those cells of the matrix where the intervening party is permitted or exhibits a particular form of control in one of the stages of dispute resolution. Exactly how this can be done is probably best illustrated with some examples. Consider the results of the preliminary set of managerial interviews described earlier.

DESCRIBING MANAGERIAL
CONFLICT INTERVENTION

Two variations of an interview were utilized in this research to elicit managers' descriptions of how intervention occurred in the various disputes. In the first 39 interviews, managers were presented in matrix in Table 11.3 in a somewhat modified form and were asked to describe their own intervention in a recent dispute vis-a-vis this representation. Validity was assessed in this technique by asking interviewees if they felt this representation sufficiently described how they intervened and what additional information, if any, was necessary to describe what they did. The second interview procedure involved asking 21 managers to describe how they intervened in a

TABLE 11.3   A Matrix Representation of Managerial Conflict Intervention Procedure

	Timing of Third-Party Control	Process			Content			Request	Motivational		
	Definition										
	select resolution procedure	A			A			C	A		
	feel out parties		B			B				B	
	what is in dispute?			C			C	A	A		C
	what information exists?										
	what are the alternatives?										
Timing of Third-Party Control	**Discussion**										
	present relevant information	A	C		A			C	A		C
	present arguments	A	C		A			C	A		C
	clarify information	A	C		A		C		A		C
	Alternative Selection										
	decide validity of arguments	A	C		A		C		A		C
	select an alternative	A	C		A		C		A	B	C
	Reconciliation										
	reconcile parties	A	C		A		C		A		C
	enforce decision	A	B	C	A	B	C		A	B	C
	hear appeals	A			A				A		

A: A cell entry of A indicates that the timing and form of control represented by that cell is exhibited by managers utilizing an inquisitorial intervention procedure.

B: A cell entry of B indicates that the timing and form of control represented by that cell is exhibited by managers utilizing a providing impetus procedure.

C: A cell entry of C indicates that the timing and form of control represented by that cell is exhibited by managers utilizing an adversary intervention procedure.

given conflict in detailed narrative form. Validity of the taxonomy was then assessed by determining how reliably two independent, trained coders could classify these verbal descriptions in terms of the taxonomy.

In both instances, the results were initially very promising. Coding could be done very reliably and additions to the framework were generally not considered necessary by the interviewees. However, conclusive evidence regarding the validity of the framework for describing managerial dispute intervention still requires completion of the larger sample survey described earlier as well as collections of more objective evidence (not involving self-report data) concerning managerial intervention strategies. With these sample and method-ological limitations in mind, how do managers appear to intervene in conflict? The three most frequently occurring intervention procedures are presented in Table 11.3

Inquisitorial Intervention

The most frequently occurring intervention procedure was charac-terized by managers taking strong and active intervention in stages II, III, and IV of the resolution process (see cell entries A in Table 11.3). Managers who used this procedure actively guided the discussion, often censoring individual disputants, and made and enforced a deci-sion much like a benevolent parent or inquisitor. Thus this procedure could be called *inquisitorial intervention.*

For example, one of the disputes described by a manager in our survey took place in a brokerage firm in which a new broker purportedly stole a client from an older broker. In this instance, the intervening manager, who supervised the two brokers, spoke with the client and confirmed that the client had in fact switched brokers. He then told the client that if she were unwilling to return to the original broker, she should take her business elsewhere. In addition, the new broker was told that if a similar incident were to happen again, he would be fired. When the client and the junior broker attempted to explain their side of the story, the intervening manager indicated that she was not interested (thus control over the presentation and clarifi-cation of argument in this instance was in the form of censor). The manager indicated that it was necessary to be tough and consistent in such cases no matter what circumstances were involved.

This type of active intervention is generally performed with little investigation by a manager regarding what really is in dispute or what information may be relevant to solving the problem. In other words, intervention does not occur in stage I (the definition stage). In at least some of the interventions in the sample, this appears to have led to snap decisions based on past experience that did not really solve the conflict or that created new conflict between the disputants, often involving additional actors.

Providing Impetus

In the second most frequently occurring procedure, managers initially contacted the disputants to determine the nature of the conflict and then sent them away with a strong incentive for reaching agreement, such as threatened removal of one of the parties (see cells entries B in Table 11.3). Thus, this procedure could simply be called *providing impetus.*

An example of this sort of intervention involved an intervention by the vice president of a retail store chain. The dispute was between the head of the data processing department, who needed to hire summer help immediately to fill the shortages in staff, and the head of personnel, who wanted to avoid circumvention of normal hiring practices for summer interns. The vice president spoke briefly with both managers and then simply told them that they had "damn well better go back and work it out." Although no action was explicitly threatened if agreement was not reached, both parties were aware of the likely uproar if their differences were not settled. In other interviews, this type of threat was coupled with active interaction in the definition stage of the resolution process. Also, positive incentives for reaching an agreement were sometimes provided (e.g., lunch out with the boss).

This procedure appears to have at least two difficulties associated with it. One difficulty is that the underlying conflict does not appear always to be resolved. Instead, differences were polished over to please the boss. In a few specific instances in our survey this resulted in further conflict. Also, the concerns of parties indirectly involved in the conflict were not well represented in this procedure. For example, minority interests might have been overlooked in the solution to the described dispute.

Adversary Intervention

The third procedure (see cell entires C in Table 11.3) is similar to inquisitorial intervention in some respects. Like inquisitorial intervention, managers using this procedure decided how the conflict was to be resolved and enforced the decision if necessary. Unlike inquisitorial intervention, however, the third party generally did not actively seek or restrict the content of particular evidence and arguments from the disputing parties. Instead, the third party passively listened to both (or several competing) sides of the dispute as they were presented by the disputants. The intervener may, however, have specified how he or she wanted the information presented (e.g., who was to go first, how rebuttals were to be dealt with) and generally have actively sought clarifying information and arguments. A second difference between this procedure and inquisitorial intervention is that the third party often did not choose the procedure for resolving the dispute but instead acceded to a request by the disputants to listen to each side and suggest a solution. Thus the choice of procedure was generally in the form of "control by request." Because the disputants argued their own cases this procedure will be called *adversary interventionn*.

An example of this sort of intervention from the interviews concerned a dispute over the need for a new boiler for a school. The dispute was between a member of the engineering department for a local school board who felt a new boiler was needed and a consultant for the federal government, called in to evaluate this stated need, who felt that a new boiler was unnecessary. The engineer and the consultant went together to the state representative, who listened at length to both sides of the case and accepted the school board's recommendation.

SUMMARY OF MANAGERIAL CONFLICT INTERVENTION

Several general points can be drawn from the results of this preliminary study. First, it does appear quite possible to describe how managers intervene in conflict in fairly rich detail. As mentioned earlier, additional responses and observational measures are necessary before we can draw any firm conclusions about how managers generally intervene in disputes. However, a very interesting trend exists in the present results. In the majority of the descriptions we collected, the third party selected the alternative for resolving the dispute. Thus there is a surprising absence of more therapeutic intervention styles in which managers guide disputants to a solution as opposed to choosing a solution for them.

There are a number of potential reasons why managers might prefer to intervene as decision makers as opposed to conciliators or therapists. First, making decisions is rather habitual for most managers and thus it may be their most natural response. Similarly, seeking a decision may be the normal mode in which employees interact with their managers, and they may approach their supervisor with that expectation when seeking help with a dispute. Second, time to resolve the dispute and disruption of normal affairs appear to be important concerns for managers when deciding how to intervene in disputes (Lissak & Sheppard, in press). Working with disputants to guide them actively in resolving their own disputes is probably just too time consuming for the average manager. This immediate preoccupation with time may, of course, backfire. For example, one manager in our study saw the same two employees repeatedly with the same conflict. In the conclusion of his interview this manager confessed that he wished he had spent more time working through the problem the first time that it arose. However, actively deciding the disposition of a dispute is probably often the most expedient means of handling a dispute as a third party. Finally, maintaining the capacity to decide the disposition of a dispute provides the third party an opportunity to protect the company's interest, as well as his or her own interest.

Whatever the reasons for the predominance of third-party decision making in mangerial conflict intervention, it is clear that how managers and professionals intervene in organizational conflict is generally very different. Most professionals who intervene in organizational conflicts (except arbitrators) do not make and enforce a decision. Instead, professionals tend to apply more diagnostic and therapeutic procedures. One response to this absence of correspondence between how managers and professionals intervene is that managers clearly need training in conflict management (see, for example, Brett and Goldberg, this volume). However, we should seriously review why managers act as they do before beginning to train managers and MBA students to mimic Carl Rogers.

Because of the poor correspondence between professional and managerial intervention, the present research on organizational conflict intervention may be of little use in guiding further work on managers. Arbitration is the only procedure closely approximating any of the managerial procedures. Fortunately, however, two of the procedures utilized by managers are very similar to the two principal forms of legal procedure from which their names were derived, i.e., adversary and inquisitorial legal procedures. This correspondence suggests that research and theory on legal procedure may be a useful guide to future research on managerial conflict intervention. To understand how legal procedure relates to managerial conflict intervention, some background about the comparative structure of the two legal procedures is necessary.

In an inquisitorial system (used in varying forms in continental Europe), once one party files a suit, the judge, through a number of subordinates (court investigators), seeks out the evidence. There are no separate witnesses for the two parties. Rather, the witnesses testify for the court, and the parties are not allowed to prepare or affect the witnesses prior to the trial. The judge, equipped with a summary of the basic facts of the case, calls on the witnesses to give their testimony in narrative form. Following the judge's interrogation the contending parties are permitted to ask clarifying questions or bring out omitted points favorable to their case. After final arguments from both sides, the judge renders a decision.

In an adversary system (derived from English Common Law), however, the two disputants (or their representatives) are responsible for developing their own evidence, including interviewing witnesses, and to varying extents actually preparing them for trial testimony. At the trial the party who calls the witness attempts to elicit, in a quasi-narrative fashion ("examination-in-chief"), information favorable to his or her side. Thereafter, the witness is subjected to cross-examination by the opposing party. The judge remains an essentially passive listener during the presentation of evidence (except for deciding disputes about procedure in response to an objection by one of the participants) and becomes active only when the decision phase begins.

In summary, in an inquisitorial system the judge or his or her representatives are responsible for discovering and eliciting evidence, whereas in the adversary system, disputants or their attorneys are responsible for evidence discovery and presentation. However, in both systems the judge is responsible for making the decision. Let me caution the reader that this overview of the basic characteristics of the two systems oversimplifies some complex structural and ideological issues differentiating them (see Damaska, 1973, 1975a, 1975b). Nevertheless, it is sufficient background for the purposes of this chapter.

UTILITY OF LEGAL WRITING TO MANAGERIAL CONFLICT INTERVENTION

A strong parallel between two procedures utilized by managers and procedures used in a legal setting should be evident from these brief descriptions. Given this parallel, does research on comparative law contain any useful leads for furthering our understanding of managerial conflict intervention?

The first potential application of comparative law concerns hypotheses regarding the relative strengths and weaknesses of the managerial conflict intervention strategies portrayed in Table 11.3, cells A and C. According to legal research, adversary intervention should have at least three advantages over inquisitorial intervention. First, *adversary intervention will be perceived by the disputing employees as more fair than inquisitorial intervention* (Thibaut & Walker, 1975). Research in several cultures has repeatedly indicated that disputants consider pure adversary legal procedures more fair than pure inquisitorial procedures. One explanation for this perception is that individuals consider it only fair to permit the disputing parties' "say," unencumbered by control from some noninvolved outside party (Lind, 1982). Similar perceptions of fairness have been found in other settings as well, e.g., reward allocation (Folger, 1977) and grading decisions (Tyler & Caine, 1981).

A second probable strength of adversary intervention procedures is that *more information relevant to the task of the intervening manager will be generated using adversary intervention than will be generated using inquisitorial intervention.* Because disputants present their own cases in adversary legal procedures, Freedman (1970) suggested that they are driven through self-interest to present more information than a generally disinterested third party would elicit. In other words, adversaries try harder.

Finally, since in adversary intervention the manager listens passively to all sides of the dispute before making a decision, *managers using adversary intervention will be less likely to become prematurely biased and draw premature conclusions than will managers using inquisitorial intervention* (Adams, 1973). In contrast, more active third parties might find that the initial evidence favors one of the disputants and from that point on simply look for evidence confirming that initial impression, disregarding contrary facts. Thibaut, Walker, and Lind (Lind, 1975; Lind, Thibaut, & Walker, 1973; Thibaut, Walker, & Lind, 1972) have provided research evidence supporting these last two suggested strengths of the adversary legal procedure.

Similarly, the inquisitorial legal procedure, and thus presumably inquisitorial managerial intervention, has it strengths as well. First, *inquisitorial intervention will generate less distorted or biased information than adversary intervention will* (see Frank [1949] for a legal discussion, and Sheppard & Vidmar [1980] for research evidence). Adversaries may be equally driven by self-interest to present distorted or withhold harmful information as they are to generate more information, thus leaving the manager with potentially contradictory, unhelpful information. In addition, inquisitorial legal procedures appear to lead to less conflict during the resolution process than do adversary procedures (Sheppard, 1982a). Thus one final hypothesis to be drawn from legal research is that *inquisitorial intervention will result in less conflict during the resolution process than will adversary intervention.*

In summary, legal writing suggests at least five hypotheses that can begin to form the basis of a contingency model of managerial conflict intervention. In other words, there are some fairly clear suggestions regarding when inquisitorial intervention procedures might be preferred (i.e., when reduced conflict and information quality are important) and when adversary intervention procedures might be preferred (i.e., when perceived fairness, decision fairness, and information quantity are important).

A second way in which legal writing can aid thought about managerial conflict procedures is in terms of how legal procedures are modified to minimize the impact of their respective weaknesses. Most of this discussion is taken from Damaska (1973, 1975a, 1975b). Regarding the propensity for an active intervening party to conclude a case prematurely, many inquisitorial systems have included pretrial investigative reports and easier appeal processes to compensate. Easier access to higher court appeal than in the United States and even random review of lower court decisions is purported to caution lower court judges against drawing premature conclusions as well as permit a vehicle for redress if a premature decision has been made. In addition, the proper use of an unbiased pretrial investigative report should provide the inquisitor some reasonable idea about the range of information bearing upon a case and lessen any tendency to follow only one lead.

These same modifications are also directed at increasing the amount of information presented at a trial. The threat of higher court review should motivate thorough questioning by a judge. Also, investigators, whose performance evaluations are dependent upon the quality of the reports they file, are driven by self-interest to seek out information. In fact, there is some indication that more evidence is gathered by two neutral inquisitorial investigators than by two opposing adversary attorneys (Sheppard, 1982b).

Finally, as a partial remedy to the problem of perceived fairness, the disputants or their representatives are generally allowed to tell their side of the case in inquisitorial legal procedures. It appears that such an opportunity to present one's side, even without total control over half the trial and the questioning of witnesses, may be sufficient to ensure perceived fairness (Sheppard, in press). One final point regarding perceived fairness is that citizens in countries having inquisitorial procedures are much less likely to seek litigation as means to resolving a dispute (Hayden & Anderson, 1980). Therefore, the great loss of disputant control present in inquisitorial procedures occurs only for individuals who have shown a real incapacity to solve their own problems. Thus such limited disputant control is probably less unfair than in the United States, where more conflicts are brought to litigation.

Each of these variations in inquisitorial procedures can, with modification, be applied as ways of engineering the style of managers utilizing inquisitorial intervention strategies. Scott (1965), for example, discusses at length the sad absence of appeal procedures in most organizations. Managers can, without much loss of control, permit each disputant some time to give his or her piece. Employees or peers can be encouraged and taught how to solve their own disputes. Finally, as suggested earlier, more detailed early investigation of disputes brought to a manager is probably highly desirable to avoid premature, misguided solutions to disputes. Similarly, modifications to adversary intervention can be derived from studying variations of adversary trial procedures. For example, one reason for the development of strict rules of evidence in adversary legal systems is to compensate for some of the biases and distortions prevalent in these systems

(Wigmore, 1937). Managers should perhaps review the principles underlying evidentiary rules.

In conclusion, it appears that the study of managerial conflict intervention procedures can probably be improved by considering analogous procedures utilized in other settings. Clearly, wanton borrowing from other fields may be as harmful as ignoring the correspondence between conflict intervention in organizations and other settings. Analogues other than the law should also be examined, if only because not all managers act in a manner similar to judges (see Table 11.3, cells B, for example). However, if done judiciously, communication between dispute arenas should improve everyone's understanding.

REFERENCES

Adams, G. W. The small claims court and the adversary process: More problems of function and form. *The Canadian Bar Review,* 1973, *51,* 583-616.

Anderson, J. C. The impact of arbitration: A methodological assessment. *Industrial Relations,* 1981, *20,* 129-148.

Beer, M. The technology of organizational development. In M. D. Dunnette (Ed.), *The handbook of industrial organizational psychology.* Chicago: Rand McNally, 1976.

Blake, R. R., & Mouton, J. S. *The managerial grid.* Houston: Gulf, 1964.

Blake, R. R., Shepard, H. A., & Mouton, J. S. *Managing intergroup conflict in industry.* Ann Arbor: Foundation for Research on Human Behavior, 1964.

Damaska, M. Evidentiary barriers to conviction and two models of criminal procedure. *University of Pennsylvania Law Review,* 1973, *121,* 578-589.

Damaska, M. Presentation of evidence and factfinding precision. *University of Pennsylvania Law Review,* 1975, *123,* 1083-1106. (a)

Damaska, M. Structures of authority and comparative criminal procedure. *Yale Law Journal* 1975, *84,* 483-544. (b)

Deutsch, M. *The resolution of conflict.* New Haven: CT: Yale University Press, 1973.

Douglas, The peaceful settlement of industrial and intergroup disputes. *Journal of Conflict Resolution,* 1957, *1,* 69-81.

Filley, A. C. *Interpersonal conflict resolution.* Glenview, IL: Scott, Foresman, 1975.

Fisher, R. J. Third party consultation: A method for the study and resolution of conflict. *Journal of Conflict Resolution,* 1972, *16,* 67-95.

Folger, R. Distributive and procedural justice: Combined impact of voice and improvement on experienced inequity. *Journal of Personality and Social Psychology,* 1977, *35,* 109-119.

Frank, J. *Courts on trial.* Princeton, NJ: Princeton University Press, 1949.

Frankel, M. The search for truth: An umpireal view. *University of Pennsylvania Law Review,* 1975, *123,* 1031-1059.

Freedman, M. Professional responsibilities of the civil practitioner. In D. Wickstein (Ed.), *Education and the professional responsibilities of the lawyer.* Charlottesville: University Press of Virginia, 1970.

Fuller, L. The adversary system. In H. Borman (Ed.), *Talks on American law.* New York: Vintage Books, 1961.

Gottman, J. M. *Marital interaction: Experimental investigations.* New York: Academic, 1978.

Hayden, R. M., & Anderson, J. K. On the evaluation of procedural systems in laboratory experiments: A critique of Thibaut and Walker. *Law and Human Behavior,* 1980, *3,* 21-38.

Lind, E. A., Thibaut, J., & Walker, L. Discovery and presentation of evidence in adversary and non-adversary proceedings. *Michigan Law Review,* 1973, *71,* 1129-1144.

Lind, E. A. The exercise of information influence in legal advocacy. *Journal of Applied Social Psychology,* 1975, *5,* 127-143.

Lind, E. A. Procedural justice revisited. In T. Tyler (chair), *New directions in procedural justice research.* Symposium presented at Annual Meeting of the American Psychological Association, Toronto, 1982.

Lissak, R., & Sheppard, B. H. Criteria for choosing and evaluating dispute resolution procedure. *Journal of Applied Social Psychology,* in press.

Mintzberg, H. The manager's job: Fact and folklore. *Harvard Business Review,* 1975, *53*(4), 49-61.

Newman, H. R. Meditation and factfinding. In R. D. Helsby (Ed.), *Portrait of a process-collective negotiation in public employment.* Fort Washington, PA: Labor Relations Press, 1979.

Pondy, L. R. Organizational conflict: Concepts and models. *Administrative Sciences Quarterly,* 1967, *12,* 296-320.

Scott, W. *The management of conflict.* Homewood, IL: Irwin, 1965.

Sheppard, B. H. *Procedural aspects of police crisis intervention.* Paper presented at the Law and Society Association Annual Meeting, Toronto, Canada, 1982. (a)

Sheppard, B. H. Toward a comprehensive model of dispute intervention procedures. In T. Tyler (chair), *New directions in procedural justice research.* Symposium presented at Annual Meeting of the American Psychological Association, Toronto, 1982. (b)

Sheppard, B. H. Third party conflict intervention: A procedural framework. In B. M. Staw and L. L. Cummings (Eds.), *Research in organizational behavior,* Vol. 6. Greenwich, CT: JAI, in press.

Sheppard, B. H., Lesser, S., Li, C., & Mace, M. *Preliminary validation of a comprehensive framework of third party intervention procedures.* Unpublished manuscript, Duke University, 1982.

Sheppard, B. H., & Vidmar, N. Adversary pre-trial procedures and testimonial evidence: Effects of lawyer's role and machiavellianism. *Journal of Personality and Social Psychology,* 1980, *39,* 320-332.

Sheppard, B. H., & Vidmar, N. *Resolution of disputes: Some research and its implications for the legal process.* Invited address for Social Sciences Research Council Law and Psychology Conference, Trinity College, Oxford, England, 1982.

Thibaut, J., & Walker, L. *Procedural justice: A psychological analysis.* Hillsdale, NJ: Erlbaum, 1975.

Thibaut, J., & Walker, L. A theory of procedure. *California Law Review,* 1978, *66,* 541-566.

Thibaut, J., Walker, L., & Lind, E. A. An adversary presentation and bias in legal decisionmaking. *Harvard Law Review,* 1972, *86,* 386-401.

Thomas, K. Conflict and conflict management. In M. D. Dunnette (Ed.), *Handbook of industrial organizational psychology.* Chicago: Rand McNally, 1976.

Thomas, K. Manager and mediator: A comparison of third-party roles based upon conflict management goals. In G. Bomers & R. Peterson (Eds.), *Industrial relations and conflict management.* Amsterdam: Nijhof, 1982.

Torrow, W. W., & Pinto, P. R. The development of a managerial job taxonomy. *Journal of Applied Psychology,* 1976, *4,* 410-418.

Tyler, T. R., & Caine, A. The influence of outcomes and procedures on satisfaction with formal leaders. *Journal of Personality and Social Psychology,* 1981, *41,* 642-655.

Wall, J. A. Mediation: An analysis, review and proposed research. *Journal of Conflict Resolution,* 1981, *25,* 157-180.

Walton, R. E. *Interpersonal peacemaking: Confrontations and third party consultation.* Reading, MA: Addison-Welsey, 1969.

Walton, R. E., & Dutton, J. M. The management of interdepartmental conflict: A model and review. *Administrative Science Quarterly,* 1969, *14,* 73-84.

Wigmore, J. *The science of judicial proof.* Boston: Little, Brown, 1937.

Young, O. *The intermediaries: Third parties in international crises.* Princeton, NJ: Princeton University Press, 1967.

12

THE USE OF THIRD PARTIES IN ORGANIZATIONS
A Critical Response

Jeffrey Z. Rubin

Tufts University

A discussant's job is a bit like that confronting a solver of jigsaw puzzles. It is easy enough to remark upon the different shapes and sizes of the pieces; it is more interesting and challenging to find some way of fitting these pieces together. What makes this task particularly intriguing in the case of a set of essays is the fact that the individual pieces were not created with the intention of being fitted together in anything other than the most general fashion. In the private little world of the discussant, one never knows until the pieces are laid out on the table whether they will work easily into an integrated whole— or whether, perhaps, a Procrustean bed will be required instead.

It is in the spirit of this challenge that I am pleased to report that the four contributions in Part III of this volume are a puzzler's delight. Yes, there clearly are differences among the chapters; indeed, each is worthy of enjoyment in its own right. In addition, however, they conjointly provide an interesting picture of current assumptions and ideas about third-party intervention in organizational settings. These chapters thereby collectively offer some provisional suggestions for increasing the effectiveness of such interventions.

In keeping with the gestalt objectives of most puzzle solvers, this brief essay will comment on a few of the themes that appear to weave through two or more of the four contributions. Rather than focus on the numerous distinctive features of each chapter, I will comment instead on the implications of their collective form. I do so in the comforting knowledge that these individual essays are printed for one and all to see and to integrate as *they* see fit.

One final preliminary comment is necessary. Although organizational settings are the proper focus of this book, and third-party intervention in such settings is the focus of this part in particular, it would be unnecessarily restrictive to comment upon organizational implications alone. The following comments are therefore an amalgam of general observations about third-party intervention, generally, as well as about the nature of such intervention in organizational settings more specifically. These comments are summarized as a partial set of seven needs for further work.

NEED FOR AN "INTERVENTION ESPERANTO"

Third-party intervention in conflict takes place in an impressively diverse array of settings, ranging from the international arena to labor/management negotiations to intraorganizational disputes to the details of divorce mediation. Equally impressive is the absence of a common language that can be used to describe—in all these settings simultaneously—what it is exactly that third parties do. Indeed, there is not even agreement to this point about what constitutes a third party.

In this regard witness the definitions of a "third party" that appear in the four chapters. Sheppard describes a third party as "an initially uninvolved party who later intervenes to help manage the dispute." (Why must such a person be uninvolved initially? What about the numerous instances in international politics of third parties who intervene effectively despite involvement from the outset?) Notz, Starke, and Atwell, although never explicitly defining a third party, seem to have in mind an individual who is superior in power to the disputants and who imposes some sort of compromise upon them. (What about the many third parties who lack such superior clout and who nevertheless intervene, often with great effectiveness?) Brett and Goldberg's analysis proceeds from the assumption that there are two traditional third-party roles, that of facilitator/counselor (who encourages autonomy) and that of adjudicator (who imposes settlement). But what about fact finders? Or go-betweens? Clearly our efforts to understand the nature of effective third-party intervention will be influenced by our preliminary assumptions about the nature of the beast.

NEED FOR A BETTER ACCOUNT OF HOW THIRD PARTIES INTERVENE

To be sure, the shared objective of those of us who are interested in dispute settlement is to find ways of enhancing third-party effectiveness. Even as this quest continues, however, it is essential that better descriptions be obtained of what it is, exactly, that third parties actually *do.* There are many wise men and women around these days, each of whom is a world's expert regarding some particular anatomical part of the great elephant. What we sorely need are more people with expertise (even if it is lesser expertise) about the contours of the beast as a whole.

To this end, I am particularly impressed by the taxonomy proposed in Sheppard's chapter. A direct descendant of the Thibaut and Walker (1975) framework for analyzing procedural justice, Sheppard's taxonomy provides a more ambitious, elaborate, and comprehensive system that can be used to locate virtually all forms of third-party intervention. Like all taxonomies, this one invites attention to both of those factors that have been chosen for inclusion—as well as those stepchildren that have been left out in the cold. (The Sheppard analysis, for example, proposes a series of stages—definition, argumentation, decision, and finally reconciliation—that all intervention procedures move through. But such a framework, although useful, oversimplifies what is in fact probably more often a cyclical arrangement, let alone a pattern that may be entirely different.)

Nevertheless, when all is said and done, Sheppard's taxonomy of third-party intervention is impressive because of the many behaviors that can be readily coded using this system—and the reliability with which such coding can apparently be accomplished. Given my interest in the emergence of an Intervention Esperanto, the Sheppard taxonomy is most encouraging. To repeat, the idea is not to explain why some interventions work better than others; this important concern must be addressed continually. Rather, the idea is to find some common language that can be used to describe interventions across the enormous variety and number of settings in which they occur. Sheppard's taxonomy constitutes a significant step in this direction.

NEED FOR MORE RUNGS ON THE ESCALATORY LADDER

In their treatment of grievance mediation, Brett and Goldberg do a compelling job of arguing for the virtues of introducing mechanisms that retard the rate of escalation in disputes. As conflicts escalate, there is a powerful tendency for the disputants to make positional commitments from which they are subsequently unable or unwilling to extricate themselves. It is as if once an escalating conflict develops a momentum of its own, the protagonists become captives of the system, unable to find a perch from which they can spring to escape without being skinned alive. What is needed, therefore, is some mechanism for increasing the number of rungs on the escalatory ladder, and the grievance mediation system described by Brett and Goldberg suggests one route for accomplishing this objective.

Brett and Goldberg describe an arrangement in the bituminous coal industry that requires a conflict to move through a number of stages before being settled through arbitration. Thus the lodging of a complaint is followed by review by a mine committee; the grievance is then referred to representatives of union and management before (assuming voluntary mediation is chosen) a mediator first attempts to help find a mutually satisfactory solution and then—if necessary—gives an oral advisory opinion about how the dispute is likely to be settled if it goes to arbitration. Then, and only then, after the dispute has failed to be settled at any one of these many junctures along the way, does the dispute go to arbitration. To repeat, the general importance of this grievance procedure is that it suggests a way in which escalatory increments can be built into a dispute settlement system. And as the findings of Brett and Goldberg's research amply indicate, the effect of increasing the number of rungs is to bring more disputes to settlement at less cost in time, money, and emotion.

NEED FOR A LIGHT INTERVENTION TOUCH

I have argued elsewhere (Rubin, 1980, 1981) that there is likely to be an inverse relationship between the amount of control a third party exercises in an effort to forge an agreement and the degree to which that agreement is deep-seated and long lasting. In general, the rule of thumb here appears to be: apply as little power as is necessary in order to move the disputants out of deadlock toward a settlement of their differences.

The rationale underlying this generalization is that people in conflict generally want to be in control of their own fate—not always, mind you, but often enough that such a sentiment must be taken into account in devising an intervention regimen. Agreements that disputants reach as a result of third-party leverage are likely to work, but only so long as such leverage is applied on a continual basis. When disputants come to agreement because of third-party pressure or imposition of a settlement, their motivation may best be characterized as extrinsic: They have done so because they were forced to or because they were rewarded for doing so. In contrast, when disputants reach agreement of their own accord, their motivation is intrinsic: They have done so not because they had to but because—based on a appraisal of the situation—they chose to. Under these circumstances, it is not only the disputants' behavior that may be modified but also the attitudes underlying this behavior—and the result may well be an involvement and set of insights into the underlying process that makes more likely an agreement that will endure.

Brett and Goldberg argue convincingly for the importance of a light intervention touch. Mediation does not simply work as well as arbitration in the coal industry; it works better. This finding is particularly impressive in light of the mediators' brief and informal training in their role. Similarly, Sheppard observes that the heavy-handed "inquisitorial" style of many managers may work in the short term, but it often fails in the long run. I was particularly struck in this regard by the observation of the mediator studied by Brett and Goldberg who reported trying to bring disputants to negotiate by trying to "advise the weaker party of the weakness of its position" while trying "to avoid advising the stronger of its strength." Analogously, perhaps what we need to do is find some way of advising powerful third parties not to use the leverage they have available to them—while simultaneously reminding relatively weak third parties of the need to devise procedures that involve the disputants in the settlement of their own conflict.

NEED TO EDUCATE THIRD PARTIES

Should anyone have doubted this fact, these chapters make amply clear the fact that dispute intervention is what Fisher and Ury (1981) described as a "growth industry." Wall and Schiller point out that the court system is overloaded with civil cases and that there is an ever-increasing need to find ways of mediating out-of-court settlements. Such negotiated settlements stand to benefit both the clients and the court system in a variety of ways—quality and cost of agreement reached, degree of control afforded the disputants themselves, and so forth—each of which is articulated by Wall and Schiller.

Similarly, in their analysis of resource allocation conflicts, Notz, Starke, and Atwell point out that organizations are typically characterized by the existence of a number of domains in which conflicts habitually arise. Among other things, these conflicts typically focus on the setting of organizational goals, the distribution of budgetary resources, and the differences of interest among the organization's subgroups. Notz, Starke, and Atwell go on to observe that these conflicts, endemic to organizations, are exacerbated by the continual dwindling of economic resources. This is an exceedingly important point, one that merits attention in its own right. As organizational resources decline, already existing tendencies to compete in a variety of ways will be greatly amplified—placing greater pressure than ever before on those individuals who can intervene effectively in intra-organizational disputes.

But if dispute intervention is a growth industry, as evidenced by an overloaded court system and organizations that are confronted with dwindling resources, then what of the third-party interveners themselves? Effective intervention is clearly necessary, but has it been forthcoming? The answer, at least as indicated in three of the four essays presented here, apparently is no. Wall and Schiller point out that judges occupy an extremely powerful and influential position; their role is whatever they want it to be. Yet despite this possibility for significant input, the preliminary indications in the Wall and Schiller chapter are that judges are uncertain about what they ought to do as third parties. Even though judges seem to know that they should intervene in an effort to avoid costly court trials, they seem reluctant to do so and instead tend to adopt a relatively passive position. Clearly, these judges, and the lawyers who appear before them, need to be better informed about the range of options available to them—some of which are inappropriately heavy-handed in a legal system, to be sure, but other techniques that might well help move protagonists toward out-of-court settlements.

Similarly, the evidence presented by Sheppard, and implied in the Notz, Starke, and Atwell chapter, indicates that managers in organizational settings are using their considerable clout as interveners to impose agreements rather than help disputants find solutions for themselves. The so-called "inquisitorial" style that characterizes the most frequently used managerial intervention procedure relies, writes Sheppard, on the heavy-handed practice of "enforcing a decision much like a benevolent parent." The next and most popular procedure is one in which managers imply that positive incentives will be forthcoming, or negative incentives withheld, if agreement is reached. Note that once again the managerial assumption seems to be one of "me chief, you Indian"; the forms of intervention used most frequently rely on managerial imposition of their greater power.

As I argued earlier in this essay, such heavy-handed intervention tactics are likely to prove effective in the short run but are apt to be quite ineffectual in the long term. What is needed, therefore, is some way to educate the likely interveners in organizational settings about both the probable effects of their interventions and some ways of doing things a bit differently. The key to such educational attempts, I suggest, will be to relate them to managers' current interests and inclinations. As implied by Sheppard, and also by the Notz, Starke, and Atwell chapter, managers appear to intervene as heavily as they do because they do not see any reason to do things differently. They have the power to impose agreement, they do not wish to take the time necessary to intervene more patiently, and they are used to settling the disputes that arise in the brisk fashion of a "decisive" person. Why should they change?

They should change because a heavy-handed intervention style is likely to settle differences only in the short run. Managers need to be shown that it is in *their* long-term interest to utilize intervention techniques that are more likely to involve the disputants as autonomous actors who must reconcile their own differences. The intraorganizational conflict described by Notz, Starke, and Atwell makes it all the more important that interventions be found that are likely to do more than extinguish the latest brush fire. When the number of such conflagrations is on the rise, it is in the firefighters' interest to develop a more effective means of combating them. As Brett and Goldberg point out, dispute settlements that occur through relatively light-fingered mediational efforts are likely to be more durable and less costly, and they may well enhance disputants' satisfaction and morale as well.

NEED TO TAILOR INTERVENTIONS TO THE INTENSITY OF CONFLICT

In our forthcoming book, Dean Pruitt and I argue that conflict intensity is a dimension of great importance, one that must carefully be taken into account in planning third-party intervention. Laboratory research over the last several years has amply indicated, for example, that interventions that prove effective when conflict is at a relatively low level of intensity may prove ineffectual—or may even backfire— in the throes of a more intense exchange (see Deutsch & Krauss, 1962; Erickson, Holmes, Fey, Walker, & Thibaut, 1974; Johnson, 1967; Krauss & Deutsch, 1966; Rubin, 1980).

This general observation is applicable to several of the chapters in Part III. Thus I was struck by the apparent inconsistencies of Brett and Goldberg's recommendations on the one hand, and Notz, Starke, and Atwell's on the other. Brett and Goldberg make a strong case for the virtues of an approach that introduces additional rungs into the escalatory ladder—thereby inviting the disputants to terminate the conflict before positional commitments become excessive. In contrast, Notz, Starke, and Atwell speak to the virtues of a deterrent approach to dispute settlement. This position, a bit analogous to the stance of deterrence theorists in international affairs, asserts that a third party who wishes to prod disputants into reaching agreement should confront them with the specter of costs that each side will wish to avoid. This is the essential rationale behind the dispute settlement procedure known as final offer arbitration, whose effectiveness has been well documented by Notz and Starke over the past few years. In effect, FOA assumes that the *fewer* the rungs on the escalatory ladder, the greater the possible cost of not reaching agreement and, therefore, the more likely the disputants are to settle.

My simple, integrative bit of commentary with regard to the apparently discrepant advice suggested by these two chapters is that both are true—depending on the intensity of conflict. When escalation is in its early stages and the accompanying conflict intensity is relatively small, it makes considerable sense to introduce additional rungs on the escalatory ladder: the more, the better. On the other hand, if and when it happens that the conflict escalates out of control—or is very likely to do so—it may be necessary to put an end to the conflict—even if only in the short term—in any way possible. It is at this point that FOA is likely to have its day in the sun.

Similarly, when conflict is of relatively low intensity, it may be advisable to follow Brett and Goldberg's suggestion of "expanding the scope of the issue in dispute." In this way, the disputants may be encouraged to examine the underlying issues in their conflict and to devise ideas that not only settle the conflict but resolve it. On the other hand, when conflict is protracted or exacerbated, it may make more sense to follow another bit of Brett and Goldberg's advice: "Narrow the scope of the issue in dispute." By tackling specific issues that appear to be workable or soluable, it may be possible to generate momentum toward settlement that would otherwise not occur. Similarly, by focusing on short-term agreements—which do not involve the establishment of precedents that each side prefers to avoid—movement toward settlement may once again be generated.

NEED TO TAILOR INTERVENTIONS
TO THE SYSTEM'S FLEXIBILITY

One final comment, this one stimulated by the Sheppard chapter. As his analysis of the inquisitorial and adversarial legal systems makes clear, there are often structural constraints in a system that make it unlikely, even impossible, to modify dramatically the ways in which intervention occurs. When such conditions obtain—when intervention styles are intractable, when systems do not tolerate extensive modification, and so forth—the best that can be hoped for is a bit of tinkering here and there in an effort to modify the system ever so slightly. As suggested by Sheppard, these techniques may entail finding ways of weakening the absolute grip of a powerful third party, perhaps by making this person accountable to others in the system, possibly by providing this person with a welter of objective information that is difficult to overlook or circumvent, and so forth. Similarly, there may be ways to shore up, at least temporarily, the credibility and persuasive powers of a relatively low status, low power third party.

Finally, if a third party or a third-party role is simply not modifiable, even to the slightest degree, it may be possible to invent new third parties for purposes of intervention. To take but one example, if organizational managers as described by Sheppard turn out to be intractably inquisitorial in their intervention methods (something that I very much doubt will prove to be the case since, as I have argued, it is in their interests to change their behavior), it is time to consider different possibilities for organizational intervention. These may be outside consultants who ride into town as needed, do their work, are paid, and then disappear into the sunset. Or they may be joint commissions or panels. And so forth, and so on, as far as the mind can reach. Since dispute intervention is, indeed, a growth industry, it stands to reason that those of us with an interest in this process should be continually vigilant about the possibilities of new and more effective techniques for moving people to a settlement of their differences.

REFERENCES

Deutsch, M., & Krauss, R. M. Studies of interpersonal bargaining. *Journal of Conflict Resolution,* 1962, *6,* 52-76.

Erickson, B., Holmes, J. G., Frey, R., Walker, L., & Thibaut, J. Functions of a third party in the resolution of conflict: The role of a judge in pretrial conferences. *Journal of Personality and Social Psychology,* 1974, *30,* 293-306.

Fisher, R., & Ury, W. *Getting to yes: Negotiating agreement without giving in.* Boston: Houghton Mifflin, 1981.

Johnson, D. W. Use of role reversal in intergroup competition. *Journal of Personality and Social Psychology,* 1967, *7,* 135-141.

Krauss, R. M., & Deutsch, M. Communication in interpersonal bargaining. *Journal of Personality and Social Psychology,* 1966, *4,* 572-577.

Pruitt, D. G., & Rubin, J. Z. *Social conflict: Escalation, impasse, and settlement.* Reading, MA: Addison-Wesley, in press.

Rubin, J. Z. Experimental research on third-party intervention in conflict: Toward some generalizations. *Psychological Bulletin,* 1980, *87,* 379-391.

Rubin, J. Z. (Ed.). *Dynamics of third party intervention: Kissinger in the Middle East.* New York: Praeger, 1981.

Thibaut, J. W., & Walker, L. *Procedural justice: A psychological analysis.* New York: John Wiley, 1975.

—IV—

NEGOTIATIONS IN THE ORGANIZATIONAL ENVIRONMENT

13

ORGANIZATIONAL MICROCOSMS AND IDEOLOGICAL NEGOTIATION

L. David Brown

Boston University

Jane Covey Brown

Institute for Development Research

This chapter examines negotiations in organizations that reflect forces in the larger society. All organizations to some extent, and some organizations to a large extent, replicate in microcosm salient features of their environments. We will argue that intraorganizational bargaining rests in large part on shared ideologies, that ideological consensus in organizations may be undercut by changes in the larger society, and that ideological negotiations differ in important ways from bargaining over resource distributions or task definitions. Ideological negotiation is quite common in organizations such as churches or political parties that rely on ideological motivations and integration mechanisms. But many organizations historically free from ideological dissensus may become subject to ideological negotiation in the near future. Better understanding of the characteristics and management implications of ideological conflict will then be highly useful.

This exploration is based on our work in a variety of contexts where ideologies contribute importantly to organizational functioning. The chapter raises more issues about ideological negotiation than it resolves, for our understanding of the issues and their implications at this point remains rudimentary. First, we examine organizations as microcosms of the larger societies within which they are embedded. Then we discuss organizational ideologies and their impact on bargaining inside the organization. Characteristics of ideological negotiation are described in the third section, and ideas about the management of ideological conflict are proposed in the fourth. Finally, the relevance of ideological negotiation to hitherto immune organizations and a research agenda are suggested.

ORGANIZATIONS AS MICROCOSMS
OF EXTERNAL CONTEXTS

Organizations that are dependent on external origins of resources often map important aspects of their external environments onto their internal structures and processes. Consider the following case:

> The Relief and Development Agency (RADA) is devoted to promoting development and alleviating catastrophes in the poorest populations in the Third World. Although its initial goals were focused on disaster relief, it has become increasingly concerned with promoting equity, encouraging self-reliance and self-help, and catalyzing local participation and control in development projects. The agency and its members are strongly committed to social justice, self-determination, and Third World development.

> RADA does not accept money from governments. Its financial support comes from corporations, foundations, and individuals, and from fund drives that generate support from many small donors.

> In pursuit of its relief and development goals, RADA undertakes a number of activities. It promotes grassroots relief and development projects that are intended to promote long-run local participation and

self-reliance. It undertakes educational campaigns in affluent countries to raise awareness of development needs and issues. It also works to influence media, governments, and public opinion on behalf of Third World development and social justice.

Rapid growth over the last several years has expanded RADA's full-time staff from about a dozen to more than fifty. The new personnel are educationally, ethnically, and nationally diverse, and many of them are not initially familiar with the goals and activities of the agency. Departments charged with fund-raising, overseas projects, administration, policy research, and development education have been created to handle diverse task and external constituencies.

Problems with decision making and interpersonal conflict within the agency have also emerged in recent years. It is no longer clear that all the staff agree about the organization's basic goals and policies. There have been departmental coordination problems, and there are rumblings about organizing a staff union among some lower-level employees.

One interpretation of RADA's recent history is the internal conflicts and ambiguities about organizational ideologies are simply "growing pains" that might be experienced by any expanding organization, quite independent of external pushes or pulls. But the most disruptive internal conflicts have focused on issues of development ideology and white racism—ideological issues that have generated intense controversy in the larger environment. We believe that many of RADA's internal organizational problems are a microcosmic reflection of its relations with the outside world. These relations are influenced by rapid growth, but growth alone does not account for the ideological content of the issues raised.

Microcosmic reproductions of external issues may be explicit or implicit, intentional or unplanned. At least three factors contribute to microcosm creation: (1) personnel characteristics and loyalties, (2) divisions of labor among departments, and (3) direct intervention by external agencies. Each of these factors influences events at RADA and is discussed briefly below.

Concerns from the larger society may be brought into the organizations by personnel who are new or closely linked to diverse reference groups in the larger environment. New personnel may bring different characteristics that were previously unrepresented in the organization; RADA's success called for more clerical staff, and the new workers came from different social and educational backgrounds than did previous staff. Some new clerical staff resented being excluded from overseas travel; others thought the development concerns of many staff members naively idealistic. Staff diversity can replicate societal tensions, such as concerns about discrimination on the basis of gender and race (Knowles & Prewitt, 1969). RADA personnel came from many racial and national backgrounds, and many lower-level personnel wondered whether their largely white male superiors were biased on race and gender grounds.

Microcosms may also be produced by divisions of labor. Different tasks and specialties may, in themselves, encourage departmental differences in perspective and interests (Lawrence & Lorsch, 1967). Organizations with diverse external constituencies often require departments to maintain close relations with very different groups. Effective RADA fund raisers empathize with affluent donors; effective project organizers are committed to the interests of the Third World poor; effective lobbyists with governments are political realists; effective public relations requires attention to "newsworthiness." These perspectives are sometimes consistent, but RADA departments often disagree about what should be done, reproducing between departments the relational characteristic of the different external constituencies.

Issues from the larger context may also appear in the organization as a consequence of direct intervention by outside forces (Pfeffer & Salancik, 1978). Issues that mobilize strong feelings in the larger society may result in external pressures on organizations, such as demands to provide equal opportunities for disadvantaged groups or to meet community standards for health and safety. RADA's spectacular growth was largely the consequence of increased funds tied to its leadership role in dealing with a widely recognized emergency in the Third World. The agency also is subject to pressures from governments—from varying degrees of disapproval from U.S. authorities to physical attacks on its staff by Third World regimes.

In short, organizations often mirror concerns and reproduce in microcosm conflicts that are salient in their environments. The resulting disputes and dynamics may be seen as central to organizational tasks and get much attention, or they may be perceived as peripheral distractions to be avoided or suppressed with minimum costs in time and energy. Some of the most important and least understood negotiations in organizational microcosms involve the ways in which individuals and organizations explain and evaluate their experiences—negotiations over individual and organizational ideologies.

ORGANIZATIONAL IDEOLOGIES

The concept of ideology has a long and lurid history, but only recently has it come into the foreground in organization theory. Definitions of ideology abound. Some investigators seem to equate ideology with organizational culture: Starbuck (1982, p. 3), for example, defines ideology as "logically integrated clusters of beliefs, values, rituals and symbols." Others have somewhat more limited definitions, such as "a relatively coherent set of beliefs that bind some people together and explain their worlds in terms of cause-and-effect relations" (Beyer, 1981, p. 166). For the purposes of this chapter, ideologies are defined as *sets of beliefs that provide explanations for phenomena, suggest appropriate actions, and bind together their adherents* (Beyer, 1981; Diesing, 1982).

Each aspect of this definition is important. First, ideologies provide beliefs about critical variables and cause-and-effect relations that explain events. RADA staff believe, for example, that exploitive social forces best explain the conditions of Third World poor (as opposed to theories about the apathy or inadequate skills of poor individuals). Such ideological explanations provide bases for action and understanding. Second, ideologies have evaluative and perscriptive components that differentiate among alternative actions. RADA ideology prescribes change strategies that will help poor people help themselves (rather than aid to upper classes that will eventually "trickle down" to the rural poor). These prescriptions define problems and provide criteria for their solution. Third, ideologies also have a social consequence—they bind together individuals who share them: Economists work best with other economists who share similar theories (Diesing, 1982), and RADA overseas staff understand each other more easily than they do their fund-raising colleagues. Common ideologies help define and unite social groups.

Although ideologies have prescriptive implications, they are not the same as values. Values are sets of normative preferences for actions and outcomes (Beyer, 1981) and constitute more general and abstract concepts. Ideologies provide explanations for situations and guidelines for attaining values (Lodge, 1975)—they offer connections between abstract statements of "the good" and concrete expressions of "reality." The same events take on different meanings in different ideological perspectives. For example, managers explain work redesigns as "efforts to improve the quality of work life," and union leaders argue that the same redesigns require "more work for the same pay." Management and union may (or may not) agree on the *value* of workers having a high quality of life but differ ideologically about how that value may be achieved. Management and union ideologies offer different perspectives on work redesign, and those perspectives may bind managers and unions together as groups at the cost of ideologically based conflict with each other.

What are *organizational* ideologies? There has been little research on organizational ideologies in comparison with the attention devoted to organizational technologies, structure, or environments. But organizations develop sets of beliefs that explain events, prescribe and justify actions, and hold their memberships together. Beyer (1981) reviewed a volume of literature to analyze the impact of ideologies and values on organizational decision-making processes. Starbuck (1982) argued that ideological factors outweigh the impacts of structure and technology for organizations in crisis. Shared beliefs about the organization, its role, and relevant cause-and-effect relations is probably universal, though the impact of such ideologies on events and behavior probably varies widely across situations.

Organizational ideologies are seldom, if ever, established by explicit intention. The *sources* of organizational ideology are both internal and external. Some components of organizational ideology are rooted in beliefs and concerns of the larger culture; other components come from external developments in technology and theory relevant to organizational goals. Heginbotham (1975), for example, found that the ideologies that shaped activity in Indian development agencies were rooted in Indian and British cultures and in traditional and modern theories of development. Many difficulties in promoting development policies sprang from internal ideological conflicts, and those conflicts were based in cultural traditions and prespectives on development imported from the environment.

Other components of organizational ideology emerge from attributes internal to the organization, such as leadership, divisions of labor, and operating technology. Organizational leadereship shapes future ideologies by creating myths, rituals, and languages by which organization members will subsequently interpret and evaluate events (Pettigrew, 1979). Strauss's (1982) analysis of psychiatric services within a large hospital stresses the interactive process by which technologies and interpersonal relations create a "negotiated order" of beliefs and prescriptions about effective patient care and appropriate therapy that is unique to each service unit.

External and internal sources together produce organizational ideologies, and those ideologies provide the ground against which interests are negotiated in organizational decision making. Beliefs shared by opposing interests limit and shape conflict between them. Collective bargaining, for example, is more productive when the parties recognize each other's legitimacy (management accepts the importance of unionization; unions accept the importance of private enterprise) and do not hold ideologies that are seriously incompatible (National Planning Association, 1953, reported in Deutsch, 1973, pp. 380-381). On the other hand, very different explanations and evaluations of the situation are associated with escalating conflict (Blake & Mouton, 1961; Sherif, 1966). Thus organizational ideologies that are widely shared may limit acceptable tactics by parties and constrain conflict escalation.

All organizations evolve some minimal ideological definitions of events and concerns, but ideological elements vary in their importance for shaping and controlling member behavior. Etzioni (1961) distinguished three bases for organizational control: coercive, utilitarian, and normative. Prisons emphasize *coercive control,* using physical sanctions to extract compliance from prisoners. Industrial organizations more often emphasize *utilitarian control,* offering combinations of rewards and punishments in exchange for employee compliance. Churches typically employ *normative control,* shaping the behavior of members and staff by appeal to common values and beliefs. Ideologies are central to motivating and coordinating activity in organizations that rely on normative control, since they provide the crucial link between values and action. Health systems, for example, rely on a "negotiated order" of shared values, ideologies, and expectations to shape interaction among diverse subunits (Strauss, 1978; Day & Day, 1977). Educational organizations (Pettigrew, 1980) and agencies that promote development in disadvantaged populations (e.g., Heginbotham, 1975; Brown, 1980b) also depend on common values and ideologies for organizational cohesion and coordination.

CHARACTERISTICS OF IDEOLOGICAL NEGOTIATION

Definitions and Example

Negotiation is one process by which decisions and agreements are reached. Alternatives include persuasion, education, manipulation, appeal to rules or authoirty, and coercion. Negotiation brings together two or more parties with differing interests in a voluntary exchange of proposals and counterproposals in order to establish agreement about their expectations of each other (see Rubin & Brown, 1975; Strauss, 1978). Negotiations are particularly important when these alternative processes will not work: when the parties have conflicting interests, so that education and persuasion will not produce agreement; when shared rules or authorities do not exist to produce agreement; or when the information available and power equalities do not allow manipulation or coercion.

Ideological negotiations present special problems, for they may challenge fundamental explanations and evaluations of organizational realities or reshape basic assumptions about how organizational activities—including negotiations themselves—should be carried on. Consider some of the controversies at the Relief and Development Agency.

By 1982, the Relief and Development Agency had nearly quadrupled the size of its staff. Many highly skilled and educated new staff members chose to work for RADA because of its ideology and values, even though the material rewards it could offer were modest. But RADA staff began to experience considerable internal turmoil as these new staff members tried to work together.

Some employees felt that many staff members, particularly the white males who dominated upper-level management, were at best insensitive to the concerns of women and blacks. Lower-level staff reported feeling ignored as people by some managers. Some black employees were particularly outraged by an anonymous "humorous" memo that made joking reference to South Africa—a reference that reflected in the eyes of some readers an insensitivity to the oppression suffered by South Africa's black population.

Many employees felt that RADA did not practice its own preaching—that it failed to live up to its own ideology in its internal management. They argued that organizational commitments to equity and equality, for example, were inconsistent with the large salary differences that separated upper and lower echelons: The lowest salary was reported to be only a little more than one-quarter the highest.

More important, lower-level employees felt that organizational governance and decision making violated its oft-expressed commitment to participative decision making. "Peruvian peasants participate more in RADA decisions than we do," claimed one secretary. Lower-level staff especially wanted to participate in decisions that directly affected their work, such as redefinition of work responsibilities and performance evaluations. These staff members had begun to meet together informally, and with encouragement from management they elected representatives to a staff advisory committee, which was charged with identifying and raising issues of concern to employees.

Forms and Consequences of Ideological Negotiation

The controversy at RADA brought together groups—black females and white males, clerical workers and managers—with quite different ideological perspectives on organizational governance and rewards. There is a long history of racism in U.S. society, and the life experiences of whites (particularly white males) and blacks produce very different explanations and evaluations for race relations (Alderfer, 1982). These different ideologies influence events in many organizations beyond RADA. Similarly, some development ideologies emphasize growth and efficiency while others emphasize equity and equality, and debates about the distribution of power and resources within RADA mirror worldwide controversies over development strategies (Goulet, 1977).

Ideological negotiations may take at least two forms. In some cases negotiations involve *direct* discussion of ideological differences, such as the employee accusation that RADA managers espouse participation in the field but act autocratically in the organization. Direct negotiation of ideological differences can produce changed explanations and prescriptions. Negotiation can clarify differences and similarities between field and organizational situations at RADA and so illuminate how much participation is appropriate in both. Direct ideological negotiations may become debates over value positions, which are difficult to resolve (Fisher, 1964). Even in the relatively concrete context of managing RADA, satisfactory resolution of the debate over growth and efficiency versus equity and equality cannot be easily achieved.

A second pattern for handling ideological differences is *indirect* negotiations that employ specific issues as surrogates for ideological differences. Agreement on specific behaviors or decisions can have ideological significance to one or both parties, and ideological concessions or low-visibility changes may be achieved without explicit debate of beliefs and prescriptions. Black personnel at RADA, for example, felt ignored and unheard by many white male managers, and they attributed this problem to white racism. The managers, on the other hand, sincerely believed that there was no serious "racism problem" in the organization. Like other white males, RADA managers often conceived race-related problems in terms of individual characteristics rather than institutional forces (Alderfer, 1982). Under these conditions it was difficult for black employees and white managers to discuss directly, let alone resolve, their differences in explanation or evaluation of racial events. The blacks focused instead on the issue of recognition. They successfully altered managers' behavior—though not their ideology—when senior managers voluntarily joined a group of black secretaries, actively listened to their concerns, and visibly thought about the issues raised. The leader of the black secretaries later expressed delight that she had been "heard" by managers for the first time.

Characteristics of Ideological Negotiations

Ideological negotiations have some special characteristics derived from the particular character of ideologies. In this section we suggest characteristics of ideological negotiations rooted in external pressures.

Characteristic 1: Ideological disputes strongly felt in the larger society promote external agency involvement in intraorganizational negotiations. Organizational ideologies are at least partially based in societal contexts, so negotiations within organizations may be significant to external agencies. External constituencies may support or undermine organizational groups that represent ideological positions. Although RADA staff generally adopted equity and equality views of development, much of the organization's financial support came from donors more interested in relief activities. Donors committed to growth and efficiency or to disaster relief would not always support development work clearly committed to radical social change.

Sometimes ideologically based groups in organizations seek assistance from external supporters to protect themselves or to gain organizational influence. The staff advisory committee at RADA, for example, began to send minutes of committee meetings directly to the RADA Board of Trustees, so their concerns would be clearly understood (and perhaps supported) by board members.

Even when external parties are not directly involved in ideological disputes in organizations, their potential for involvement may influence the course of negotiations. RADA employees joked about how newspapers would love a story about a RADA clerical union and how damaging such reports would be to the organization's image. Ideological negotiations that involve microcosms of larger issues are particularly vulnerable to influence from and exploitation by external agencies.

Chacteristic 2: Ideological negotiations are subject to misunderstandings based on inconsistent explanations. Ideologies provide explanations of causes and effects that are important to organizations and their members—a "paradigm" in Kuhn's (1962) sense that defines variables and relationships relevant to understanding events. The connotations of an event may be very different when explained in different ideological frameworks, and such cognitive differences can make agreement difficult (Alexander, 1979). White male managers, for example, often emphasize individual merit and hard work in explaining organizational rank and success; black secretaries at RADA, in contrast, were highly aware of social and institutional factors that hamper organizational success for minorities.

When parties operate from inconsistent explanations, misunderstandings are inevitable. Cognitive differences may be complicated by unsynchronized recognitions of ideological differences. Cultural minorities or lower power participants in organizations recognize ideological differences earlier than do dominant groups, and the latter may be greatly surprised by ideological challenges (Brown, 1982). White males, in RADA as elsewhere, are often the last to recognize how their explanations for race and gender relations differ from those of women or blacks (Alderfer, 1982). Such unrecognized or misunderstood differences can produce unexpected explosions and instabilities in ideological negotiations.

Characteristic 3: Ideological negotiations are subject to distortion based on divergent prescriptions and evaluations. The prescriptive element of ideologies can generate powerful distortions of information exchanged in ideological negotiations. Research suggests that groups in conflict develop evaluations and prescriptions that are biased in favor of themselves and against their opponents (Blake & Mouton, 1961). Managers and clerical workers in RADA developed emotionally charged and value-laden stereotypes of each other: some workers described managers as "Stalinist" or "autocrats," while some managers saw workers as "crazy" or "incompetent." Such stereotypes can be used to justify aggressive tactics and to further distort new information. Strongly held normative positions make ideological negotiations particularly subject to information distortion (Diesing, 1982).

Negotiations that involve ideological prescriptions easily evolve into disputes over values, and value conflicts are notoriously difficult to resolve (Fisher, 1964). Ideological discussions at RADA often included inflammatory evaluations: Lower-level personnel spoke of manager "hypocrisy," and managers spoke of lower-level "naivete." Such judgments tend to increase the stakes of negotiation and the emotional involvement of the parties.

Characteristic 4: Ideological negotiations are subject to emotional polarizations based on threats to group cohesion. Ideologies bind together their adherents and provide integrating beliefs and prescriptions. Ideological challenges can therefore threaten the internal cohesion of parties as well as their evaluations and prescriptions for operating in the organization. Alderfer (1982) found that white male academics protected each other from challenges to their behavior and implicitly racist ideology. When ideology provides a uniting force for adherents who wish to remain cohesive, ideological challenge may evoke emotional responses based on strong group identifications.

Challenge to organizational ideology in RADA gathered momentum after clerical staff began to meet regularly, and a staff advisory committee was elected. The clerical group and (to a lesser extent) the committee developed common explanations and evaluations of their situation, and their ideological solidarity enabled them to challenge management. Initial management disarray became ideologically clarified as a senior management group began to meet regularly. Thus the third aspect of ideology—its binding quality—also shapes ideological negotiations, endowing those interactions with energies derived from group solidarity as well as from information and evaluations from different ideological perspectives.

Taken together these factors suggest that ideological negotiations can be more problematic than other forms of negotiation. External party involvement, explanatory misunderstandings, distorted evaluations and prescriptions, and emotional investments based in group dynamics can combine to make ideological negotiations particularly complex. They may be especially subject to escalation, on the one hand, as parties become emotionally polarized and increasingly competitive. Or they may be especially subject to suppression, on the other, as parties become less willing to deal with differences explicitly and become more selectively "blind" to their existence.

Contexts of Ideological Negotiation

Ideological negotiations, like other decision processes, occur within *negotiating contexts* derived from histories of past interactions and decisions. Individuals and group representatives have beliefs and expectations about the negotiation process itself—the extent to which accurate information will be exchanged, the trustworthiness of other parties, the utility of different bargaining tactics, the likelihood that agreements will be kept. These beliefs and expectations are a consequence of previous negotiation experience (Strauss, 1978). The *process* of negotiation affects expectations for the future as well as immediate agreements or disagreements.

The context of negotiations is shaped by both direct and indirect negotiation of ideological issues. When lower-echelon RADA staff directly questioned the fit between organizational ideologies and compensation differences, they implicitly raised a question about the negotiability of such issues. Management's (somewhat reluctant) willingness to discuss the issue reinforced (or perhaps established for the first time) a context in which organizational ideology could be enforced (or at least raised) by employees. This implication also affects employee questions about organizational ideology with respect to participation. Management's willingness to discuss their behavior implicitly indicates willingness to be influenced—to permit at least some employee participation in organizational decisions.

Indirect negotiations also affect future negotiating contexts. Recognition of black worker concerns by white managers potentially legitimates black challenges of white authority in the future. While it was not clear that the discussion produced immediate ideological changes, it did enable more information exchange and less distorted evaluations by both sides.

The characteristics of negotiation contexts depend on the history of negotiations in the organization (Strauss, 1978; Brown, 1982). When negotiations have a long history (e.g., collective bargaining between labor and management in the private sector), formal and informal structures and processes provide a well-developed context that guides and constrains interaction. Where the issues are new, the parties recently defined, or the negotiation process unfamiliar, structures and processes may have to be invented to organize the negotiation context. Ideological negotiations are relatively familiar problems in RADA, but not in many other organizations.

IMPLICATIONS FOR MANAGING IDEOLOGICAL NEGOTIATIONS

Ideological negotiations differ from other forms of negotiation in several ways. What do these differences imply for managing ideological negotiations, either as a participant with an ideological position to advance or as a third party concerned with constructive negotiations? The following speculations are based on this analysis and our experience with ideological negotiations in organizations.

Creating Contexts for Ideological Negotiation

Ideological negotiations are at once products of past experience and precursors of future interactions. The results of past negotiations live on, both as decisions about specific issues and as expectations for the future—such as attitudes and belief about opponents and their negotiation behavior. So the ideological negotiations of today, whatever their outcomes in terms of immediate beliefs and behavior, set the stage for the negotiations of tomorrow. If RADA managers stonewall protests from lower-echelon employees today, they may have less ideological challenge in the future, at the expense of less ideological commitment by employees to the organization.

RADA has a long history of ideological discussion and controversy and so has developed a negotiations context within which ideological elements are recognized and discussed. But ideological disputes are foreign to many other organizations, particularly those that have histories of control through utilitarian and coercive means. Prisons have had difficulty controlling ideologically united inmates (e.g., Jackson, 1970), and public and private organizations have been unable to stop whistle-blowing by ideologically committed professionals (Parucci, Anderson, Schendel, & Trachtman, 1980).

When organizations do not have an existing context for ideological negotiations, precedents and constraints for future negotiations will be created during initial discussions of ideological differences. Individuals in unfamiliar ideological controversies negotiate on two levels: They deal with problems explicitly at issue, and they create expectations and constraints for future negotiations. It is easy in such situations to win the battle and lose the war, for negotiating contexts set unintentionally have as much subsequent force as do those created by design.

All negotiations, to some extent, set contexts for the future, but context setting is particularly important in ideological negotiations for two reasons. First, the *unfamiliarity* of ideological disputes in many organizations increases the likelihood that ideological differences will not be recognized or accepted as legitimate subjects for negotiation. In such circumstances, suitable negotiation contexts will not be established. Second, ideological negotiations are *volatile,* so negotiating contexts that promote constructive discussion reduce the chances of destructive escalation or suppression. The combination of volatility and unfamiliarity make it easy to have unproductive ideological negotiations unless attention is paid to developing a suitable negotiating context.

In addition to providing guidance and constraints for negotiation activities, negotiating contexts may also provide standards for evaluating alternatives and for choosing among them. *Principles for "fair" resolution* of ideological negotiation allow decisions to be made even when superordinate concepts cannot be recognized or invented. Fisher and Ury (1981) described "principled negotiations," in which the parties search for mutually agreeable standards against which the fairness of a solution can be judged. Ideological negotiations in particular need the legitimacy conferred by "fair decision making" because they potentially undermine the legitimacy of the organization as a whole. Kuhn (1962), for example, describes processes by which scientific "paradigms" (sets of beliefs that bind together and guide the activities of scientific schools and communities) replace one another: Work under old paradigms produces anomalies; new paradigms develop support as they better explain those anomalies. Scientific values and principles (e.g., parsimony, prediction, replicability) offer shared standards by which paradigm disputes are eventually "fairly" resolved.

Managing Special Characteristics of Ideological Negotiations

The nature of ideological differences increases the likelihood of misunderstandings based on different explanations, distortions based on different normative perspectives, and emotional reactions based on strong group identifications. While these aspects of ideological differences interact closely in the heat of negotiations, they offer conceptually separable avenues by which negotiators may influence events.

Different ideological perspectives offer different explanations— alternative variables and cause-and-effect linkages to account for problems and propose solutions. When negotiators pursue their own analyses without attending to alternative explanations, misunderstanding and confusion abound. Negotiators who *recognize and understand alternative explanations* are better positioned to find common ground, to see possible concessions, or to craft "yesable" propositions (Fisher & Ury, 1981). Given understanding of the explanations and concerns of both sides, these explanations can be synthesized into mutually acceptable *integrative theories* (Eiseman, 1978). The differences between white manager and black employee explanations for race relations at RADA, for example, are less problematic when both sides recognize that dominant groups are less likely to be challenged for insensitivity and so may remain ignorant in spite of good intentions.

Ideological prescriptions and evaluations can produce distortions of information exchange and moral evaluations of the other's perspective that make mutual influence impossible. Negotiators can reduce the impact of such distortions by *focusing on issues and behaviors that do not fit stereotypes.* The willingness of black secretaries at RADA to speak out, and the willingness of white male managers to listen and think seriously about preceptions of white racism in the organization, served to reduce stereotypes on both sides and to set the stage for better communication in the future. The parties may also share prescriptions that provide opportunities for ideological synthesis. Studies of intergroup conflict indicate that superordinate goals, shared by both groups but requiring joint activity, can reduce conflict and promote cooperation (Sherif, 1958). An analogous notion in ideological negotiations is a *superordinate* principle that prescribes actions deemed necessary by both parties. All the parties to the disputes at RADA agreed that the organization should promote "equity" and "development" for disadvantaged groups. Agreement on that principle limited conflict to matters of implementation rather than to permit ideological polarization.

When ideological homogeneity provides the glue that holds groups together, negotiations that threaten ideologies may also threaten the parties. When parties are symmetrically mobilized and/or powerful, *synchronizing group expectations and organizations* to prevent surprise challenges can reduce instability in ideological negotiations. Dominant groups are often less aware than subordinate groups of their own or others' ideologies (Brown, 1982), and they feel confused, surprised, and threatened by ideological challenges. Even in RADA, where ideological discussions were common, top management was surprised and somewhat hurt by lower-echelon accusations of hypocrisy. Settings in which ideological differences can be explored without threatening the existence of participating groups can be created.

Where some groups are ordinarily less cohesive and organized than others, providing alternative bases *for cohesion* can reduce the threat implicit in ideological negotiations. Regular meetings and internal organization of RADA employees enabled them to broach ideological issues and to discuss them without taking "party lines" that were unbreachable without harm to group solidarity.

Managing Microcosms

This chapter began with the notion that the ideological tensions inherent in relations among external agencies and social systems may be reproduced and negotiated within organizations whether or not they are organizationally relevent. The last two sections have focused on managing the resulting negotiations inside the organization. Another alternative is to manage organizational boundaries to alter the impact of external forces and so reshape microcosmic reproductions of external problems.

In recent years, countless studies of strategies and tactics for managing relations between organizations and environments have been suggested (Thompson, 1967; Pfeffer & Salancik, 1978; Brown, 1982). Organizations can actively *defend themselves from external pressures* and so reduce internal reproduction of external problems. Information flows can be controlled to reduce uncertainties, and supplies of critical resources can be altered to reduce important dependencies. RADA has decided to generate a mass donor base rather than be dependent on single-source funding. Hence they have gained relative political independence by diversifying their sources of funds. Organizations may intentionally *choose to work with diverse or similar external constituencies* and so expand external pressures for internal ideological diversity. The combination of tasks selected by RADA—development education in the First World, development projects in the Third World, political lobbying with governments in both worlds—makes ideological negotiation within the organization inevitable.

More generally, organizations react differently to the ideological tides that run through their societal contexts. For some organizations, those tides run against their "real business," and so ideological negotiations are annoying distractions that interrupt more important activities. Others *conceptualize their missions to fit external trends.* By recognizing external ideological trends, they capitalize on explanations and prescriptions from external sources and bind energy current in the larger society. Japanese organizations, for example, have apparently mobilized nationalism and martial ideologies on behalf of economic productivity (Pascale & Athos, 1981; Ouchi, 1981). In spite of its internal challenges, RADA evokes fierce support and high levels of commitment from most of its personnel, who are committed to somehow solving the development problems that lie at the heart of the organization's operation.

FURTHER RESEARCH

This chapter argues that organizations that bring together people from different social constituencies may internally reproduce ideological conflicts characteristic of the larger society. We have illustrated this notion with the case of an international relief and development organization. We believe that ideological negotiation is characteristic of some other contemporary organization (e.g., health, education) and will become increasingly common in many new sectors in the future. Several trends suggest that ideological negotiations will become increasingly important.

One important trend with implications for organizational ideologies is *changing expectations and increased diversity of the workforce.* In the United States, workforce attitudes and beliefs are changing, and the diversity of the workforce is increasing. Young people are less respectful of "established authority" and less willing to postpone gratification than their predecessors were; women and people of color bring quite different perspectives to previously white, male-dominated organizations. These new workers will require changes in organizational perspectives and expectations—in short, ideological negotiations.

A second trend is *the struggle to improve worker productivity.* Participative management, quality of work life experiments, organization development, and quality circles are all productivity-enhancement strategies that carry with them sets of beliefs that differ from dominant U.S. business ideologies. They suggest that workers and management should collaborate, as in Japan. Implementing such innovations will require renegotiating presently adversarial ideological postures for both management and workers.

Finally, the *rise of multinational corporations* compels attention to ideological differences across cultures. Such corporations cannot be efficiently coordinated without recognizing and managing ideological diversity rooted in the cultural origins of organization members. Global corporations will build ideologies that appeal across cultural boundaries and encourage constructive ideological negotiations or compete with more ideologically sensitive corporations under formidable handicaps.

Within organizations where ideological negotiations are common and effective, we need studies of the strategies, tactics, and contexts that produce constructive resolutions of ideological differences. We have suggested some of the facets of ideological negotiations that distinguish them from more commonly studied bargaining situations, and we have speculated about activities by which a negotiator or a third party might promote better negotiations. But more specific and conclusive answers about the strategies and tactics of ideological negotiations, and the contexts in which those strategies and tactics are appropriate, must await more focused research.

We need to know more about how strategies and tactics from ideologically sophisticated settings can be used in less experienced organizations, and how experience from other kinds of negotiations can be used in ideological disputes. How can RADA's experience with ideological negotiations, for example, be used to help resolve tensions among divisions of a multinational corporation? How can the collective bargaining experience of U.S. unions and management be adapted to managing tensions between socialists and capitalists in international settings? Such studies can provide the insights needed for constructive response to ideological differences and so liberate the enormous energies and talents human beings can mobilize in support of their central beliefs.

REFERENCES

Alderfer, C. P. Problems of changing white males' behavior and beliefs concerning race relations. In P. S. Goodman and Associates (Eds.), *Change in organizations.* San Francisco: Jossey-Bass, 1982.

Alexander, E. The reduction of cognitive conflict. *Journal of Conflict Resolution,* 1979, *23*(1), 120-138.

Apter, D. E. *Ideology and discontent.* New York: Free Press, 1964.

Beyer, J. Ideologies, values and decision making in organizations. In P. Nystrom and W. H. Starbuck (Eds.), *Handbook of organizational design,* Vol. 2. New York: Oxford University Press, 1981.

Blake, R. R., & Mouton, J. S. Reactions to intergroup competition under win-lose conditions. *Management Science,* 1961, *4.*

Brown, L. D. Planned change in underorganized systems. In T. G. Cummings (Ed.), *Systems theory for organization development.* London: John Wiley, 1980. (a)

Brown, L. D. *Organizing for development.* Working paper, Institute for Development Research, 1980. (b)

Brown, L. D. *Managing conflict at organizational interfaces.* Reading, MA: Addison-Wesley, 1982.

Day, R. A., & Day, J. V. A review of the current state of negotiated order theory. In J. K. Benson (Ed.), *Organizational analysis.* Beverly Hills, CA: Sage, 1977, 128-146.

Deutsch, M. *The resolution of conflict.* New Haven, CT: Yale University Press, 1973.

Diesing, P. *Science and ideology in the policy sciences.* Chicago: Aldine, 1982.

Eiseman, J. W. Reconciling incompatible positions. *Journal of Applied Behavioral Science,* 1978, *14,* 133-150.

Etzioni, A. *A comparative analysis of complex organizations.* New York: Free Press, 1961.

Fisher, R. Fractionating conflict. *Daedalus,* Summer 1964, 920-941.

Fisher, R., & Ury, W. *Getting to yes.* Boston, MA: Houghton Mifflin, 1981.

Goulet, D. *The cruel choice.* New York: Atheneum, 1977.

Heginbotham, S. J. *Cultures in conflict: The four faces of Indian bureaucracy.* New York: Columbia University Press, 1975.

Jackson, G. *Soledad brother: The prison letters of George Jackson.* New York: Bantam, 1970.

Knowles, L. L., & Prewitt, K. *Institutional racism in America.* Englewood Cliffs, NJ: Prentice-Hall, 1969.

Kuhn, T. S. *The structure of scientific revolutions.* Chicago: University of Chicago Press, 1962.

Lawrence, P. R., & Lorsch, J. W. *Organization and environment.* Homewood, IL: Irwin, 1967.

Lodge, G. C. *The new American ideology.* New York: A. A. Knopf, 1975.

Ouchi, W. *Theory Z.* Reading, MA: Addison-Wesley, 1981.

Pascale, R. T., & Athos A. *The art of Japanese management.* New York: Simon & Schuster, 1981.

Perrucci, R., Anderson, R. M., Schendel, D. E., & Trachtman, E. Whistle-blowing: Professionals' resistance to organizational authority. *Social Forces,* 1980, *28*(2), 149-164.

Pettigrew, A. On studying organizational cultures. *Administrative Science Quarterly,* 1979, *24*(4), 570-589.

Pfeffer, J., & Salancik, G. *The external control of organizations.* New York: Harper & Row, 1978.

Rubin, J. Z., & Brown, B. R. *The social psychology of bargaining.* New York: Academic, 1975.

Sherif, M. Superordinate goals in the reduction of intergroup conflict. *American Journal of Sociology,* 1958, *63,* 349-358.

Sherif, M. *In common predicament.* Boston: Houghton Mifflin, 1966.

Starbuck, W. H. Congealing oil: Inventing ideologies to justify acting ideologies out. *Journal of Management Studies,* 1982, *19*(1), 3-27.

Strauss, A. *Negotiations.* San Francisco: Jossey-Bass, 1978.

Thompson, J. D. *Organizations in action.* New York: McGraw-Hill, 1967.

14

NEGOTIATION
An Escape From Strategic Stalemate

Edwin A. Murray, Jr.

Boston University

My objective in this chapter is to explore the role of external negotiations in strategic management. Specifically, I shall identify areas of strategic management that appear to be underserved by the application of negotiation processes and that as a consequence, deserve further study. I also shall discuss the emergence of new types of third-party organizations that offer new potential for shaping and aiding interorganizational negotiating processes. Throughout, I am seeking ways to manage more effectively corporate enterprises, not only so that individual companies might achieve their objectives but so that legitimate societal norms and expectations will be met as well. Only when both conditions are satisfied simultaneously can corporate performance be said to be genuinely optimal.

STRATEGIC MANAGEMENT

Top-level managers, responsible for managing entire enterprises, are increasingly interested in managing their organizations strategically. Strategic management is that "process that deals with fundamental organizational renewal and growth, with the development of the strategies, structures, and systems necessary to achieve such renewal and growth, and with the organizational systems needed to effectively manage the strategy formulation and implementation processes" (Hofer, Murray, Charan, & Pitts, 1980, p. 7). Strategic management is based on the concept of strategy. A typical definition of strategy holds that *strategy* is a coherent, integrated set of objectives and actions for using an organization's resources to gain and secure a sustainable position of advantage (Hammond, 1981).

Conventionally, this type of definition has been interpreted as a call for the comprehensive and systematic planning of long-term corporate objectives, strategies, policies, and programs, all designed to achieve a position of superiority over the competition (Ansoff, 1965; Steiner, 1969). Such an interpretation implies that corporate management alone can chart a course for the corporation, apparently independent of serious internal resistance or external constraints. Managerial discretion is presumed. However, management does not have unbridled discretion in its decision making. In practice, strategy formation is more accurately characterized as the cumulative result of at least three influences:

(1) top-level strategists attempting to define and direct the company's business;
(2) other managers and organizational subunits within the corporation seeking to influence that definition and direction; and
(3) external parties seeking to motivate, constrain, and otherwise influence the company.

I shall focus on this third influence and corporate responses to it.

STRATEGIC STALEMATE

Although corporations—especially large ones—are perceived as powerful because of their concentrated economic power, they are not necessarily powerful vis-a-vis other actors in their environment. Other companies of equal size, or with superior technology, or with greater financial resources, or with some other form of distinctive advantage can neutralize a firm's power and even threaten its competitive position. Such competitive pressures may affect and even limit management's strategic choices.

In addition, management's decision may be contingent upon acquiescence or approval of other parties outside the firm. Most notably for firms in regulated industries, but for many more companies as well, a host of government and other external agencies with various degrees of oversight responsibility may need to be consulted. The effect of this is to take decision making somewhat out of management's hands and disperse it among a variety of agencies external to the firm, thus fragmenting and complicating the strategic decision-making process.

In some extreme cases, either because of market and competitive pressures or because of government regulations and the intervention of social and political interest groups, companies may find themselves in a strategically stalemated position. *Strategic stalemate is the inability of management to make a substantial series of productive strategic choices or moves without the support, concurrence, and/or acquiescence of one or more significant parties external to the firm.* An illustration of this type of deadlock would be a company that cannot secure the external financing necessary to modernize its plant and equipment so as to compete more effectively. Another example would be the inability of management to proceed with a plant construction program because of the unwillingness of government agencies to grant permits for pollution control devices.

Causes and Effects of Stalemate

Four major factors, singly or in combination, contribute to strategic stalemate.

(1) Competitive countermoves. If, for every competitive initiative a firm takes (such as new product introductions, plant capacity expansions, new marketing campaigns), one or more of its competitors matches the move, a competitive deadlock may result. Evidence of stalemate may show up in the form of stymied sales levels, stagnant

market shares, and a plateau in earnings. As a result of these outcomes, competition may become much more fierce, leading to price wars, overbuilding of productive capacity, industrial espionage, and raiding competitors for key technical and managerial talent. On the other hand, a collusive type of accommodation might be reached with price fixing and the dividing up of markets. The first types of reaction can be harmful to the companies involved, and the second class of responses is deleterious to their customers.

(2) Resource scarcity. If adequate resources, in the forms of capital, human resources, technology, and raw materials, are unavailable, a company may find its strategic options limited or foreclosed. Evidence of this type of adverse resource-dependent condition (Pfeffer & Salancik, 1978) would typically been seen in banks withdrawing company lines of credit, high turnover and low morale among employees, repeated failures in new product development, and chronic shortages of raw materials and/or increasing costs of procurement. As a result, a company could find its sales, market share, and profits all flat or falling. In extreme cases of scarcity, the success of turnaround or diversification efforts become less probable and selling out to another company or liquidation becomes more likely. Any company so involved is obviously adversely affected, and industry competition, as a result, may be reduced.

(3) Limited market demand. If there develops insufficient market demand for a company's products or services, it may find its strategic options limited or foreclosed. Evidence of this would be found in declining sales, mounting inventories, and a fall-off in order backlogs. The result, of course, would be declining profitability, slippage in employee morale, and perhaps drastic cost-cutting measures such as layoffs to contract the business. If efforts to generate sales or reduce costs are insufficient to turn the business around, divestment or liquidation of the business becomes more likely. Not only is the company adversely affected, but industry competition is likely to decline as a result.

(4) Regulatory constraints. To the extent that agencies external to a firm have legitimate oversight responsibility for it and/or its oper-

ations, a company may be restricted in its strategic choices. This condition is most evident for companies operating in regulated industries. Operating permits, licenses to build, tariff schedules, affirmative action compliance programs, and so forth all are representative of the types of externally imposed constraints under which such firms operate. Prolonged delays in granting necessary permissions and/or legal recourse through court actions often characterize deadlocks between companies and their regulators. The results can of course be serious: escalating construction costs, reduction in requested rate increases (and hence a reduction in company revenues and profits), limited market access, delayed technological innovation, and unabated pollution of the environment. These can have varying negative impacts on the companies, its customers, and the communities involved.

Responses to Strategic Stalemate

In an external environment characterized by constraints and ambiguity stemming from limitations on managerial power and decision-making authority, only three managerial responses are viable:

(1) Increase the power of management vis-a-vis the environment. Through the effective use of more systematic methods of strategic analysis and planning, many companies try to achieve growth in their revenues and shares of market so as to achieve a position of sustainable dominance over competitors and bargaining power relative to suppliers and customers, and, if possible, enough of both to deter new entrants to their markets. This amounts to emphasizing even more the traditional methods of strategic planning and decision making.

(2) Decrease the fragmentation or diffusion of decision making in the environment. The expectation is that this simplification of the environment will lead to a reduction in uncertainty about government regulation and its effects, outside interveners and their inputs, and so forth. The resulting stability, or at least greater likelihood of predic-

tability, allows companies to turn to more systematic methods of strategic analysis, forecasting, and planning. Again, this is tantamount to simplifying and stabilizing the firm's surroundings so that rational, comprehensive planning can be made to operate more effectively.

(3) If neither is possible, or is achievable only to a limited extent, accept the fact that most managerial power vis-à-vis other environmental actors and forces is limited and decision making is diffuse. In response to the shortcomings of conventional strategic planning, develop policies, structures, processes, and techniques to anticipate and cope with such an environment more effectively. This will require genuinely innovative approaches to strategic management.

I will now discuss each of these responses in greater detail.

EMPHASIZING STRATEGIC PLANNING

Many senior managers (and consultants to those executives) value the logic of rational, comprehensive analysis and planning. Accordingly they emphasize the application of competitive strategies and modern planning techniques in order to enhance the performance—and hence power—of their companies. The power they seek is often a function of growth and stability rather than profitability alone. Despite the espoused primacy of "profit maximization" in their objective, most corporate strategists act in ways that suggest that other criteria actually take precedence. Growth and stability often seem to be the real objectives of corporate performance. From a historical perspective, it has been contended that "in making administrative decisions, career managers preferred policies that favored the long-term stability and growth of their enterprises to those that maximized current profits" (Chandler, 1980, p. 10). An emphasis on growth—whether expressed in preferences for growth of revenues, market share, assets, employees, or profits—serves as a proxy for the quest for power. By increasing any one or some combination of these measures, management gains increased discretion or influence, and thus power, with respect to the fortunes of the institution. Therefore, by emphasizing strategic planning, management tries to increase the firm's (and their own) power—either over their competitors or with respect to their resources and markets via leverage over their suppliers and buyers, respectively.

Ironically, it is modern strategic planning practices, coupled with new technology, that have caused many companies to come to competitive impasses over growth, market shares, technology, and profitability. In tracing the evolution of corporate strategic planning over the last thirty years and projecting trends for the 1980s and beyond, Zakon (1982) concludes that more and more companies are becoming strategically stalemated by their competitors.

Zakon begins with three premises. First, a company's profitability is a function of its competitive advantage over rival companies. Second, the number of ways advantage can be gained and the potential size of the advantage will vary from industry to industry. Third, the nature and magnitude of these advantages will change during an industry's evolution.

The strategic implications of these premises can be portrayed in matrix form (Figure 14.1). On the vertical axis, the number of ways in which competitive advantage can be obtained are arrayed, from many to few. For example, restaurants have many ways in which they may differentiate themselves—location, cuisine, price, service, decor, and so on. By contrast, companies selling commodity products like basic steel have relatively few ways to distinguish themselves; hence price becomes their chief competitive weapon.

On the horizontal axis, the size of competitive advantage is portrayed—from small to large. In the uncoated paper business, for example, large paper mills used to provide significant costs advantages for their owners. Now, with big mills the norm for all large competitors in the industry, economies of scale associated with large plants provide virtually no relative advantage.

Using this matrix, companies may be categorized according to the different industry groupings shown. *Fragmented industries* are those such as restaurants that have many sources of competitive advantage, none of which helps in a decisive way. Companies in *specialization industries* also have many sources of competitive advantage and typically have achieved significant advantage from one or more of them. Zakon cites the example of the Japanese success in penetrating the U.S. auto market by specializing in high-quality, fuel-efficient compact cars. *Volume industries* are companies that have sought competitive dominance primarily through increasing economies of scale and cost reduction. Traditionally, firms in process industries such as paper, steel, aluminum, and synthetic fibers have sought

Size of Competitive Advantage

	Small	Large
Many	Fragmented Industries	Specialization Industries
Few	Stalemated Industries	Volume Industries

Number of Ways Competitive Advantage Can Be Obtained

Figure 14.1   Industry Status as a Function of Competitive Advantage

greater market power and higher profits by investing in capital equipment to achieve their industry's low-cost position. In the 1950s and 1960s, these volume strategies worked well, but the oil shock of 1973 changed many factors. The slowing growth of demand made it difficult and costly to load huge new plants fully. Inflation outweighed scale savings in accounting terms. Invested capital pressured competitors to stay on in order to earn back their investments. The spread of technology and experience attracted new competitors with low labor costs from the lesser developed countries. Technologically, scale limits were reached.

As a result of these several trends in combination, many volume industries have become *statemated industries.* As noted in the case of the uncoated paper industry, the techniques of increasing economies of scale in order to reduce costs now have been largely exhausted as a means of deriving competitive advantage. Another illustration of this can be found in the case of the basic steel industry. Because new technologies for steel production and facility construction were available around the world and because strategic planning methodologies also were available, virtually any company that wanted and could afford to build a cost-efficient, world-scale steel mill could do so with the assurance that it was a strategically "correct" move—at that time. But now that so many competitors are similarly positioned, industry stagnation has set in. The few sources of competitive advantage that remain are relatively small. As a result, steel companies face stable or declining sales levels and market shares. Underutilized capacity and stubbornly high fixed costs adversely affect profitability.

Traditionally, companies have responded to such competitively stalemated situations in several ways. Price cutting (to increase volume) and cost reduction (to increase profits) are classic moves. Research and development is stressed in the hope of making a breakthrough in product design or process technology, either one of which could create a new and sizable source of competitive advantage. Diversification into other businesses may be attempted and/or the stalemated business may be divested. In some cases, the business may be "refocused." For example, some chemical and steel companies, rather than become competitively deadlocked in basic, commodity-like products, may concentrate on specialty products with higher growth and profit potential. Alternatively, some competitors may dramatically "change the rules." Air Products, for instance, circumvented Union Carbide's stable dominance of the industrial gas market by reconceptualizing the business. Instead of copying Union Carbide's distribution system and delivering its gas products by truck and rail, Air Products built on-site industrial gas production facilities to service large industrial customers. It thereby developed a unique product/service alternative to its key competitor's traditional products and services.

Such responses are likely to remain a necessary—even primary—subset of strategic options drawn upon by corporate management. However, they may not always suffice. Furthermore, the business environment is changing. In a world economy experiencing slowing growth, resource shortages, increased inflation, and rising levels of pollution, more regulation of business in the forms of tariff barriers, import quotas, antitrust laws, pollution level controls, and so forth is sought.

This portends greater uncertainty for corporate planners and makes dependence on traditional, deterministic strategies potentially less viable in the future. In today's world, government regulation and intrusive community-based groups are but two of the many forces that limit management's discretion in planning; managerial choices increasingly are bounded by a variety of limitations imposed from outside the firm.

DEALING WITH OUTSIDE REGULATION

The modern corporation typically encounters a variety of externally based, "intrusive" elements (Dill, 1976). Government regulatory agencies, legislative bodies, church-sponsored organizations, community-based coalitions, and other types of interest groups all seek to influence a firm's policies and operations. Generally, the most important of these is government and its regulation of business. Moreover, the most common relationship between business and government (as well as other external groups) has been adversarial in nature (Fox, 1981, p. 97):

> Today, most of the dealings between business and government in the United States are adversarial, as government probes, inspects, taxes, influences, regulates, and punishes. In this setting, trade-offs evolve haphazardly as the often unforeseen and unintended effects of regulation work their way through the economy. Business managers at all levels negotiate delays, develop means for partial compliance, defend themselves in lawsuits, and otherwise seek to minimize the impact of government on their operations while responding to the many disparate agencies with which business comes into contact.

As a result of this, and in order to facilitate the formulation and execution of conventional competitive strategies, corporate managers may try to reduce the fragmentation and diffusion of externally based decision making that affects their companies.

Recent efforts at deregulation—or, more properly, "regulatory reform"—have been based in part on the premise that reducing and/or simplifying the external decision making affecting corporations would enable them to plan with greater discretion. And by having greater latitutde in their strategic planning, businesses could be operated more efficiently and effectively.

Nevertheless, for all the rhetoric about deregulation, there is much evidence to suggest that regulation—for many companies and industries—still remains very much a fixture in the business environment. What actually appears to characterize regulatory trends is a shift from industry-specific "economic regulation" to industry-spanning "social regulation." All companies in all industries are being affected by regulation with respect to equal employment opportunities, environmental protection, occupational safety and health, and so forth. Regulation before 1960 focused on particular industries (for instance, transportation, banking, airlines, and communications), but now there is a wide range of agencies to respond to social demands. Just a partial listing of them includes organizations as varied as the Consumer Product Council (CPSC), the Environmental Protection Agency (EPA), the Equal Employment Opportunity Commission (EEOC), the Department of Energy (DOE), the National Highway Traffic Safety Administration (NHTSA), and the Occupational Safety and Health Administration (OSHA; Fox, 1981, p. 98).

Those companies destined to remain in heavily regulated environments or subject to a large number of external pressures need to work at three levels of strategy (Mahon & Murray, 1981):

(1) *a traditional, economically oriented business strategy* defined in typical product- or service-market terms;
(2) *a political strategy* or negotiated approach to manage relationships with regulatory and/or other outside bodies; and
(3) *a social or public policy strategy* to address the broader concerns of multiple, diverse constituencies.

An illustration of a company engaging in the latter two types of strategy would be one of AT&T's local operating companies. It must apply to the appropriate state regulatory agency for any significant modification of service offerings, pricing structures, or marketing programs. Not only must the telephone company receive the approval of the appropriate state regulatory commission(s), but it must also receive the concurrence of the Federal Communications Commission. Throughout this approval process, maintaining and managing political relationships is of crucial importance. The telephone company also enters into negotiations (if not directly, then implicitly, via state rate commission hearings) with various consumer groups and/or other intervener organizations. Here a well-designed and -implemented public relations campaign—including dialogue with consumer groups—could aid the company in securing public support for its case.

Political and social sensitivity are very important to all companies in regulated industries because they must reach accommodation with a variety of external parties. In earlier research I found that plans of strategic significance to an electric utility were not formulated strictly within the firm, as traditional planning models suggest. Instead, in response to some roadblocks thrown up by outside intervener groups and state regulatory agencies, the company negotiated a settlement. Specifically, after extensive bargaining management agreed to a compromise plan regarding the company's newest power plant location, its scheduled capacity additions, selection of power sources, and pollution control policies (Murray, 1980).

Despite the apparently constrained nature of even highly regulated industries, there can be surprising degrees of latitude. This is partly a function of corporate management's skill in negotiating and maintaining productive relationships with its various external stakeholder groups and, in particular, with the relevant government agencies exercising regulatory oversight. Heikoff (1975, p. 145), for example, concludes that "legislators, elected administrators and business executives . . . are representatives of contending constituencies whose political interaction determines the balance between public and private interests." Thus rational models of regulation (Holden, 1966) must be qualified because the effectiveness of the regulatory process depends in part on the consent of the regulated—not solely on the policies, programs, or actions of the regulators. Regulatory agencies, as it turns out, must bargain with the regulated "until they find a settlement that is mutually tolerable" (Heikoff, 1975, p. 146).

Such negotiations have long been an important part of the regulatory process. In cases of more traditional "economic" regulation, such major issues as market entry, pricing, fair rates of return, service standards, and route structures were subject to extensive bargaining by the companies involved and federal, state, and local regulatory agencies. Even other parties intervened in the hearings. Competitors, new entrants, suppliers, customers, and community-based groups often participated, directly or via their legal representatives. Now, with more "social" regulation in existence, the major issues have become those of affirmative action, occupational safety and health, product safety, protection of the environment against pollution and hazardous wastes, nuclear plant safety, and so on. As in industry-specific regulation, the affected companies and their regulators engage in extended negotiations, and they are joined in their hearings and proceedings by even more intervening groups. Not only may several industries now be represented by their trade associations, but a wider array of special interest groups, consumer advocates, social activists, and public interest groups may also be representated. Furthermore, the regulators themselves have changed. Instead of being specialists in the industries they regulated, the new regulators are specialists in functional fields such as environmentalism, nuclear safety, and the like. As a consequence, the negotiations have become more complicated and extensive than before.

Typically, in both "economic" and "social" regulation, public hearings precede the deliberations and rulings of regulatory agencies. Increasingly, however, these government-made decisions are challenged in the courts by special interest groups, including business. This is not only because of the increased complexity of the issues but because of some procedural and structural problems that have led to a series of stalemates.

According to Reich (1981), the regulation of business has suffered through a long history of bitter confrontation, tactical infighting, and strategic delay and deception. Business, for its part, has a negative, defensive, and reactive attitude. It often denies that problems exist, places the blame elsewhere, or argues that government interference is not needed. Regulatory agencies also contribute to the animosity. They often direct adverse publicity toward the companies, arbitrarily set unrealistically stringent standards, devise cumbersome compliance procedures, and threaten massive subpoenas. The result has been paralyzing confrontation instead of negotiation directed at problem solving.

Reich argues that a major contributing factor is the large and relatively new group of professional intermediaries between business and government. Washington-based lawyers representing companies before regulatory agencies and the courts (the former of which have their own lawyers and public relations specialists), lobbyists, trade association staff members, public relations specialists, public affairs consultants, and special interest group journalists all make up an army of people with vested interests in helping to manage the tensions between business and government. Reich suggests that they even help create and maintain the tensions by sharply defining and magnifying controversies between their clients and their clients' opponents, exaggerating the dangers in the opponent's activities and designs, prolonging and intensifying the controversies, and keeping business executives and regulatory officials apart from one another.

Fox (1981) argues in a somewhat similar vein. He notes that existing regulatory procedures encourage conflict among the parties involved. With only the courts as a formal mechanism to settle differences, businesses have taken rigid positions and then fallen back on delays, partial compliance, and ultimately lawsuits to oppose constraining and conflicting regulations. Likewise, some regulatory agencies and many opposing groups such as consumer advocates and environmentalists take equally unyielding and adversarial stands. The result often is a bitter and protracted impasse.

Where there are multiple government agencies responsible for decisions affecting corporate operations, it certainly seems preferable—from the corporate strategist's view—to reduce the number of intervening influences. Arguably, such a reduction could even improve the effectiveness of government operations. However, as we have noted, significant reductions in regulation seem unlikely—notwithstanding some of the recent reforms and moves to "deregulate" industries such as the airlines and interstate trucking. Despite the sometimes dysfunctional effects of regulation, it appears destined to remain very much a factor to be dealt with by company managements. Significant simplification of the corporate environment by reducing the diffusion of external decision making is not indicated.

NEGOTIATION AS AN ESCAPE FROM STALEMATE

The issue for the corporate strategist is not simply how to formulate better competitive strategies so as to increase managerial power. The deterministic nature and widespread "availability" of such strategies cause them to be conceptually played out. The sole remaining source of advantage in an increasing number of competitive strategies seems to lie largely in a firm's ability to execute them, i.e., its caliber of operational, not strategic, management. Nor is the issue for the strategist one of somehow reducing the diffusion of decision making in the environment. That aspiration runs counter to the reality of greater intrusiveness into corporate affairs by outside regulatory agencies, interest groups, courts, or individuals claiming a legitimate interest, or "stake," in the strategy and operations of the firm.

New creative approaches to situations that in the past have led to strategic stalemate are needed. By entering into negotiations with external stakeholders, innovative *cooperative strategies* can be developed. This direction appears particularly promising in a period of resource shortages, slowing growth, and the increasing internationalism of business because the interdependencies among institutions have become so critical. The need will grow for more interconnections, networks, dialogues, and interactions among societal institutions—corporations included.

Already, Lodge (1976) and Novak (1982) have argued, there seems to be a significant change occurring in the ideology of Americans—one that brings us into closer alignment with the thinking of Western Europe, Japan, and other parts of the industrial world. We are a country moving from "individualism" to "communitarianism," and accompanying this shift in values there is a greater tolerance, appreciation, and even expectation of decisions arrived at through broader-based participation than before. Business, labor, government, and other elements of society all are coming to see the need to be represented in major societal choices if they are to be lastingly accepted and effective.

OVERCOMING COMPETITIVE STALEMATES

To deal with competitive stalemates, some companies have tried to work together to create an "industry strategy." Through trade associations such as the National Electric Manufacturers' Association (NEMA), for example, electrical manufacturing companies have established product and manufacturing quality standards in an effort to advance their collective interests. Generally such efforts have only modest impacts because of two limiting factors. First, there is the inhibition of antitrust law, which causes companies to be wary of behavior that could be construed as collusive and in any way designed to be in restraint of trade. Second, there is the problem of reaching some type of actionable consensus among a large number of disparate companies, even though they all participate in the same industry. Very often competitive leaders welcome standardization because it helps *their* designs and quality standards become the norm. This could serve to enhance their competitive advantage over more marginal competitors and even serve as a potential barrier to entry, thus deterring new firms from joining the industry. Naturally, smaller or relatively disadvantaged firms would resist these efforts, and conflict is likely to result. Nonetheless, when problems loom large enough, this type of factionalism may give way to new, even more far-reaching forms of collective effort.

Recently, for example, a rather direct form of collaboration within the electronics industry was explored. Control Data Corporation convened a meeting of sixteen major U.S. electronics companies for the purpose of forming a collective research and development venture tentatively called Microelectronics & Computer Technology Enterprises (*Wall Street Journal,* March 1, 1982). Despite the obvious antitrust implications of the venture, William Norris, chairman of Control Data, asserted the need for creative solutions. Otherwise, the industry would be left with "IBM and Japan and precious little else." He said that Japanese companies' collective research, tariff barriers, and partitioning of product lines had wrought "massive distortion of the world competitive scene which can only be dealt with by extraordinary action." In his view, older and more common forms of intercompany cooperation such as cross-licensing of technology patents and even the more recently announced Semi-Conductor Research Cooperative targeted for universities would not be sufficient.

There may even be a need for collaborative efforts that cut across several industries, leading ultimately to a "national economic strategy." According to observers like Reich (1981) and Scott (1982), there is a clear need to formulate a more cogent, viable national industrial policy. Such a policy, though, requires extensive analysis and public debate if it is to succeed. Collaboration and agreement among business, labor, and government interests will be required at a minimum. Harbingers of such cooperation may be present in government efforts to moderate or simplify some regulations for particular industries and labor unions taking less belligerant stands in contract negotiations. Companies—beset by the recession, foreign competition, and the dire straits of certain key industries—also are taking a more conciliatory stand (New York Times, April 14, 1982).

OVERCOMING REGULATORY STALEMATES

To overcome regulatory stalemates, Fox (1981) has proposed public/private "partnerships" in which differences lead to negotiations instead of confrontations. Borrowing from the dominant European and Japanese models of close coordination, he recommends the establishment of organizations outside the formal judicial process to deal with controversial issues. These forums, if held without conflict-generating press releases and media coverage, could be the basis for arriving at more sensible rules and standards than current adversarial procedures. In support of his proposal, Fox cites the effective relationships and accomplishments achieved by the National Institute of Building Sciences, the Joint Labor-Management Committee, the National Coal Policy Project, and the Health Effects Institute.

There is also a need for regional, state, and local forums to deal with issues such as taxation, rising health care costs, transporation planning, regional energy demands and supplies, and the education and training of the work force. One example of a successful response by an association of companies is that of the Massachusetts Business Roundtable, a coalition of Massachusetts-based companies that devised a new reimbursement formula to contain rising health care costs in the state. This was attained by proposing and negotiating a solution with several groups: the Massachusetts Rate Setting Commission, the Massachusetts Hospital Association, Blue Cross, private insurance companies, the governor's office, several members of the Massachusetts legislature, and federal agencies in Washington (Boston Globe, August 24, 1982). Other examples of "roundtable" business associations and their activities have been described by McQuaid (1981) and Bemis and Cairns (1981).

Not all companies are willing to enter into partnerships with government agenices and community groups to resolve controversial issues. The Reserve Mining Corporation and its protracted wrangling with the U.S. Environmental Protection Agency, U.S. Justice Department, various state and federal courts, and Minnesota state agencies and community groups is a classic case in point (Schaumburg, 1976). As early as December 1978, the Stoddard Report (prepared by the U.S. Department of the Interior) asserted that taconite tailings (i.e., the residue from iron ore refining operations) from the Reserve plant at Silver Bay, Minnesota, were seriously polluting the waters of Lake Superior. There then ensued a federal enforcement conference convened by the Department of Interior, a suit filed by Reserve in Minnesota State Court against the Minnesota Pollution Control Agency, and—after a second and third federal enforcement conference session—a series of federal court lawsuits.

Reserve engaged in a long history of reactionary avoidance, delay, obstruction, and obfuscation on the one hand and proactive—at times manipulative—initiatives on the other. For example, counting only the major events between February 17, 1972, and April, 8, 1975, when the case finally ended after an appeal to the U.S. Supreme Court, Reserve was involved in no less than 33 legal actions. Such an approach is clearly at variance with the open-minded, problem-solving, and genuinely interactive stance required to make negotiations acceptable to all interested parties.

To reform or circumvent this type of corporate behavior, Reich (1981) argues for the development of an attitude of problem-solving instead of confrontation. To facilitate this, he suggests the development of intelligence systems to give early forewarning of critical issues. He also recommends the careful monitoring and review of the performance of business/government intermediaries to ensure they are helping to *solve* the problems, not *exacerbate* them. Like Fox, he urges entering into public negotiations before formal regulatory proceedings begin.

FROM INTERNAL TO EXTERNAL POLICY

Productively overcoming competitive or regulatory stalemates requires an interdependent and interaction view of corporate relationships with other institutions in society. It is a view based less on pure competition and increasingly on cooperation. Traditionally, the study of management policy has focused primarily on those policies *internal* to the organization that were viewed as *instrumental* to achievement of the company's competitive and economic objectives. This is the realm of internal or "instrumental" policy. Commonly, these policies involve the standard functions of business: product design, research and development, pricing, distribution, personnel, financing, manufacturing, and so forth. However, there is mounting evidence that policymaking should be oriented more toward the firm's *external* environment. Such policymaking is designed to *facilitate* the company's operations and achievement of its economic and other social objectives and is coming to be of critical importance. This area is one of "facilitative" policy.

IBM is one example of a company that has prospered because of its willingness and ability to blend strategic "external" negotiations effectively with more conventional, "internal" forms of management. It has very successfully augmented a rational, well thought out corporate strategy and highly developed planning process with an array of political strategies and socially responsive postures that aid it in a series of negotiations and understandings with governments around the world. These interactions are enormously important to IBM in that they have become interwoven into the fabric of the company's strategic management. According to one recent account (Pollack, 1982, p. 1):

> Government actions can help or hurt I.B.M. as much as, if not more than, actions of other companies. Certainly the most serious threat to I.B.M. until recently has not been Honeywell or Burroughs, but the United States government antitrust suit. Now it is Japan's government-backed thrust into the computer business.
>
> "The competitive issues and the government issues have been merged both in Europe and Japan," said Yves Doz, professor at INSEAD.
>
> Over the years, I.B.M. has developed an elaborate system for managing its dealings with national governments. I.B.M. blends into the background of the countries in which it operates like a chameleon and then makes its appeals to governments based on the national interest rather than on I.B.M.'s interest. It generally behaves ethically—no bribery scandals mar its past—yet is not above playing one government against another, using the law to its fullest advantage or bringing into play its own considerable power and resources, which stem from its size and its dominance of the market for a vital product.

FUTURE RESEARCH ON NEGOTIATED STRATEGIES

What we know about and how we treat external policymaking as opposed to internal policymaking still seems quite uneven in its scope and depth. Therefore, the following areas are proposed for futher research.

(1) *Are* there discernible and operationally significant differences between what I have termed "facilitative" (external) and "instrumental" (internal) corporate policies? If, as seems plausible, the firm's external policies are significantly different in scope, character, and implications from its internally focused, instrumental policies, they probably need to be treated differently. This may amount to any

one or a combination of several different requirements for a corporation's external strategic planning:

- involving different, or at least supplemental, inside managers;
- bringing in expertise from outside;
- going through a different type of policy formation process;
- undertaking new or different types of analysis.

On the other hand, if there is no significant difference between internal and external policies, conventional management structures and methods should serve satisfactorily for both forms.

(2) Sociopolitical strategies by businesses are increasingly common and seem to be predicated on the assumption that external pressures can be dealt with in a way analogous to competitive strategy. Therefore, analytical techniques and "planning" methodologies—adopted for use in a sociopolitical arena—are commonly prescribed for the management of emerging critical issues. MacMillan (1978), for example, writes of "strategic anticipation" in the formulation of corporate political strategies, and Post (1978) explores the consequences of reactive, proactive, and interactive modes of response by companies to public issues. Radford (1980), treating strategic interactions as a complex decision situation, sees decisions as subject to a number of successive "rounds" during which bargaining takes place until a stable outcome is achieved. All of these approaches share a fundamental perspective of firms—as individual entities—conceiving and executing strategies in relationship to other, external entities, and/or forces. The mechanisms used and even the calculus employed in designing and carrying out these moves is by and large the same as is used for more traditional business planning and operations. Moves, countermoves, and various gaming techniques are employed. In this sense, existing managerial structures and procedures are adapted for new uses—the formation and implementation of *facilitative* (external) versus *instrumental* (internal) policies. An obvious question arises as to the suitability of this adaptation. Are organizational structures and methods sufficiently adaptable to yield facilitative policies as effectively as they yield instrumental policies?

(3) One indication of the inadequacy of traditional forms and processes may be in the development and utilization of new organizational structures. From research on public affairs management in U.S. corporations (Mahon, 1982; Post, Murray, Dickie, & Mahon,

1982), there is evidence to suggest the growing prominence of public affairs offices as important supplements to corporate planning efforts. Even in those firms characterized as using long-range *strategic* planning methods, public affairs is a significant function. Most public affairs offices fulfill a role of "window out/window in," serving as a highly interactive corporte link to and from the external environment. In this manner, public affairs management serves a boundary-spanning role, quite like senior levels of general management, in that the managers of public affairs typically represent the organization (or subunits of it) as a whole. Further study of the contributions and limitations of the public affairs function could contribute to their more effective utilization. Improving the operations of public affairs units arguably would serve both corporate management and the public at large.

(4) In addition to examining the nature, activities, and influence of new organizational forms within corporate organizations, there is much to learn about external coalitions, or business associations. These mediating institutions traditionally have been of two types: the industry trade association (which sets certain technical standards) and the professional association (which becomes involved in certification and licensing, thus influencing professional behavior norms). A third, newer type of association exists and has been termed the "peak association." It is defined as "a heterogeneous [non-industry-specific] coalition of top executives voluntarily organized to develop 'business' or community positions and to assess top government officials on issues of economic, business, or community interests" (Ladd, 1981). Studies focusing on the number, characteristics, organizational processes, and influences of these types of organizations would be most appropriate as a way to understand their roles in the formulation of external policies and negotiated strategies.

SUMMARY

I have tried to show that in managing their firms, corporate executives for a variety of reasons run the risk of strategic stalemate. Because of resource shortages, limited market demands, competitive impasses, or regulatory deadlocks, management may be stalemated. It is not enough, however, to simply try to do more strategic planning of a conventional nature to anticipate and cope with the first three of these problems. Nor is it an adequate response to attempt a simplification of the regulatory environment to avoid confrontational deadlocks.

Instead, an active problem-solving approach can be undertaken through creative negotiations. Business coalitions, or partnerships, among companies within industries, across industries, and in combination with government agencies and other outside interest groups provide the vehicles for this type of interactive dialogue. In order to make it work, attention needs to be focused on external, or facilitative, policymaking, rather than internally-oriented, or instrumental, policymaking. In order to study external policies and their roles in negotiations to avoid stalemate, a research agenda is proposed.

REFERENCES

Ansoff, H. I. *Corporate stragegy.* New York: McGraw-Hill, 1965.

Bemis, J., & Cairns, J. A. "In Minnesota, business is part of the solution." *Harvard Business Review,* July-August 1981, pp. 85-93.

Chandler, A. D. *The visible hand.* Cambridge, MA: Harvard University Press, 1980.

Dill, W. R. "Strategic management in a kibitzer's world," in I. Ansoff, R. Declerck, & Hayes (Eds.), *From strategic planning to strategic management.* New York: John Wiley, 1976.

Fox, J. R. "Breaking the regulatory deadlock." *Harvard Business Review,* September-October 1981, pp. 97-105.

Hammond, J. S. *Strategic planning presentation.* North American Society for Corporate Planning, Boston Chapter, Waltham, Mass. 1981.

Heikoff, J. M. *Management of industrial particualtes.* Ann Arbor: Ann Arbor Science Publishers, 1975.

Hofer, C. W., Murray, E. A., Jr., Charan, R., & Pitts, R. A. *Strategic management: A casebook in business policy and planning.* St. Paul: West, 1980.

Holden, M., Jr. "Pollution control as a bargaining process: An essay on regulatory decision-making." Cornell Water Resources Center, Ithaca, New York, October 1966. Cited in Heikoff, J. M., *Management of industrial particualtes.* Ann Arbor: Ann Arbor Science Publishers, 1975.

Knox, R. A., "Business' push to put a cap on hospital costs." *Boston Globe,* August 24, 1982, p. 45.

Ladd, L. J. *Analyzing peak associations: A look at strategy in the business round-table.* Presentation at National Academy of Management meetings, San Diego, August 1981.

Lodge, G. C. *The uses of ideology for environmental analysis* (ICCH 9-377-147). Intercollegiate Case Clearing House, Boston, Massachusetts, 1976.

MacMillan, I. C. *Strategy formulation: Political concepts.* St. Paul: West, 1978.

Mahon, J. F. *Corporate public affairs offices: Structure, behavior, and impact.* Unpublished doctoral dissertation, Boston University School of Management, 1982.

Mahon, J. F., & Murray, E. A., Jr. "Strategic planning for regulated companies." *Strategic Management Journal,* 1981, *2*(3), 251-262.

McQuaid, K. The roundtable: Getting results in Washington. *Harvard Business Review,* May-June 1981.

Murray, E. A., Jr. "Strategic choice as a negotiated outcome." *Management Science,* 1978, *24*(9), 960-972.

Novak, M. Mediating institutions: The communitarian individual in America. *Public Interest,* Summer 1982, pp. 3-20.

Pfeffer, J., & Salancik, G. R. *The external control of organizations.* New York: Harper & Row, 1978.

Pollack, A. The far-flung wars of mighty I.B.M. *New York Times,* September 19, 1982, Section 3, pp. 1, 26.

Post, J. E. *Corporate behavior and social change.* Reston, VA: Reston Publishing, 1978.

Post, J. E., Murray, E. A., Jr., Dickie, R. B., & Mahon, J. F. The public affairs function in American corporations: Development and relations with corporate planning. *Long Range Planning,* 1982, *15*(2), 12-21.

Radford, K. J. *Strategic planning: An analytical approach.* Reston, VA: Reston Publishing, 1980.

Raskin, A. H. "The cooperative economy." *New York Times,* April 14, 1982, Business Section, p. 1.

Reich, R. B. "Regulation by confrontation or negotiation?" *Harvard Business Review,* May-June 1981, pp. 82-93.

Reich, R. B. "Why the U.S. needs an industrial policy." *Harvard Business Review,* January-February 1982.

Schaumburgh, F. D. *Judgment reserved: A landmark environmental case.* Reston, VA: Reston Publishing, 1976.

Scott, B. R. Can industry survive the welfare state? *Harvard Business Review,* September-October 1982, pp, 70-84.

Steiner, G. A. *Top management planning.* New York: Macmillan, 1969.

Zakon, A. J. *Strategic planning for the 1980s and beyond.* Presentation to the Business Policy and Planning Division at the Annual National Academy of Management meetings, New York, August 17, 1982.

15

TO BARGAIN OR NOT TO BARGAIN?
The Case of Hospital Budget Cuts

V. V. Murray
T. D. Jick
P. Bradshaw

York University

In the study of bargaining and negotiation in organizational settings, there is a natural tendency to take several matters for granted in the haste to get down to the interesting questions of how the parties deal with each other. In particular, it is usually assumed that at least one of the parties believes:

(1) That there are one or more issues over which there is conflict between that party and another.
(2) That the other is a *cause* of the situation that it finds dissatisfying.
(3) That the other party is *intentionally* causing the undesirable situation.
(4) That *negotiation* is the best means for dealing with the conflict.
(5) That this negotiation is best carried out in a *direct,* face-to-face manner with the opponent.

In actual fact, of course, each of these five assumptions is problematic. In any relationship between two parties, different answers to each of these issues are possible (see Rubin & Brown, 1975). It is therefore very important in considering bargaining and negotiation in or between organizations to understand what leads to the point at which traditional face-to-face, two-party bargaining begins. One must understand something about what gives rise to the perception of conflict, the causes of conflict, and the choice of means for dealing with it, as these antecedent conditions will determine whether or not negotiations will take place at all. Similarly, to understand these antecedent conditions may, from the point of view of conflict management, obviate the need for negotiations in the first place.

This chapter does not attempt to provide a thorough and systematic review of all the theory and research surrounding the emergence of conflict and the conditions leading to the commencement of negotiations.[1] Rather, it seeks to illustrate the evolution of a relationship, where issues of difference exist from the point where these issues are recognized to the point where negotiation begins, and indicate some of the variables affecting this process. We do this by means of tracing the response of six Canadian hospitals to five years of continuous "underfunding" by a government funding agency.

Most public organizations are dependent on government funding bodies for their basic existence. In recent years, such organizations have become increasingly vulnerable to severe, externally imposed budget cuts that threaten required inputs. An environment of munificence has been dramatically replaced during the past decade by one in which every shrinking dollar must be painstakingly justified. Some organizations, however, fare better than others—in part, because some effectively fight back and resist the cuts. One strategy that is often utilized by key decision makers is to try to persuade the funding source to increase allocations through bargaining. But this approach is not the only one, and there are several basic forms of bargaining possible. Our chapter thus begins with a conceptual framework based on Jick and Murray (1982) that captures some of the different strategies and tactics, as well as the contextual and antecedent conditions, that shape the actions of organizations faced with externally imposed pressure to shrink.

A CONCEPTUAL FRAMEWORK FOR
THE ANALYSIS OF STRATEGIC DECISION
RESPONSES TO BUDGET CUTS

In recent years, a number of organizational researchers have begun to pay considerable attention to the issue of how organizations react to, and enact, their environments (e.g., Adams, 1975; Pennings & Goodman, 1977; Weick, 1979; Bromily, 1981). The adaptation of organization to periods of growth, changing market conditions, and new legal restrictions have been popular topics of interest. But as the resources for organizational inputs have diminished, the study of how organizations adapt or adjust (Miller & Friesen, 1980) to their environments has focused largely on decline and scarcity (e.g., Whetten, 1980; Levine, 1980; Jick & Murray, 1982; Zammuto & Cameron, 1982; Nottenburg & Fedor, 1982; Miles & Cameron, 1982). Unfortunately, although the number of war stories in the literature associated with crisis and decline has grown, there is a remarkably small body of empirical research grounded in analytic or theoretical frameworks (e.g., Billings, Millburn, & Schaalman, 1980; Starbuck, Grever, & Hedberg, 1978; Dunbar & Goldberg, 1978). More specifically, the literature related to strategic decision responses (of which choosing to enter into organizational negotiations is one) is especially sparse (Cameron, in press, is a good exception as is Stevens & McGowan, 1982). This chapter will test in a preliminary way some of the hypotheses in the limited extant literature on this subject.

In brief, the analytic framework on which this study is based (Jick & Murray, 1982) suggests that the strategic and tactical decisions of how to handle an externally imposed budget cut are shaped largely by the nature of the decision-making process used by those setting policy in organizations. The nature of this process (what is considered, who is involved, and so on) is a result of the actual nature and extent of the environmentally induced financial crisis and a series of critical assumptions, interpretations and perceptions held by the key decision makers. These critical assumptions are in turn influenced both by a variety of organizational and contextual conditions existing at the time of the cutback and by the results of previous strategic and tactical cutback decisions (if any). This simple analytic framework is illustrated in Figure 15.1.

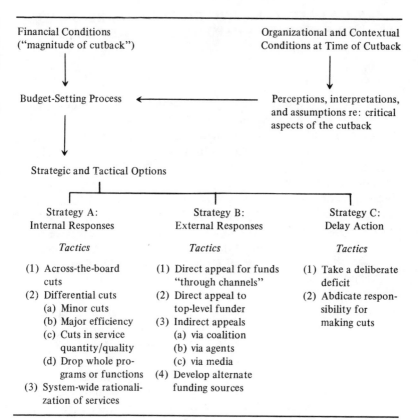

Figure 15.1   **General Framework for the Analysis of Strategic Decision Responses to Budget Cuts**

This chapter will primarily discuss the *externally* oriented strategic and tactical decisions made by a group of Canadian hospitals and illustrate the decision-making processes that lead them from one tactic to another, including that of entering into direct negotiations with their funding agency. The remaining elements of the model in Figure 15.1 will be introduced only insofar as they shed light on explanations for the types of decisions taken.

BASIC STRATEGIES AND TACTICS FOR RESPONSE TO EXTERNALLY IMPOSED BUDGET CUTS

When it comes to responding to externally imposed budget cuts, there are really only three basic strategies possible for the dominant coalitions in pubic sector organizations. One is internally oriented and involves trying to save money by means of various efficiencies or a paring back in the quantity of services offered. The second is externally oriented and involves attempting to persuade the funding sources through tactics (including negotiations) to end their cutbacks or to find alternative sources to make up the difference. The third "strategy" is to delay action, at least temporarily. Within each of these basic strategies, there is a limited number of tactics that may be adopted, although the *combinations* of strategies and tactics that form the overall *patterns* of response can be quite large. Although the focus of this chapter is on external strategies, the choice of such strategies can be understood only in the context of all the strategic alternatives or patterns.[2] Based upon a few studies (Manns & March, 1978; Glassberg, 1978; Levine, 1978, 1980; Stevens & McGowan, 1982), each of the strategies is discussed below.

The primary tactics within the *internally oriented* money saving strategy are: across-the-board cuts, differential cuts, and systemwide rationalization of cuts. Within each of these are numerous subtactics identified in Murray, Jick, and Bradshaw (1982). Together these tactics reflect a focus on organizational efficiency, i.e., a concern with resource allocation—who will get how much less (Cameron, in press).

In contradistinction, the *external* strategy is directly concerned with organization/environment relations, specifically, resource acquisition—how to get more money. The primary tactics for the externally oriented money raising strategy are as follows:

(1) Direct appeal through channels. This involves asking the primary funding source for more money. The source is usually a

branch of the state apparatus. Within this apparatus there is usually some person or unit designated as the primary contact for dealing with the focal organization regarding its funding. Thus this tactic involves appealing for more money through the designated channels by means of rational, data-based presentations of the needs of the institution and/or its existing efficiency and productivity. Such appeals usually contain little or no bargaining or negotiating behavior.

(2) Direct appeal to higher levels. This involves making appeals "over the heads" of those directly responsible for dealing with the focal organizations. This could be directed to persons one or two levels up, to heads of the ministries or government departments concerned, or to elected politicians who have ultimate authority over the funding bodies. These appeals may or may not involve bargaining behavior.

(3) Indirect appeals. This involves trying to get others to act as allies or agents on behalf of the focal organization to bring influence to bear on those who have direct-line responsibility for funding. This is different from the above tactics, which involve direct approaches to those who have official involvement in the decisions on funding for the focal organization. There are three basic mechanisms of indirect appeal:

(a) The use of coalitions of similarly affected organizations that together will strive to influence the funding source(s) on behalf of all members. Where no coalition exists, the biggest effort comes in trying to form one (among all the hospitals in a given region, for example) or, in other cases, to revive and redirect existing associations toward lobbying on behalf of underfunded members.

(b) A more independent form of indirect appeal occurs when the organization approaches other individuals or organizations that are not allies in the same field (in the sense of being similarly afflicted organizations) but could be expected to have sympathy for the focal organization's plight and some influence with the funding source(s). Examples include local politicians, business or labor leaders, associations of client groups or other organizations that have a symbiotic relationship with the focal organization.

(c) A special case of the use of "other influentials" would be the use of the media as a means of creating popular discontent with the way the funding source has been treating the focal organizations and thereby create pressure on it to improve the situation. Use of the media involves a variety of activities designed to get attention directed to the *effects* of lowered funding.

Note that none of these indirect appeals involves the focal organization in direct face-to-face negotiations.

(4) Alternate sources of funds. Finally, there is the tactic of not trying to increase funding from the major existing sources of funds but to go after money from *alternative* sources of funds. This means creating either completely new sources or obtaining a significantly increased proportion of funding from formerly minor sources. Typical here are the actions of imposing (or increasing) fees paid by users of the service or of launching major charity appeals to the public.

This array of external strategies, all of which could be categorized as influence (but not negotiating) strategies, is consistent with a study by Aplin and Hegarty (1980). These researchers differentiated four political influence strategies employed by organizations to affect legislation in business and economic matters: (1) information, (2) public exposure/appeal (e.g., media campaign), (3) direct pressure, and (4) political pressure (i.e., coalition building). The techniques within each of these categories were identified by political figures as most commonly utilized by groups attempting to influence legislative action, but they also fit directly with the first three external tactics described above.

The third basic strategy is to *delay action.* While it may seem to be a passive or reactionary strategy, it need not be. Its chief tactical manifestation is in the form of deliberately not saving or not raising sufficient money to equal the budget cut but instead going into a deficit position. In either case the hope is usually that the funding agency will not allow a deficit to occur and will step in to "bail out" the organization. Thus it is indeed a rather subtle bargaining ploy. A second tactic for delaying action is to simply abdicate responsibility to making the cuts. This can take the form of the key decision makers resigning their positions. More assertively, they may also state that they will not make the necessary cuts but that those who provided the inadequate funds will have to do so instead (and take the responsibility for the consequences as well).

The above catalogue of strategies and tactics for responding to externally imposed budget cuts is deliberately stated at a high level of abstraction and is meant to be sufficiently general to be inclusive of all the available methods for saving money, raising money, or delaying decision. It must be noted, of course, that *within* most of the tactical areas noted above, a wide variety of *specific actions* may be chosen. Thus, for example, there are various specific ways of making direct appeals through channels or working with coalitions to press for more money. These more detailed considerations become an interesting subsidiary concern in the analysis of cutback management.

Summary

The above discussion highlights two issues. First, what is the comparative use of internal, external, and delay strategies in the hospitals under study? And what would explain the pattern of results? Second, within a strategy such as the externally oriented one, is there an overall pattern of tactic use over time? And what would explain this pattern of results? The specific hypotheses in each of these areas drawn from some of the literature will be discussed in the context of the results section but follow from the conceptual framework in Figure 15.1.

THE RESEARCH STUDY—SAMPLE AND METHOD

The research to be reported here is based on six case studies of hospitals in the province of Ontario, Canada. Hospitals in Canada are part of a national health program and are about 80 to 90 percent funded by the ministries of health in each province, using money provided from the province's funds as well as from transfer payments from the federal government administered by the provinces. Remaining funds are provided by means of charges to patients (for private rooms, parking fees, cafeteria services for staff and visitors, endowments, research grants, and so on).

The six hospitals participating in this study were chosen so as to be representative of the typical sizes and location in the province. Two were large city-based teaching hospitals, two were middle-sized sub-urban general hospitals, and two were small general hospitals in a small town considerably removed from large urban areas.

The method used was a combination of archival analysis of original documents, structured questionnaires, and interviews. It was hoped that this methodological triangulation (Jick, 1979) would minimize some of the problems inherent in retrospective analysis.

In analyzing the results of this data-gathering procedure, the researchers were fully cognizant of the inherent difficulties and limitations in both the short-term case study approach and the retro-spective nature of much of the data obtained (Yin, 1979). Only information that was in written form or corroborated by at least two respondents is used in the discussion to follow. Even so, it is possible that what we have, especially for undocumented events three to five years old, may be more an *ex post facto interpretation* of what happened than an accurate account of what actually did happen.

RESULTS

The Nature of the Financial Pressure

A major determinant of the impact of financial constraints on an organization is the extent to which they represent a perceived crisis. As discussed elsewhere (Jick & Murray, 1982), while there are several definitions of the concept of crisis, it is generally agreed that a crisis is created by three phenomena: (a) severity of threat to needs, objectives, or conditions that are important to those affected by it; (b) degree of suddenness, in the sense of having little or no warning of the threat and/or little or no time to produce a response to it; and (c) uncertainty as to the likely duration of the threat. These variables are actually continuous in nature, hence the degree of crisis can vary from minimal (not too severe, relatively predictable duration, nonsudden) to severe (harsh conditions with little response time and uncertain future).

Unfortunately, the present research does not permit a test for differing reactions under a variety of differing crisis conditions.

TABLE 15.1 Extent of Cutbacks in Hospitals Under Study, 1978-1981

Year	Funding Increase	Inflation Rate	Demand for Services
1978-79	+5.2%	+9.1%	–1.2%
1979-80	+5.6%	+10.2%	–1.1%
1980-81	+11.5%	+12.5%	–0.1%

However, it does permit us to say something about one of the more common patterns of cutback found in many situations. This is the pattern of what can only be called "moderate long-term crisis." It is a pattern characterized by:

(a) moderate degree of severity, i.e., funding consistently but not greatly below the rate of inflation with the demand for services remaining essentially steady;

(b) moderate degree of suddenness, i.e., a period of about three months between being notified of the amount of money to be received for any given year and the date of budget submission;

(c) moderate degree of certainty of continuing duration, i.e., a five-year pattern suggesting that the funding source will continue in the same vein for several years in the future.

Specifically, in the case of the six hospitals in the present study, figures on the severity of crisis were available for all of them for only the 1978-1981 period (see Table 15.2). In the budget year 1978-1979, the average net increase in funding from the Ministry of Health for the hospitals in question was 5.2 percent, whereas the consumer price index for that year rose to 9.1 percent and the demand for hospital services (as represented by the average number of patient days in the six hospitals) declined by only 1.2 percent. In the year 1979-1980, the average funding increase was 5.6 percent, while the rate of inflation in general was 10.2 percent and the demand for hospital services declined by 1.7 percent. In 1980-1981, funding was at the level of 11.5 percent, inflation was 12.5 percent, and demand increased on average by .1 percent.

Discussion

This type of moderate crisis situation has confronted many organizations in health, education, and social services in western countries for the past several years. It must be noted emphatically, however, that it is different from the situation that confronted a number of agencies of the U.S. government, for example, shortly after the Reagan administration took control of the civil service. In that situation, cuts were deeper and made more suddenly than those that confronted the Ontario hospitals in the present study. On the other hand, the situation in the Ontario hospitals differs again from that confronting certain school systems in various countries, in which there has been a slow and predictable decline in the school population that was forecast five or more years prior to the start of the cutbacks. While this latter situation has undoubtedly been difficult, it could only be said to represent a minimal level of crisis, objectively speaking. (The fact that organizational leaders do not always *perceive* crisis characteristics objectively is an important phenomenon affecting the nature of these responses and will be discussed separately.)

STRATEGIC RESPONSES TO CUTBACKS

The first question to be considered is the patterns of use over time of the three basic response strategies to externally imposed budget cuts: the internally oriented (saving) strategy; the externally oriented strategy of raising money by trying to influence the funding agency or some other source of funds, or delaying action. A simplified picture of these patterns is presented in Table 15.2. For this table, the researchers looked at the complete records of all tactics adopted over the five-year period and made a judgment about the relative degree of intensity or frequency with which each of the three basic strategies was used for each year.

Minimal use of each strategy is represented by the letters S (saving), R (raise money), or D (delay action). Moderate use is indicated by the letter with one plus sign (+) after it, and heavy use by the letter and two plus signs (++). The saving strategy, for example, would be judged to have been minimally used if a hospital did no more than close a ward for several weeks in summer when demand is usually lower or become slightly more careful about the use of supplies. A moderate use of the strategy would involve more major efficiency measures such as saving $80,000 per year by introducing new techniques for floor cleaning or a small cut in staff (less than 2 percent). Heavy use of the strategy would involve larger staff cuts and/or several other major cost-cutting tactics.

Similarly, a minimal use of money raising strategy would be something like increasing user fees by the equivalent of the annual rate of inflation or making a single appeal to the funding agency for a small amount of extra money using normal channels of communication. A moderate use of this strategy would involve appeals for larger amounts of money, still going through channels. Heavy use would involve appeals for large sums and the use of other than normal channels along with one or more other tactics in this group.

While there is inevitably a certain amount of arbitrariness in judgments of this kind, the researchers remain convinced that the criteria used were sufficiently clear to allow at least a general picture to emerge. In addition to showing the relative emphasis placed on each strategy by each hospital, Table 15.2 also shows the cumulative use of each strategy over all hospitals for each year. It does so by giving a numerical weighting to the three degrees of use (++ = 3; + = 2; letters only = 1). The total score for the use of each strategy is noted at the bottom of the table. A score of 18 would mean that all six hospitals had used the strategy heavily in the year in question; a score of 1 would indicate that only one hospital had used the strategy at a minimal level.

From Table 15.2, it can be seen that there are two major trends in the patterns of basic strategy use as the moderate cutbacks recurred from year to year over the five-year period.

(1) There is a curvilinear pattern in the use of the *internally oriented* (saving) strategy. As cuts got underway in 1976, it was used heavily by two hospitals, moderately or minimally by two, and not at all by one (the sixth hospital was new and not yet on the so-called global budget, giving it full control over the distribution of its funds). As the cuts continued, the use of the saving strategy became stronger until last year, when it began to diminish.

TABLE 15.2 Basic Strategies of Cutback Response in Six Hospitals, 1977-1982

Hospital	1977-1978	1978-1979	1979-1980	1980-1981	1981-1982
A	S++; R+*	S++; R++	S++; R++; D++	S+; R++; D++	S; R++; D++
B	S++	S++; R+; D+	S++; R++; D+	S++; R++; D++	S; R++; D++
C	New Hospital N.A.	S++; R+; D+	S++; R+; D+	S+; R+; D++	S; R++; D++
D		D	S; R; D+	S++; R; D++	S; R+; D++
E	S+; R; D	S+; R+; D+	S++; R+; D+	S++; R++; D+	S++; R+; D+
F	S	S++; R	S++; R	S++; R+	S++; R+
Save	9**	13	16	16	10
Raise money	3	10	12	14	15
Delay action	1	7	11	14	14

NOTE: ++ = top priority strategy; + = significant strategy; (no sign) = minor strategy; (no letters) = strategy not used at all.

*S = Save money by means of internal cuts; R = Raise money from the environment; D = Delay action.

**Weights derived as follows: ++ = 3; + = 2; letters only = 1; no letter = 0. Total score for each strategy for each year is the total of the weighted numbers for that strategy across all the hospitals.

(2) In contrast, the use of the *externally oriented* (raising money and delaying action) strategies show a constant increase over the years with moderate to heavy use becoming the norm after the 1979-1980 budget year. This means that most hospitals chose to go into a deficit position in their projected budgets for the year and then appealed to the Ministry of Health for additional money to cover the projected debt, clearly a bargaining ploy.

Discussion

In the review of existing literature on the topic of cutback management (Jick & Murray, 1982), we posited (as did Levine, 1978) that the choice of response strategies would be strongly affected by the decision makers' interpretation of the *causes* of the cutbacks. If it is believed that the organization brought the cuts upon itself by its own actions, it would tend to adopt the internally oriented saving strategy; if it is believed that the cuts are due to forces external to the organization, it would adopt strategies aimed at persuading and influencing the environment to be more munificent—*provided,* as Jick and Murray pointed out, that it feels it has sufficient power to give it a fair chance of success.

The use of the delaying action strategy is not explicitly discussed by Levine (1978) but can be seen to be a logical outcome of the extent to which the cutbacks are seen to be "rationally or politically motivated," (Levine's terms). A *rational* cause is perceived when the decision makers believe that the funding agency accepts the overall goals and objectives of the focal organization but is concerned with making it more efficient and effective in achieving those goals through technical/economic improvements. A *political* cause is perceived when the funding agency is believed to be acting out of pure self-interest (where those interests do not complement those of the focal organization) or is being forced to act against the interests of the focal organization by more powerful outside forces. Clearly, the strategy of delay is more likely to be used in two circumstances. First, it occurs when it is felt that the funding agency may be *trying* to act rationally but is making a serious mistake in severe cutting of the focal agency (hence a deficit is incurred while the focal organization tries to persuade the funding agency to change its mind). Second, it occurs when the funding agency is seen as acting for purely political reasons, in which case delaying cutbacks or reducing their severity by taking a deficit becomes an act designed to lend force to the money-raising strategy—e.g., "They won't let us go bankrupt; they'll have to step in and give us more money to keep our deficit down."

The situation described in Table 15.2 supports the Levine hypotheses well. As the first cutbacks were made, the explanations from the Ministry of Health were couched in exclusively rationalistic, internally oriented terms—namely that the health-care system was too "fat" and had overexpanded. What was necessary, therefore, was a reduction in the level of service and improved internal efficiency. The majority of our interviewees in the six hospitals studied believed the ministry's position and accordingly devoted most of their efforts to trying to save money internally. In several cases, however, though the hospital administrators accepted the general argument that there was fat in the system and a need for retrenchment, they felt the ministry had erred in its decision on the sum granted their particular hospital because it was already more efficient than others and/or had special needs and demands that would prevent service reductions. In these cases, it made sense to appeal to the ministry through channels for more money to rectify the "error." This could be thought of as the beginning of bargaining and negotiation between the two organizations, but actually they did not view it this way. These appeals were perceived by most as part of a logical, rational process designed to overcome the inadvertent ignorance that led to too great a budget cut.

As the years passed, however, two things happened: The cuts continued at the same rate of moderate severity, and it was discovered that appeals for more funds were paying off, i.e., the ministry would grant some additional money when an appeal was made. Thus the belief that the cuts were internally caused and had a rational basis began to fade and was replaced by a stronger belief that they were externally caused for *political reasons* and that hospitals had sufficient influence with the ministry to elicit extra money from it. Respondents recalled feeling that they no longer trusted the ministry, that the ministry was being forced into damaging the health care system by the elected politicians, that "the squeaky wheel gets the grease," and so on. Hence it was reasonable that one would see a steady increase in externally oriented fund-raising attempts using more intentional and intense bargaining tactics and planned deficits aimed at "forcing" the ministry to cover them. Attempts at internal savings were maintained until the 1981-1982 budget year, during which more and more administrators took the attitude of "that's it, there's no more fat in *our* organization. Services are pared back as far as they can go without seriously endangering the level of health care available to the public." From that point on, the number of memos exchanged, and the number of formal and informal meetings with ministry officials increased significantly, as did the use of the delaying action strategy.

In fact, in the hospitals studied, it is clear that the deficit tactic was used at this stage as an aggressive, proactive device, a deliberately implicit threat to the funding agency that carried the message:

> We cannot provide a proper standard of care on the money you have given us, and the deficit reflects the amount needed. If you don't provide the extra resources to cover it, the responsibility for the results in terms of political repercussions will be yours.

This message was rarely stated explicitly, though it was conveyed in veiled form in some of the letters of appeal each year.

MONEY-RAISING TACTICS USED IN RESPONSE TO CUTBACKS

In Table 15.3, we present an overview of the specific tactics used in saving, raising money, and delaying action. For simplification, the years studied are collapsed into two periods: that between the budget of 1976-1977 and the end of the financial year 1979 (i.e., 1978-1979 budget), which was when the pattern of consistent underfunding was established (the "early" period), and the period between the budget of 1979-1980 and 1981-1982, which could be called the "later" period.

Perhaps the most striking overall finding revealed in Table 15.3 is the large growth in the externally oriented money-raising tactics over the two periods in question. The tactic of a simple appeal made through those persons in the Ministry of Health designated as the first line of contact for each hospital was utilized by all but one hospital in

TABLE 15.3 Tactics Used in Response to Cutbacks, 1977-1982

Tactics in Support of the Money-Raising Strategy	1976-1977 to 1978-1979							1979-1980 to 1981-1982						
	Hospital						Total	Hospital						Total
	A	B	C	D	E	F		A	B	C	D	E	F	
● Direct appeals through channels	X	X	X	X	X		5	X	X	X	X	X	X	6
● Direct appeals to higher levels	X						1	X		X			X	3
● Indirect appeals:														
—thru coalitions	X	X					2	X	X		X			3
—thru other influentials							0						X	1
—thru media							0				X			1
● Alternative sources of funds:														
—user fees				X			1	X	X		X			3
—public appeal							0	X						1
—others							0				X	X		2
Total Money-Raising Tactics	3	2	1	2	1		9	5	3	2	5	2	3	20
Delay Tactics														
● Planned deficits		X	X	X	X		4	X	X	X	X	X	X	6
● Abdication														
Total Delay Tactics		1	1	1	1		4	1	1	1	1	1	1	6

—288—

the early period and by all six in the later period. These appeals were strongly rationalistic in nature, providing various comparative cost or demand statistics to support the argument that the hospital in question needed more money than that contained in the original ministry allocation for the year. This finding is consistent with the results of Aplin and Hegarty (1980), who reported that "information-based influence attempts" were utilized more extensively than any other approach by organizations.

The two teaching hospitals studied were active members in a formal association of Ontario teaching hospitals, representatives of which met regularly with the minister of health and the deputy minister to discuss developments in hospital treatment programs. Respondents in our interviews frankly stated that a major purpose of such meetings was to convince the relevant officials that funding should be provided to ensure that the teaching hospitals were able to implement new advances as they occurred and generally to ensure that teaching hospitals remain leaders in providing the highest quality of health service. Only one hospital mentioned that it tried to deal with the Ministry of Health other than through its first-line representatives, and that incident occurred in 1978-1979 and involved a letter to the director of the institutional branch (responsible for overseeing all public hospitals) seeking clarification of the reasons for an additional grant that did not reach the level requested.

Finally, although the data were weak on this point, only one hospital mentioned that it deliberately raised various fees for "extras" such as parking, cafeteria food, and private bed rates. These fees were raised by the amount of the inflation rate for the year. Had all hospitals used all the means potentially at their disposal to get more money, there would have been 48 X's (8 tactics by 6 hospitals) in Table 15.3 for the 1976-1978 period. As it is, there were only 9, half of which were of the least-assertive variety.

By contrast, in the 1979-1982 period, there were 20 such efforts. This is still not quite half of the potential (reflecting the moderate nature of the cutback pressure) but over twice as many as in the previous period. The case records show three hospitals resorting to appeals to higher levels in the funding agency, two of which arranged to see the minister or deputy minister of health and one that allowed its annoyance with funding to be reported in the local newspaper. In addition to the two teaching hospitals who used their association, one (with several others) attempted to form a coalition of all the hospitals in the city in which it was located for the purpose of pressuring the ministry to provide improved funding (the effort was not successful). Another hospital said it had begun to make a point of ensuring that the mayor and other elected officials of the town were fully informed of the difficulties it was having as a result of reduced funding. There was also an increase in the reported use of higher fees, and two cases were reported where effort was made to increase the use of volunteers to provide certain services (such as information desks) formerly carried out by paid staff. (This action, while not directly raising money, is externally oriented and has the effect of making money available for other services.)

Discussion

As financial constraints continued over time, the increased use of externally oriented, *political* money-raising tactics (i.e., the increased use of higher-level approaches, media, and coalitions) reflects the decision makers' convictions that internal savings were almost used up and that the cause of the financial problems was external. An interesting aspect of the externally oriented appeals, however, solidly confirms the contention of March and Olson (1976), Weick (1979), and others that whatever is the "real" reason for a given activity in organizations, it is critical to make it *seem* "rational"—i.e., based on technoeconomic logic in support of generally accepted principles and objectives. Just as all communications from the ministry were couched in terms of rational explanations for the cuts, so all appeals were written with maximum emphasis on factual data. The problem, of course, is that there was (and still is) little or no agreement among the hospitals or ministry officials as to what criteria are definitive in terms of showing needs and comparative cost/benefit positions.

Though the actual use of externally oriented tactics of bringing political pressure to bear on the funding agency certainly increased substantially from the early to late periods, the attitudes of the decision makers toward the ministry changed even more radically. At the time of our interviews in July 1981, they had reached new heights in terms of beliefs that the hospitals would not receive a fair and full hearing of their cases. Such attitudes would likely presage an even greater tendency to resort to politically oriented, money-raising, and delaying tactics if the current funding practices continue.

The most interesting finding with respect to the internally oriented money-saving tactics with implications for external relations is that none of the hospitals adopted what might be termed an "ultrarationalistic" position. In no case was there an instance of an overall review of the major treatment programs and functions leading to a decision to actually eliminate one or more of them. The kind of basic change in overall strategy, which in business organizations is represented by the elimination of a product line or a major market redirection, was simply not done during the period in question. Nor was there any move on the part of the hospitals studied to join with others in the area to engage in systemwide forms of rationalization, e.g., putting all obstetrics in one hospital, all psychiatric cases in another, major cardiac surgery in a third, and so on. (It must be stated that in two cases, there already was a limited amount of system rationalization for medical programs, and two other hospitals had entered into a regional laboratory arrangement, putting all lab facilities for the district in one hospital.) But in general, as would be consistent with moderate levels of crisis, the effort was made to save money only by more or less traditional attempts at increasing internal efficiency.

CONCLUSION

The total health care system for a large region like the province of Ontario is vastly complex. To understand how effective and efficient it is in providing health care to its 6 million inhabitants requires elaborate knowledge of the nature and frequency of illness and recovery and of the myriad costs associated with treating it. There is no well-understood means for obtaining this knowledge or even agreement as to the best method for developing such means. Rather, there is a vast array of reports and statistics, each of which is collected and distributed by the parties interested in the health care system. The parties do not all collect the same statistics and those that are collected can be interpreted in various ways. The result of this situation is that each of the major groups who are part of the system (such as elected politicians, health care professionals and their associations, the heads of various health care institutions, civil servants, and various organized groups in the general public) has its own interpretation of the standards of care, current quality of care, relative priorities of different aspects of care, and so on.

In our study, it appeared as though in the mid-1970s (between about 1976 to 1978) there was a remarkable degree of consensus among at least the politicians, civil servants, and health care administrators that the system was "fat" in the sense that there were more beds per 1000 population than was necessary and too many people with not enough to do. It was generally accepted that cutbacks and efficiency measures in the system as a whole were necessary, and for the first two or three years after 1976, most hospitals tried vigorously to save money internally (though from the beginning concern was expressed about how the particular budgets for their specific institutions were calculated). This is consistent with Cameron's (in press) prediction that administrators in declining institutions tend to emphasize internal budgeting and fiscal concerns.

At this point, there were two directions in which the system could have moved—toward greater rationalization or greater politicization. Greater rationalization would have meant spending a lot of time working out a set of criteria that could be generally accepted by the funding agency and the hospitals for judging efficiency *and* effectiveness in the context of a set of previously agreed-upon goals and objectives. (This is the successful private sector model discussed by Zammuto and Cameron, 1982.) Such a model would have required leading participants from the ministry and the hospital to work closely together to achieve a minimum level of consensus on a set of standards (realizing, of course, that pure objectivity would never be achievable) and possibly to consider some domain changes.

The other direction was that of greater politicization, which would have meant increasing conviction on all sides that no common objectives could exist, nor could any consensus on standards of measurement be agreed upon. Therefore, the relationship between the funding agency and the individual hospitals would have been adversarial. *The ensuing conflict could only have been resolved by negotiations involving the use of power, influence, and information, which would omit or distort anything that failed to support the preferred point of view.*

In the present study, it is apparent that the politicization model predominates in the minds of hospital managerial staff and the upper-level Ministry of Health managers who decide on funds. The more health care administrators have come to view the funding decisions as political and adversarial, the more they have moved away from internally-oriented money-saving strategies and toward money raising or planned deficit strategies. Thus budgeting became subservient to the ongoing process of negotiating with the environment for more money. It became an activity for reflecting expectations and judgments about standards for the quality and quantity of health care provided by the hospital, which then became part of the ongoing negotiating process with the ministry—as opposed to its earlier role as an internally oriented tool for bringing about, and enforcing, the greatest level of internal cost efficiency. This latter role still existed, but was distinctly secondary by 1981-1982.

It seems clear, then, that unless extraordinary measures are taken by the funding source, sustained moderate cutbacks can lead to a strong increase in the politicization of the process. Those on the receiving end undergo a substantial change in their perceptions of the cause of the cutbacks and, given a little reinforcement, will quickly change their response strategy pattern from one emphasizing internally oriented, rationally based savings measures to externally oriented, politically based money raising measures.

While the study reported here draws attention to the broad distinctions between internal versus external and rational versus political responses to cutbacks, there is still much that remains unknown. As yet, there is no clear picture of what it is that leads an organization to commence direct face-to-face negotiations with an opponent as opposed to adopting one or more of the indirect influence attempts discussed above. The details of the bargaining process itself under conditions of a constraint crisis, which were not even addressed in this study, also remain largely unknown. Finally, it must be noted that the situation discussed here is itself only one power configuration—that in which one party (the Ministry of Health) is in a generally strong power position over the other (the individual hospitals) and initiates the actions that cause the conflict. Needless to say, other basic power configurations could well produce different strategic decision responses and action patterns.

NOTES

1. Readers interested in general reviews of conflict in organizations should see Thomas (1976). For more practical examples of alternatives to conflict, see Reich (1981) and Drayton (1981).

2. Interestingly, Stevens and McGowan (1982) found that the distinction between internal and external strategies can best be described as a continuum rather than as a dichotomy because some of them have both internal and external objectives.

REFERENCES

Adams, J. S. *The environmental context of negotiation between human systems.* Paper delivered at the Negotiation Conference, Center for Creative Leadership, Greensboro, N.C., 1975.

Aplin, J., & Hegarty, W. H. Political influence: Strategies employed by organizations to impact legislation in business and economic matters. *Academy of Management Journal,* 1980, *23*(3), 438-450.

Berger, M. Two paradoxes in managing decline. *Proceedings of the Academy of Management,* 1982, 334-338.

Billings, R. S., Millburn, T. M., & Schaalman, M. L. A model of crisis perception: A theoretical and empirical analysis. *Administrative Science Quarterly,* 1980, *25*(2), 300-316.

Bromily, P. Task environments and budgetary decison-making. *Academy of Management Review,* 1981, *6*(2), 277-288.

Cameron, K. Strategic responses to conditions of decline: Higher education and the private sector. *Journal of Higher Education,* in press.

Drayton, W. Getting smarter about regulation. *Harvard Business Review,* July-August 1981, 32-38.

Dunbar, R., & Goldberg, W. Crisis development and strategic response in European corporations. In C. F. Smart & W. T. Stanbury (Eds.), *Studies in crisis management.* Toronto: Butterworth, 1978.

Hermann, C. F. Some consequences of crisis which limit the viability of organizations. *Administrative Science Quarterly,* 1963, *8*(1), 61-82.

Jick, T. D. Mixing qualitative and quantitative methods: Triangulation in action. *Administrative Science Quarterly,* 1979, *24*(4), 602-611.

Jick, T. D., & Murray, V. V. The management of hard times: Budget cutbacks in public sector organizations. *Organization Studies,* 1982, *3*(2), 141-169.

Levine, C. H. Organizational decline and cutback management. *Public Administration Review,* 1978, *38*(2), 316-325.

Levine, C. H. (Ed.). *Managing fiscal stress.* Chatham, NJ: Chatham House, 1980.

Manns, C. L., & March, J. G. Financial adversity. Internal competition and curriculum change in a university. *Administrative Science Quarterly,* 1978, *23*(4), 541-552.

March, J. G., & Olsen, J. P. *Ambiguity and choice in organizations.* Oslo: Universitetsforlaget, 1976.

Miles, R. H., & Cameron, K. *Coffin nails and corporate strategies.* Englewood Cliffs, NJ: Prentice-Hall, 1982.

Miller, D., & Friesen, P. Momentum and revolution in organizational adaptation. *Academy of Management Journal,* 1980, *23*(4), 591-614.

Murray, V. V., Jick, J. D., & Bradshaw, P. *Managerial responses to sustained moderate levels of financial constraint in public organizations.* Paper presented at the 10th World Conference of the International Sociological Association, Mexico City, 1982.

Nottenburg, G., & Fedor, D. B. Organizational responses to decline. *Academy of Management Proceedings,* 1982, 255-259.

Pennings, J., & Goodman, P. Toward a workable framework. In P. Goodman, J. Pennings, & Associates (Eds.), *Perspectives on organizational effectiveness.* San Francisco: Jossey-Bass, 1977.

Reich, R. B. Regulation by confrontation or negotiation. *Harvard Business Review,* May-June 1981, 82-93.

Rubin, J. Z., & Brown, B. R. *The social psychology of bargaining and negotiation.* New York: Academic, 1975.

Smart, C., & Vertinsky, I. Design for crisis decision units. *Administrative Science Quarterly,* 1977, *22*(4), 640-657.

Starbuck, W. H., Greve, A., & Hedberg, B. Responding to crisis: Theory and the experience of European business. In C. F. Smart & W. T. Stanbury (Eds.), *Studies in crisis management.* 1978.

Stevens, J., & McGowan, R. Dimensions of managerial strategies in governmental organizations. *Academy of Management Proceedings,* 1982, 344-348.

Thomas, K. Conflict and conflict management. In Marvin Dunnette (Ed.), *Handbook of industrial organizational psychology.* Chicago: Rand McNally, 1976.

Weick, K. *The social psychology of organizing* (2nd ed.). Reading, MA: Addison-Wesley, 1979.

Whetten, D. A. Organizational decline: Sources, responses and effects. In J. R. Kimberly, R. H. Miles, & Associates (Eds.), *The organizational life cycle.* San Francisco: Jossey-Bass, 1980.

Yin, R. The case study crisis: Some answers. *Administrative Science Quarterly,* 1981, *21*(1), 51-65.

Zammuto, R. F., & Cameron, K. S. Environmental decline and organizational response. *Academy of Management Proceedings,* 1982, 250-254.

16

NEGOTIATIONS IN THE ORGANIZATIONAL ENVIRONMENT

A Framework for Discussion

Robert G. Eccles

Harvard Business School

A FRAMEWORK FOR NEGOTIATION

The three chapters in Part IV cover a broad range of topics. The negotiation issues addressed by these chapters and questions that arise in attempting to integrate them can be outlined through the use of the matrix presented in Figure 16.1. Figure 16.1 shows that negotiations are of two basic types: resource based and ideologically based. Both of these types can occur within the organization (internal) and between the organization and an actor in its environment (external). I have placed the three chapters in the boxes corresponding to their explicit and implicit content. The resulting pattern suggests that in spite of the apparent variety in topics, together they suggest a general framework.

	Type of Negotiation	
	Resource	Ideological
Internal	V. Murray et al. 4	Brown & Brown 1
External	3 V. Murray et al. E. Murray	2 Brown & Brown E. Murray

Focus of Negotiation

Figure 16.1

IDEOLOGICAL NEGOTIATIONS: INTERNAL AND EXTERNAL

Brown and Brown make the very useful distinction between ideological negotiations and bargaining over resource distributions or task definitions. They treat ideologies as sets of beliefs that bind people together and that explain cause-and-effect relationships. Their central argument is that the embedding of organizations in the larger society (i.e., the external environment) influences internal ideological negotiations. In particular, external agencies may intervene directly in internal ideological negotiations and members' actions may be heavily influenced by strongly felt external loyalties that shape their individual ideology. Brown and Brown explore the factors contributing to ideological similarity and diversity among members. They also explore the various levels at which intervention can be made to facilitate these internal ideological negotiations. One of these levels is the link with the external environment.

While Brown and Brown are primarily concerned with the impact of external relationships on internal ideological negotiations, Murray is directly concerned with external negotiations per se. Brown and Brown's treatment of ideological negotiations can easily be generalized to relationships with external actors, but this is largely implicit in their chapter. The ideological component of external negotiations is more explicit in Murray's essay, as is evident from his discussion of "'external' policymaking" and individualistic and communitarian ideologies. Cell 2 does not receive the same direct attention as Cell 1; the reader may wish to consider the varioius forms that explicit arguments would take here. Another useful set of questions suggested by these two chapters relates to the nature of the relationship between internal and external ideological negotiations.

EXTERNAL NEGOTIATIONS: IDEOLOGICAL AND RESOURCE

The central point of Murray's chapter is that conventional strategies may lead to various forms of "strategic stalemate," i.e., low performance. He argues that the options for getting out of this situation—based on increasing power over the environment or consolidating diffused decision-making responsibility in the environment—are not always viable. Instead, the firm must learn how to negotiate with environmental elements such as government agencies.

Murray argues that the nature of these negotiations is affected by the shift in America from an individualistic to a communitarian ideology. This shift, in turn, affects the use of resources. He gives as an example a collective research and development venture formed by 16 major U.S. electronics companies. Here negotiations would be required for determining what resources each firm would contribute and how each firm would benefit from the collective effort. Negotiations with government agencies also involve resources, such as the costs incurred by the firm in meeting regulatory requirements.

Murray's chapter suggests the need to examine in more depth the relationship between resource and ideological negotiations with the external environment. One important issue is the extent to which negotiations of one type constrain and shape negotiations of the other. This issue needs clarification both in the external case and in the internal one explored by Brown and Brown. At the same time, similarities and differences between the internal and external cases need to be established.

RESOURCE NEGOTIATIONS: EXTERNAL AND INTERNAL

Like E. Murray, V. Murray, Jick, and Bradshaw are also concerned with external resource negotiations. In a nicely done empirical essay, they contribute to building a theoretical framework linking external and internal resource negotiations. They studied the responses of six hospitals to funding cutbacks in a situation they termed "moderate long-term crisis." This situation is characterized by (1) moderate degree of severity, (2) moderate degree of suddenness, and (3) moderate degree of certainty of continuing duration. For all situations, they identified three basic responses: (1) an internal strategy of budget cutting that requires internal negotiations over resources, (2) an external strategy of negotiating for restoration of funds or obtaining funds from alternative sources, and (3) a delaying strategy that seeks to avoid responsibility for making cuts by putting this on the external agency, thereby pressuring it to "bail out" the hospital if it is unwilling to take this step.

Murray et al. found a curvilinear pattern in the internal budget-cutting strategy and increasing use of the external negotiating and delaying strategies as reduced funding persisted over time. Thus they explicitly show a relationship between internal and external resource negotiations. More implicit in their chapter are the ideological conditions in which these external negotiations occur and the consequences of the delaying strategy to internal ideological negotiations. The delaying strategy entails the direct intervention of external agencies, one of the four factors identified by Brown and Brown as contributing to internal ideological negotiations.

By identifying the variables of severity, suddenness, and uncertainty of duration, Murray et al. suggest the possibility of a more general theory linking internal and external resource exchanges. How are these related according to variations in these three variables? The third strategy of "delay" can be seen as adding a third dimension of time to the table shown in Figure 16.1. Obviously, timing is crucial in negotiations, and they rightly single it out for special attention. This general theory of resource negotiation can then be combined with one for ideological negotiations. The chapters in Part IV suggest some specific issues that would be involved in accomplishing this.

INTERNAL NEGOTIATIONS:
RESOURCE AND IDEOLOGICAL

The need for further exploring the relationship between internal resource and ideological negotiations has already been suggested. As depicted in Figure 16.1, the chapters in this session provide the least linkage from this perspective. This is not surprising given the focus of this session on negotiations in the organizational environment. But it is telling that when these chapters are taken together, they clearly show that a better understanding of external negotiations will contribute to a better understanding of internal negotiations.

—V—

ORGANIZATIONAL APPLICATIONS

17

AN INFLUENCE PERSPECTIVE ON BARGAINING WITHIN ORGANIZATIONS

David Kipnis
Stuart M. Schmidt

Temple University

Empirical studies of bargaining typically focus on outcomes. This research tradition has usually examined the connection between bargaining contexts and the nature of outcomes, to the exclusion of the actual bargaining process. Yet as Kochan (1980) points out, there is a need to examine the behavioral process of bargaining rather than treating it as a "black box." The purpose of this chapter is to describe what happens inside this black box of the bargaining process. The specific focus is on the interpersonal tactical actions taken by managers when influencing superiors and subordinates.

While not necessarily labeled bargaining, these tactical actions, or influence attempts, occur on a daily basis. Whenever people seek to influence each other at work, there occurs, implicitly or explicitly, a

Authors' Note: *The assistance of Carol Carynnyk is gratefully acknowledged.*

process of negotiation. The process remains implicit if both parties agree with each other. However, this negotiating process becomes explicit when disagreement occurs.

Influence is exercised for a variety of reasons. Sometimes it is used to satisfy personal objectives such as securing benefits or better work assignments. Other times it is used reactively to prevent interference with one's own activities. Most often influence is used to pursue organizational objectives, as, for example, to encourage others to perform effectively, to promote new ideas, or to introduce new work procedures (Schmidt & Kipnis, 1982). Frequently, a combination of these personal and organizational reasons underlies the use of influence in organizations.

Within organizations, influence may be exercised in a variety of ways. These attempts include changes in the target's work environment (Kipnis & Cosentino, 1969), the use of nonverbal behavior and symbols (Pfeffer, 1981), behavior modification (Babb & Kopp, 1978), and direct verbal influence. This chapter focuses on three interrelated aspects of direct verbal influence among organizational participants. These are the range of influence strategies used by managers to influence both their superiors and subordinates, the parameters governing the use of the strategies, and the effects of using various strategies on subsequent interpersonal relations among the persons involved.

PREVIOUS DESCRIPTIONS OF INFLUENCE

Social scientists have been interested in developing a parsimonious system for classifying the various ways by which people attempt to influence others. The reason for this interest is that if we are to understand how influence is exercised and the consequences associated with its use, it is necessary to be able to classify forms of influence into meaningful categories. However, despite the many years of research on social influence, we know very little about how people actually exercise influence. Our most prevalent ideas about compliance-gaining behavior are based on armchair speculations that have been organized into rational classification schemes. Examples of such schemes include those based on the nature of controls

(Etzioni, 1961), the amount of control and manipulation (Tedeschi, Schlenker, & Bonoma, 1973), or the bases of power (French & Raven, 1959), to name a few of the many current deductively derived classification schemes.

A number of problems with these deductive classification schemes have been noted. One problem, as Raven (1974) has observed, is not only that they overlap each other, but also that each has a different number of dimensions specified. For example, if influence tactics are derived from the French and Raven (1959) bases of power, five influence strategies will emerge: rewards, coercion, expertise, legitimacy, and charisma. Alternatively, if influence tactics are derived from Kelman's (1958) scheme, three influence strategies will result based on the use of sanctions, personal charm, and credibility.

Another problem with many of the existing classification schemes is that they blur the distinction between "resources controlled," which provides the potential for exercising influence, and the actual influence tactics used. With few exceptions (e.g., Cartwright, 1965; Dahl, 1957), the distinction between resources and influence strategies has not been made explicit. As a result, an assumption has developed that when the bases of power are known, the influence tactics are also known (see, for example, Tedeschi et al., 1973). It is assumed that threats are used when the base of power is coercive and that promises are used when the base of power is reward. This assumption may be incorrect. It may be that there is little relationship between the nature of the resources controlled and the tactics used. One possibility is that control of practically any resource needed by a target person provides an influencer with many options for behavior. Not only may users of sanctions promise and threaten, but they may also coax, hint, and argue as well. Perhaps control over many resources expands the range of influence tactics powerholders use, rather than simply dictates which tactics will be chosen.

Yet another problem with deductive classification schemes is that they are both deficient and excessive. When influence tactics are actually studied, it is found that people do not use all of the tactics described by the classification schemes. Not only that, but people use influence tactics not even mentioned in these schemes. This point was first revealed in a study by Goodchild, Quadrado, and Raven (1975), in which college students wrote brief essays on the topics, "How I got my way." Many of the influence tactics described by these students could not be easily classified into preexisting categories. Indeed, several influence tactics, such as the use of expert power, were not even mentioned.

INDUCTIVE STUDIES OF INFLUENCE

Due to the many problems with deductive classification schemes, recent studies of influence have adopted the methodology of first asking people in a given setting to describe the actual tactics that they use. These descriptions are then used to construct questionnaires that contain the influence tactics described by respondents. Factor analysis and other multidimensional analyses of these questionnaire data have found underlying structures that could not be deduced from existing classification schemes. In studies of interpersonal influence in nonorganizational settings, two or three dimensions of influence tend to emerge (Cody & McLaughlin, 1980; Falbo, 1977; Falbo & Peplau, 1980; Kipnis & Cohn, 1979). These dimensions involve using assertive tactics, rational tactics, and nondirective or manipulative tactics. Clearly, these dimensions differ from those that have been derived from deductive classifications of power (Student, 1968; Perreault & Miles, 1978).

The above methodology was also used by Kipnis, Schmidt, and Wilkinson (1980) to study managerial use of influence within organizations. In that study, managers described actual incidents in which they attempted to change the behavior of subordinates, peers, and superiors. Based on these descriptions, a questionnaire was constructed containing 58 influence tactics. Then, new groups of managers used the questionnaire to describe how frequently they used each tactic when attempting to influence their superiors, peers, or subordinates. Up to seven dimensions of influence were found, depending on the target of influence. Combining the results from the three target groups, seven influence strategies were isolated as shown in Table 17.1. A new scale, the Profile of Organizational Influence Strategies (POIS), was developed to measure these seven influence strategies (Kipnis & Schmidt, 1982).

Again it is apparent that the dimensions, or strategies of influence, in Table 17.1 differ from any that could be derived from existing

TABLE 17.1   Strategies of Organizational Influence

Strategy	Behavior
Reason	This strategy involves the use of facts and data to support the development of a logical argument. Sample tactic: "I explained the reasons for my request."
Coalition	This strategy involves the mobilization of other people in the organization. Sample tactic: "I obtained the support of co-workers to back up my request."
Ingratiation	This strategy involves the use of impression management, flattery, and the creation of goodwill. Sample tactic: "I acted very humbly while making my request."
Bargaining	This strategy involves the use of negotiation through the exchange of benefits or favors. Sample tactic: "I offered an exchange (if you do this for me, I will do something for you)."
Assertiveness	This strategy involves the use of a direct and forceful approach. Sample tactic: "I demanded that he or she do what I requested."
Higher Authority	This strategy involves gaining the support of higher levels in the organization to back-up requests. Sample tactic: "I obtained the informal support of higher-ups."
Sanctions	This strategy involves the use of organizationally derived rewards and punishments. Sample tactic: "I threatened to give him or her an unsatisfactory performance evaluation."

classifications. As previously mentioned, for instance, influence tactics deduced from French and Raven's (1959) classification would use rewards, punishment, expertise, legitimacy, and charisma. Such a set of influence tactics would be both redundant in terms of the underlying factor structure, and deficient, because it would not contain strategies of coalitions, ingratiation, or appeals to higher authority.

In order to explore patterns of influence usage in organizations, a three-nation study of managerial influence was conducted. The POIS was administered to first- and second-line managers in England (N = 121), Australia (N = 126), and the United States (N = 113). In each country, two versions of the POIS scale allowed managers to indicate how frequently they used each of seven strategies to influence subordinates and superiors. Additionally, respondents completed a supplemental questionnaire describing their work and attitudes toward their work situations.

MOST FREQUENTLY USED STRATEGIES

It is reassuring to find great similarities among Australian, U.S., and English managers in how they exercise influence. Furthermore, in all three countries the frequency of using the influence strategies was virtually identical. When seeking to influence their superiors, managers reported that they relied most often on reason, followed by coalition, and then ingratiation. Going over the "boss's head" or resorting to higher authority was used least often to influence superiors.

The rank order of preferred strategies was somewhat different when influencing subordinates. Once again managers reported that the most frequently used strategy was reason. What was of interest, however, was that the second most popular strategy was assertiveness. While perhaps not surprising, it confirms the common belief that managers can aggressively demand compliance from their subordinates but not from their superiors. These findings are shown in Table 17.2.

FACTORS AFFECTING THE
CHOICE OF INFLUENCE STRATEGIES

Having identified seven influence strategies, the next question concerned the factors that affected their use. Why do managers demand compliance in one instance, plead in another, and rationally argue in a third? Available research on this topic suggests that a complex of personal, organizational, and situational factors may determine which strategy is used. These factors include a manager's relative power, objectives for wanting to use influence, and expectations of the willingness of targets to comply.

TABLE 17.2   Most to Least Popular Strategies Used in All Countries

	When Managers Influenced Superiors*	When Managers Influenced Subordinates
Most Popular	Reason	Reason
	Coalition	Assertiveness
	Ingratiation	Ingratiation
	Bargaining	Coalition
Least Popular	Assertiveness	Bargaining
	Higher Authority	Higher Authority
		Sanctions

*The strategy of sanctions is omitted in the scale that measures upward influence.

Power

Power enters into the selection of influence strategies in two ways. First, managers who control resources that are valued by others or who are preceived to be in positions of dominance use a greater variety of influence strategies than do those with less power. Second, managers with power use assertiveness with greater frequency than do those with less power.

(1) Variety of influence strategies. Perhaps the most striking illustration of the variety of influence strategies used by managers with power can be found by examining how they influence superiors and subordinates. In all countries, managers use the following four strategies more frequently to influence subordinates than to influence superiors: assertiveness, ingratiation, bargaining, and higher authority. Only reason was used more frequently to influence superiors. While perhaps not too surprising, this finding indicates that managers apply substantial pressure on subordinates to comply because they potentially have a larger range of strategies available. Thus if one strategy does not gain compliance, pressure is maintained on subordinates through the use of an alternative strategy.

Another example of this relationship between power and variety of influence strategies is found by comparing the approaches of managers who direct units of varying technological complexity. Hickson, Hinings, Lee, Scheneck, & Pennings (1971) and Perrow (1967) have pointed out that managers who supervise nonroutine technology are relatively powerful because other units depend on their expertise to solve important organizational problems. In comparison, managers who direct routine kinds of work are generally taken for granted because the contributions of their units tend to be of less consequence. Consistent with this reasoning, we found that managers who directed nonroutine technologies used a greater variety of strategies when attempting to influence their superiors. In particular, they frequently used reason, assertiveness, and higher authority. It may be that managers of nonroutine technologies use reason because their work generates information and ideas that must be communicated, assertiveness because their control of uncertainty provides them with a base of power, and high authority because they are less concerned with retaliation from their superiors.

(2) Assertiveness. In addition to using a greater variety of influence strategies, managers who have power are more likely to invoke assertive and directive strategies. While the relationship between power and assertive tactics is hardly surprising, it is found with unceasing regularity within both organizations and general social relations. For example, it is reported in studies among children attempting to influence younger children, peers, and adults (Goldstein, Miller, Griffin, & Hasher, 1981), among lovers attempting to influence each other (Kipnis & Cohn, 1979), and among business organizations (Wilkinson & Kipnis, 1978). In all instances, those with more power (or resources) are likely to use directive tactics to influence others. We speculate that there is an "iron law of power" such that the greater the discrepancy in power between influencer and target, the greater the probability that more directive influence strategies will be used.

This does not necessarily mean that powerful managers use assertiveness as their first strategy. Given a choice, most managers initially seek to exert influence through simple requests and reason. Assertiveness is used when the target of influence refuses or appears reluctant to comply with a request. When such resistance is encountered, managers with power tend to use more directive strategies. Typically they shift from using simple requests to insisting that their demands be met. In contrast, managers without power are more likely to stop trying to influence when they encounter resistance or shift to other influence strategies such as coalition or ingratiation. This is because they feel the costs associated with assertiveness are unacceptable. For example, they may be unwilling to provoke the ill will of the target.

Objectives

Our findings clearly indicate that managers also vary their strategies in relation to their objectives. When managers seek benefits from a superior, they often use "soft" words, impression management, and the promotion of pleasant relationships—tactics measured by the strategy of ingratiation. In comparison, managers attempting to persuade their superiors to accept new ideas usually rely on the use of data, explanations, and logical arguments, that is, tactics measured by the strategy of reason. In addition, they are likely to use assertiveness to obtain organizational objectives but not personal objectives.

Similarly, this matching of strategies to objectives holds true when managers influence their subordinates. For example, reason is used to sell ideas to subordinates and ingratiation is used to obtain favors. As a general rule, the more reasons managers have for exercising influence, the greater will be the variety of strategies that they will use.

Expectations of Compliance

Managers also vary their strategies according to how successful they expect to be in influencing their target. Where past experience indicates a higher probability of success, managers use simple requests to gain compliance. In contrast, when success is less predictable, managers are increasingly tempted to use assertiveness and sanctions to achieve their objectives.

Lowered expectations for successful influence frequently are based on a realistic appraisal by managers of the targets' potential resistance. In other instances, however, managers' expectations are not based on reality. Thus, for example, the social psychological literature consistently reports that as individuals become increasingly dissimilar in terms of attitudes, race, sex, and social orientations, they expect that others will be less cooperative (Byrne & Griffitt, 1973). Given these lowered expectations, it is understandable that there are frequent complaints that managers use more assertiveness and sanctions with minority employees. This behavior may be attributed to managers' mistaken notion that reason will not yield compliance. Hence they feel that it is necessary to use more directive tactics.

Other personal variables that can distort expectations for successful influence include the degree of liking the target (Wartman & Linsenmeier, 1977), trusting the target (Deutsch & Krauss, 1962), and lacking self-confidence (Kipnis & Lane, 1962; Mowday, 1978). In all instances, these lowered expectations increase the probability that managers will shift from reason to assertiveness and sanctions in attempting to influence targets who they do not expect to be compliant.

Summary of Factors Affecting Choice of Influence

Integrating the findings presented in the preceding sections, we hypothesize that managers will use *assertiveness* when they have a predominance of power, their objectives are organizational (rather than personal), and their expectations about their ability to influence the target are low. Managers will use *reason* when the target and the manager approach equality in power, organizational objectives are sought, and they have high expectations about their abilities to exercise influence. Finally, *ingratiation* is most likely to be used when managers have less power than the target of influence, personal objectives are sought, and expectations of successful influence are low.

COMBINATIONS OF INFLUENCE STRATEGIES

Managers were found to vary the combination of influence strategies that they typically use. Cluster analyses of data from the Profile of Organizational Influence Strategies instrument indicated that managers in England, Australia, and the United States fall into the following three clusters of influence usage: *shotgun* managers, *tactician* managers, and *bystander* managers.

Shotgun Managers

This group of managers had higher scores on all seven influence strategies than did tactician or bystander managers. Shotgun managers, then, attempt to get their way by using the full range of influence strategies. One possible explanation for this behavior is that they want much from others and as a result have to try out different strategies.

To test this possibility, discriminant analysis was used to analyze the questionnaire data of all managers. This analysis indicated that shotgun managers reported having significantly more unfulfilled objectives in terms of ability to sell their ideas, obtain personal benefits, or get others to work more effectively. In addition, they are the ones in each country with the least organizational experience. In summary, shotgun managers are inexperienced, probably ambitious, and want much. To this end, they openly attempt to obtain what they want through the indiscriminant use of influence strategies.

Tactician Managers

This group of managers relied heavily on reason to influence others, though they had at least average scores on the remaining strategies. That is, tactician scores on the use of reason were as high as shotgun managers'. Their remaining strategy scores, however, were lower than shotgun managers' but higher than bystanders'. Tacticians, then, get their way primarily by using facts in logical arguments. The image portrayed here is that of rational organizational managers exercising organizational influence in a deliberate manner.

Discriminant analysis indicated several organizational and personal characteristics that distinguish tacticians from other managers. Perhaps most important is that they have power in their organizations. This was shown in several ways. First, tacticians manage work units that do technologically complex work. Their employees are skilled, and the work requires considerable planning before it can be carried out. As noted earlier, managers of "high tech" units should have power in their organizations. Our data confirmed this. Tacticians stated that they have considerable influence over such matters as setting budgets, influencing company policy, and dealing with personnel matters. In general, they expressed satisfaction with their ability to perform their work.

In sum, it seems that tacticians are flexible in their use of influence, find their organizational objectives generally met, and rate themselves effective in carrying out their tasks. At the same time, they occupy positions of power based on their skills and knowledge, which allows them to influence others by relying mainly on the strategy of reason.

Bystander Managers

This group had the lowest scores on all seven influence strategies. They exercise little influence in their organizations, despite the fact that they occupy managerial positions. There are two alternative explanations for their inactivity. One alternative is that bystanders occupy such powerful positions in their organizations that others continually anticipate their needs. Hence they do not have to exercise influence, because they get their way without effort. The other alternative explanation for their inactivity is that they lack power in their organizations. Therefore, bystanders feel it is futile even to try to influence them.

The results of the discriminant analysis support the second explanation. Bystanders are managers who direct organizational units that do mostly routine work. They also supervise the greatest number of subordinates, which is another indication of routinization. Given this kind of work, it is not surprising that they rate themselves as having little organizational power. They are unable to influence decisions about budget, personnel, and company policy. Further, in each country, the managers in this group are those who have been in the same job the longest.

In sum, our impression is that bystanders are managers who are marking time in mundane jobs and who see themselves as helpless, because they have little or no organizational impact. This interpretation is consistent with Seligman's (1975) description of "learned helplessness." This condition is produced by having little personal control over important life events. The result of this loss of control is that individuals stop wanting and stop trying. Such inactivity was also shown by bystander managers. They no longer attempt to influence others in their organizations, either to obtain personal benefits or to achieve organizational objectives. Not surprisingly, as a group they express the least satisfaction with their abilities to work effectively.

DIFFERENTIAL CONSEQUENCES OF INFLUENCE STRATEGIES

The choice of strategies used in the influence process affects the influencer's perceptions of the target in predictable ways. Successful use of strategies such as sanctions or assertiveness increases an influencer's perception of control over the target. In such cases, compliance is attributed by influencers to their own demands and orders rather than to the free choice of the target. For instance, if a manager said to a subordinate, "I insist that you do what I say," and the subordinate subsequently complied, a reasonable inference by the manager is that the order caused compliance. Such an inference is less likely to be made if a manager said (and meant), "Here's what I would like you to do, but you decide for yourself." Compliance subsequent to this second tactic is more likely to be attributed by the manager to the subordinate's own decision to comply. In terms of attribution theory (Kelley, 1967), one consequence of using assertiveness and sanctions is that the target's behavior is perceived as externally rather than internally controlled. The use of reason and ingratiation are less likely to produce such attributions (Kipnis, 1976) because they allow target persons freedom to decide for themselves whether or not to comply. Another consequence of successfully using assertiveness and sanctions is that the target is less favorably evaluated. This is because the target is seen as externally controlled. To illustrate, in a recent experimental simulation of an organizational work experience (Kipnis, Schmidt, Price, & Stitt, 1981), subjects were appointed as leaders of small work groups and instructed to act as either authoritarian or democratic leaders. Authoritarian leaders were instructed to use assertive and directive tactics in which all decisions were made by themselves. Democratic leaders used reason and nondirective tactics. They also delegated decision-making power to group members. At the end of the work session, autocratic leaders perceived group members as externally controlled. That is, they were *less* likely than democratic leaders to attribute group members' performance to "group members own motivation to perform well." Further, authoritarian leaders evaluated the task performance of group members less favorably than democratic leaders did.

The apparent explanation for these less favorable evaluations is that the behavior of the target (workers), no matter how excellent, is seen as guided by the leader's orders rather than by the target's abilities and motivation. Hence the target is not given full credit for his or her performance. Evidence supporting this negative relationship between beliefs about control of the target's behavior and evaluations of the target are found consistently in field studies among dating and married couples (Kipnis, Castell, Gergen, & Mauch, 1976; Kipnis & Cohn, 1979) and in experimental studies of work groups (Kipnis, 1972; Kipnis et al., 1981). In all instances, the more a person perceived unilateral control over another, the greater the devaluation of the other.

IMPLICATIONS FOR BARGAINING

The literature concerned with bargaining generally focuses on the outcomes of bargaining, the resources of the contending parties, and the social-psychological context in which bargaining occurs. Actual strategies of influence used in bargaining have, for the most part, been neglected. Emerging research suggests that this is an important omission, because tactical action is at the heart of bargaining (Bacharach & Lawler, 1981). Influence in bargaining is not limited to offers, threats, and inducements as is so often portrayed in the gaming literature (Chertkoff & Esser, 1976). At a methodological and substantive level, knowledge of the bargaining process would be strengthened by empirical studies of the variety of influence tactics that are actually used, as well as by analyses of their underlying structure (see Wall and Schiller, this volume).

In general, recent research (Kipnis et al., 1980; Mowday, 1978; Tedeschi et al., 1973) suggests that the choice of tactics will vary according to the objectives involved, the relative power of the contending parties, and their general expectations of the willingness of each other to comply. Other chapters in this book have also provided information about one or another of these variables. What we would like to stress is that these social psychological variables not only serve to guide the choice of tactics initially, but also guide subsequent forms of influence if the contending parties do not reach an immediate settlement. That is, there appear to be predictable shifts in the use of tactics that require study. Such shifts do not simply involve escalation, but also the use of coalitions, ingratiation and other strategies.

We also suggest that there may be important individual differences in styles of bargaining. Some negotiators may attempt to overwhelm their opponents by using all available influence strategies as was true of shotgun managers. Still others may rely mainly on reason. Still others may do very little (for instance, bystander managers). The implication of these variations in negotiating style for the bargaining process needs to be explored.

Finally, we suggest that the choice of influence strategies has predictable consequences for the process of bargaining over time. The use of assertive and directive strategies may cause long-term disruptions in social relations through their effects on a negotiator's attributions of control. In a general way, Deutsch (1969) spoke of these long-term effects in his discussions of destructive and productive conflicts. However, his work had not examined the long-range effects that are actually caused by the choice of influence strategies. An understanding of this contingency appears to depend on the development of a general taxonomy of influence strategies within the bargaining paradigm.

REFERENCES

Babb, H. W., & Knopp, D. G. Application of behavior modification in organizations: A review and critique. *Academy of Management Review,* 1978, *3,* 281-292.

Bacharach, S. B., & Lawler, E. J. *Bargaining.* San Francisco: Jossey-Bass, 1981.

Byrne, D., & Griffitt, W. Interpersonal attraction. *Annual Review of Psychology,* 1973, *24,* 317-336.

Cartwright, D. Influence, leadership, control. In J. March (Ed.), *Handbook of organizations.* Chicago: Rand McNally, 1965.

Chertkoff, J. M., & Esser, J. K. A review of experiments in explicit bargaining. *Journal of Experimental Social Psychology,* 1976, *12,* 464-486.

Cody, M. J., & McLaughlin, M. L. A multi-dimensional scaling of three sets of compliance-gaining strategies. *Communication Quarterly,* 1980, *3,* 34-36.

Dahl, R. A. The concept of power. *Behavioral Science,* 1957, *2,* 201-215.

Deutsch, M. Conflicts: Productive and destructive. *Journal of Social Issues,* 1969, *25,* 7-41.

Deutsch, M., & Krauss, R. M. Studies of interpersonal bargaining. *Journal of Conflict Resolution,* 1962, *6,* 52-76.

Etzioni, A. *A comparative analysis of complex organizations.* New York: Free Press, 1961.

Falbo, T. Multidimensional scaling of power strategies. *Journal of Personality and Social Psychology,* 1977, *35,* 537-547.

Falbo, T., & Peplau, L. A. Power strategies in intimate relations. *Journal of Personality and Social Psychology,* 1980, *38,* 618-628.

French, J.R.P., Jr., & Raven, B. The bases of social power. In D. Cartwright (Ed.), *Studies in social power.* Ann Arbor: Institute for Social Research, University of Michigan, 1959.

Goldstein, D., Miller, K., Griffin, M., & Hasher, L. *Patterns of gesture and verbal communication in a tutorial task.* Unpublished manuscript, Department of Psychology, Temple University, 1981.

Goodchilds, J. D., Quadrado, C., & Raven, B. H. *Getting one's way.* Paper presented at the meeting of the Western Psychological Association, Sacramento, California, 1974.

Hickson, D. J., Hinings, C. R., Lee, C. A., Scheneck, R. H., & Pennings, J. M. A strategic contingencies' theory of intraorganizational power. *Administrative Science Quarterly,* 1971, *16,* 216-229.

Kelley, H. H. Attribution theory in social psychology. In D. Levine (Ed.), *Nebraska symposium on motivation.* Lincoln: University of Nebraska Press, 1967.

Kelman, H. C. Compliance, identification and internalization: Three processes of opinion change. *Journal of Conflict Resolution,* 1958, *2,* 51-60.

Kipnis, D. Does power corrupt? *Journal of Personality and Social Psychology,* 1972, *24,* 33-41.

Kipnis, D. *The powerholders.* Chicago: University of Chicago Press, 1976.

Kipnis, D., Castell, P., Gergen, M., & Mauch, D. Metamorphic effects of power. *Journal of Applied Psychology,* 1976, *61,* 127-135.

Kipnis, D., & Cohn, E. S. *Power and affection.* Paper presented at the meetings of the Eastern Psychological Association, Philadelphia, 1979.

Kipnis, D., & Cosentino, J. Use of leadership powers in industry. *Journal of Applied Psychology,* 1969, *53,* 460-466.

Kipnis, D., & Lane, W. P. Self-confidence and leadership. *Journal of Applied Psychology,* 1962, *46,* 291-295.

Kipnis, D., & Schmidt, S. *Profile of organizational influence strategies.* San Diego: University Associates, 1982.

Kipnis, D., Schmidt, S., Price, K., & Stitt, C. Why do I like thee: Is it your performance or my orders? *Journal of Applied Psychology,* 1981, *66,* 324-328.

Kipnis, D., Schmidt, S. M., & Wilkinson, I. Intraorganizational influence tactics: Explorations in getting one's way. *Journal of Applied Psychology,* 1980, *65,* 440-452.

Kochan, T. A. *Collective bargaining and industrial relations.* Homewood, IL: Irwin, 1980.

Mowday, R. T. The exercise of upward influence in organizations. *Administrative Science Quarterly,* 1978, *23,* 135-156.

Perreault, W. D., & Miles, R. H. Influence strategy mixes in complex organizations. *Behavioral Science,* 1978, *23,* 86-98.

Perrow, C. A framework for the comparative analysis of organizations. *American Sociological Review,* 1967, *32,* 194-204.

Pfeffer, J. *Power in organizations.* Boston: Pitman, 1981.

Raven, B. H. The comparative analysis of power and influence. In J. T. Tedeschi (Ed.), *Perspectives on social power.* Chicago: Aldine, 1974.

Schmidt, S. M., & Kipnis, D. *Managers' pursuit of individual and organizational goals.* Paper presented at the American Psychological Association National Meetings, Washington, 1982.

Seligman, M. E. *Helplessness.* San Francisco: Freeman, 1975.

Student, K. R. Supervisory influence and work-group performance. *Journal of Applied Psychology,* 1968, *52,* 188-194.

Tedeschi, J. T., Schlenker, B. R., & Bonoma, T. V. *Conflict, power and games.* Chicago: Aldine, 1973.

Wilkinson, I., & Kipnis, D. Interfirm use of power. *Journal of Applied Psychology,* 1978, *63,* 315-320.

Wortman, C. B., & Linsenmeier, J. A. Interpersonal attraction and techniques of ingratiation in organizational settings. In B. Staw & G. Salancik (Eds.), *New directions in organizational behavior.* Chicago: St. Clair Press, 1977.

18

IMPROVING INDIVIDUAL PERFORMANCE

David W. Grigsby

Clemson University

To date, discussion of bargaining and negotiation in organizations has been associated almost exclusively with the resolution of substantive disputes. Bargaining principles have been successfully applied to a wide variety of conflict situations including interorganizational disputes, intergroup rivalries, and interpersonal conflicts. A growing number of organizational researchers and theorists have, however, begun to consider more diverse applications of the principles of bargaining in organizational settings. Among these applications is the improvement of employee performance through bargaining strategies.

Formal appraisal systems have become the rule as organizations have grown in size and complexity. A well-developed performance appraisal system increases the probability that productive people will be retained, motivated, and promoted. Organizations that have formal systems are also in a better position to demonstrate compliance with equal employment opportunity laws (Latham & Wexley, 1981).

The performance review process as carried out in most organizations consists of a periodically recurring series of activities. Elements usually included are (a) setting performance standards, (b) measuring individual job performance, (c) comparing the individual's performance to the standard, and (d) "feeding back" the performance review results to the individual employee.

One drawback of formal appraisal systems is that they treat the performance of all employees, regardless of their situations, with the same series and timing of procedures. (One notable exception to this problem is the practice of conducting more frequent performance reviews with new or probationary employees.) For the most part, however, the same process is used for individuals under a wide range of conditions, many of whom may have very different needs to be addressed by the review process.

With regard to meeting these different needs, there are three major tasks to performance evaluation. One is to respond to new employees and their evolving expectations as they develop into productive workers. The expectations of individuals at this early career stage are critical to their motivation and eventual success and are therefore an important product of the performance monitoring system. The second major task of performance review is to improve the performance of already established employees. By providing feedback about the level of achievement and an opportunity to discuss performance goals with a superior, the review process provides valuable information for setting new goals and targeting future efforts. The third task of performance review is to provide a means of dealing with "problem employee" behavior. The performance feedback session affords an opportunity to counsel the poorly performing worker and to assist him or her in correcting work behavior toward organizational objectives.

These three tasks, each of which deals with different individual circumstances, all contain some elements of the classic negotiation process. This chapter will develop a framework for investigating these and other performance review situations in light of contemporary bargaining theory. Following that, some suggestions will be offered for improving the performance of individuals and organizations by making more explicit the bargaining aspects of each of the situations outlined above.

BARGAINING MODELS

A given relationship is commonly characterized as a bargaining one according to its adherence to some given set of criteria. Rubin and Brown (1975) offer the following list of five criteria:

(1) At least two parties are involved.

(2) The parties have a conflict of interest with respect to one or more different issues.

(3) Regardless of the existence of prior experience or acquaintance with one another, the parties are at least temporarily joined together in a special kind of voluntary relationship.

(4) Activity in the relationship concerns: (a) the division or exchange of one or more specific resources and/or (b) the resolution of one or more intangible issues among the parties or among those whom they represent.

(5) The activity ususally involves the presentation of demands or proposals by one party, evaluation of these by the other, and concessions and counterproposals. The activity is thus sequential rather than simultaneous.

The first of these definitional elements fits the performance relationships we are interested in well enough. Performance review and improvement, although conceivably an individual effort, normally includes at least two individuals, usually a superior and subordinate.

A pure conflict of interest, Rubin and Brown's second criterion, is sometimes evident in performance review. If so, a quantity or quality dimension may be involved wherein the subordinate's interests lie in accomplishing or staying with a lower quantity or quality of work performance for a given reward, while the superior's interests lie in having the subordinate's quantity or quality of work performance reach a higher level. In these cases, work performance may be linked, explicitly or implicitly, to rewards in the organization, and the superior's and subordinate's interests may be similarly divergent.

Normally, however, a pure conflict of interest will not be the case. The two parties will instead simply hold different preference orders for various outcomes. For instance, both superiors and subordinates want the organization to prosper and grow, but either because of attitudinal differences or the organization's reward structure, profits will probably be less important to the subordinate. The differences in preference, however, are usually only vaguely understood by the two parties.

Rubin and Brown's third criterion—the existence of a voluntary relationship—is also minimally met. Although restrained by institutional or economic barriers, the employee/employer relationship is essentially voluntary by nature. Rubin and Brown's fourth and fifth characteristics of bargaining relationships, rather than defining preconditions for bargaining, describe the interaction that takes place in bargaining. These characteristics offer us some guidance for designing interaction activity in the performance review system that will exploit the advantages of defining them as bargaining problems.

The fourth criterion from Rubin and Brown's list, when applied to performance improvement, implies that organizational resources, in the form of rewards, should be explicitly linked to performance by some feature of the review system. Also implied is the fact that the activity should be oriented toward the resolution of "psychological factors" such as image or self-esteem that may be at stake.

The fifth criterion describes the type of activity associated with bargaining. In applying this to employee performance appraisal, it suggests the use of rather free give-and-take between superior and subordinate in arriving at a performance plan that is acceptable to both parties.

UNEQUAL POWER

Perhaps the most troublesome problem in applying bargaining concepts to the superior/single subordinate performance relationship lies in dealing with the seemingly unequal distribution of power between the two parties to the relationship. Rubin and Brown conclude that equal power between bargainers is, generally, more likely than unequal power to result in effective bargaining. Moreover, Bacharach and Lawler (1981) place power in a critical role in their general theory of bargaining: "Power pervades all aspects of bargaining and is key to an integrative analysis of context, process, and outcome." The manner in which bargaining principles can be applied to the superior/subordinate relationship depends, therefore, on assessing the power aspects of the relationship.

Most definitions of power focus on the role of resource dependency in creating power. Emerson (1962) defines power as control over the things that another values. Thibaut and Kelley (1959) define it as the range of outcomes (positive and/or negative) through which one person can be moved by another. Pfeffer's (1981) extensive treatment of power in organizations is essentially in agreement with these earlier definitions.

Resource dependence and control are pervasive aspects of the superior/subordinate relationship that inhibit the characterization of these actors as bargaining equals. However, the relationship often possesses other characteristics that may enhance the subordinate's role toward a more equal division of power. Pfeffer (1981) identified four sources of power in organizations in addition to the ability to control resources:

(1) power derived from successful coping with uncertainty;
(2) irreplaceability;
(3) ability to affect the decision process;
(4) power of consensus.

The ability and the need *to cope with uncertainty* are unequally distributed in most organizations and may often be located in the hands of otherwise low-power individuals. A classic example of this source of power is the technician with specialized knowledge on whom others depend to restore malfunctioning equipment. Adams (1980) identified a similar source of power in boundary-role persons, stemming from their ability to interpret the environment for other organization members. Individuals who possess the requisite skills or who are afforded unique opportunities to assist the organization in coping with a complex environment are therefore afforded increased power; this power is frequently extended to being able to influence their own outcomes on a footing more equal to their superiors'.

The second source of power is *irreplaceability.* The subordinate whose skills are in short supply commands more power and, consequently, increased ability to bargain effectively with superiors. Power through irreplaceability may also be achieved over time by individuals who are willing to take on unpleasant or unpopular tasks in the organizations. Power gained in this manner is also likely to affect the performance/reward relationship.

Pfeffer's third point, that power achieved through *affecting the decision process,* may take two forms that relate to the superior/subordinate performance relationship. First, individuals who have the ability to control other outcomes may use that ability (implicitly or explicitly) to control performance expectations or rewards. For example, where individual productivity is measured in quantitative terms, an individual may use qualitative variables to bargain implicitly over performance standards. The individual may say, in effect, "Sure

I can produce that many units of output, but the quality will have to suffer." Adams (1963) demonstrated that individuals use both quantity and quality dimensions to restore equity in pay relationships.

A second way in which individuals may affect the decision process is through control of information. An individual who has the ability and opportunity to control information about his/her performance can achieve bargaining power in negotiating goals and rewards. A classic example of this informational power is "rate restriction" activity, used to alter management's perception of an adequate standard work performance. Subordinates may also hide information about production that, if revealed, would increase standards or production rates.

Pfeffer's fourth alternative source of power, the *power of consensus,* refers to the ability of subunits in an organization to achieve power by presenting a united front. An obvious application to performance and rewards is the collective bargaining relationship. The concept of consensus power may also be applied to the superior/single subordinate relationship in regard to performance and rewards by substituting the word "consistency" for "consensus." An individual whose demands to his or her superior are consistent stands a greater chance of achieving positive bargaining outcomes than does one whose demands are inconsistent. Consensus power may also derive from one's referent power (French & Raven, 1968); a popular subordinate may be afforded more bargaining power with a superior by virtue of the subordinate's ability to influence peers.

Given these possibilities for modifying the inherently unequal distribution of power between superior and subordinate, power may approach a rough equivalency in many instances. Thus principles of equal-power bargaining may satisfactorily apply to the organizational performance relationship.

Why, then, is negotiation not often used in the performance review process? Probably for two reasons. First, managers may tend to approach performance reviews from a traditional high-power perspective. As they see it, the superior's role is to evaluate and to provide prescriptions for corrective action, either through what Maier (1976) called the "tell-and-sell" approach or through some type of pseudo problem-solving approach. Second, they view negotiation solely as a dispute resolution mechanism for use between parties of equal "power" (in the traditional sense). The negative consequences of failing to recognize and respond to the subordinate's informal power has been amply demonstrated and can be generalized to include the performance review process as well.

While the recognition of enhanced subordinate power points to the adoption of more explicit negotiating in the performance review process, it would be a mistake to assume that negotiation would work well in situations in which subordinates are decidedly low in power. From Kipnis and Schmidt's (this volume) study of tactics used by subordinates to influence their superiors, it may be inferred that low-power subordinates are more likely to engage in resistance tactics or ingratiation than are high-power subordinates, and they are more likely to seek to establish coalitions with other low power individuals.

The discussion of Pfeffer's (1981) informal power sources gives us reason to believe, however, that subordinates often do possess sufficient power to affect the performance review process. The superiors' awareness of this power, coupled with the problems associated with traditional "tell-and-sell" performance review, should lead them to favor more explicit negotiation processes. The point is to improve individual performance. If negotiation can achieve this, procedures should be adopted that include negotiation.

Based on what we know about the use of negotiation in other settings, several other benefits can be predicted to ensue from performance review bargaining. One of these is a high commitment to the results on the part of both parties, since negotiation involves a mutual influence process and give and take of ideas. Negotiation also provides an acceptable nondestructive method for turning problematic conflict situations into productive ones.

GUIDELINES FOR APPLICATIONS

A set of guidelines is proposed here for the application of bargaining procedures in the area of employee performance improvement: A negotiation model may be applied to performance review:

(1) where circumstances point to enhanced power of the subordinate;
(2) when a conflict of interest exists in regard to employee performance standards and the distribution of rewards;
(3) where job performance may be measured effectively along quantitative dimensions;

(4) where rewards may be effectively mediated on an individual basis and linked to specific performance objectives;

(5) where bargaining activity can be effectively controlled and limited to the performance/reward activity of the individual.

These guidelines will now be applied to the three situations we proposed earlier: new employee orientation and socialization, employee performance goal setting, and problem employee counseling.

NEW EMPLOYEE PERFORMANCE

The psychological contract, a concept first introduced by Argyris (1960), and later expanded by Levenson (1962) and Schein (1965), is an implicit agreement between an individual and the employing organization. An employee has expectations about what he or she will receive from the organization (salary benefits, advancement opportunities, intrinsic satisfaction, and so on) and about what he or she expects to give to that organization (skills, long hours, effort, attitudinal commitment, and so on). The organization also has expectations of what it will receive from the employee and what it expects to give to him or her. These four sets of expectations constitute the psychological contract.

While superiors may discuss a number of important aspects of the psychological contract with a new subordinate, the entire complex set of expectations may be so extensive that it can never be exhaustively deliberated. Furthermore, the psychological contract is, by its very nature, being constantly modified. This is a more pronounced problem for mangerial jobs than for nonmanagerial ones; the latter job descriptions often contain fairly detailed information about job duties and activities. Nevertheless, virtually all jobs involve at least some ambiguous or conflicting expectations.

A new employee may meet with the supervisor shortly after employment to discuss the employment relationship. At this point, the employee's concept of the psychological contract has already begun to form through information gained in the employment process; the expectations of the new employee and those of the supervisor are likely to be close. However, few aspects out of the total set of expectations are likely to be verbalized at this point. Furthermore, continuing dialogue concerning the eventual interpretation of each other's expectations is the exception rather than the rule in most supervisor/ subordinate relationships. Over time, the parties' concepts of the psychological contract often evolve into ones that are quite dissimilar. This leads to situations in which either the manager or subordinate perceives the other party as having violated the contract (Dunaheff & Wangler, 1974).

Using the psychological contract as a conceptual basis, Kotter (1973) analyzed the experiences of a group of managers in their initial employment following graduate training. The following are some of his findings.

(1) Correspondence in the expectations of organizations and individuals was positively related to greater job satisfaction, productivity, and reduced turnover. Managers who established a contract that contained more matches in expectations had a more satisfying and productive first year and remained longer with the company than did those who had fewer matches between their expectations and those of the organization.

This finding is consistent with other research (Wanous, 1973) regarding the success of "realistic job previews" in lowering unrealistically high expectations of new recruits. Recruits often begin the initial employment period with unrealistically optimistic views of many factors: the degree to which one's skills will be valued, the opportunities for advancement, and so on. Mismatches can have disastrous consequences for the maintenance of the psychological contract. The employee begins to view mismatches as failures of the organization to live up to its agreement and then responds by breaking his or her side of the bargain.

(2) The probability of a match between the employee's expectations concerning a given item and the organization's expectations concerning that item is greater if the employee clearly understands his or her own expectations. In other words, if the employee is aware of his or her expectations, they are more likely to match those of the organization. Individuals apparently modify their expectations when they choose to confront them realistically. Perhaps unspecified high hopes become more realistic under close scrutiny. This argues for a process whereby the individual would be encouraged to specify and examine in detail what he or she expects to receive from, and give to, the company.

(3) If an employee and a company representative explicitly discuss the range of their individual expectations, mutual understanding is

increased, as is the probability of matching. Although employment interviews and initial meetings between the employee and superior appear to accomplish this, there are a number of reasons why important aspects of the working relationship are often not addressed. Norms develop in most organizations that define some items as not legitimate to talk about. Also, new employees are often reluctant to voice the full range of their concerns for fear of being thought overly cautious. Also, the superior may be poorly trained in interviewing or not rewarded for initiating an open discussion of the new employee's perception of the job and responsibilities.

Another interesting aspect of this initial relationship is that the new employee may possess informal power by virtue of his or her "newness" in the organization. There may be a period of time, shortly after the employee joins the organization, during which he or she can exercise a great deal of discretion in job behavior since expectations are not yet fully formed. This "honeymoon" period would, therefore, be a time when it is easier to negotiate standards for performance. This might be done by establishing an initial dialogue between the new employee and the superior regarding the employee's expectations and the expectations that the organization has for that individual, as interpreted by the superior. Periodic follow-up to monitor changes in the employee's perception of the psychological contract would also seem appropriate. Kotter's (1973) findings suggest that successful efforts aimed at getting new employees to confront their expectations early on, and to discuss these with key superiors, would improve employee satisfaction and productivity and thereby decrease turnover.

Bargaining approaches can also ensure a continuing dialogue. Subordinates could be encouraged to think of their relationship with the organization as an exchange relationship (i.e., what am I giving to, and what am I receiving from this organization?). Supervisors would also be asked to evaluate each subordinate in these terms. As a part of each new employee's orientation procedure, the manager would present his or her expectations. The aim here is to make explicit those aspects of the psychological contract that are rarely, if ever, acknowledged. The new employee would then be encouraged to evaluate these comments and respond to them. The ensuing dialogue would form the basis for working out a mutually satisfactory superior/subordinate relationship.

Although an initial meeting might vary little from a standard orientation interview, the new employee would be encouraged to adopt a workable paradigm for conceptualizing his or her relationship to the organization and a basis for articulating perceived mismatches between these expectations and reality. Real benefits to the organization might be forthcoming during this socialization period, since the manager could also renegotiate expectations with the new employee as he or she becomes accustomed to the job. For example, valued rewards could be linked to productivity increases.

Managers and new subordinates might meet periodically and review this exchange relationship. This approach would be especially useful where employees possess highly valued skills they might use as a basis for establishing bargaining power in the organization and where successive increments in productivity are measurable.

PERFORMANCE GOAL SETTING AND BARGAINING

Just as the performance expectations of new employees may be addressed through bargaining, so may the performance of other organizational members be enhanced by a similar approach. The positive effects of goal setting on individual performance have been well established in the literature (Locke, 1968). Management by objectives (MBO), a concept originated by Drucker (1954) and refined by Odiorne (1965) and others, provides a means of incorporating goal setting into the individual performance relationship through individualized goal setting, measurable objectives, accountability, and feedback. The extent to which subordinates are allowed to participate in the setting of their own goals, however, vary widely in practice.

Carroll and Tosi (1973) examined research on the relationship between productivity and subordinate participation in the goal-setting phase of MBO. They concluded that the extent to which subordinate participation in goal setting resulted in increased productivity is dependent on the subordinate's perception of the participation as legitimate. If an individual has control over the manner in which goals are set and over the means of achieving them, positive results can be predicted.

This finding has implications for the utilization of bargaining procedures in MBO systems. When individuals have control over the means by which they can achieve objectives, bargaining procedures may provide another essential ingredient for perceived legitimate participation, i.e., a process for participation in goal setting.

Werther and Weirich (1975) suggest incorporating negotiation into MBO by using a combination top-down and bottom-up approach to goal setting. Management states overall objectives for the organization but allows considerable flexibility in setting specific performance objectives for each employee, as long as these specific objectives contribute to accomplishment of the organization-level plans. Superior and subordinate may then negotiate goals within this range defined by the organization.

Two basic types of issues may be in dispute in any bargaining situation: distributive and integrative (Walton & McKersie, 1965). Distributive bargaining issues are those that deal with the allocation of a fixed amount of limited resources. Pure conflicts of interest are at stake, and resolution of distributive issues can come about only through concession making and compromise. Integrative bargaining issues are those in which the common interests of both parties may be served and even expanded. Solutions are available for integrative issues that satisfy each party's concerns without sacrificing the concerns of the opposing party. To employ an overused metaphor, distributive issues deal with how a pie is to be cut up, and integrative issues address the possible ways of creating an additional or larger pie.

While there are, apparently, some distributive issues in performance goal negotiation (e.g., amount of direct pay), there are also numerous important integrative issues. Individual productivity goals, for example, may be largely integrative in nature. The superior, seeking to maximize overall unit-level goals, favors high individual productivity and therefore a high goal for the subordinate. While the subordinate also desires high productivity, he or she is also concerned about accountability for results and the consequences of an unfulfilled high goal. This suggests differences in the order of preferences for outcomes, rather than a purely distributive dispute.

A bargaining procedure, whereby the subordinate presents his or her proposed goals as an initial offer, might supplement the usual goal-setting session. These are then responded to by the superior, who presents his or her plan as a counteroffer. A session of give and take resulting in the final agreed-upon goals follows. This plan should result in more realistic goals since any unreasonable initial position can be expected to be modified in the process. Moreover, the dialogue that is fostered by bargaining could result in a better understanding of each other's positions. For example, a bargaining session designed to develop sales goals for an individual sales manager would, quite naturally, involve discussion of the special characteristics of the sales territory, customers' probable responses to new products, and the like. Goal-setting participation through bargaining could, therefore, achieve some rather significant "side benefits" in addition to enhanced productivity.

Whether or not bargaining procedures can be incorporated successfully into goal-setting activities depends upon a number of factors. As we have already mentioned, the ability to distinguish several means by which goals are to be achieved is a prerequisite. This suggests reserving performance goal bargaining to jobs requiring judgment and discretion in their performance. Also necessary is the existence of multiple individual performance criteria, since the attempted bargaining over a single distributive issue will most likely lead to impasse. Therefore, it may not be advisable to attempt performance goal bargaining for routine, single-facet jobs. Also, as mentioned earlier in the discussion on bargaining in general, some semblance of equivalent power enhances bargaining effectiveness. Therein lies a third reason for limiting performance goal bargaining to more complex, nonroutine jobs.

Adoption of performance goal bargaining raises the possibility of bargaining impasse. The distributive qualities of certain goals may cause superiors and subordinates to deadlock at some point in the negotiation. If they cannot agree on a set of goals and measurement means, how should goals be set?

Third-party resolution procedures such as mediation and arbitration have been the dominant means of resolving impasses in collective bargaining settings (Kochan, 1980). Although their use in performance goal setting could be viewed by superiors as undermining managerial authority, we have seen earlier that traditional notions of authority and power must be modified in order to adopt bargaining procedures in the first place. Given that an appropriate scheme could be developed for selecting unbiased third parties to be mediators or arbitrators, third-party intervention seems to promise a good means for ending impasses in this area as well.

Arbitration offers a degree of finality not found in mediation arrangements. An arbitrator is given the authority to impose a final settlement on the disputing parties. While this may be attractive from the standpoint of ending the impasse quickly, arbitration can often cause the parties to feel as if they have a reduced voice in the outcome and, therefore, less commitment to the final performance goals that are established (Notz & Starke, 1978). The availability of arbitration as a dispute resolution mechanism has also been shown to lead parties to bring extreme positions to arbitration, resulting in a "chilling effect" on the process (Feuille, 1975).

Mediation, whereby the third party assists the primary parties in reaching their own settlement, offers less speedy resolution but seems better suited to the process of performance goal setting. Because of the integrative nature of the issues involved, goal setting seems to call for more of a problem-solving approach. A mediator could assist parties in sorting out their preferences and exploring areas of mutual concern. Furthermore, the performance goal-setting task requires commitment to the final outcome on the part of both parties if the goals are to be carried out. High commitment is more likely when goals are jointly bargained and agreed to than when goals are set by an outside arbitrator.

In addition to the problems of impasse resolution, other problems exist in attempting to install effective performance goal bargaining. For instance, there is the problem of accommodating both organizational and individual goals. The possible benefits accruing to organizations in the form of increased employee satisfaction and productivity, however, make the proposition well worth further investigation on a case-by-case basis.

CONTRACT COUNSELING

A third application of bargaining procedures for individual performance enhancement lies in the area of counseling the problem employee. A technique referred to as "contract counseling" (Sperry & Hess, 1974) may be applied to a wide range of employee problems including performance deficiencies.

The contract is used as a goal-setting tool. It is an agreement between the helper (in this case the superior) and the person receiving help (the subordinate with a performance deficiency). The employee agrees to practice a certain desired behavior and the manager agrees to provide assistance. The contract, which may be stated either orally or in writing, makes it clear that the employee "owns" the problem and emphasizes that in order to use the manager's time and energy, the employee must take some constructive action. The following example, adapted from Calhoon and Jerdee (1976), illustrates the use of behavioral contracting:

> George Brown is a clerical employee supervised by Helen Clark. Work has been piling up on his desk causing difficulties for others in the department. George tells Helen that he is overloaded and cannot catch up. In a discussion of the problem, Helen reviews each unfinished item and notices that most require George to check with some higher level official before they can be completed. George eventually agrees that this is so and admits to avoiding those items because he feels uncomfortable talking to higher-ups. In the ensuing discussion, Helen is somewhat sympathetic but makes it clear that this deficiency in George's work must be corrected. They agree that George will get to know the officials he must deal with in his work by personally calling on two of them each day for two weeks.

In contract counseling, the employee agrees to do something specific and then report the behavior to another person. Generally, the steps are the following (Loughary and Ripley, 1979):

(1) A goal is defined.
(2) A plan is discussed, and the actual tasks to be done are defined.
(3) The person responsible for doing the tasks makes a commitment to follow through.
(4) The action is taken (or not taken).
(5) A report is made to the helper regarding the action.

Contracting places the responsibility for performance improvement on the employee. As a helper, the manager provides support, encouragement, and assistance in defining the specific behavior to be carried out, but it is clear that the subordinate must act. The role of the manager is also clear in regard to follow-up. Once the contract is negotiated and agreed upon, the manager does not intervene until a report is made. When the report is made, the manager may offer support, confront the individual with his or her failure to perform, or renegotiate the contract, depending on what is reported.

The terms of the contract should be stated simply and directly, so that both parties can easily determine whether or not its terms were carried out. In the example, if George calls on two higher-ups per day, the contract is fulfilled. Room for disagreement is minimized. The desired behavior has either occurred or it has not.

More intractable performance deficiencies may also be addressed using this method. For these more serious problems, the manager would work with the subordinate through a series of successively higher goals over a longer time period in order to reach the final performance objective of satisfactory job performance.

Proponents of contract counseling stress the objective nature of the approach as compared to traditional counseling methods. In the example, Helen might have simply talked to George about the problem and tried to assess the causes of his reluctance to confront higher-ups. Instead, Helen, as helper, suggested a plan by which she could actively seek to improve George' performance. An important consideration is that the employee receiving the help does in fact make a decision about corrective behavior. Without this commitment on the part of the employee, the use of contract counseling in performance improvement is inappropriate.

Bargaining procedures can be used to obtain commitment to a behavioral goal in counseling. The manager uses successively higher levels of promised support to obtain successively greater concessions from the employee to attempt the desired behavior. The emphasis here is on jointly reaching a measurable goal for the employee that he or she is confident of achieving and that will correct the deficiency, thereby satisfying organizational requirements for satisfactory job performance.

Of the preconditions required for true bargaining, the one that is least likely to be present in situations requiring contract counseling is the assumption of equivalency in bargaining power. The need for correcting deficient performance by a subordinate is not as likely to occur where those individuals have attained substantial power in the organization. Because of this, the manager should be especially cautious regarding the way in which agreement is obtained from the employee. Managers may, through the use of superior position power, unknowingly force agreement to their demands. Consequently, the resulting contract is less likely to succeed since the employee's felt involvement is not as great.

CONCLUSION

The three applications discussed above each involve a characteristically different approach to bargaining. In the new employee's case, evolving expectations form the focus of discussion, and bargaining offers a convenient process for making explicit a wide range of otherwise implicit (but perhaps misunderstood) aspects of the psychological contract. In performance goal setting, the focus is on providing a constructive atmosphere for genuine problem solving. Recognizing the informal power of subordinates and putting them on a more equal footing with superiors improves the probability that such an atmosphere will develop. In employee problem counseling the focus is on getting the individual involved in his or her own performance improvement. Bargaining serves as a vehicle for bringing about the involvement.

For the subordinate, the implications of using bargaining approaches in these ways are decidedly positive. The individual is afforded a clearer picture of his or her rights and responsibilities upon entering the organization, is recognized as having a legitimate right to play a role in determining his or her own outcomes, and is given more responsibility for improving inadequate performance.

The implications for managers are somewhat more ambiguous. Perceptions that bargaining undermines authority and thereby depletes a manager's power to control the organizational unit are inevitable. The question, then, is whether or not this apparent abdication of formal position power seriously threatens a manager's ability to manage. If the organization relies on formal authority, job titles, and directive communication and measures results by compliance to that authority, then the answer is yes. If, on the other hand, the organization measures results by other criteria, such as improved performance, enhanced employee satisfaction, and individual development, the formal authority relinquished when managers employ bargaining procedures seems a small price to pay for achieving those goals.

REFERENCES

Adams, J. S. Wage inequities, productivity, and work quality. *Industrial Relations,* 1963, *3,* 9-16.

Adams, J. S. Interorganizational processes and organizational boundary activities. In B. M. Staw & L. L. Cummings (Eds.), *Research in organizational behavior* (Vol. 2). Greenwich, CT: JAI, 1980.

Argyris, C. *Understanding organizational behavior.* Homewood, IL: Dorsey, 1960.

Bacharach, S. B., & Lawler, E. J. *Bargaining: Power, tactics, and outcomes.* San Francisco: Jossey-Bass, 1981.

Calhoon, R. P., & Jerdee, T. H. *Coaching in supervision.* Chapel Hill: University of North Carolina Institute of Government, 1976.

Carroll, S. J., & Tosi, H. L., Jr. *Management by objectives: Applications and research.* New York: Macmillan, 1973.

Drucker, P. *Practice of management.* New York: Harper, 1954.

Dunaheff, M. H., & Wangler, L. A. The psychological contract: A conceptual structure for management/employee relations. *Personnel Journal,* 1974, 518-526.

Emerson, R. M. Power-dependence relationships. *American Sociological Review,* 1962, *27,* 31-41.

Feuille, P. Final offer arbitration and the chilling effect. *Industrial Relations,* 1975, *14,* 302-310.

French, J.P.R., Jr., & Raven, B. H. The bases of social power. In D. Cartwright (Ed.), *Studies in social power.* Ann Arbor: University of Michigan Press, 1968.

Hansen, J. C., Stevic, R. R., & Warner, R. W., Jr. *Counseling: Theory and practice* (2nd ed.). Boston: Allyn & Bacon, 1977.

Kochan, T. A. Collective bargaining and organizational behavior research. In B. M. Staw & L. L. Cummings (Eds.), *Research in organizational behavior* (Vol. 2). Greenwich, CT: JAI, 1980.

Kotter, J. P. The psychological contract: Managing the joining-up process. *California Management Review,* 1973, *15*(3), 91-99.

Latham, G. P., & Wexley, K. N. *Increasing productivity through performance appraisal.* Reading, MA: Addison-Wesley, 1981.

Levenson, H. *Men, mangement and mental health.* Cambridge, MA: Harvard University Press, 1962.

Locke, E. A. Toward a theory of task motivation and incentives. *Organizational Behavior and Human Performance,* 1968, *3,* 157-189.

Loughary, J. W., & Ripley, T. M. *Helping others help themselves: A guide to counseling.* New York: McGraw-Hill, 1979.

Maier, N.R.F. *The appraisal interview* (2nd ed.). LaJolla, CA: University Associates, 1976.

Morley, I., & Stephenson, G. *The social psychology of bargaining.* London: George Allen & Unwin, 1977.

Notz, W. W., & Starke, F. A. The impact of final offer vs. conventional arbitration on the aspirations and behaviors of bargainers. *Administrative Science Quarterly,* 1978, *23,* 189-203.

Odiorne, G. S. *Management by objectives.* New York: Pitman, 1965.

Pfeffer, J. *Power in organizations.* Boston: Pitman, 1981.

Rubin, J. Z., & Brown, B. R. *The social psychology of bargaining and negotiation.* New York: Academic, 1975.

Schein, E. H. *Organizational psychology.* Englewood Cliffs, NJ: Prentice-Hall, 1965.

Sperry, L., & Hess, L. R. *Contract counseling: Developing people in organizations.* Reading, MA: Addison-Wesley, 1974.

Thibaut, J. W., & Kelley, H. H. *The social psychology of groups.* New York: John Wiley, 1959.

Walton, R. E., & McKersie, R. B. *A behavioral theory of labor negotiations.* New York: McGraw-Hill, 1965.

Wanous, J. P. Effects of a realistic job preview on job acceptance, job attitudes, and job survival. *Journal of Applied Psychology,* 1973, *58,* 217-232.

Werther, W. B., Jr., & Weirich, H. Refining MBO through negotiations. *MSU Business Topics,* 1975, 53-59.

19

HUMAN RESOURCE MANAGEMENT

Douglas T. Hall

Boston University

Negotiation has been defined as "a form of decision making in which two or more parties talk with one another in an effort to resolve their opposing interests" (Pruitt, 1981, p. xii). Most of the literature focuses on settings in which a clear, explicit, mutually recognized negotiation process exists: labor/management relations, internal communications, and marketplace decision making. However, as Pruitt (p. xi) observes,

> It is actually a much broader phenomenon, occurring within and between business and government offices, in homes, and among friends and relatives. Indeed, it is found at so many levels of society and is so frequently encountered that its impact on human welfare can hardly be underestimated.

Although discussions of bargaining and negotiation often start with an acknowledgment of underdefined bargaining situations, these analyses usually waste very little time moving on to one of the more common formal bargaining settings. In contrast to this approach, the present discussion will focus on a situation in which bargaining is frequently subtle and often not explicitly recognized: the area of management/management relations. To be specific, we will examine the process by which managerial decisions regarding human resources are made.

THE PROBLEM

With the exception of some textbooks that show organization charts and listings of personnel functions, there has been little systematic analysis of how organization decisions are made about the structure, activities, and resources of the personnel or human resource function. There has also been little attention paid to different orientations or styles of human resource units as they evolve and relate to the line organization. In some organizations, the human resource department is seen as totally removed from mainstream organizational activities: a low-status staff activity. In other firms, personnel is a much more active partner in running the business. What accounts for such differences?

In viewing the structure of a human resource unit, we are dealilng with a dual-faceted problem: (1) the *autonomy* of the human resource function, and (2) the *integration* of the human resource function with line management. In many organizations, the human resource function suffers from deficiencies in either or both of these areas. By autonomy, we mean the ability to exercise self-direction, to operate with a certain level of independence from the rest of the organization. Integration refers to collaborative activity with the line organization in the pursuit of common goals.

Figure 19.1 illustrates the different types of human resource orientations that can result from different combinations of high and low autonomy and integration. In organizations in which the human resource (HR) function has both low autonomy and low integration with the line organization (Cell I), the result is a *clerical* orientation. This is a situation in which there is a personnel area (often not with even the status of a formal department) that is devoted solely to routine procedures of people processing: handling employment applications, administering salaries and benefits, and perhaps delivering an occasional orientation session. Longer-term HR activities such as employee development or proactive tasks such as planning would be foreign to this type of HR function. This Type I HR function

Integration of Human Resources
With Line Management

	High	Low
High	Cell IV Mission Orientation	Cell III Procedures Orientation
Low	Cell II Fire-fighting Orientation	Cell I Clerical Orientation

Human Resource Autonomy (row label spanning High/Low on the left)

Figure 19.1   A Matrix of Human Resource Functions

is often found in young, small organizations (in early stages of development) and in older organizations with routine, predictable, easily met "people needs," such as retail stores, certain public agencies, and small mass production plants.

In Cell II we move to an HR function that is more closely tied to the line organization, but it is "tied" in the sense of being captive to line management. In this *fire-fighting orientation,* the HR function exists to serve line management, responding quickly to any and all demands and crises of the line organization. It could be an employee-relations-oriented HR function whose main mission is to maintain a good labor relations climate and to deal with frequent grievances, potential grievances, contract negotiations, strikes, and the like. Or it could be a more organization-development-oriented unit, acting primarily in a consulting role to top management but working with an agenda defined by management. And the problems presented by top management might be constantly changing, so that staff are pulled from one crisis to another, with little sense of accomplishment in any of them.

In Cell III, where HR is a fairly free-standing department with its own direction, we see a *procedure orientation.* This is old-fashioned personnel administration at its worst. Often the independence of the department is perceived by other parts of the organization as being used in a negative way, to present barriers to action by the line units. Examples of such barriers would be numerous forms to be completed in precise ways for hiring, firing, transfer, salary adjustments, benefit changes, and the like. For example, in the author's university, certain promotion and tenure actions were delayed because material from outside letters was not typewritten and double-spaced. These procedures may have originated from legitimate external considerations, such as legal requirements and affirmative action regulations, but such requirements may become far more tedious than these external mandates may warrant. With this departmental insulation from line units develops an attitude or climate within the function that leads these human resource procedures to become functionally autonomous—an end in and of themselves. Many university personnel departments are such a force to be reckoned with.

In Cell IV, with good integration with line management and high autonomy, we see a true *mission orientation;* here, HR is dedicated to whatever is the main business of the enterprise. Human resources are there to work in collaboration with management, as part of a management team. They have the power to help define a human resource agenda for the organization and often act in a proactive consultative role.

As a human resource function develops, there is often a progression through the various cells. When the organization or HR function is new, there may not be a separate HR department, but perhaps just one or two clerical or administratiave people who perform some personnel activities (Cell I). As the function grows into a separate department, it could still remain in a clerical mode for some time, but with expanded clerical functions (e.g., more sophisticated selection procedures). As its capabilities expand, it can move toward either greater independence from the line organization (Cell III) or toward greater utilization by the line (Cell II). The most mature state is the collaborative Cell IV.

One of my objectives in this chapter is to determine how an organization can move to Cell IV integration. Few do. Human resource practitioners in a Cell I department, in their attempts to upgrade the status of their unit, often choose a strategy of either increasing their power and autonomy of developing stronger links with the line organization. The risk of the first approach is that increased power and autonomy alone will only land them in Cell III (a procedures orientation). On the other hand, the second strategy (increasing integration or centrality) may lead them to be coopted by line management, placing them in Cell II (fire-fighting). However, it may be necessary to move through one or both of these other cells in order to achieve Cell IV.

CONFLICT AWARENESS

L. Dave Brown (1983) has introduced the concept of conflict at organizational interfaces, which is extremely useful for the purposes of the present essay. Although Brown raises the possibility that organizational interfaces might be lubricated with graphite, injected with penicillin, or polished with Turtle Wax, he goes on to consider other approaches to improving interunit relations. Brown defines conflict as "incompatible behavior between parties whose interests differ" (1983, p. 4). Interests are defined as "recognized *and unrecognized* stakes that are affected by the interaction of parties" (p. 4, emphasis added).

Generally the bargaining literature had dealt with situations in which clear differences of interest exist between parties. Where management has been concerned, the focal conflicts have been with labor or an external entity, such as a seller, buyer, competitor, or regulator. In this analysis, we will need to examine *management/ management bargaining.* In particular, we are considering bargaining among line management units and the management of the human resource function. Since the goals and responsibilities of these two parts of an organization differ (Lawrence & Lorsch, 1967), there are many operational matters in which their interests differ, thus producing potential conflict by Brown's definition. In this context, bargaining would be the appropriate and commonly used method of reducing conflict.

Consider, for example, employee transfers. A line unit may have a vacancy for a division manager in Denver, and the regional director may want to fill it with the person she considers best qualified: an up-and-coming department head now in Houston. However, as part of a corporate management development program, that department head (let's call him Jim Green) is slated by human resource management to put in a tour at headquarters in New York. Furthermore, Green was just moved to Houston last year, and the corporate policy (while not rigid) is to keep fast-trackers in assignments for at least two years whenever possible.

This incident is an example of clear conflict between human resource management and the regional director. The goal of the HR function here is to maintain corporate policy and to promote management development to meet long-term, overall corporate needs. Meeting the immediate staffing needs of the region is important, but not as important as corporate-wide responsibilities.

Now consider a more subtle situation. What if the best next move for Jim Green were in fact the division manager's slot in Denver, and the slot were open. And say the regional manager wanted another person in that job, a person who could easily be moved. If the regional manager is not aware that the human resource executive is thinking about Green as a candidate, the regional manager is not aware of any conflict between her interests and the HR functions in this situation. If the power of HR is low (Cell I or II), HR might not even think to propose Green as a candidate, creating no conflict. However, if the HR head had more power and was considering pushing for Green, he or she could anticipate future conflict with the regional manager. And the *unilateral awareness of conflict* would in turn give the HR head even more power in this situation (through the opportunity to map out an advance strategy).

Let's make this situation one step more general. What if the HR head recognizes that there will be a whole range of situations in which the interests of the HR function will differ from those of line management: e.g., the development of new performance appraisal systems, employee surveys, new compensation systems, revised hiring practices. Many of these activities disrupt the status quo of line management in ways that the line management may not anticipate, but that human resource managers may. If the HR head is aware of the inherent conflicts between the HR functions and line units, this awareness gives him or her tactical advantage in dealing with line units.

Thus one important element of the bargaining strategy of the effective human resource manager is to recognize the existence of conflict situations and the potential need to bargain, even when his or her line counterpart does not yet recognize the need. As described by Bachrach and Lawler (1981, p. 74), the first step in bargaining strategy is to recognize the existence of "tacit bargaining":

> Tacit bargaining occurs when the bargaining relationship is not officially recognized or consenually defined by the parties. It takes the form of parties attempting to influence each other informally without necessarily being conscious that they are in a bargaining relationship. The conflict may be open and severe, but it often takes very subtle forms of mutual manipulation. This form of bargaining often connotes loyalty, since it pre-supposes a commitment to the organization and a willingness to avoid making explicit conflicts that can be left implicit.

One may wonder how any human resource manager might be unaware of these interdepartmental conflicts. There are several ways. In a Cell II personnel unit, the human resource manager totally accepts the goals of the line management and does not conceive of somewhat different goals for the HR function. As Brown (1983) points out, there may be *too little conflict* in this captive HR situation. The need in Cell II, then, is to heighten the HR manager's awareness of interunit conflict. *Bargaining awareness* is one way to increase the power of HR in Cell II and move it toward Cell IV. This could be done by recognizing that *the captive status of HR in fact also represents a dependence of the line organization on HR,* since HR is meeting an important need of line management. As Kotter (1977, p. 131) points out, one of the ways of increasing A's power over B is to increase B's awareness of dependence upon A. In the case of managers,

> an effective manager often gains power . . . by feeding others' beliefs that they are dependent on the manager either for help or for not being hurt. The more they perceive they are dependent, the more most people will be inclined to cooperate with such a manager.

The two methods Kotter found used by managers to create perceived dependence were: (1) finding and acquiring resources required by the other and (2) affecting other's perceptions of one's resources.

The insightful HR manager will be able to recognize which HR functions are most critical to line management (e.g., recruiting in a fast-growing firm). The next step is to subtly make the delivery of these functions to a particular line manager less unconditional and more contingent upon certain kinds of cooperation with HR, as it pursues its goals.

An example of bargaining awareness took place in a large international commercial bank that had a fairly low power, captive personnel department (Cell II). A new personnel vice president was rotated in from an operating unit of the bank. Although he had had little experience in personnel, he had considerable experience in corporate policies. He quickly recognized that the prime resource delivered by personnel was its college recruiting and training program. At the same time, his mandate from the bank's chairman was to promote management development through more lateral, cross-functional employee transfers. However, department managers scoffed at the idea of accepting unknown people from other departments. (The bank had a very strong functional structure.) Then the personnel vice president converted what had been a routine HR college trainee assignment process into a bargaining situation: He let line managers know that the number and quality of college recruits they would receive from the training program would henceforth be directly related to the number of transfers they would accept from other departments. Soon the other routine personnel services became subject to bargaining: consultation, assistance with salary administration, training opportunities, and so on. The potential to bargain had been there all along, but bargaining arousal was a necessary first step.

CREATING BARGAINING AROUSAL: ORGANIZATIONAL UNLEARNING

Creating a new role definition that incorporates the ability to bargain requires *unlearning*. Both the organization and the role incumbent must unlearn old responses to old stimuli before new responses can be adopted. As Hedberg (1981) indicates, unlearning involves three types of disconfirmation of connections, each of which will be discussed in this case of role transition:

(1) Disconfirmation of connnections between selecting and interpreting stimuli. This means the perceiver no longer knows what is perceived. The meaning of perceived events and actions is no longer the same as it used to be. An example of this in the human resource area would be the new meanings attached to geographical relocations and promotions. The "old" meaning of a rejection of a relocation and promotion recommendation by a candidate was that the candidate

was not committed enough to the career and the organization to take the risks associated with the move and new job responsibilities. Now, however, the meaning may say more about the competing commitments that the candidate must manage: a spouse's career, family ties, financial investments in the present house, and so on. The commitment to one's own career could be extremely high, but the competing commitments could be even higher. Human resource managers are learning to revise their interpretation of stimuli such as transfer refusal. Executives are doing the same and in the process are learning to look toward the human resource function to help make sense of this "world turned upside down."

(2) Disconfirmation of connections between stimuli and responses. This means the person or organization no longer knows what responses to make to identified stimuli. An example would be the earlier illustration of a manager's expectation of receiving his or her regular allocation of college trainees. What if, instead of having a request for trainees routinely met, the response were something like, "It is difficult to justify sending you three trainees when only last month you did not have any need for the experienced second-level person who wanted to transfer in from Department X"? Or, what if a line manager's request to a personnel manager were met by a counterrequest? As organizations train personnel and people become even scarcer resources, personnel managers will have ample reason (indeed, need) to connect new responses to old stimuli.

(3) Disconfirmation of connections between responses. This means the person no longer knows how to assemble response to new situations, so that the person's theory of action (Argyris & Schon, 1975) may be threatened. This is most likely to be troublesome for complex problems with a detailed "subroutine" of responses and many contingencies and subtleties. An example here might be the contrast between the so-called new industrial relations and the earlier form. Traditionally, the relationship between management and the union centered primarily on the union contract—its creation and its operation. Other issues related to the work environment, such as job design, employee participation, and team management, were seen as quite separate or perhaps even by the union as antagonistic attempts at union busting. Attempts to redesign jobs and give employees more responsibility sometimes were met with union demands for more pay. Now, however, because of extreme environmental economic threats, both parties—labor and management—are seeing new connections

among these once separate or antagonistic responses. Employee participation is more often seen by the union as a means of promoting its members' goals, not as a violation of the contract. Human resource managers' attempts to redesign work are seen by management not just as "good employee relations" but as "good management." Tough bargaining and cooperative work redesign are now more connected responses than they were earlier.

And, in fact, even the *actors* are more connected now. In one large manufacturing firm (part of the auto industry), the employee relations department dealt with union/management issues, and the personnel training and development department (two *very* unconnected departments) conducted work redesign and organization development activities. Now the work of these two departments is much more connected. Union relations is now defined to include cooperative organization development activities, while training and development are conducted increasingly in partnership with key union leaders.

Thus through various forms of organizational unlearning, organizations are being unfrozen to new roles and responsibilities for the human resource function. Most of this unlearning has been triggered by *problems,* as opposed to people or opportunities, as Hedberg (1981) would predict. These problems have come in the form of financial losses, decreasing market shares, foreign competition, and declining product quality. The better-managed companies, such as Delta Airlines, General Electric, and IBM, saw these new connections early as a way to seize competitive opportunities and in response to the leadership of key senior people (Pascale & Athos, 1981), but these changes have been adopted elsewhere in "bandwagon" proportions only as a result of critical problems (such as, "How are we ever going to *survive?*").

This theme of organizational unlearning through disconnections is also supported by Van de Ven, Delbecq, and Koenig's (1976) findings that the factor that correlates most strongly with organizational coordination is task uncertainty. Put in our context, this would mean that we would be most likely to see human resource activities become more integrated with "mainstream" line management when these various stimuli and response connections break down and the familiar become suddenly foreign. Task interdependence was the second strongest factor related to coordination, and again as line managers and human resource managers recognize the extent of their mutual interdependence, the motivation to coordinate (through bargaining, joint planning, and rule-setting) increases.

PERSONAL QUALITIES FOR
INTRAMANAGEMENT BARGAINERS

What are the personal characteristics necessary in order for a human resource manager to be effective in an ill-defined bargaining situation, such as the one proposed here? The following are some of the more important qualities:

(1) Confrontation skills. This is probably the most important ingredient of all. The person would have to be able to shake up a comfortable interdepartmental status quo, in which the personnel department was playing a captive administrative, or clerical role (Cells I, II, or III). He or she would need to clearly assert the human resource needs and the critical role for HR considerations in influencing business decisions (not just vice versa).

(2) Stress capacity. As McCann and Galbraith (1981) point out, the effective person in an organizational boundary role (such as the HR/line management interface), will experience high levels of stress and must be capable of working comfortably with stress.

(3) Capacity to develop trust. This is another skill identified by McCann and Galbraith. Trust development is important because high trust is more likely to lead to win/win solutions and to long-term satisfying relationships than is low trust.

(4) Coping skills. Elsewhere, the author has identified three strategies for coping with role conflict and stress (Hall, 1972). Type I coping—problem-solving with role senders to redefine the sent role in a mutually satisfactory way—is seen as especially useful for effective human resource bargainers. A person with these skills would also be able to confront difficult issues with line management and to *increase organizational conflict* where necessary (Brown, 1983). Type II coping—independently defining and resolving one's own role in a conflictful or ambiguous situation—would also assist a person to operate effectively in a human resource boundary role. Type III coping—reactive role behavior (attempting to meet all external role demands)—may be effective in a Cell II or Cell I organization but would lead to great stress and frustration in Cell IV.

(5) Internal locus of control. In order to lead a department to a state of self-direction, the individual must possess this quality. Furthermore, Type I and Type II coping, as described above, presupposes that the person has a strong inner sense of direction and control.

(6) Interactive planning skills. As described by McCann and Galbraith (1981), this quality entails the, ability to deal with high levels of cognitive complexity and ambiguity, to think tentatively, and to "play with" various "what-if" scenarios. It means being able to treat problems as tasks, not as occasions to allocate responsibility and blame. It also means being able to shift time horizons, to consider both short-term demands and long-term implications, and to be comfortable in occasionally making tradeoffs between the two.

(7) Appropriate personal needs. Drawing on the work of Schutz (1966), three types of needs might be relevant to the role of the human resource manager: inclusion, control, and affection. Regarding the appropriate level of motivation for *inclusion* and *affection,* these might vary with the stage of integration that the organization has achieved. If it is in the early stages, with strong internal boundaries, a more independent, low-inclusion person might be more effective at playing the "troublemaker" or conflict-arousing role. If a level of integration has already been achieved and the human resource function is already in a bargaining-coordinating role, a person with moderate affection (social) and inclusion needs would probably be more effective. Moderate *control* (power) needs would probably be important, too. The reason for *moderate* social and control needs is that if the social needs are too high and the control need is too low, the person would "cave in" too frequently to his or her counterparts in other departments. If the social needs are too low and control needs too high, the person might have insufficient motivation to bargain and work collaboratively as part of a management team and attempt to build an empire instead (Cell III).

How is it possible to identify or develop a person with this imposing set of qualities? Can these qualities, in fact, be developed, or are they stable personality characteristics? Some are probably deeply rooted in the personalities, such as stress capacity and need strength, and thus might be very difficult to change. These characteristics could be identified either through testing, through an assessment center, or through observations of on-the-job behavior. Other qualities, such as coping skills, confrontation skills, and trust building, are probably interpersonal skills that could be increased through training such as behavior modeling and on-the-job coaching (Wexley & Latham, 1981).

NEGOTIATION AND INFLUENCE STRATEGIES

Once we have the right type of person in charge of a function such as human resources, what strategies lead to effectiveness as he or she negotiates with other units in the organization? In considering this issue, let us examine a case of an organization that moved recently from a combination clerical/administrative personnel function (somewhere between Cell I and Cell III) to a mission orientation (Cell IV.).

The organization in this case is a large international commercial bank located in the Midwest. Since branch banking is not allowed in its state, consumer banking has not been of primary importance in this bank, and it has instead concentrated on nationwide commercial and foreign markets. The bank had always had a comfortable number 2 market position in the Midwest, with a conservative, traditional approach to investment and loan decisions. Human resource activities such as recruiting, training, job assignments, and rewards were rather routine, with an emphasis on long service, corporate loyalty, and job move decisions made by senior management based upon what they felt was best for the employee and for the bank.

In the 1970s, the world of banking changed fundamentally. "Disconnections" were rampant. What had been the "right type" of banker was often 180 degrees out of phase with emerging needs for risk taking, uncertainty, conflict management, and individual creativity and accountability. New types of services and organizational subunits, such as an exploding array of financial services, venture operations, leasing activities, and energy-oriented subsidiaries were created, calling for differentiated employee skills, career paths, and rewards. The chairman and CEO of the bank reasoned that a novel, proactive personnel function would be essential to the organizational changes necessary for future success.

A young, fast-track manager was chosen to head up the personnel function. He had grown up in the city as a tough, street-wise kid and put himself through college as an employee of the bank. Thus even though he was in his late 30s, he had twenty years' service with the bank, an important loyalty factor in this organization. His background had been in systems and operations, which gave him credibility with the task-oriented managers of the line units, such as commercial lending. His personal style was affable and cooperative, but at the same time, no-nonsense, thorough, and confronting. He was well aware of the change taking place in banking, and he had a vision of the new organization that would be necessary. He was also aware of the low-power role of personnel in this organization, as well as the need to negotiate with and influence the line organization. In the sections that follow, we will describe various strategies that he used to increase his negotiation power.

Personal Power of Subunit Leader

As has been said, the personal credibility of this person was critical. First, he was a "fast-tracker," a "star" in this system. He had "hard" experience in systems and operations. He was mainstream. No "warm and fuzzy" type was he. He had gone to one of the good, respected Catholic colleges in the city. His physical qualities reinforced his interpersonal style qualities: tall, trim, ruggedly attractive; an immaculate, conservative dresser; tough; able to "bore in" to the other person in conversation with intense concentration; a dynamic, persuasive, somewhat earthy speaker. While forceful, he also could "read" people beautifully. A major advantage in his negotiations was his ability to diagnose the motives and interests of the adversary and to generate win/win solutions to help meet many of these unstated aims. In short, he had good perspective-taking ability, a critical factor in effective conflict resolution (Bazerman & Neale, 1982). He showed many of the "face-to-face" qualities identified by Kotter (1977): expertise, creation of dependencies, persuasion, and creation of obligations.

Relational Power

Of course, the most important source of power this individual had was his support from the CEO, who had been and still is his mentor.

This relationship does not translate into unconditional support on every issue, but it does mean good access to the top and a good opportunity to influence at this level. The perceptions by others of this identification with the CEO greatly enhanced this person's power (Kotter, 1977).

He is also well connected to the network of other formal and informal leaders in the organization (he is one of the "old boys," a "right type"). In addition to the relationships formed by "growing up together" in the bank, he has also consciously worked at developing good working relationships with key line managers. Over time, a history of mutual respect and trust has developed.

Thinking Strategically

The remaining methods involve what Kotter (1977) called *indirect* strategies. A critical starting point was having a clear sense of the organization's mission and strategy (which came from the CEO). The mission is a statement of the organization's reason for existing. Strategy is the process whereby resources are consciously allocated to those users that will be most effective in achieving the objectives related to that mission (Tichy, Fombrun, & Devanna, 1982).

In strategic thinking, an organization can be considered to possess three levels (see Figure 19.2). The top, or *institutional,* level is that at which the organization is ultimately directed and at which it interacts with its environment. It is at this level that policies and long-term strategies and plans are developed. The middle is the *managerial* level, where the operations of the organization are controlled and directed. At this level, control and information systems are critical, as are a variety of integrative devices. Plans and strategies imposed from the institutional level become objectives at the managerial level, which in turn must develop its own shorter-term plans and strategies to attain these objectives. The lowest level is the *technical or operational level,* where the actual goods or services of the organization are produced. Again, the strategy of the middle level constitutes objectives for the operational level, which in turn must develop its own strategy to attain these end results.

To think strategically, as our personnel head did, several activities are important. First, one must have a *strategy for one's own function,* one that fits with the organization's mission. In this case, the manager's

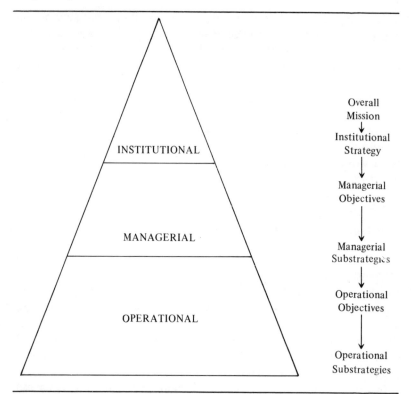

Figure 19.2   Three Levels of Organizational Strategy

strategy was to create a personal role and a personnel function that would create the required organization of the future.

Second, it is necessary to have *different substrategies for each of the three organizational levels.* In this case, the HR strategy for the institutional level was to influence the CEO and the top management team to adopt new personnel policies and to inject human resource considerations into the business plans for the operation. At the managerial level, his strategy was to develop modern personnel systems (such as selection and performance appraisal), and to work with line managers to implement these systems bank-wide. At the operational level, the strategy was gradually to replace many staff who had been "dumped" in personnel either because they had failed elsewhere or because they were "good with people." New personnal staff would have to be trained as personnel specialists *or* they would be high-potential management trainees on rotation from "mainstream" departments.

For this human resource manager, the key intervention was the *development of the institution-level strategy for human resources.* As Tichy, Fombrun, and Devanna (1982) point out, personnel managers often fall into the trap of becoming so preoccupied with management-level systems that they fail to devote enough energy to the high-impact institutional level.

Influencing Top Management

How, specifically, did this institutional-level influence take place? First, there was a process of *"educating" top management.* This took the form of direct personal influence, through discussions of critical corporation problems and key personnel moves. It was also done through the *strategic use of outside consultants.* Another variant here was the *development of a role as counselor to the CEO.* This role would be different from the regular management team role, in that it often meant just being available to listen, to act as a sounding board while the CEO let off steam or weighed alternatives. Sessions with the CEO were often not actual decision points, but the opportunities for influence were nevertheless great.

A critical way of influencing the top was the *involvement of top management in human resource issues.* Using committees of senior line management to select key managers or to develop personnel selection policies was a strategy not for abdicating personnel's influence but to "infiltrate" personnel thinking into line management. Another way to influence top management was to *influence future top management* (i.e., today's "fast-trackers"). By adopting the policy of rotating stars through personnel, this meant that in future years, most of the top people in the organization would have served a tour in personnel, which presumably would have affected their thinking.

Impacting the Culture

Just as strategy and policies have far-reaching and long-term effects, the culture of an organization, its pivotal norms and values, permeates all thinking and action in the system. By recognizing that the present culture would greatly impede the necessary changes, the personnel head attempted to influence the culture. A series of climate surveys provided a diagnosis of the current cultures in various units of the bank. Managers were left with decisions of how to act upon the survey results, and thus a whole network of line management "change agents" was created throughout the bank. Of course, this created a need for personnel specialists to help interpret results and to provide consultation on appropriate actions. The need to change was clear from the data, as was the need for help from personnel. Result: one more bargaining chit for HR.

The culture was also affected through new selection and socialization practices. More MBAs were hired to provide a more professional, technically competent work force throughout the bank. More planning went into job assignments and selection of supervisors for trainees.

Impacting Information Systems

At the managerial level, new information systems greatly enhanced the key role of personnel. A new performance appraisal system—made uniform, bank-wide, and with all reports maintained by personnel—affected a critical aspect of line management: the administration of rewards. Many chits had to be cashed in to sell this new system, but once it was in place, the return on that investment— i.e., the increased stature of personnel for upgrading the quality of organizational performance—was striking.

The organizational surveys, mentioned earlier, were a key information system, and the impact of survey feedback on a line manager was considerable. It was clear that surveys were not just a management tool but a practical instrument for personnel as well.

Publications such as employee newsletters, periodic reports to employees, shareholders, and outside constituents also became effective means of communicating and promoting management's objectives. As the area responsible for this valuable communication, the stature of personnel was again enhanced.

A critical type of power is power over a person's career. The personnel head created a new function, *internal placement,* which was responsible for internal job transfers. The personnel department became a broker for people who wanted to make interdepartmental moves or for managers who wanted to attract good people from another department. This put personnel in a clear bargaining position as it had to reconcile often competing interests of various line managers.

Cooptation of the External Environment: Use of Boundary Role

Central to many of the strategies discussed so far was the effective utilization of the *boundary-spanning function* of the human resource activity. Because part of the HR role is to interact with external agents such as unions, various government organizations, sources of labor, and professional associations, the HR manager can often utilize demands and pressures from the external agents to support the HR agenda. Affirmative action, health and safety, tight labor markets, and maintaining nonunion status are some of the more familiar examples of this use of the boundary spanning role to support HR interventions in the line organization. Through the process, as well, HR became an important agent in helping the organization cope with uncertainty in its environment and in facilitating the resulting management decision process; these are two critical sources of power (Pfeffer, 1981).

Furthermore, as the need to communicate more effectively with outside constituencies increased—especially government regulators and the general public—the personnel function was expanded to include personnel and corporate relations or external affairs. This included critical public relations and government lobbying agencies. By expanding the boundary of his activities outside the organization at the institution level, his internal influence expanded as well.

Strategic Use of Personnel's Resoures

As these various attainments and resources of the HR function were being created, they became in part resources to be used to enhance the future negotiating power of personnel. They were not simply offered charitably to the organization, but they were given with a message: The personnel function intends to be an integral part of the running of this business. And, in fact, this is what has happened. There was an early stage of tension and resentment on the part of some line managers about the growing power of personnel, but this was overcome by the clear benefits HR was providing to the line organization.

CONCLUSION

As Brown(1983) has indicated, issues of conflict and bargaining at organizational interfaces have received inadequate attention in the organizational literature. In this analysis we have examined strategies by which a traditionally low power function in an organization, through awareness of conflict and bargaining situations, increases its negotiating power. A primary ingredient of success here is the ability to function *strategically,* with a primary focus on the institutional level of the organization (e.g., impacting top management and corporate culture, and utilizing the external environment). In addition to strategic behaviors, the proper personal characteristics (such as confrontation, trust, and coping skills, internal locus of control, and appropriate needs) are also essential to enable the person to identify and use the appropriate strategies. This process of virtually creating something out of nothing is an exercise in outstanding organizational leadership.

REFERENCES

Argyris, C., & Schon, D. A. *Theory in practice.* San Francisco: Jossey-Bass, 1975.

Bacharach, S., & Lawler, E. J. *Bargaining: Power, tactics, and outcomes.* San Francisco, Jossey-Bass, 1981.

Bazerman, M. H., & Neale, M. A. *Improving negotiation effectiveness under final offer arbitration: The role of selection and training* (Working paper 11/82), Boston: School of Management, Boston University, 1982.

Brown, L. *Managing conflict at organizational interfaces.* Reading, MA: Addison-Wesley, 1983.

Hall, D. T. A model of coping with role conflict: The role of behavior of college-educated women. *Administrative Science Quarterly,* 1972, 471-485.

Hedberg, B. How organizations learn and unlearn. In P. C. Nystrom & W. H. Starbuck (Eds.), *Handbook of organizational design* (Vol. 1). Oxford: Oxford University Press, 1981.

Kotter, J. Power, dependence, and effective management. *Harvard Business Review,* 1977, *55,* 125-136.

Lawrence, Paul R., & Lorsch, J. W. *Organization and environment.* Cambridge, MA: Harvard Business School, 1967.

McCann, J., & Galbraith, J. Interdepartmental relations. In P. C. Nystrom & W. H. Starbuck (Eds.), *Handbook of organizational design* (Vol. 2). Oxford: Oxford University Press, 1981.

Pascale, R. T., & Athos, A. G. *The art of Japanese managment.* New York: Simon & Schuster, 1981.

Pfeffer, J. *Power in organizations.* Boston: Pitman, 1981.

Pruitt, D. G. *Negotiation behavior.* New York: Academic, 1981.

Schutz, W. *The interpersonal underworld.* Palo Alto: Science & Behavior Books, 1966.

Tichy, N., Fombrun, C., & Devanna, M. A. Strategic human resource management. *Sloan Management Review,* Winter 1982.

Van de Ven, A. H., Delbecq, A. L., & Koenig, R. J., Jr. Determinants of coordination within organizations. *American Sociological Review,* 1976, *41,* 322-338.

Wexley, K. N., & Latham, G. P. *Developing and training human resources in organizations.* Glenview, IL: Scott, Foreman, 1981.

20

BARGAINING WITHIN ORGANIZATIONS

Samuel B. Bacharach

Cornell University

Conventional organizational theory has had a rational, cohesive notion of organizations. For the sake of parsimony, scholars have made particular assumptions about organizations and actors in them which appear to be incongruent with the way organizations operate in the real world. Bacharach and Lawler (1980) have recently pointed out that students of organizations have tended to cast them as normatively integrated systems, thereby ignoring political conflicts and other tensions. Students have tended to view the organization as a holistic entity, overlooking such organizational subunits as interest groups and coalitions, which are crucial to the development of a political perspective of intraorganizational behavior. This apolitical orientation is indicative not only of macroorganizational analysis, but also of much of the work by organizational and industrial psychologists. Organizational psychologists have focused primarily on integrative organizational processes (e.g., motivation, control, leadership), while ignoring the diversified interests that tend to pull organizations apart. As Kochan and Verma point out in their chapter in this volume, a growing number of theorists have begun to emphasize conflict in organizations (Strauss, 1978, Bacharach & Lawler, 1980; Pfeffer, 1981). It is critical, however, that we distinguish between a cooperative model, a conflict model, and a bargaining model of organizations (Bacharach & Lawler, 1981a). To maintain that organizations need to be analyzed as systems made up of diverse interest groups and actors with unique goals and aspirations is not by definition to accept organizations as arenas of continuous bickering and chaos. Indeed, one could accept the empirical reality of differential interests and at the same time stress the normative mechanisms that sustain organizational unity. Indeed, intraorganizational conflict occurs within the context of a reified, normative apparatus and is therefore constrained in duration and in scope. That is, an organization that experiences intraorganizational conflict at all points in time and over all issues will be unable to sustain itself.

A radical notion of conflict assumes it to be a zero-sum game, that is, that the outcomes among various interest groups are negatively related. This model of conflict is offered by the most radical critics of organizational theory. Clearly, it is offered in direct opposition to the positive-sum assumptions made by those who see organizations as cooperative entitites where what is good for one subgroup is necessarily beneficial for the whole. As Bacharach and Lawler (1981) point out, bargaining has little place in either of these two models. A positive-sum situation, being inherently cooperative, requires little negotiation. Conflicts can be resolved by education or communication, because through such activities opposing parties recognize their common interests and see the deleterious consequences of conflict for both. Given an acknowledged positive-sum relationship, who needs bargaining? In contrast, zero-sum relationships may be sustained for a time with power and threats: the only issue for theorists in this tradition is who dominates or can muster the greatest power? Organizations, however, are for the most part mixed-motive settings. In other words, parties have tenatively consented both to cooperate and compete. It is through the bargaining process that parties resolve the competition versus cooperation dilemma. However, as Bacharach and Lawler further note, the mixed-motive setting implies a constant process of renegotiation over time.

As such, a bargaining perspective applied in intraorganizational analysis makes the following assumptions:

(1) The power structure of organizations at different points in time and over different issues is negotiable. Simply put, this assump-

tion implies that we no longer cast organizations as centralized or decentralized but rather make an assumption of some fluidity over issues and over time. One particular issue at one particular point in time may be highly negotiable while another issue at the same or different point is nonnegotiable. Indeed, as Hall points out in his chapter, the power of an organizational subunit can vary dramatically over time.

(2) Actors can mobilize bargaining power to execute their will. This assumption implies that through calculated tactical actions actors can mobilize even limited resources in pursuit of a particular end. Each of the chapters in Part V is illustrative of a tactical use of power in a bargaining setting. Each author has assumed that actors in organizations are not simply the passive recipients of formal authority but can actively mobilize bargaining power.

(3) Tactical and countertactical bargaining is critical in organizational life. This assumption implies that the bargaining process has an active and reactive component. That is, actors do not simply mobilize power as implied by assumption 2, but do so in response to the actual and expected bargaining positions of their opponents. It is around this assumption that we begin to become sensitive to the tactical dimensions of bargaining strategies in organizations.

(4) Organizations are dialectical bargaining systems. This assumption is based on the previous three and implies that organizations dialectically change through offers and counteroffers. Whether we view an organization as stable or not, whether we view management or labor as powerful or not, will depend upon at which point of this dialectic we examine organizations. Clearly, a cross-sectional analysis is insufficient

Each chapter in Part V explicates and illustrates each of the assumptions we have listed. The Hall paper appears at first reading to be situationally unique. A quick reading would suggest that this is an essay simply about the management of a human resource department. The body of this chapter, however, extends beyond its empirical referent. Hall picks up on a theme in the work of Lawrence and Lorsch

(1967) and Hickson et al. (1971): departmental power and its relationship to the problem of coordination. Implied in the Hall chapter is the assumption that departments in organizations, while trying to sustain themselves as units integrated with the overall organizational function, at the same time seek their own autonomy based on the perpetuation of their power vis-a-vis the power of other units in the organization. As such, Hall accepts the basic premise that organizations are mixed-motive settings. In specific reference to human resource departments, Hall maintains that "they often choose either a strategy of increasing their power and autonomy, or a strategy of developing stronger links with the line organization."

Within the context of what we proposed as a bargaining approach to organizations, Hall maintains that the bargaining power of a human resource department is not static but rather is historically specific and constrained by the personality of the human resource manger. He goes on to illustrate the importance of personal characteristics necessary if one is going to bargain successfully in such a situation. Among the skills that he accentuates are confrontation skills, stress-coping skills, and interactive skills. The comments about personal qualities are useful observations, but there is the unspoken assumption that these are inbred personality characteristics rather than dimensions of strategic thinking that can be taught or structured by the demands of higher management.

Hall is more persuasive when he discusses bargaining strategy as a means of enhancing the power of the human resource department. An effective bargaining strategy, according to Hall, is dependent on the ability of the human resource manager to recognize the emergence of a bargaining situation. Successful bargaining will depend on the ability of the human resource manager to see the relationship between his or her department and the line organization as a dependent relationship, not simply as a coordinative relationship. The fluid nature of bargaining in organizations is highlighted by casting power in terms of dependence rather than in terms of absolutes. It is the ability of the human resource manager to accentuate this dependence relationship, through what Hall calls "bargaining arousal," that shifts a mechanistic power relationship to a form of negotiated order.

In the second half of his chapter, Hall deals with negotiation and influence strategies. Hall offers a fascinating account of one manager's approach, but there is a genuine question of whether Hall confuses strategy and tactics. It can be maintained that there is only one strategy (his "strategy") that incorporates numerous tactics. The major failing of this section, however, is that Hall ignores what for us is a critical third assumption, i.e., the countertactical maneuvers of opponents. Implicitly, he treats other organizational members as passive targets of the human resource manager's maneuvering. If they were simply targets, incapable of countertactical moves, an argument could be made that no real bargaining occurred. More likely, the others not only had objectives of their own (as Hall does acknowledge) but also opportunities to exercise power. Hall gives no sense of how his human resource manager may have adjusted his strategy and tactics to take these counterinfluence attempts into consideration. In all likelihood, the true brilliance of his bargainer was reflected in his ability to combine objectives and power of his own with estimates of how other parties' objectives and power might affect "getting there from here." While this is implicit in Hall's presentation, a more thorough analysis would have explicated the cognitive calculations involved in tactical bargaining.

It is this dimension that Kipnis and Schmidt accentuate in their chapter. Kipnis and Schmidt are primarily concerned with the selection of influence strategies by which managers attempt to influence the behavior of subordinates, peers, and superiors. Seven different so-called strategies are identified: reason, coalitions, ingratiation, bargaining, assertiveness, higher authority, and sanctions. Unlike previous work, which tended to deduce influence tactics from a given scheme (e.g., Bacharach & Lawler, 1981), Kipnis and Schmidt derive their categories empirically. As they report:

> When seeking to influence their superiors, managers reported that they relied most often upon reasons, followed by coalitions, and then ingratiation. Going over the 'boss's head' or making appeals to higher authority was used least often to influence superiors.

> The rank order of preferred strategies was somewhat different when influencing subordinates. Once again managers reported that the most frequently used strategy was reason. What was of interest, however, was that the second most popular strategy was assertiveness.

Having identified the influence strategies, Kipnis and Schmidt concentrate on factors associated with the selection of influence strategies. In this regard, they identify three critical elements: (1) a manager's relative power, (2) a manager's objectives, and (3) a manager's expectations of the willingness of the targets to comply. These three factors are the critical cognitive elements involved in strategy selection. It is these factors that have been omitted in the strategic section of the Hall chapter. In terms of relative power, Kipnis and Schmidt find that those with greater power use more directive tactics to influence others. In terms of objectives, they find that managers varied their strategies in relation to their objectives. For example, managers use reasons to sell ideas to subordinates and ingratiation to obtain favors. In regard to expectations of willingness of targets to comply, they maintain that "where past experience indicates a high probability of success, managers use simple requests to gain compliance. In contrast, where success is less predictable, managers are increasingly tempted to use assertiveness and sanctions to achieve their objectives."

A cluster analysis of their data revealed a distinction between three types of managers: shotgun managers, tactician managers, and bystander managers. Shotgun managers are those who use the full range of the seven influence strategies. Tactician managers rely heavily upon reason to influence others but have at least average scores on the remaining strategies. Bystander managers have below-average scores on all seven strategies.

The contribution of the Kipnis and Schmidt chapter is in their effort to delineate the dimensions that govern the cognitive calculations that bargainers must carry out before selecting tactics. However, while they conceptually distinguish between relative power, objectives, and willingness of targets to comply, it should be noted that these are empirically interrelated issues. If there is anything clear from the confusion concerning bargaining power, it is that we cannot answer the question "what is a party's power?" without answering "what is that party seeking?" and "where is the other party coming from?" By identifying these dimensions, Kipnis and Schmidt have made a significant contribution to the bargaining literature, elaborating that which Hall, in his chapter, has left unspecified. The interrelationship of these three dimensions, however, needs to be pursued.

Although being primarily concerned with tactical calculation, the Kipnis and Schmidt chapter also falls prey to the same problem in the second half of the Hall chapter. The opposing party is treated solely as a passive target, a victim. As stated before, if the other party is passive, bargaining is unnecessary. Bargaining strategy, for both theorists and bargainers themselves, must focus on anticipation of the other party's responses and his or her ability and readiness to use leverage to pursue objectives of his or her own.

Unlike the Hall and the Kipnis and Schmidt chapters, the Grigsby chapter attempts to identify elements in bargaining models that can be applied to performance management settings. Grigsby wants to improve employee performance through bargaining. Three specific applications are discussed: (1) negotiating performance goals with new employees, (2) negotiation in management by objectives (MBO) systems, and (3) negotiating performance improvement with the poorly performing employee.

The strongest part of the Grigsby chapter is its description of how subordinates might possess or acquire power vis-a-vis superiors and use performance management settings as forums for bargaining. The weakest part is its use of Rubin and Brown's descriptive observations as prescriptive, normative statements. It is a huge leap from saying that superiors might *have* to bargain in performance management settings to saying that superiors *should structure* such settings as forums for bargaining. The weakness in Grigsby's approach is most apparent in his prescription of explicit bargaining in new employee counseling. One would expect this to be the setting in which management would least want to expose itself to the implication that prescribed exchanges are open to question. Most certainly management would not want to cast that forum in terms of interests that are assumed to be in conflict. There is a basic distinction between exchange bargaining, where two sets of resources are open to question, and distributive bargaining, where one party's interests are taken as givens and the other's are being divided up.

If one wants prescriptions to make managers better managers, then what should be drawn from Grigsby's discussion is a *warning*—actually, *two* warnings.

- *To immediate supervisors:* Be aware that when performing performance management functions, subordinates may have leverage to turn such encounters into bargaining sessions where they make demands on you.
- *To higher management:* Be aware that such settings may involve two-way give and take and that supervisors may have personal

interests, apart from organizational interests, just as their subordinates do. Those points are entirely different from the prescription that management should purposefully *turn* such encounters into bargaining sessions. If bargaining is defined as settings where exchange outcomes are (implicitly or explicitly) being determined (i.e., they're not predetermined by organizational rules, structures, and the like), it is much more likely that *subordinates* would want to use performance management settings for that purpose.

But Grigsby's notion cannot be dismissed altogether. There is a danger in assuming that an "authority structure" automatically specifies exchanges that are in management's current interests. Authority is the legitimated product of past decisions, and as demands on the organization change, it is possible that prescribed exchanges may work against higher management's interests. So higher management may have to initiate bargaining to produce a new configuration of legitimated exchanges. One would still expect, however, that it would try to do so tacitly, not explicitly. Explicit bargaining would call its own authority too clearly into question. Kipnis and Schmidt's finding that "reason" was almost invariably the opening tactic of managers suggests such a tacit-bargaining approach.

The main contribution of Grigsby's chapter is that, unlike the other two chapters, this one views bargaining as a sensitizing mechanism for management. Bargaining and the bargaining process for Grigsby become tools that can be applied to practical management. Unfortunately, we do not concur with Grigsby's basic assumption that the "principles" of bargaining are so clear that they can be readily applied.

Each of these chapters has made certain contributions to the intraorganizational bargaining literature. Hall, in viewing organizations from a bargaining perspective, casts power relations in coordination as dynamic processes rather than as mechanistic structures. He illustrates the two introductory assumptions regarding intraorganization bargaining: that the power structure of organizations at different points in time and over different issues is negotiable and that actors can mobilze bargaining power to execute their will. He also implicitly illustrates the fourth assumption that organizations are dialectical bargaining systems. Hall's chapter fails to deal with the third assumption that tactical and countertactical bargaining is critical in organizational life. Kipnis and Schmidt illustrate that actors in organizations select different tactical alternatives, depending upon their situations, but they too neglect the strategic interaction inherent in bargaining situations. Finally, Grigsby deals with the always thorny question of "So what does it mean for practitioners?"

The contributions and limitations of these chapters highlight several issues in the general bargaining literature as it is applied to organizations:

(a) *There is a need to distinguish between bargaining and the broader sociological concept of exchange.* One of the few premises in organizational theory on which there is any consensus is that all organizations are systems of exchange. The cohesive component of organizational life is the fact that all organizations are semi-constructed systems of dependence. If we compare the bureaucratic structural model of organizations as developed in the work of Blau and Schoenherr (1971), Pugh et al. (1968), and Hage and Aiken (1970) with the cognitive and process-oriented work of March and Simon (1958) and Weick (1969), we note that although they vary in their assumptions regarding the predictability of patterned behaviors in organizations, they all assume that intraorganizational life is sustained by systems of exchange based on dependence. This assumption does not simply hold true for the intraorganizational literature, but in recent years has been developed in the examination of organizations in their environment (Jacobs, 1974; Aldrich, 1979). Many of the chapters in this volume seem to focus more on the exchange relationship than on bargaining behavior as such. Bargaining is based on an exchange relationship grounded in dependence but cannot be equated with it. Bargaining in organizations is important because the formally specified exchange relationship is not all-inclusive; there are gaps between the formal exchanges and their daily manifestations. Bargaining is important because structural dependencies often go unspecified or break down. Bargaining is important because one or more parties may want to change existing exchange relationships.

(b) *There is a need to specify the meaning of bargaining power.* The idea of power is critical in most of the chapters in this volume, as it is in most studies of bargaining, but the idea itself too often goes unspecified. Bargaining power is equated with authority, with influence, with tactics, with strategy, with bargaining itself. The classic Weberian definition of power maintains that power is the probability that one party can carry out his or her will despite the resistance of the opposing party. In this context, bargaining becomes the manifestation of power. Bargaining power, when measured in terms of outcomes, is the ability to get an opponent to do something in spite of the opponent's resistance. More often than not this ability is defined as the ability of one party to control a resource. A party's bargaining power is correlated with that party's control of resources, but more importantly, it exists by virtue of the other party's dependence on the resources controlled by the first party (Bacharach & Lawler, 1981b). Clearly, this notion of bargaining power is closely linked to the above discussion of dependence in organizations. It is important to draw such a link, because the concept of power can help us understand how bargainers come to understand and act within a bargaining situation.

(c) There is a need to distinguish between tacit and explicit bargaining. Explicit bargaining implies a common recognition and acknowledgment that the parties are engaged in bargaining; tacit bargaining implies a bargaining relationship that is neither recognized nor acknowledged as such (Bacharach & Lawler, 1981a). Under tacit bargaining we are more likely to see informal influence attempts rather than any formal mode of negotiation. The field of industrial relations has tended to focus on explicit bargaining, while organizational behavior, especially when looking at intraorganizational relations, implicitly concentrates on tacit bargaining. As a result, both fields have developed concepts of bargaining and either has developed an adequate understanding of how its explicit or tacit focus may have limited the applicability of its concept. That failure is illustrated by the chapters in this volume: tacit and explicit bargaining are examined interchangeably, and rules that govern explicit bargaining are (implicitly) assumed to be the same as those that govern tacit bargaining. An issue of common and major interest for industrial relations and organizational researchers would be to examine empirically the relationship between explicit bargaining and tacit bargaining. Cross-sectionally this can be done by examining the scope of one versus the scope of the other, and longitudinally it can be done by examining the dialectical relation between the two. Specifically, one could examine when or for what kinds of issues does tacit bargaining go beyond explicit bargaining, and when and how does tacit bargaining become so recognized as to become explicit bargaining.

(d) There is a need to recognize the significance of the unit of analysis. Simply put, at what level and among what units does bargaining occur? Chapters dealing with interorganizational bargaining tend to reify and anthropomorphize the organization; chapters that deal with intraorganizational bargaining do the same for departments or interest groups. They tend to assume that the collectivity itself is the key actor, rather than examining constituent representatives who bargain on its behalf. An organization does not bargain; people do. But it is as important to recognize that people bargain *on behalf* of larger collectivities as it is to recognize that individuals do the bargaining. A bargaining analysis of organizations maintains explicitly that conscious action is critical in understanding organizations. Individual actors are not simply passive receptacles of structure, nor are they unfettered manipulators of their situations. They both affect and are affected by the contexts in which they act. This emphasis on the action component of organizational analysis accentuates the problem of the unit of analysis. It accentuates the importance of examining the relationship between the negotiating representative and the unit he or she represents. A bargaining perspective, therefore, implies an examination of mixed units of analysis. Of course, this is not the case when we are speaking about individual bargaining; however, in reality, with the possible exception of executive corporate levels, the scope of individual bargaining in organizational life is minimum.

(e) There is a need to distinguish explicitly theoretical models of bargaining and the idea of bargaining as an implicit metaphor or sensitizing device. To date most of the broad work on bargaining (Bacharach & Lawler, 1981a; Pruitt, 1981; Walton & McKersie, 1965) has worked within the formal deductive framework. That is, formal axiomatic propositions have been built one upon another around a common framework. But when these theories are applied to empirical settings, be they real world or experimental, what is tested are their separate propositions and not their framework as such. The necessary connections between and among formal axiomatic propositions are not empirically established, resulting in incomplete bargaining models. A complete bargaining model will only be achieved if a methodology can be found to apply to these propositions, not individually but collectively, to the study of organizations.

For the most part, the authors in this volume do not build on previous work in formal bargaining theory, nor do they set out to construct a bargaining theory as such. Their chapters, while loosely speaking of models and theories, tend to accentuate bargaining as a metaphor that will somehow bring to the forefront issues we have previously ignored, such as power tactics, conflict, and negotiations. Such an approach, by itself, is unlikely to contribute to any cumulative model. The strength of this approach, however, is that it has led these authors to concentrate on situations and interrelated patterns of behavior, rather than on isolated acts. If the research strategies they have developed can be directed and informed by deductive theory, significant advances in our theoretical and practical understanding of bargaining can be expected.

(f) Before we can make such advances, however, we must recognize yet another need: the need to distinguish between bargaining tactics and bargaining strategy. Tactics are what bargainers do; strategies are what bargainers think. The one is behavioral, the other cognitive. Occasionally, that distinction is dismissed as "merely semantic." More often, it is dismissed as unnecessary: If what we want to understand is what bargainers do, and if tactics are the behavioral manifestation of strategy, then isn't it sufficient, indeed more valid, to infer whatever logic may lie behind a set of tactics by simply observing tactics themselves? Without sufficiently appreciating the importance of their contribution, the authors of the chapters in Part V provide an answer to that question: no. No, because the same tactics may be used in different bargaining settings, for altogether different reasons. No, because bargaining frequently involves the use of a number of tactics, one after another; if "earlier" tactics anticipate "later" ones and achieve the outcomes that a bargainer is pursuing, we may miss the significance of the sequential pattern. No, because there may not be a logic behind some bargainers' use of tactics. Kipnis and Schmidt's shotgun managers and bystander managers clearly had no strategy; Hall's human resource manager formulated a strategy out of everyday transactions and demands that his predecessors had treated as routine; Grigsby's managers are called upon to recognize the bargaining potential in performance management interactions that occur on a daily basis, with or without such recognition.

Strategy, then, is not simply what bargainers think; it is a way of thinking that involves consideration of one's power, one's objectives, and how the one can most effectively be used to secure the other, given that one's opponent has objectives and sources of power of his own. The chapters in Part V illustrate that it is possible to treat objectives, power, and interaction as separate or routine considerations; they also illustrate that the strategist will not treat them separately or routinely. By providing us with illustrations of the null set—the nonstrategist—these three chapters help us clarify the distinction between strategy and tactics. By providing us with evidence and a rationale to expect that the strategist will be more successful than the nonstrategist at achieving his or her objectives, they illustrate why it is important to draw such a distinction.

As I noted earlier in my comments on the Kipnis and Schmidt chapter, the questions "what is a party's power?" "what is that party seeking?" and "where is the other party coming from?" are interrelated. Different objectives and different relationships with one's opponent imply different sources of power. Different relationships and different sources of power constrain the objectives one can reasonably expect to attain. Depending upon his or her actual situation, a bargainer may have no control over one or more of those factors; the internal politics of his or her constituent organization or the position of his or her opponent may dictate an answer. The nonstrategist is one who flails away at such constraints (Kipnis and Schmidt's shotgun manager) or else is paralyzed (their bystander). The strategist, by contrast, is one who asks where he or she may yet have maneuvering room and sets out to identify mutually consistent answers to those questions over which he or she does have some control and those over which he or she does not (Shedd, 1983).

What we are suggesting, therefore, is that we treat the interrelationships between power, objectives, and interaction with an opponent as empirical issues. "Which comes first?" is a practical issue that bargainers must resolve for themselves. In recent research on teacher unions, for example, Shedd (1983) found that some union leaders formulated their objectives based on calculations of what their current power and the other party's objectives and power appeared to be; others identified their objectives and then set out to develop the power to secure them. Both types of union leaders were strategic thinkers: both recognized that the three questions are interrelated and consciously worked out answers that reflected their connectedness.

Bargaining theorists, like most social scientists, get uncomfortable when their subjects are allowed to think. The reason we have so many different models of bargaining—and the reason we have paid so little attention to the concept of bargaining strategy—is that each theorist has insisted on doing all the thinking for his or her bargainers. Each model's assumptions specify how bargainers think and specify that both will necessarily think alike. The notion that bargainers might have to decide consciously what to make of their situations and to adjust their strategies accordingly is thereby overlooked. If we are prepared to treat existing bargaining theories not as all-sufficient explanations of bargaining but as different strategies—different ways of thinking about a bargaining situation—we might be prepared to acknowledge that all the theoretical issues that have been bedeviled theorists and researchers are practical issues for bargainers themselves. We could then make strategy making the focus of our attention. Kochan (1982) recently suggested that strategy making is an important area of future bargaining research. The point needs to be made more forcefully: A focus on strategy making would fundamentally alter our appreciation of existing bargaining theory and would allow us to make important advances in our theoretical and practical understanding of bargaining (Bacharach and Shedd, 1983).

Focusing on bargaining and negotiations in organizations represents an acceptance of the need for a political theory of organizations. From a bargaining perspective, we begin to introduce the calculating free actor (Crozier & Frieberg, 1980; Bacharach & Lawler, 1980). We move away from structural sociological determinism and deemphasize the passive actor as he or she has been perpetuated by industrial and organizational psychology. We assume that actors have different interests; we assume that actors think; we assume that actors calculate; we assume that actors coalesce; we therefore assume that they make strategy and bargain. The application of bargaining in organizations is a simple acceptance of the fact that actors are no less political in their organizational life at work than they are in life outside their organizations.

REFERENCES

Aldrich, H. E. *Organizations and environments.* Englewood Cliffs, NJ: Prentice-Hall, 1979.

Bacharach, S. B., & Lawler, E. J. *Power and politics in organizations.* San Francisco: Jossey-Bass, 1980.

Bacharach, S. B., & Lawler, E. J. *Bargaining: Power, tactics, and outcomes.* San Francisco: Jossey-Bass, 1981. (a)

Bacharach, S. B., & Lawler, E. J. Power and tactics in bargaining. *Industrial and Labor Relations Review,* 1981, *34,* 219-233. (b)

Bacharach, S. B., & Shedd, J. B. *Power, conflict and change in labor-management bargaining.* Presented at the Academy of Management Association symposium *Conflict In Organizations/Organizations in Conflict: Radical Explanations,* Dallas, 1983.

Blau, P. M., & Schoenherr, R. A. *The structure of organizations.* New York: Basic Books, 1971.

Crozier, M., & Friedberg, E. *Actors and systems: The politics of collective action.* (Arthur Goldhammer, trans.). Chicago: University of Chicago Press, 1980.

Hage, J., & Aiken, M. *Social change in complex organizations.* New York: Random House, 1970.

Hickson, D. J., Hinings, C. R., Lee, C. A., Schneck, R. E., & Pennings, J. M. A strategic contingencies theory of intraorganizational power. *Administrative Science Quarterly,* 1971, *16,* 216-219.

Jacobs, D. Dependency and vulnerability: An exchange approach to the control of organizations. *Administrative Science Quarterly,* 1974, *19,* 45-49.

Kochan, T. A. Collective bargaining and industrial relations. *Industrial Relations,* 1982, *21,* 73-122.

Lawrence, P. R., & Lorsch, J. W. *Organization and environment.* Cambridge, MA: Harvard University Press, 1967.

March, J. G., & Simon, H. A. *Organizations.* New York: John Wiley, 1958.

Pen, J. *The wage rate under collective bargaining.* (T. S. Preston, trans.). Cambridge, MA: Harvard University Press, 1959.

Pfeffer, J. *Power in organizations.* Marshfield, MA: Pitman, 1981.

Pruitt, D. G. *Negotiation behavior.* New York: Academic, 1981.

Pugh, D. S. et al. Dimensions of organizational structure. *Administrative Science Quarterly,* 1968, *13*(2), 65-105.

Strauss, A. *Negotiations: Varieties, contexts, processes, and social order.* San Francisco: Jossey-Bass, 1978.

Shedd, J. B. *Internal politics and external bargaining: Strategy in school district labor-management relations.* Unpublished Doctoral Dissertation, Cornell University, Ithaca, New York, 1983.

Walton, R. E., & McKersie, R. B. *A behavioral theory of labor negotiations.* New York: McGraw-Hill, 1965.

Weick, K. *The social psychology of organizing.* Reading, MA: Addison-Wesley, 1969.

—VI—

SUMMARY

21

STUDYING ORGANIZATIONAL NEGOTIATIONS

Implications for Future Research

Roy J. Lewicki

Duke University

Max H. Bazerman

Massachusetts Institute of Technology

The theme of this volume reflects our perceptions that managers do a great deal of negotiation every day—purchasing, selling, mergers and acquisitions, budget determination, performance appraisal, settling a liability claim, meeting federal regulations, and so on. While negotiations permeate organizational life, managers often fail to realize the importance of negotiation to their position. As Raiffa (1982, p. 357) notes:

> Executives . . . frequently assert that they're not interested in the role of the intervenor in conflicts because that's not what they do as business-

men. It always gives me special pleasure when, during seminars on negotiation, such executives realize that mediating conflict is what they do all the time in the internal management of their organizations. Executives rarely think of themselves as mediators, even while they mediate.

Paralleling Raiffa in spirit, by addressing the deficiency to the research community, Kochan and Verma started this volume by challenging organizational scholars with the following:

> The thesis developed here is that we have reached a stage of evolution in both organization and industrial relations theory that allows us to move beyond abstract conceptualizing about negotiation phenomena to more concrete analysis and practical application. Indeed, unless those who believe that a negotiations perspective has something to offer organization theory and practice can successfully translate their broad theoretical points of view into useful guides for organizational participants, these theories will continue to remain aloof from organizational application.

Given this void by managers and researchers concerning the prevalence of negotiation inside organizations, we asked the authors of this volume to present (1) new theoretical developments generalizable across negotiation tasks in organizations and (2) unique applications of the concepts in the existing and emerging negotiations literature that provide a new perspective to organizational behavior problems. With this as background, this summary chapter examines each of the subtopics of this volume in terms of the progress made by the contributions and, perhaps more importantly, sketches a research agenda for the future.

NEGOTIATION DECISION MAKING

The five chapters in Part II identified a number of specific aspects about how individual cognition affects the process of negotiation. Greenhalgh and Neslin added to our methodological understanding of how to "capture" the preferences of negotiators. Ebert and Wall made us aware of the role of the other party in our decision processes in a negotiation context. The other three chapters provided conceptual advances about basic decision processes that speak to how negotiation decision processes can be changed. Pruitt clarified specific, implementable strategies for improving the search for integrative solutions between negotiators.

Bazerman and Neale identified a number of deviations from rationality (that are common to negotiators) that decrease negotiations effectiveness and the likelihood of two parties reaching a mutually agreeable resolution. Lewicki provided a description of the factors affecting a negotiator's ethical choices, considerations a manager must face in dealing competitively with another party. Overall, these three chapters provided new conceptual ideas that generalize across negotiation tasks within organizations. In addition, these chapters identify deficiencies in negotiator decision making and thus provide an outline concerning the changes that are necessary to improve negotiation effectiveness.

The chapters on negotiator decision making have guided our search for improving negotiation effectiveness by *describing* how negotiators currently make decisions. Each chapter also includes implicit ideas for how to incorporate these ideas into prescriptive strategies for change. For example, Pruitt suggests that we need to get negotiators to break their fixed-pie assumptions and consider possible trade offs between issues. Bazerman and Neale suggest that we need to help negotiators recognize the deviations from rationality that exist in the judgments of negotiators. However, Part II does not provide much guidance for how to make these changes take place and become institutionalized into the competitive strategies of negotiators. Future research needs to incorporate the decision content of the chapters in this volume with what the field of organizational behavior knows about planned change, in order to develop prescriptive strategies for making the changes that will have a real impact on negotiation effectiveness.

Another limitation that permeates these chapters is the boundaries of the research—in each case there is an assumption that the two parties have agreed to negotiate in a relatively fixed format. This assumption hides much of the richness of the context of negotiation. Negotiators often have a choice. They can negotiate, they can search for competitive offers, or they can avoid making the transaction because of the awkwardness of negotiation. Viewing negotiation as a form of coordination between two parties with divergent interests (Pruitt, 1981), what are the determinants of whether or not negotiation is initiated? This question is central to a descriptive model of negotiation.

The authors of the chapters on negotiator decision processes have also limited their scope by imposing a single negotiator for each side. What are the decision processes involved within a party when that party is being represented by a negotiating team? How will the answers to this question affect the ideas developed in this volume? Ebert and Wall provide a skeleton to the answers to these questions—but the topic remains a black box.

Finally, all of the papers have assumed a two-party negotiation process. We need look no farther than the recent Bendix/Martin-Marietta/Allied merger example to see a vivid illustration of a multiparty context. The social psyschological coalition formation literature may add to our understanding of these situations. Many of the ideas in this volume would need to be modified with the introduction of additional parties.

These missing links address important theoretical issues that generalize across a wide range of negotiating contexts. They may have been ignored in the negotiation literature because some of them are not relevant to the labor/management context that has dominated the applied negotiations literature. In addition, these missing links may help provide the bridge between the theoretical developments in this volume and organizational applications.

THE USE OF THIRD PARTIES IN ORGANIZATIONS

War, General Clemenceau said, is too important to be left to the generals. Similarly, civil disputes, more and more business executives are concluding, have become too expensive and complex to be left to the lawyers. . . . In response, a quiet revolution in the way corporations handle lawsuits has been unfolding over the past year [Business Week, August 23, 1982].

These firms are managing conflict through voluntary third-party intervention. This is consistent with Supreme Court Chief Justice Berger's recent conclusion that alternative third parties must partially replace the courts. To increase the use of third parties within and between organizations, we need to develop a clearer understanding of how third parties can successfully be used in organizational settings. The four chapters in the volume on third-party intervention begin this effort.

Brett and Goldberg identify the benefits of grievance mediation—a new topic in the labor/management domain. Wall and Schiller investigate the prevalence of mediation in the courts. Notz, Starke, and Atwell take an intriguing look at the manager as a third party—consistent with Raiffa's perspective. Finally, Sheppard provides a generic taxonomy of alternative forms of third parties. These chapters successfully identify (1) the wide range of applications possible of our knowledge of third parties and (2) evidence of the potential for success that the use of third parties provide.

Again, we raise the issue of implementation. How do we get civil disputes into the more efficient system of mediators, rather than the courts? How do we get managers to recognize the complexity of their third party duties? How do we convey to society that this literature has something to tell them about the resolution of conflict? The answers to these questions will determine the extent to which there is a diffusion of third-party intervention from the labor/management domain to broader contexts.

What would happen if this diffusion occurred rapidly over the next 5 to 10 years? We would have a tremendous shortage of trained third parties. Unfortunately, as Brett and Goldberg note, "the skills of generating and sustaining conflict appear to be more widely distributed in the population than are skills in managing and resolving conflict." Thus we need to train managers in their role as third parties. This is, for example, happening as volunteer-staffed dispute resolution centers spring up around the country. We need to train external third parties for contexts other than labor/management relations. Unfortunately, the existing literature on professional third-party intervention views their task as an art form. In fact, Sheppard's chapter reports that managers resolve disputes all the time—and in ways that do not necessarily resemble "professional" third-party descriptions. Are these procedures effective? Which models are best suited for which types of disputes? The *scientific* study of these questions is central for educating new third parties effectively.

The four chapters in Part III have clarified the tremendous potential for the use of third parties. The limitations to the use of the content of these chapters lies in identifying the characteristics of effective intervention procedues, the diffusion of third-party techniques, and how to provide training for the increased use of these procedures.

NEGOTIATIONS IN THE
ORGANIZATIONAL ENVIRONMENT

The chapters in Part IV attempted to grapple with the larger perspective of negotiation as a mechanism by which an organization manages and relates to its environment. Each chapter tackles the problem from a different perspective and with a differing degree of theoretical/empirical emphasis. David Brown and Jane Brown report a case study of an international agency—the Relief and Development Agency—and use that case as a vehicle for proposing a model of "ideological negotiations." An ideological negotiation is a process by which differences in ideological beliefs and orientations are discussed and debated within an organization. Brown and Brown discuss the various types, forms and characteristics of ideological negotiation, and suggest mechanisms for their effective management. Moreover, they show how such negotiations in organizations are frequently microcosms of various forces and pressures in the organization's external environment. Hence while much of the negotiated resolution is achieved internally, a great deal of the impetus and pressure for such negotiation may be external to the organization. Ted Murray, in a theoretical essay, suggests that negotiation is a proactive strategy that organizations can use to "enact" and respond to their environments. As the environment of the firm becomes increasingly complex—rapidly changing economic conditions, technology, new foreign and domestic competition, government regulation, and so on—management's strategic options become more and more limited. These increasing limitations increase the risk that a firm may become subject to "strategic stalemate"—in Murray's words, an "inability of management to make a substantial series of productive strategic choices or moves without the support, concurrence, and/or acquiescence of one or more significant parties external to the firm." In order to avoid such stalemate, Murray suggests that management strategies must actively pursue alternatives that restore power and decision-making authority to the firm's leaders. Negotiation is one of those alternatives. An opportunity to observe these strategies in action is provided by the Murray, Jick and Bradshaw paper on hospital budget cuts. Although the hospitals studied by these researchers are public organizations (contrast to the private firms assessed by Murray), we have an opportunity to understand how public organizations respond to their own environmental threats—externally imposed budget cuts. The authors clearly show how hospital administrators used distinctly different strategies, and with differing frequency over time, to respond to these external threats to their operating efficiency and effectiveness.

While the level of analysis of these chapters enhances our understanding of how organizations strategically interact with their environment, several questions may be asked to direct further research. First, the organizational actions and reactions described in these chapters are the result of individual and collective efforts—yet we gain no insight as to the individual and group processes responsible for conceiving and implementing this strategy. *Who* are the key people who monitor and scan the environment? Who determines the company's strategic behavior and by what procedures? Similarly, in the Murray, Jick, and Bradshaw hospital cases, who were the decision makers that were determining how to respond to the budget cuts? What assumptions, information, and procedures were they using to make decisions about how to respond? Is their behavior typical or atypical of public administrators in comparable cost-cutting and revenue-cutting circumstances?

A second question may also be raised regarding negotiation as an organizational from of strategic response. Murray suggests that negotiation is an effective strategic response to the environmental uncertainty and complexity that he describes. Similarly, Brown and Brown describe ideological negotiation in RADA as a microcosm of the greater conflicting social ideologies that exist in society. In both cases, the authors are describing negotiation as one of several options for strategic response—but perhaps without a full exploration of the other opinions for response or of the factors that would determine when those options would be likely to be implemented.

In all cases here, we are asking two fundamental questions. First, is it possible to use individual models of strategic human behavior to understand the scope and range of organizational action and reaction? We need more information about who makes strategy in organizations, and the process by which it is made, before we can comfortably discuss in detail an organization's strategic behavior. Second, we also need to understand whether organizations have the same range of options as individuals do for strategic action and response (or whether those options are greater or lesser in scope) and what factors determine when an organization (or individual) decides to *negotiate,* as opposed to delay, withdraw, counterattack, and so on. Deeper understanding of this process at the individual level, and a clearer understanding for how and when organizations respond with similar or different processes, will greatly enhance our understanding of organizational-level strategic actions and reactions.

ORGANIZATIONAL APPLICATIONS OF NEGOTIATION

In commenting on the previous sets of chapters we have frequently raised the questions of implementation and application—how, specifically, principles, theories, and models of negotiation can be applied to specific organizational settings and processes. The chapters in Part V are unified by that common orientation. Each paper in Part V enriches our understanding of an aspect or organizational life by proposing a negotiation/influence model to account for behavior. As with the array of chapters in the other sections, these also cover the range from theoretical to empirical.

David Kipnis and Stuart Schmidt summarize their research on influence tactics that are commonly used by managers in organizations. Rather than propose a single model of influence, Kipnis and Schmidt conducted inductive studies of influence: They asked managers to describe the methods that they used to influence others in their organizations and then extensively analyzed and coded those descriptions to derive a new classfication of influence tactics. Subsequent research has been able to determine the nature of influence strategies that managers use with subordinates, peers, and superiors; the factors affecting the choice of influence tactics; and the "types" of managers based on the pattern of influence tactics that they use. The research has exciting implications for an inductive understanding of how managers decide to exercise influence and the factors that affect their own individual selection of stategies. Many of these strategies are consistent with a broad definition of a negotiation model.

David Grigsby selects one setting in which mutual superior/ subordinate influence is frequently exercised—the performance evaluation process. Grigsby suggests that a negotiation model might be effectively used to better understand performance appraisal. If both the goal setting and performance appraisal can be viewed from a negotiations perspective, Grigsby suggests that negotiation strategies can be effectively used to set the original performance goals with new employees, to renegotiate old objectives with experienced employees,